# MEMORIES OF A FOREGONE ERA

### BURTON • DIMPERIO • MUSILIN • MALINS • WEBB

BY

## CARMEN PELLEGRINO

# MEMORIES OF A FOREGONE ERA

*Burton • Dimperio • Musilin • Malins • Webb*

The Storied History of Football
at Westinghouse High School
Pittsburgh, Pennsylvania

## Carmen Pellegrino

**Word Association Publishers**
1-800-827-7903
www.wordassociation.com

ISBN 13: 978-1-59571-215-8
Library of Congress Control Number: 2007937597

Word Association Publishers
205 5th Avenue
Tarentum, PA 15084
www.wordassociation.com

# TABLE OF CONTENTS

*Acknowledgements • 7*
*Dedication • 9*
*Foreword • 11*
*Introduction • 3*

PART 1 – THE EARLY YEARS

Chapter 1      *"Pro" Burton Arrives in Homewood • 31*
Chapter 2      *The 1920's – First Championship Season • 44*
Chapter 3      *The 1930's – "Pro" Drives The Bulldogs • 68*
Chapter 4      *The 1940's – "Pro" Passes Reins To Pete Dimperio • 85*

PART 2 – A DYNASTY EMERGES

Chapter 5      *The 1950's – Dimperio Leads The Way • 127*
Chapter 6      *The 1960's – The 25 Game Winning Streak • 181*
Chapter 7      *A Testimony To Pete Dimperio • 209*
Chapter 8      *The 1970's – Worthy Successors Musilin and Malins • 233*

PART 3 – CHANGES AND CHALLENGES

Chapter 9      *The 1980's – Passing of a Legend • 251*
Chapter 10     *The 1990's –Webb Leads House To a Milestone • 263*
Chapter 11     *Beyond The 20th Century • 302*
Chapter 12     *My Personal Reflections • 315*

PART 4 – RECORDS AND SUMMARIES
A Special Tribute • 415
Epilogue • 437

5

**NOTE: Many long hours of research have been spent putting together this historical book. It covers more than 80 years of football history. There may be some errors and other discrepancies, but all the data and events are factual and to the best of my knowledge. Please excuse the dark smudge marks on some of the old newspaper clippings and photos. I apologize for any reading inconvenience.**

**Thank You,**
**Carmen Pellegrino**

# ACKNOWLEDGEMENTS

To my wife Pat Pellegrino who supported me in every possible way with her patience, understanding, typing and assistance in the drafting of this book.

To my step-son Lou Tedesco, Jr. who inspired me to write this book.

To Joseph Pronio for his inspirational support, dedication and efforts in garnering reference materials and contacting several of our alumni for human-interest accounts of their playing days at Westinghouse High School.

A special thank you to my classmate, Georgeanne Dye Stitt for letting me borrow her late father's albums reflecting his athletic achievements at Westinghouse High School; a collection that really helped immensely in getting this book written.

To George Webb, Head Football Coach, and Lance Carter, Athletic Director, at Westinghouse High School for their help and support.

To Angelo Aliberti, my cousin, who did the deposition for Coach Pete Dimperio's retirement testimonial at the Pittsburgh Hilton; a priceless document that appears in Chapter 7.

A special thank you to Pete Dimperio, Jr. and Peggy Dimperio; they graciously shared with me some of their memories and mementos of their late father.

Much thanks to both Tom Costa, Jr. (entrepreneur) and my nephew Tony Zampella, Jr. (coach/strategist) for their support and valuable input.

To many of my alumni friends and relatives who let me borrow their yearbooks for reference purposes. A special thank you to Herb Amen, Albert Bo Silvio, Robert Merletti, Ray Gorman, Joseph Folgarelli, Paul Mazzei, Bill Nicoletti, Leonard Gallo, John Girdano, John Ebbitt, Chauncey Morse, and Michelle Lee who shared their experiences and and/or school memories with me. Thank you to a special group...WHS 1947, 1948 and 1949 football alumni for inviting me to be a part of their annual reunions.

To the following sources of reference: Westinghouse High School year books; Old Timers' Golden Jubilee Souvenir Brochure 1900-1956 Football Edition, By C.A.Herman, Historian-Editor; Pittsburgh Post-Gazette Sports Department; Pittsburgh Press Sports Department; Pittsburgh Sun-Telegraph Sports Department; Pittsburgh Courier Sports Department; East Liberty Tribune Sports Department; and the Pittsburgh Tribune-Review Sports Department.

Special thank you to Ken Davidson, WHS 1938, for his artistic assistance.

7

# DEDICATION

To my wife Patricia, for giving me love, family, and a new lease on life.

To my late mother Margaret Vaccarelli Pellegrino, for raising me with countless values of life. God called for her at age forty-five in 1959. Also to my father Joseph Pellegrino who taught me the importance of an honest day's work. He is still going strong at 95 years of age.

April 11, 1930
My parents on their wedding day
Mom was sixteen and Dad was seventeen

# FOREWORD

*"Memories of a Foregone Era"* could just as easily be from a memory of your not-so-distant past – a heartfelt reflection of a time marked by the stories within a community, shaped by role-models who stood for it from within its local high school. The teachers, administrators, coaches and parents all came together to encourage the hearts and minds of its student body through the rituals and attitudes fostered in the classroom and on the field. And in many of those communities the manifestation of commitment, passion and determination awakened to create a culture where all who attended those four years of high school experienced a special human bond that helped to build an enduring community, and year after year, developed a successful student body. This is a story of one such inner city high school, which since its inception became an integral part in shaping a proud community.

For me this connection produced a plethora of priceless memories. Every town or community across America may lay claim to such a traditional connection of foregone years. The recollection of Friday night lights attracting the many proud and loyal supporters, making their way into the local stadium to watch and cheer on their youthful athletes as they enthusiastically prepared to play the game of football. This was Americana with all the excitement and pageantry. The marching bands of both schools presented the colors of our nation and struck up a sincere rendition of the "Star Spangled Banner", and the sound of the public address system blared the voice of our friendly announcer who introduced the captains of both teams amid the cheers of loyal supporters as they advanced to the center of the field for the official coin toss. Yes, those autumn days of yesteryear carried many fond memories. They were soon to be forgotten as we proceeded on with life's journey. High school football across our land has and always will bring us together as it is an influential part of our American tradition.

Many times over those memories are recaptured with much joy and laughter, especially at class reunions. This is a journey that carries with it many values that grace our great country. I liken this story as an open book to any town or community that has heartfelt memories of their high school alma mater. Those memories seem to find a way back into our lives at times when we least expect it as we greet old friends from time to time during our life's journey.

Over the years many admirers have dubbed my hometown of Pittsburgh, Pennsylvania as "The City of Champions" – such folklore status cultivated a spirit that spilled over into many communities surrounding our great city. The spirit of high school football carries with it a tradition that never fades away. It passes on from generation to generation with all the pageantry that goes with it. Pittsburgh

11

being the sports town that it is has touched so many lives from each generation. Over and over again a person receiving an award or an accolade will acknowledge with much pride the school and the city where they grew up. They never forget where it all started; reaching back for nostalgia to help make sense of this precious moment in our life's journey.

*"Memories of a Foregone Era"* epitomizes my memories, feelings and pride of the football fortunes and misfortunes of Westinghouse High School. There were a number of personal experiences and events that motivated me into putting this book together. During my early years I was fascinated by the pride and spirit that our community had for Westinghouse High School. Much of it came from the proud tradition of the school's successful programs in athletics and music. It was really the heart and soul of our neighborhood and produced many individuals who went on to succeed in many fields of endeavor. It was a special blend of people that pulled together and made it all happen.

Let me begin my story of this inner city high school, located in Homewood, an eastern community of Pittsburgh, Pennsylvania. It is a school that possesses one of the finest scholastic football traditions in America. Steadily rising from a relatively unknown to one of the most respected football programs in Pennsylvania, the Bulldogs became the envy of many throughout its storied history. Through the efforts of some ***patient and excellent*** coaching along with the talent and efforts year after year of a dedicated array of gridiron warriors eager to uphold a very proud tradition. A tradition that has put together well over 500 wins, 35 Pittsburgh City League Titles, one WPIAL Title, a winning percentage of .720 and a reputation that exemplified the true meaning of PRIDE. That winning percentage is one that rates with much respect at any level of competition.

This is not a story about statistics; it is about a dedicated and loyal community that produced a school that developed a blend of talent and pride. It was a special blend that only those who experienced it can really appreciate. Unless you were a part of that special era it is hard to explain, and yet understanding some of these experiences seems a worthwhile project as we explore what might be missing in our shared communities today. I invite you to join me as I highlight one such sustainable recipe through my experiences and memories.

• • • •

By the turn of the century when the early elite Pittsburgh families constructed country estates on undeveloped land in Homewood they began to build strong traditions. Between 1910 and 1950 a steady stream of immigrants moved into Homewood to form a little league of nations. They had strong traditions that continued to revitalize the community. They were traditions of values and lifestyles that survived opposition and tension of several culture and ethnic differences. With the realization that loyalty and respect for each other was required in order to blend together they developed a strong bond of unification. Up until the 1950's, the Homewood-Brushton community had been integrated with relatively little racial conflict. The population had about 25% black and by the year 1960, it had risen to more than 70%. The trend steadily increased and spilled over into the surrounding communities of Lincoln-Lemington and Larimer, and Westinghouse continued to win. Those shared ethnic values and traditions shared by the early classes had begun to show each generation that followed how to enjoy this journey of life both on and off the field. This is what was required in order to be the winner that Westinghouse High School was. Regardless of race, creed or color, the Westinghouse loyalty will always remain in the hearts of the many that passed through those hallowed halls.

A local television station WQED in Pittsburgh (February of 2004) aired a one hour special tribute entitled *"The House a Black Horizons Special."* It epitomized the sense of pride that has for years existed at Westinghouse High School, a.k.a. "The House"- A documentary that was narrated by Chris Moore, and produced by both Moore and Minette Seate. It contained several interesting interviews of alumni (both black and white) who graduated from the House. Seeing the enthusiasm and pride they had for their alma mater was both heartwarming and amusing. From former football coach George Webb and his daughter Dawn Webb-Turner, former cheerleader Esther Bush (Urban League President), former teacher Mr. Joseph Capone and keyboardist Patricia Prattis Jennings of the Pittsburgh Symphony Orchestra expressed heartfelt reflections of their years at Westinghouse. The stroll down the main corridor adorned with portraits and biographies of the many successful alumni was quite impressive. It is appropriately named, the "Wall of Fame;" a reflection of pride that has existed throughout the storied history of Westinghouse High School.

Moore's interviews with former football players George Webb, Lloyd Weston, John Girdano, Joseph Pronio, Mark Ellison and Hawthorne Conley was a real treat as they elaborated on what it took to play football for Westinghouse. Alumnus Herb Amen, our entertainment historian, named several Westinghouse alumni who went on to outstanding careers in music and entertainment. He also expressed how much the pride factor existed within our community as well as our school. WQED did an excellent job in creating a most interesting documentary.

13

Many of our alumni to this day still express how proud they were having been a part of that fine tradition, and I am one who is proud to share its storied history with you. The twentieth century was a historical one that saw the proud Bulldogs put together that impressive winning record. Quite an accomplishment considering what the inner city schools have endured throughout many cities in America. Those three communities (Homewood-Brushton, Lincoln-Lemington and Larimer) that made up the student body of Westinghouse High School shall always stand tall in the folklore of that big House in Homewood. The early years ('30s, '40s, and '50s) of the twentieth century were more controlled and disciplined, but the years that followed were challenged by unruly distractions that America is dealing with to this very day. Traditional values are what made this country what it is today and the game of football is very much like life. There are setbacks and rewards in both and the desire to prevail goes to those who persevere. I will long remember those three communities as I traveled those streets and avenues many times over during my years at Westinghouse.

The community of Larimer where I was born and raised was predominately Italian. We had it all – family owned groceries, specialty and amenity shops, bakeries, churches, schools, social societies, entertainment and night spots, and most of all life-long friendships. We had all the basic needs to make life on the Avenue a village of pride and contentment. Our grandparents and parents came over from Europe and put their skills and ambitions to work, and by the time our generation came along we were able to benefit from their efforts. They paved the way for us to continue on with the American dream that they worked so hard to realize, and we were fortunate to follow their lead. So many of us left that little Italian village behind, but the memories of where we came from will always remain in our hearts. Friendships were formed that still remain and will continue to remain until the end of time.

"*Memories of a Foregone Era*" epitomizes my memories, feelings and pride of the football fortunes and misfortunes of Westinghouse High School. There were a number of personal experiences and events that motivated me into putting this book together. During my early years I was fascinated by the pride and spirit that our community had for Westinghouse High School. Much of it came from the proud tradition of the school's successful programs in athletics and music. It was really the heart and soul of our neighborhood and produced many individuals who went on to succeed in many fields of endeavor. It was a special blend of people that pulled together and made it all happen.

Every football season was an exciting experience for me. At an early age I began collecting newspaper clippings and pictures of every Westinghouse football game and put together several scrapbooks that became my main source of memories. My close cousin "Sonny" helped me a lot during those early years – we would meet with our bicycles and ride once a week to Aunt Rose's house to pick up week-old newspapers that she would save for us. Back then there were three daily Pittsburgh newspapers (Post-Gazette, Press and Sun-Telegraph). We would remove the sports sections of each paper, and load them into our bicycle baskets. Then we would ride back home to clip out pictures and articles that were of interest to us and put them in our scrap books. I remember my mother telling me to clean up all the scraps of paper that were left over or else the scrap book hobby was going to come to an end. I listened because some of those newspaper articles are still neatly stored away in those scrap books.

I saw Westinghouse play in many games with the first one being in 1944 at Pitt Stadium. Every year brought a new team that was eager to uphold the tradition. Some names were new and some were familiar as many families produced yet another member of the team to carry on the tradition. I still remember the first time I saw them lose a game and how I had a tough time dealing with it. Back then when a certain team beat Westinghouse it made headlines in all the local newspapers. A loss was always tough to take, but the winner knew that they had beaten the best. In fact, one year a local school declared a day off from school after upsetting the Bulldogs. The best always gets respect and Westinghouse gained that respect through the many years of being a winner.

At one of my class reunions a former teacher who began her teaching career at Westinghouse and later taught at another city school expressed to me that teaching at Westinghouse was her most rewarding time. She said that the spirit and pride at Westinghouse was very special to her. Year after year our football teams were very

14

instrumental in motivating our student body. We seemed to feed off of their winning ways.

To this day I am proud to say that I am a product of Westinghouse High School as it prepared me well for life's work and challenges. Back then getting your high school diploma was considered an honor. On that day of Commencement in June of 1954, I can still remember the mixed emotions I had when we marched into our auditorium for the last time as our orchestra led by our band director, Mr. Carl McVicker, played an inspirational rendition of "Pomp and Circumstance." Our school motto, *"Here Youth and Opportunity Meet"* was never more true in meaning as when I reached out to receive my diploma. It was a time in my life that I will always remember. Thanks to all my classmates and faculty for sharing with me those fond memories. Our class was very close and I keep in touch with many of them to this very day. I only hope that the youth of today can overcome some of the negative elements that have threatened what should be the happiest years of their lives. I am deeply saddened when I read and hear about some of the tragedies that have taken place so close to this very high school that so many of us called our home away from home. What was a comfort zone for my generation has become one that has security keeping a watchful eye on those who strive to tarnish the image of our school motto.

Year after year, class after class left behind a proud tradition. It remained within its' portals waiting for a new generation to seize it, respect it and prosper from its values. The many memories my generation had of Westinghouse High School are surely going to be forgotten after we are gone. The very thought of this happening inspired me even more into writing this book so that later generations will be able to read about the storied football history of the Westinghouse Bulldogs. As the Twentieth Century was coming to an end I could plainly see that the enrollment changes taking place in the City of Pittsburgh Public School System was affecting the winning ways of Westinghouse. Today the scholastic football headlines reflect the emergence of Perry Traditional Academy as the perennial football powerhouse in the City League of Pittsburgh – a status that Westinghouse High School once held so proudly for a better part of the twentieth century. Times have changed and that is to be expected, but the Bulldog teams of yesteryear will never be forgotten. My generation will take those coveted memories with us to the other side when it is time for us to meet our Maker. We shall leave behind a legacy that will always remain in the folklore of the storied history of our alma mater.

15

We made the most of what we had. Today the generation has so much more, but many of them still complain and expect more. This quote that originated many generations ago by former president John F. Kennedy is one that each of us should strive to live by – **"Ask not what your country can do for you, but ask what you can do for your country."** There is more to gain in giving than there is to taking. Sacrifice, respect and the desire to persevere are three attributes that some of our young people are finding difficulty in developing. But thank goodness most of them are making the most of their opportunities, and have exemplified so much talent and intelligence.

Parents are finding it difficult to control the behavior of their children because of a variety of reasons. Today the challenges are of a different nature that did not exist in our culture years ago. Young parents are to be commended for their efforts, and many times grandparents and great grandparents are stepping up to support their needs. Somehow, some way, our society must overcome the many negative elements that are challenging our young people today. There are many single parent families that are struggling to make ends meet, and that is an ongoing problem.

Every generation has cherished memories that they treasured and appreciated in some special way. My generation, and I for one, would relive it all over again, and not change one thing. When I say I would not change one thing I realize that not every stage of my life was without disappointments and/or setbacks. I was able to recover and move on with my life. The generation before were survivors, and we followed by taking their lead and appreciated what they left for us to build on. Because of them we were able to see and enjoy so many historical gains and advancements that enhanced our lifestyle. From medical breakthroughs to industrialized advancements our generation has been blessed. To top it off we were entertained by some of the most talented of entertainers – too many to mention by name. They helped us to enjoy some of the values of life. Many of them are gone, but their legacies will remain with us forever.

My generation survived World War II, Korea and Vietnam and have much to be thankful for. Thousands and thousands of young people and veterans have sacrificed their lives so that our country will enjoy the freedom of life and the pursuit of happiness. They will never be forgotten as so many families have suffered the loss of loved ones. Enjoy the fruits of our free nation. Today we must do whatever it takes to protect that freedom.

As I reflect back into my reservoir of memories and recount some of my life's priceless moments the traditional values that I gained at Westinghouse High School had given me the motivational tools that I needed to meet the many challenges throughout my life. From time to time I have sat around the dining room table with my grandchildren sharing some of those memories with them and they seem to realize why I repeat myself so much. To them it was light years ago, but to me it seems like it happened a short while ago. They laugh with me as I describe what it was like during those early years of my journey and one of them will say, ***"Pappy has his gold and blue colors on again."*** They know me like a book and I would not have it any other way.

17

Our Namesake
George Westinghouse
1846-1914

18

Follow along with me as I journey back to my Alma Mater

John Kaplan/The Pittsburgh Press

## To the men who made it possible,
## The Coaches

**PETE DIMPERIO**

**PRO BURTON**

19

**Pro Burton:**
1916 -1945 * Record: 149-65-23 * 11 Pittsburgh City Titles * 1 WPIAL Title

**Pete Dimperio:**
1946 -1966 * Record: 151-29-5 * 17 Pittsburgh City Titles

**Rudy Musilin:**
1957-1970 * Record: 28-7-0 * 1 Pittsburgh City Title

**Fred Malins:**
1971-1977 * Record: 41-15-3 * 1 Pittsburgh City Title

**George Webb:**
1978-2001 * Record: 156-82-5 * 5 Pittsburgh City Titles

**GEORGE WEBB**

20

*"Championship teams do not just happen. They are the result of unselfish effort, cooperation and hard work. Our coaches taught us how to play like champions."*

**RUDY MUSILIN**

**FRED MALINS**

21

*Best Wishes to Carmen Pete Dimk*

ATHLETIC
DEPARTMENT

Willard  Fisher

Peter  P.  Dimperio

Joseph  K.  Harsky

Austin  K.  Grupe

## THE SKETCHBOOK

### Our Beloved Mascot

*Bulldog, Bulldog, come to see our Bulldog,*
*You can hear him yelling Yeah team!*
*Stop him, never, Bulldog is too clever,*
*He's as fierce as ever!*
*He's a Bulldog, Rah! Rah! Rah!*

# INTRODUCTION

## NEVER TOO LATE

It has been said ***"it's never too late to pursue an endeavor,"*** and I found that to be true when I decided to go back to school to further my education. After ten years of hitting the books I was able to accomplish my goal by earning my Engineering Degree at the age of forty. Today as I reach the age of seventy, I am challenging ***"it's never too late"*** again; this time pursuing an endeavor to write a book. Maybe it was the realization that I am getting a lot older, and time is not waiting for me to express what I have carried in my heart for many years. Recapitulating memories of a storied history that ranks high in the annals of high school football is something that has consumed every autumn of my life. This desirable endeavor has rewarded me with so many meaningful friendships. Going way back to the early beginning of my research and continuing on throughout the entire twentieth century, the experience of interviewing so many alumni has been an absolute joy. It is truly amazing how so many of them welcomed a heart to heart conversation reflecting on their high school days at the big house in Homewood. Many of those who I spoke with are no longer with us today, but I will always value the memories of our conversations. Time passes and marches on, but those memories will last forever.

As we all know time waits for no one. I have been hard pressed to find quality time in pursuance of this endeavor, but I have managed to do so by burning the midnight oil. I only wish that I could have started a lot sooner, but nevertheless I have enjoyed the late start. One of my classmates, Georgeanne Dye Stitt, expressed to me that her late father, Bob Dye, would have appreciated my desire to complete this book while he was still alive. Much of my material has come from his scrap book collection that she was kind enough to let me borrow. He was one of the finest all around athletes to have graduated from our alma mater. I know he would have been a big help to me, and I do feel that his spirit is nearby.

• • • •

Many times over I have had dreams that I was back in school fulfilling what I had longed to accomplish, but never could. Missing out on something that has haunted me to this very day, and that was to play varsity football at Westinghouse High School. There were circumstances back then that deprived me of this desire, and it carried over into much resentment during and after my school days ended. It was very hard for me to sit back and watch my friends and family members play the game

23

that I truly loved. Those who were close to me while I was growing up realized why I felt so much resentment. My close cousin "Sonny" who did play football was the only one who was able to console me. He knew why I was hurting, but there was nothing he could do to help me. I sat in those bleachers and watched game after game, following closely every play that was executed on the playing field. I was really into the game and could feel the thrill of victory and the agony of a loss. My mind was so focused that I had a hard time relaxing while sitting and watching my classmates playing the game that I really loved.

I had a very demanding father. When I reached the age of twelve I was always busy helping Dad with his projects. Digging foundation footers by hand with pick and shovel was how it all started. I highly resented those two hand tools, but I learned how to use them well. Each time I picked and shoveled it was done with much the same attitude as someone working out in the weight room. I missed out on a lot of sports activities with my friends. It was very frustrating for me, but I was his only son and he needed my help more than I needed football. That was the way he brought me up and I had to accept it. On the positive side Dad is still with us today and doing well at the age of 94, and I thank God for that. He works in mysterious ways and for some reason He felt that my father needed me more than I was willing to realize. It was not easy to give up my football and baseball glove for a pick and shovel, but I had no choice. That was not a pleasant memory. Life goes on and I learned to accept the hand that was dealt to me. I learned how to work hard at a young age and thus I was well prepared for my life's work.

• • • •

During those early years I was able to collect article after article and keep close tabs on the football fortunes of my alma mater. It was the next best thing for me to do at the time. Fifty years have passed and that collection of articles has become a priceless source waiting for a book to be written. Many times over I have shared my recollections of those articles with friends and family, and then *one day my stepson "Lou" asked me "What are you going to do with all these scrap books and articles ... Why not write a book?"* I just paused and looked at him shaking my head, and then it finally hit me. By putting all of this collection together I had a plethora of memories that I could share with others. The realization that I could finally fulfill my dream in another way was suddenly staring back at me. It was time for me to write about those priceless memories that have been with me for so many years. But it will never replace my desire to put on the pads and slip into that gold and blue uniform of the Westinghouse Bulldogs. I have been told many times over to let go of the past, but I have been driven to fulfill what has allured me for so many years.

All four parts of this book epitomizes how Westinghouse had risen to be one of the most respected football programs in Western Pennsylvania. Pennsylvania is a hotbed for high school football. Many of the legends that grace the Pro and College Football Halls of Fame have come out of Western Pennsylvania. The Bulldogs earned a reputation that became the envy of many throughout their storied history. The early years saw **Coach Pro Burton, *"The Builder of Champions,"*** put together an athletic program that paved the way for his successors to build on, and they did as the Bulldogs dominated the City League of Pittsburgh for many years during the twentieth century. They also held their own against the tough W.P.I.A.L. along the way. This was accomplished through the efforts of some **patient and excellent coaching** along with the talent and efforts year after year of a determined and dedicated array of gridiron warriors who were always eager and ready to uphold a very proud tradition. This proud football program has put together well over **500 wins, 35 Pittsburgh City League Titles and one W.P.I.A.L. Title** while winning over seventy percent of it's games. An unforgettable time period that spanned for over 90 years. Those gridiron warriors knew what it was like to perform on a hard oil soaked terrain where no grass root system could ever grow. The home field of the Bulldogs was in dire need of a makeover that never came. The luxury of playing on natural grass was a real treat that only came when they traveled outside of the city limits to play a Friday night game under the lights at one of the suburban school stadiums. That was a real treat for all of us.

## LOVE FOR THE GAME

My love for the game of football was something to look forward to every autumn. When September rolled around and another new school year began, football was in the air. Our fine marching band, led by Mr. Carl McVicker was getting ready for another gridiron season. Musical renditions could be heard throughout those hallowed halls. That marching unit of gold and blue did itself proud at all the games season after season. The cheerleaders were out on the courtyard mastering cheer after cheer. The football team under the watchful eyes of Coach Pete Dimperio was down on the field working hard to get ready for another banner year. The atmosphere within our school was filled with much enthusiasm and we let it all hang out at every pep rally. It was a special time of year as our student body fed off the winning ways of our football team. The spirited fan support from both students and alumni was quite impressive and winning gave us every reason to be proud. It was so heart warming to see alumni coming back to see the Bulldogs play game after game. They never forgot where they came from.

## LOOKING BACK IN TIME

Back in the mid -1850's, Homewood was a valley of wooded fields and swamps with a few houses and farms and a small railroad station. Before the turn of the century several of the early elite Pittsburgh families constructed country estates on this undeveloped land, and they began to build strong traditions. One of those early aristocrats was George Westinghouse who later became our high school namesake. He was a very proud successful industrialist in our country's folklore of history and having our school named after him certainly reinforced our pride and loyalty.

When Westinghouse High School was organized in 1912, it was situated on Brushton and Baxter Avenues. Back then it was called Brushton High School. During that year one hundred and thirty-five freshmen entered its portals. The building was not yet completed, but the students were eager to attend classes. The faculty at that

25

time was twenty-seven in number, Mr. W.L.Leopold was Principal and Miss Eleanor Wood was Chief Clerk. Then baseball, football and hiking were the main sports. There was still a lot of undeveloped land nearby and so hiking was a popular activity for many of the students to enjoy.

Later on, between 1910 and 1950, a steady stream of immigrants moved into Homewood to form a little league-of-nations. Italian, Irish, and German immigrants faced discrimination along with the blacks from the early white settlers. Prior to 1950 the Italians had the largest ethnic group and they had strong traditions that continued to revitalize the community. There were traditions that survived opposition and tension of several culture and ethnic differences with the realization that loyalty and respect for each other was required in order to be successful. Up until the 1950's, the Homewood-Brushton community had been integrated with relatively little racial conflict. The key movement occurred when the Civic Arena was built displacing several thousand residents from the Lower Hill district of Pittsburgh. Most of those residents were black. Many of them moved to Homewood and the whites began to move out to the suburbs. Not all the whites moved out of Homewood as many stayed in the area south of the railroad tracks in Point Breeze. Before this movement the population had about 25% black and by 1960, it had risen more than 60%. The trend steadily increased and spilled over into the surrounding communities of Lincoln and Larimer and Westinghouse continued to win in a big way.

In 1948, my first year at the House, the Bulldogs starting eleven had only one black – halfback Charles "Porky" Jones, but by 1959 the starting eleven had only one white – fullback Mike Bisceglia. The winning tradition was always there as each generation strived to carry on what the early classes had worked so hard to establish.

During that time span, the Bulldogs captured nine city championships, as the winning tradition never wavered. Regardless of race, creed or color, the Westinghouse loyalty prevailed. We were blessed with dedicated young men who respected leadership and dedication and were willing to go the extra mile. During this extreme population change, legendary coach Pete Dimperio never let it affect the dedication and loyalty he had for his players. White or black it never made any difference to him. When anyone would ask him about the number of blacks or whites on his team he would smile and say "They could be green, yellow, purple, and black or white as long as they have the desire, dedication, loyalty and respect for each other is all that matters to me." Just as it is in life – the family that prays together stays together and that is what he preached to his players. A winning team is one that plays together striving to reach a common goal, and no one player is bigger than the game of football.

## PROGRAM CHANGES HAVE AFFECTED THE HOUSE

In recent years as the twentieth century was coming to an end the House has experienced hard times on the gridiron, but it is not from the lack of effort. The odds have favored cross town rival Perry Traditional Academy as the open enrollment policy/magnet programs in the Pittsburgh City School System has strongly supported their football fortunes. I have been following high school football for well over fifty years and it does not take a postal clerk to sort out all the different zip codes that have graced the talented Perry Commodores football program in the past twenty years.

When Westinghouse High School enjoyed those many years of success in the City League they did so with talented athletes that resided in the Homewood-Brushton, Lincoln-Lemington and Larimer neighborhoods under the zip codes that were within its jurisdiction. It was three proud neighborhoods that provided the Westinghouse Bulldogs with a winning tradition. Today those same neighborhoods are taking advantage of choice programs that are being offered elsewhere in the city of Pittsburgh. Unfortunately, the students are making choices to attend school elsewhere. Sometimes in life you have to make your own opportunities by supporting the hand that is dealt to you.

Today I see the old traditions and loyalty slowly drifting away, and I am saddened by this discouraging development. Back in our day the curriculum was the same at all the city schools, therefore you were expected to attend the school where you lived. That school was the heart and soul of each community, but today that is no longer the case. Today the bond of community and the school is lost. The values we gained from that bonding were priceless.

Those echoes of our past could be heard across the entire community - "You can be sure if it's Westinghouse." Today there are echoes of violence that have really affected this proud community. God forbid if those who care should lose the battle of maintaining the pride of Westinghouse High School. Her alumni shudder every time a disaster occurs within that community, and I am one who is deeply saddened when such events do occur.

With the open enrollment magnet programs and the negative street behavior the likelihood of Westinghouse regaining the glory days of football success will be a monumental challenge. The latter years have been a real struggle for the football program of the Bulldogs. The local sports pages no longer highlight the winning ways of the House. How disappointing it is to see them of late in last place of the City League standings. What was once a proud football tradition that had so much pride and respect has been tarnished. Our predecessors worked hard to establish our legacy. They did it with a strong loyal community and a desire to make Westinghouse High School, the best that it could be. There was no need to bus across town to find a better opportunity for scholastic or athletic endeavors. School and community loyalty was once her strength, but today that has been challenged.

## ACCOLADES AND MEMORIES ARE COUNTLESS

As we continue through the storied football history of Westinghouse High School I may have omitted naming your favorite player or have not praised your favorite team, and I must apologize for that. Every young man who wore the gold and blue colors deserved to be recognized. Each and every one of them (including the student managers) has contributed in some way to the fine tradition of Westinghouse High School. It took a lot of dedication, pride, sacrifice and much more than most people realize to make the football team. There were demands that would never have been tolerated by todays youth. "If you wanted to play for the Bulldogs there was a tough

27

road to travel with no short-cuts." Many of those who traveled that road who are still with us today and those who have departed this life will always be remembered for upholding the special loyalty of Westinghouse High School. Football was the one sport that brought us all together. Every football season was like a community reunion as the Bulldogs rolled on to victory.

I have been to many class reunions, alumni functions and socials and we proudly reflect on those foregone years. A lot of it has to do with Westinghouse High School playing such an important role in the communities of Homewood, Brushton, Lemington, Lincoln and Larimer. Back then the school was literally our home away from home. My six years at Westinghouse were very fulfilling and rewarding. We learned our lessons well from a faculty that was second to none. They prepared us well for the outside world.

It has been many years since many of us have received our diplomas, but the experience will be with us for the rest of our lives. It is a case of never forgetting where we came from to remind us how far we have come in our life's journey.

**28**

# PART 1

## THE EARLY YEARS

*The community of Homewood-Brushton portrays a long diverse history of one of the oldest neighborhoods in the City of Pittsburgh, Pennsylvania. Dating back to the years 1860-1910 Pittsburgh's elite constructed great Country Estates on lands which had been forests and fields. By 1912 they organized a new high school for one hundred thirty freshmen eager to attend. That high school became the focal point of that community. The next four chapters will take us through a time period that reflects how that little school became well known in the City of Pittsburgh.*

# 1 | "PRO" BURTON ARRIVES IN HOMEWOOD

Every success story has a beginning, and the beginning of our success story goes all the way back to the year 1912 - when Westinghouse High School was organized and opened its portals for one hundred thirty freshman eager to attend classes. The faculty at that time was twenty-seven in number. Mr. W.L. Leopold was Principal and Miss Eleanor Wood was Chief Clerk. They were the pioneers who began developing the educational and athletic foundations for the future classes to build on. The school was located on Brushton and Baxter Avenues in a secluded area east of the outskirts of the City of Pittsburgh. They did not have the spacious facilities that many of the more established schools of the city had, but they persevered. They had no facilities to carry on their athletic interests but this only inspired work of a determined order that achieves the impossible, and won for our teams an unimpeachable record. Patience is a virtue that those early classes possessed and they made the most of each opportunity to excel. They challenged and competed against the best and gained ground with each passing year. They (the Class of 1916) paved the way by developing a tradition that was an inspiration to the future classes of Westinghouse High School. Before we get too far along with historical facts let us be reminded that Brushton High School was later renamed after a legendary inventor and businessman who at the turn of the century had made his home in Homewood joining other elites – Andrew Carnegie, Henry Clay Frick and John Heinz. That man was George Westinghouse who was a deliberate man – conscious of his power and cultivated it. Rain or shine he was known to always carry an umbrella – an old trait of his as told by early residents of the Homewood area. He was an efficient man who never wasted time, energy or motion, and was known to wave his umbrella vigorously when flagging down a train. The train conductors were instructed to stop the train until he was on board. In an era when train schedules were tight and punctual, only Westinghouse could delay a train. He was no ordinary commuter as his vast wealth and standing in the community was widely recognized and respected. Is it not surprising that Westinghouse High School would maintain such a proud perception of its' industrial namesake.

## OUR NAMESAKE EMERGES

The name George Westinghouse surfaced way back in 1846, the year he was born in a small town in New York State who at the age of fifteen had invented a rotary engine. Many years later, after having served in the Civil War, this young man excelled in becoming one of the most successful giants of the Industrial Revolution. His invention of the airbrake in 1868 opened the doors for the ever popular Westinghouse Air Brake Company in Pittsburgh in 1869. His invention transformed the American economy, permitting safe high-speed operation of trains in the transportation industry. He died in 1914, and later a Pittsburgh high school was named after him – that school being George Westinghouse High School. Several public high schools in the City of Pittsburgh were named after all but forgotten people who were historical legends of their time. Joining George Westinghouse were David Oliver (known as the father of Pittsburgh schools), Taylor Allderdice, Benjamin Peabody, John A. Brashear, Samuel P. Langley, Oliver H. Perry and Mary Schenley. They were all worthy of having schools named after them.

## PRO BURTON PAVES THE WAY

It wasn't until the year of 1916 when Mr. O.H. "Pro" Burton accepted the position of Athletic Director and Head Football Coach that the little school in Brushton was to realize how to gain the respect and recognition of a champion. Prior to Pro's arrival, Hugh Robinson - who was also a math teacher - was the first head football coach at the old Brushton High School from 1913 through 1915. He produced some pretty competitive teams that were respectable during those three years, but to many of the old timers it wasn't until 1916 that the existence of Brushton High School later renamed Westinghouse became a known fact. The arrival of Pro Burton was the beginning of our athletic fortunes. From Springfield College in Missouri, where he played guard on the football teams of 1912 and 1913, he went to the YMCA College in Springfield, Massachusetts. Accepting his first athletic employment in 1915 as Athletic Director of the McKeesport YMCA, Pro Burton arrived in Homewood-Brushton young, vigorous and determined to make good on his first coaching assignment at Westinghouse High School. He was the athletic department and the builder of our championship image. He gave a lifetime of service to our school and our community and will always be remembered as our builder of champions.

*Note: Let me point out that Coach Burton's name appeared in some of the news sources as Otis, Oliver, and/or O.H. Burton, therefore since I am not sure which is appropriate, I will from time to time do the same.*

Let us liken the building of this championship image as if we were building a house. There are three major stages of building a house - the foundation, the walls and then the roof. We saw three significant coaching eras that realistically built the football fortunes of Westinghouse High School in much the same manner. These three eras collectively produced and maintained a winning tradition that was the envy of many school districts in western Pennsylvania. It all began with a solid foundation - an era led by the legendary Otis "Pro" Burton - followed by the diversified era led by another legend, Peter Paul Dimperio, and later on the challenge era led by one of our own alumnus, George A. Webb. Today it is a historic landmark that stands with much

**32**

pride in the Homewood community of Pittsburgh, Pennsylvania. Countless alumni who have passed through this historic landmark will always remember it as Westinghouse Forever. Many years later we are looking at a high school that has won well over five hundred football games, thirty-five Pittsburgh City League Titles and one WPIAL Title, and has possessed a tradition that will go down in history as one of the finest in the country. May that tradition continue to flourish in the hearts and minds of those that pass through those hallowed halls.

In 1916, the year Woodrow Wilson retained the presidency of the United States by the slightest of margins, Pro Burton arrived at Westinghouse High School as an unknown and untried coach, but it presented no barrier to him. He soon won the hearts of the community with his quiet, friendly mannerisms. With an eager and dedicated group of young athletes he proceeded to build a future for Westinghouse in football, baseball, basketball, volleyball, and track and field. Some of those young men who helped to build the early success story for Pro Burton were Harry Grunnagle, Captain of the 1915 baseball team, Dave Longwell, Frank Youngk, Fred (Lou) Youngk, James Emery Auld, Walter Clark Bacon, Harry Clyde Doverspike, Edward Robinson Eyler, Chester Herrod, Henry Lippincott, R. Miller, George Macmillan, James Ray Nicodemis, Scott Franklin Tarner, Charley Wadsworth, W. Waite, K. Taylor, Joe Brown Steen, M. F. Berardino, A. Van-Tine Kennedy and Hammy Nunn.

Pro Burton's first football team was fielded in 1916, and only seventeen boys showed up for the first day of practice. They were eager and dedicated young men who took their lumps from the likes of Connellsville, Wilkinsburg, Allegheny, and Peabody; defeated Carnegie and tied Parnassus and posted a season record 1-4-1. Those dedicated team members were H. Beatty, P. Brittner, D. Martin, H. Dosey, D. Longwell, Frank Youngk, Fred Youngk, J. Auld, W. Bacon, H. Doverspike, E. Eyler, C. Herrod, H. Lippincott, R. Miller, G. McMillan, J. Nicodemis, S. Tarner, C. Wadsworth, W. Waite, K. Taylor, J. Steen, M. F. Berardino, A. Kennedy and Hammy Nunn.. As I look at the photograph of this team of seventeen young men I can't help but admire their determination for having played a whole season against some well established teams as Connellsville and Wilkinsburg. It had to be a very difficult season trying to prepare for each opponent with limited numbers to work with. Wilkinsburg won the WPIAL Class AA Championship that year and had no pity on the undermanned Bulldogs.

Prior to World War I many of the talented athletes dropped out of high school to go to work to help support their families. They continued to play football for some of the many sandlot teams in the surrounding districts of East Liberty. There were several good teams around who played on some of the old playgrounds that no longer exist today. Some of those old playgrounds were the Washington Boulevard Grounds, old Mellon Field, Homewood Playgrounds, D.C. and A.C. Park, Brushton County League Park and the old carnival grounds at Hamilton and Dunfermline Street. Several of the former Westinghouse gridders went on to play for the Westinghouse Alumni a tough independent team.

33

## THE AFFECTS OF WORLD WAR I

There was a lapse of a year or more in the playing eligibility of many of the young men as World War I in 1917 was raging, and it had an affect on the school and the community. Several students took advantage of the college education program while you serve military time, which was being offered by the Armed Forces of our country. The seasons of 1917 and 1918 were lacking the normal time and interest, and it showed in the final records of each of those years. Westinghouse posted a record of 2-5-1 in 1917 and played only one game in 1918 as the season was cancelled after one game was played. That war lasted from 1914-1918, and one of the side entrances to the school has a memorial plaque located above it in memory of those alumni whom served and sacrificed their lives so valiantly for our country.

With the war finally coming to an end, our community was getting back to normal activity and Coach Burton was happy to get back to working with his student athletes. He produced the first City Championship won by a Westinghouse High School varsity team in any sport with his 1919 basketball team. They were called the Marvel Team - led by such players as Paul Young, Harry Beatty, "Buckets" Bell, Henry Dosey, Andy King, and Don Martin. Even though we are covering football it is worth mentioning this outstanding basketball team. They were a product of the coaching efforts of a young Pro Burton and a group of dedicated and talented young men. Obviously, they must have been special in that era as the label, "Marvel Team," would imply.

Getting back to football, the 1919 team bounced back and recorded the first winning football season (5-1-1) at Westinghouse. Their only loss of the season was to Allegheny High School who was crowned City League Champions that year. It was the first year of crowning a city champion in football in the Pittsburgh City League. The only team to score on the Bulldogs that year was Allegheny and they did so in a big way by the score of 33-0. The five wins by the Bulldogs were shutouts with a scoreless tie against Fifth Avenue High School. All things considered, it was a successful season, and Coach Burton was beginning to see his football program making progress.

Six lettermen and eleven new candidates were put together the following year to form the 1920 team, which managed to defeat the defending city champion Allegheny for the first time in the last five years of competition. This team posted a season record 5-3-0; the three losses were to Peabody, Schenley and Fifth Avenue respectively. The newly crowned city champion for that season was Fifth Avenue High School. During this period of time (1919-1920) several young men were dedicated to Pro Burton in his efforts to build the football program and they deserve to be recognized as his early football pioneers Mike Donghue, Dick Lippincott, Glenn (Butch or Bottles) Carroll, Ed (Harp) Daly, Earl France, Harry Richards, Eddy Shook, William John Henry, Paul Youingk (who later was an All-American in his final year at Pitt under legendary Coach Pop Warner), Rolly Dale, Sam Rumbaugh, Clayton Walker, George McKinney, Curtis Brosie, Walter (Yock) Mackey, Stanley Ament, Jack Gulland, Montgomery Lantz, Frank (Red) Clark, Tom Scott Brown, and Harold (Specs) Elward.

## PATIENCE AND DETERMINATION

As Burton and his boys continued to build the foundation of the athletic program, one has to admire their determination. Many sacrifices were made as they were all striving to reach a common goal. They had to overcome a lot of adversity with the many hardships and inconveniences that existed during that era. The small school in Brushton was overcrowded with limited facilities, but somehow they learned to persevere. It was not easy to stay in school long enough to graduate as many families were experiencing hard times and needed help at home. Imagine trying to play athletics, keep up with your studies and work part-time to help support the family. This was quite common back then. Many young men played out their athletic eligibility (four-year rule), and had to drop out of school to go to work. Back then, graduating from high school was considered quite an honorable accomplishment. It was very difficult for the many young people who had to leave school because of family hardships. That entire generation is to be commended for establishing such a solid foundation for the future generations to build on. The success story of the Westinghouse football fortunes is a reflection of those early pioneers and coach Pro Burton for providing such a great beginning.

I was fortunate to be able to talk with many of those old timers that were a part of that generation. Many of them are no longer with us today, but the memories of those conversations are priceless. It was gratifying to see some of the smiling faces of those who played for Pro Burton. The mere mention of his name seemed to ignite one story after another. How proud they were to tell me of their playing days. Play by play accounts of certain games that they shared with me was fascinating. The pre-game pep talks Pro Burton orchestrated were something that they would never forget. His legacy will long be remembered as my own ninety-five year old father still likes to sit and talk about his memories of the old coach. Thank god at his age he is still able to remember his days at Westinghouse and his two favorite Bulldog greats Joe "Showboat" Ware and Bobby Dye. Once he gets started on his soapbox there is no stopping him. As I watch his facial expressions it is so gratifying to listen to him reminisce. He is very quiet at this stage of his life, but the mere mention of his days at the House really motivates him. This seemed to be so common with that generation, as fond memories of their past seems to rekindle their spirits. I must have heard the same stories over and over again, but just to see that smile appear makes it all worthwhile.

So many times over you will hear somebody say - "A picture is worth a thousand words"- and I really found that to be true as I journeyed through my research process. The school yearbooks during the early years reflected so much through photos; recognizing the challenging lifestyle they must have endured. It was hard to fathom how they were able to accomplish with so little to work with. Within those photos especially the individual portraits the facial expressions reflected more intense looks than smiles. Obviously, it was a reflection of a very challenging era. They were the true pioneers of our country. As I mentioned earlier they faced so many hardships, but still managed to persevere. When any of them try to tell the younger generation

35

to be thankful for what they have today our young people do not want to hear it. They turn on a deaf ear and laugh; I know I have been called old man a few times. Well so much for human nature, let us get on with our story line.

The following pages of photos were taken from several early Westinghouse yearbooks that reflect so much of how our tradition developed. I was always one who appreciated looking at historic photos because I enjoyed putting myself into that setting. It was like a comfort zone for me. I was able to look through those many early yearbooks for hours and enjoy the time I spent doing so. To me it was like traveling on an endless journey through time; time that really gave me much gratification in pursuing this endeavor. So many times I would recognize a person and realize that they walked the same halls and sat in the same classrooms as I did. Many of them were family friends, neighbors and also family members. To me it was a fascinating experience to flip through those pages and get the feeling of how well those past generations of students were able to achieve and persevere through such difficult times. The experiences of World War I, the Great Depression, the 1936 Flood, World War II, Korea and Vietnam were challenges that tested the determination and loyalty of so many of our people. Today we are being challenged again. It is such a monumental task throughout the world to find peace and tranquility and only the power of prayer is the only hope that we have to turn to.

36

**THE BEGINNING OF AN ERA**

"Pro" Burton

37

*Burton • Dimperio • Musilin • Malins • Webb*

**THE SKETCHBOOK**

38

# With the First Class

When Westinghouse High School was organized in 1912 it was situated on Brushton and Baxter Avenues. During that year one hundred thirty freshmen entered its portals. Although the building was not yet completed, the students were anxious to attend classes.

The faculty at that time was twenty-seven in number, Mr. Leopold was Principal and Miss Eleanor Wood, the Chief Clerk. The remaining twenty-five were: Catherine Austin, Science; Isabel Clingensmith, English; Lewis Elhuff, Science; LeMyra Gillis, English; Constance Hartgering, History; Alice Hayward, English; Carrie Kim, German; C. B. Kistler, Mathematics; G. A. Leopold, Mathematics; C. G. Reigner, Commercial; Anna Robinson, English; H. E. Robinson, Mathematics; I. A. Timlin, Science; Leroy Wolff, Latin; W. H. Rankin, Latin; G. P. Eckels, Commercial; H. L. Dorner, Commercial; J. H. Kutcher, Commercial; Anna Shuman, Art; A. W. Wilhoyte, Commercial; Harry Archer, Music; Fannie R. Woodside, Cooking; Fannie Wilson, Sewing; John Thompson, Mechanical Drawing; and J. G. Hartlieb, Shop.

Then Baseball, Football, and Hiking were the main sports.

*WHS Class of 1916*

*Burton • Dimperio • Musilin • Malins • Webb*

## THE SKETCHBOOK

**W. L. Leopold**
*Principal*

39

**C. B. Kistler**
*Vice Principal*
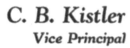

THE SKETCHBOOK

The Faculty in 1916

40

*WHS Class of 1916*

PRO'S FIRST WESTINGHOUSE HIGH SCHOOL FOOTBALL TEAM 1916

41

The following members of the team are in no special order: Harry Beatty, Preston Brittner, Don Martin, Henry Dosey, Dave Longwell, Frank Youngk, James Auld, Walter Bacon, Harry Doverspike, Edward Eyler, Chester Herrod, Henry Lippincott, R. Miller, George McMillan, James Nicodemis, Scott Tarner, Charles Wadsworth, Walter Waite, K. Taylor, Joe Steen, M.F. Berardino, Agnew Kennedy, Hammy Nunn, Coach O.H. "Pro" Burton.

1919 - WESTINGHOUSE HIGH SCHOOL CITY CHAMPIONS - 1919

42

The following members are in no special order: H.Dosey, F. Youngk, H. Beatty, Bell, King, D. Martin, P. Brittner, Shook, Rumbaugh, A. Kennedy, W. Waite, Kimes, Coach O. H. "Pro" Burton.

PITTSBURGH POST.

...ARY 1, 1911.

# SILVER LAKE AND 10 1-2 ACRES IN TWELFTH WARD PROPOSED PLAYGROUND SITE UNDER BOND ISSUE

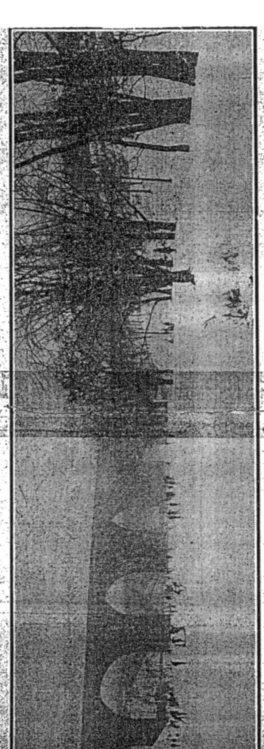

The lake itself has been for years a loved resort of East End youth and the planting and the building of bath houses, it would become a mecca for the

Silver lake and its beautiful natural surroundings will probably be condemned by the city and utilized for a playground. The Lincoln board of trade has started a movement to have the city acquire 12 acres of land, including the lake, and has made a report to Mayor Magee and the Pittsburgh Playgrounds association on the feasibility of the proposition. In the bond issue authorized in November $80,000 was set aside for acquiring playgrounds sites.

Silver lake is situated in the heart of the new Twelfth ward just below the

Brilliant cut-off bridge of the Pennsylvania railroad. The territory, which the board of trade has in mind, consists principally of a thinly wooded hollow with considerable level ground. Nine and a half acres belong to the Finley estate and 3½ acres to the Smith estate.

Rev. C. R. Zahniser, who is chairman of the board of trade committee which drew up a report on the matter, thinks Silver lake and vicinity an ideal place for a playground. He pointed out that it is within 15 minutes' walk of 40,000 people, including 6,000 or 7,000 children. The lake is within a short distance from the Lin-

coln avenue, Frankstown avenue and Hamilton avenue street car lines and Beechwood boulevard runs through the proposed site.

There is plenty of room for several ball grounds, according to Rev. Zahniser, and one corner of the site is admirably adapted for a nature garden for the children. The slopes of the hollow are wooded, affording a pleasant place for picnics and Silver lake, covering 2¼ acres, is mostly shallow but of a good quality of water.

Residents of the district think if a playground is not made of the hollow it will become a slum district like sections of

Junction hollow and other sections of the city situated near creeks. By fish

picture taken yesterday shows the surface in use by skaters. By fish children of that whole section of the city.

The Finley tract is assessed, at about $2,000 an acre. The Smith tract includes some land that could be used for building and is a little higher. No attempt has been made to find out what the owners want for the property, as it would be taken if at all, by condemnation proceedings. Councilman Charles Ross, of the Twelfth ward, is much interested in the proposition and may later introduce an ordinance to condemn the property if the city administration is agreeable to the

# 2 | THE 1920'S - FIRST CHAMPIONSHIP SEASON

The year of 1921 will always be remembered as the year of the "Champion of Champions" - Westinghouse High School's first football championship team. This team was greatly handicapped by inexperience and size at key positions, but nevertheless they persevered while compiling a record of 7-0-1, and were crowned Pittsburgh City Champions. They also tied Rochester 0-0 for a share of the WPIAL Championship and the Syracuse Trophy. That year much to his surprise - when Pro Burton called for the first practice session - seventy-five candidates reported at DC and AC Park. Compare this with the seventeen boys who showed up for the first practice in 1916, and you can see the headway that the football program was beginning to make. Among the lettermen returning from the 1920 team were Captain Rumbaugh, Farmer, Ament, Mackey, McKinney, Grunnagle, Dale, and Brosie. Some of the outstanding newcomers were Elward, Lantz, Brown and Wimmer. This team had only 14 points scored against them, and they amassed a total of 152 points. The WPIAL Championship game was played at Carnegie Tech Stadium on December 3, 1921 between Westinghouse and Rochester High Schools. In that game the Bulldogs suffered greatly with injuries early in the game to key players Farmer, Dale and Lantz and battled the heavily favored Rochester team to a scoreless tie. This tie gave Westinghouse a share of the WPIAL Title with Rochester. This was quite an accomplishment along with winning the Pittsburgh City Title and recording a season record of 7-0-1 for the little city school in Brushton. At the end of the season, several all-scholastic teams were picked by the news media, and at least three to five players from Westinghouse were selected to each team. Among those selected were: Dale, Rumbaugh, Farmer, Ament, Grunnagle, Wimmer, Mackey, Lantz and Walker, with Farmer and Rumbaugh selected for the WPIAL first team and Dale on the second team. Brown, Mackey and Elward were outstanding throughout the entire season. The general line-up for this team which back then was called the "Champion of Champions" is as follows:

| | |
|---|---|
| Left End | Ament and Brosie |
| Left Tackle | Rumbaugh (Captain) |
| Left Guard | Dale and Walter Brown |
| Center | McKinney |
| Right Guard | Mackey |
| Right Tackle | Clayton Walker |

| | |
|---|---|
| Right End | Farmer and Clark |
| Quarterback | Grunnagle |
| Left Halfback | Lantz |
| Right Halfback | Elward |
| Fullback | Dale and Wimmer |

This 1921 championship team will always be remembered for pioneering the winning tradition that preceded a number of championship teams that followed throughout the twentieth century. It was a tradition that continued to flourish and become the heart and soul of the folklore that we were quite proud to share. Loyalty, spirit and pride were always so much a part of the many successes and achievements that the Homewood school accomplished.

**1921 SEASON (7-0-1)**

| WHS | 35 | Swissvale | 0 |
|---|---|---|---|
| | 6 | Allegheny | 0 |
| | 51 | Fifth Avenue | 0 |
| | 13 | Peabody | 7 |
| | 20 | Schenley | 0 |
| | 7 | South | 0 |
| | 20 | South Hills | 7 |
| | 0 | Rochester | 0 |

Westinghouse wins City Championship (No playoff)
WPIAL Championship (Syracuse Trophy)
**WHS 0    Rochester    0**

As I reviewed some of the early year books it was quite clear that the pride of those classes was special. I was impressed and have included some of those impressions.

## TRADITION

With the opening of the 1922 autumn semester, Westinghouse High School expects to move into its new quarters in Homewood at Murtland Avenue and Monticello Street. It will be the realization of a "hope long deferred."

During the years since its organization in 1912, Westinghouse High School has built up a name to be proud of, one which has given it a peerage among other high schools – in a word Westinghouse has built up a body of honorable tradition.

We have been deprived of much of our rightful heritage of beauty and facility of equipment; but we have tried more earnestly to put beauty into our hearts and minds, and to invent when efficiency was impossible; to perform each duty, and to enter into each activity in the spirit of service and cooperation.

Our boys and girls have had no facilities for carrying on their athletic interests, but this only inspired work of a determined order that achieves the impossible, and won for teams an unimpeachable record.

45

Likewise, in our literary and dramatic work; we have persevered in spite of obstacles, and have been successful in all our efforts.

Our spirit in overcoming these hardships has given prestige to the name of our school, and the ideals for which it stands, so that now, when the name of Westinghouse is spoken, people no longer think of a small insignificant school on the outskirts of the city, but immediately they think of a body of conscientious workers, who have raised the standards of Westinghouse to rank with many older schools.

Our new building will be second to none in our city, and will in itself be an object of beauty. We must build our school on the sure foundation of the records of these past workers, which will outlive any foundation of material worth. By building thus, we shall keep tradition living within the walls as an inspiration for future classes.

## WHS CLASS OF JUNE, 1922
## FALL OF 1922 USHERS IN LONG AWAITED NEW SCHOOL BUILDING

After the successful 1921 season, it was a known fact that Westinghouse High School did indeed exist. They were now champions of the Pittsburgh City League and co-champions with Rochester High School of the WPIAL, and were looking forward to moving into a long awaited new school building in the fall of 1922. The new school building was located in Homewood at the corner of Murtland Avenue and Monticello Street and it was the realization of a long time coming. The new school was equipped with facilities that were spacious and the student body was more than ready to take its place with the more established schools of the greater Pittsburgh area. The new football field was in a natural oval-like setting surrounded by wooded slopes on two sides, bleachers on the near side (school side) and at the open end was the beautiful Silver Lake. It was a setting that would satisfy an ambitious photographer. This entire area was nestled in a deep valley located behind the school building with a long set of concrete steps leading down to the field with a perimeter cinder track. This was all in place ready for the upcoming 1922 school year. The adjacent Silver Lake was a natural resource that became a significant attraction to our school. In fact, often times Westinghouse was referred to as the "Silver Lakers" as well as the Bulldogs. The class of June, 1922 expressed in their yearbook with heartfelt pride of the traditional accomplishments by the previous generations of classes who had worked so hard to earn the dedication of the new high school in Homewood..

The 1922 team had several holdovers from the 1921 championship team - namely Elward, Lantz, Farmer, Wimmer, Ed Clark, Tubby Reister, Bobby Rylands, Jack Gulland and Barney Geilfuss. This team played two games outside the city league – beating Swissvale 27-0 and tying Monaca 0-0. In league play they lost to the eventual Pittsburgh City League Champion Allegheny 17-13 and to Schenley 6-0, and defeated Peabody 26-0, Fifth Avenue 40-7, South 34-6 and South Hills 14-0. They finished the season with a record 5-2-1. Other members of this team were Ament, Buck, Brown, Swaile, Elkfeld, Hussey, Hum Bert, Bence, W. Woods, J.R. Bentley, Nemis, B. Buncher, Llewlyn, Curry, Freeman, Blair, Conte, Robinson, and Petsinger.

## AT LAST!

If it were possible for the students who now fill the new Westinghouse High School classrooms, to visit the classes of 1915, 1916, 1917, and 1918 in the old Brushton Avenue Building, to know their hopes, their plans, their disappointments, to share in their amusement in visualizing the big, roomy building which is now ours, they would know that Westinghouse High School is more than just a picture on a postcard. Deprived of its material structure, these early classes began laying traditions, began laying foundations of success in athletics, literature and scholarship. They gave its name a meaning. Almost overnight the little East End School sprang into prominence, and took its place with the much older and more established schools of Pittsburgh.

These old classes were not privileged to get into the new school, but they have carried on with them the pioneer spirit of Westinghouse, and they have handed down from class to class that determination to build and to achieve. The present student body seems to understand the significance of their heritage. Let them take up the work. Vast possibilities lie before them. Though greatly handicapped, what were the triumphs of the early classes? What are to be the triumphs of the new classes?

*WHS Class of January, 1923*

47

### "Westinghousism"
There is Patriotism, there is Americanism, and there is "Westinghousism." Patriotism usually means loyalty to the ideals of the patriot in time of war: Americanism, loyalty to the welfare of America at all times: Westinghousism, loyalty to the welfare of Westinghouse. America is more than an expanse of territory. Westinghouse High School is more than a mass of brick, clay and mortar. Westinghouse is what her students are. What they become, she will be. They can write her name on the clouds or drag it in the dust. Her name can appear at the top only when they put it there. She can claim only as many silver cups as they win for her. In short, they determine her pulse beat of success.

*WHS Class of January 1923*

### Burton Rebuilding with Patience
The following year, 1923 saw Allegheny repeat as the Pittsburgh City League Champion. They defeated the Bulldogs 32-0 and were the best team in the city that year. Westinghouse finished the season with a record of 3-4-1. The following three years saw Schenley High School of Oakland emerge as the top team in the city as they captured city titles in 1924, 1925 and 1926. They defeated Westinghouse in all three of those seasons, but the Bulldogs managed to stay competitive and posted respectable records of 5-3-0; 5-2-0; and 4-3-1 during that same time period. By now coach Burton was encouraged as he began to see more boys coming out for football.

In 1925 his first call for practice brought out one hundred candidates. Compare this with his first call for practice in 1916 which brought out only seventeen candidates - you could see the interest and progress that football was making at Westinghouse. Patience is a virtue and Pro Burton realized it was gong to take time to develop a winning program.

**1927 Team Recaptures Long Awaited Title**

In 1927 the long awaited City League Title returned home to Westinghouse since the "Champion of Champions" team of 1921. The 1927 team defeated Schenley for the first time in four years and produced the school's first collegiate All-American – Ken Ormiston, at the University of Pittsburgh in 1934 under the legendary coach Jock Sutherland. Some of the all-time Westinghouse greats were members of this stellar Bulldog team. Edgar Patterson won All-City and All WPIAL first team tackle. Others on the team included Larry (Red) Sullivan, later quarterback on one of the famous Duquesne University teams that defeated the Rose Bowl team of the University of Pittsburgh. Sullivan later went on to coach at Homestead High School. Ed Reilly was also a member of that Duquesne team with Sullivan. The Pittsburgh newspapers picked Westinghouse's Ken Ormiston, Edgar Patterson, James (Red) Will, Lawrence (Red) Sullivan, Regis Brown, Ed Reilly, and Albert (Pat) McQuinn on the All-City team with Honorable Mention going to Ollie Hussey and Goedell.

48

This Westinghouse team was a solid aggregation loaded with talent: Ken Ormiston, Ed Reilly, Harry Ayers, Larry (Red) Sullivan, Regis Brown (captain), Albert (Pat) McQuinn, Theodore Hill, Goedell, Edgar Patterson, James (Red) Will, Joseph Grace, Walter Benzie, Norman McCormick, Dallas, John Mayberry, George Burkholder, Wilson, Lester English, Harry Groves, Harry Stroud, Klotz, Angelo Carboni, James (Wm) Matoney, Mathews, Harold Stanford, Conley, John (Ollie) Hussey, Thompson, Rockford, Ficklin, Clyde Strainer, Cornell Cooper, Fred Beckett, Ralph Pacciarelli, Albert McIllveen, Frank (Hinks) Durzo, Bob Zollinger, Michael Pucciarelli, Joe Pritchard, Charles Phillips, Bradford Isley, Henry Idzowski. Walter Ganoe, Byron Evans, William Dawson, Charles Davis, Thomas Butler, Robert (Sparky) Adams with Campbell, team manager. Below is a summary of the 1927 season:

**1927 Season (7-0-1)**

| WHS | 42 | Swissvale | 0 |
|-----|----|-----------|---|
| | 0 | Wilkinsburg | 0 |
| | 6 | Schenley | 0 |
| | 70 | South | 0 |
| | 23 | Peabody | 6 |
| | 61 | Fifth Avenue | 6 |
| | 67 | South Brownsville | 6 |
| Pittsburgh City Championship | | | |
| WHS | 13 | Oliver | 6 |

## 1928 BRINGS BACK TO BACK TITLES

The following year was another banner year for the gold and blue. Eight lettermen returned from the previous year to defend their title and defend it they did. The first three games were non-league and on the road against the likes of New Castle, Waynesburg and Indiana. The Bulldogs defeated both Waynesburg 19-0, and Indiana 12-0, but suffered their only loss of the season to always tough New Castle 25-7. Pro Burton always liked to play against the best of the WPIAL in the pre-season prior to the City League schedule as it was a good way to find out how well prepared the Bulldogs were to challenge for the city title. It is a known fact that prior to the 1999 season New Castle High School has won more football games, 628, than any other high school in the WPIAL. Westinghouse always fared well during the early years against competition outside the city league. In fact they played New Castle six times in their series winning four times and losing twice. When you play against the best you find out how good you really are. The Bulldogs learned a lot from the New Castle defeat and were prepared to defend their city title. They had a fine season winning seven, losing one with one tie against tough Allegheny. Schenley challenged the Silver Lakers before losing 6-0. It was a tough win for Burton's boys as they were looking ahead to the city title game the following week against South Hills. The championship game was played at Pitt Stadium before an estimated 10,000 spectators. Westinghouse scored early in the first quarter after an exchange of punts. With South Hills losing twenty-five on the exchange the Bulldogs with good field position scored after two plays. Halfback Joe "Showboat" Ware passed to his running-mate James Matoney in the endzone from fifteen yards out and the Bulldogs were on the scoreboard. The try for extra point was blocked and that's all the scoring there was until the fourth quarter. South Hills practically outplayed the Silver Lakers for a better part of the first three quarters after turning back a late third quarter scoring threat. By the fourth quarter the relentless Bulldog ground game began to take its toll on the game Tunnelites. Westinghouse's bruising fullback Ken Ormiston paved the way scoring two touchdowns in the final stanza as the Bulldogs defended it's hold on the city title . The final score was Westinghouse 19 South Hills 0. South Hills was a worthy contender and gave the Bulldogs a real battle. Prior to this game South Hills had been in several title games and were looking to win their first one. Schenley was always their nemesis in past years and now Westinghouse extended that for another year. The Bulldogs had won back to back city titles and were now being recognized as a worthy up and coming powerhouse.

The members of this team were as follows: George Burkholder, Ed Reilly, Gil Nowe, James DeMarchi, Edgar Patterson, John Mayberry, Klotz, James Matoney, Ken Ormiston, Theodore Hill, Bob Dye, Joe Ware, Harold Stanford, Frank (Hinks) Durzo, John McCabe, Gagagen, George (Dutch) Schaltenbrand, James (Red) Will, Dave DeMarchi, Alfred McIllveen, Wayne Woods, Dave Martin, James Mathews, Aphonse Nardulli, Harry Grove, Chester Jalott, Lawrence (Red) Sullivan, William McCluan, Bob Zollinger, Clyde Strainer, Frank Tyson, Tom Wilson, Samuel Madine, James Matoney, Walter Benzie, Cornell Cooper, Paul Gibson, Ralph Pacciarelli,

Lenny Goldman, Fred Beckett, Earl Deremer, Lewis Seigler, Homer Wadsworth, Bernard Drosnes, Harold Wendell.

This team was recognized with several players receiving All-City and All-WPIAL awards. The All-City selections were Edgar Patterson, Ed Reilly, Ken Ormiston, John Mayberry, and Harold Stanford with Honorable Mention going to Klotz, Joe (Showboat) Ware and Larry (Red) Sullivan. Edgar Patterson and Ken Ormiston were All-WPIAL choices. Below is a summary of that fine season.

**1928 Season (7-1-1)**

| WHS | 46 | South | 6 |
|---|---|---|---|
| | 0 | Allegheny | 0 |
| | 12 | Indiana | 0 |
| | 7 | New Castle | 25 |
| | 27 | Fifth Avenue | 6 |
| | 19 | Waynesburg | 0 |
| | 31 | Peabody | 0 |
| | 6 | Schenley | 0 |

Pittsburgh City Championship

·WHS 19    South Hills   0

Score by periods:

| Westinghouse | 6 | 0 | 0 | 13 — 19 |
|---|---|---|---|---|
| South Hills | 0 | 0 | 0 | 0 — 0 |

Scoring:

Touchdowns — Ormiston 2; Matoney1.

PAT — Burkholder (placement kick)

Missed PAT's Burkholder (2 placements)

## HE HAD A DREAM

It was in early September of the year 1928, when a group of young boys in gym class were playing a game of touch football on the field at Westinghouse High School. One of the boys who was a member of this class was really putting on a show with his quickness and running ability. He was only fifteen years old; all of 5' 6" tall, bowlegged and weighed about 130 pounds soaking wet. He had speed to burn and could stop and go on a dime. Coach "Pro" Burton happened to be standing on top of the hill overlooking the field and was watching as this little boy ran and dazzled his way through that touch football game. He really did not know the boy by name, but could hear his classmates calling out "nice play Joe" or "nice run, Joe". After the game was over, Coach Burton met the boy at the top of the steps leading back up to the school building. He asked him his name and if he would be interested in playing football for Westinghouse. The boy responded with a yes answer, but was quick to express to the coach about his situation at home. He had a responsibility at home that was very demanding as he had recently lost both his mother and his oldest brother within a six month time period. This was quite a blow to him and the rest of the family as he was now the oldest sibling for his father to rely upon. It made for a very tough situation for his father and three younger sisters. With only a hope and a prayer this young boy went home that evening hoping to somehow persuade his father to give him both permission and the time to play football for Westinghouse. The father was proud of the boy, but was hard-pressed to give him permission since his responsibilities at home were numerous. He was now the oldest child and very much needed by his younger sisters. Without a mother at home it was very difficult. The next day the boy returned to school and met with Coach Burton. He told him of his father's decision.

A few days passed when much to his surprise, Coach Burton appeared at his home to talk to his father and express his feelings. He felt quite helpless, as there was nothing he could do to help the family. All he could do was thank the boy's father for his time and wish him well. It was a visit that this young boy would never forget. He appreciated the interest that Coach Burton had in his athletic abilities. It was a difficult time for him. He would not be able to fulfill his dream to play on the same team with his classmates Bobby Dye and Joe Ware. In fact, the following year (his senior year) he left Westinghouse to go to work to help support the family and got married at the age of 17. He progressed in the working world and made the most of his opportunities. Through hard work and a desire to learn he became a fine craftsman and machinist. It was several years later when I came to realize how good that boy was. He was the only father in our neighborhood who took the time to play ball with me and my boyhood friends. I saw the athletic moves he had and how he enjoyed playing football and softball with us. The neighbors really enjoyed watching him play. To this day at the age of 95, he is still quite proud at the mere mention of Coach "Pro" Burton and Westinghouse High School. He was never able to fulfill his dream, but he can still be proud of what could have been. That young boy was my father, Joseph Pellegrino. I will always be proud of you Dad this one's for you.

## 1929 SEES NEW STARS ON THE HORIZON

With several of the veterans from the 1927 and 1928 championship teams gone, Coach Burton was looking at some new stars emerging in 1929 to carry on the winning tradition. Joe (Showboat) Ware, Bobby Dye and Walter Benzie were all coming into their own. They were participating in other sports as well as football and the future was looking good for Westinghouse. Cornell Cooper and little Paul Gibson were making track history for the Bulldogs at the National Inter-Scholastic Meet in Chicago. Gibson was impressive in the mile run while Cooper set a new scholastic world record in the high jump at 6'-3". Later on in his career Cornell Cooper was setting new attendance records at nightclubs across the country with his musical and singing talent. The Cooper family lived only a block away from my family and Cornell was a classmate of my father. Later on in time Cornell's younger brother Charles came along and was a great basketball talent at both Westinghouse and Duquesne University. He was an All-American at Duquesne and later after his collegiate years were over he was the first African-American drafted to play in the National Basketball Association for the Boston Celtics. We will read more about him in a later chapter.

51

Getting back to the 1929 team, they had to settle for second place in the city league final standings behind Schenley as the Spartans defeated the Bulldogs 12-0 in league play. It was one of three losses for Westinghouse – the other two were non-league to Rochester (6-0) and Jeannette (6-0) as they finished the season with a record of 5-3-0. Schenley regained the city title that year by defeating South Hills 15-0 in the playoff as they continued to be a nemesis for the Tunnelites. Several of the boys from this Westinghouse team were selected to the All-City team – they were Frank (Hinks) Durzo, Dutch Scheltenbrand, Al McIllveen, Bobby Dye, Joe Ware, James DeMarchi and Rentler.

The football program that Pro Burton was building was really beginning to look more and more respectable. The overall record since the 1913 season was 69-42-14 with three City League titles and a share of one WPIAL title. Obviously with the new school building and athletic facilities the students at Westinghouse were beginning to show more interest in the various varsity sports. Pro Burton and the entire faculty staff had to be quite pleased with the progress that was developing at the relatively new school in Homewood. The habit of winning was beginning to catch on and the development of a proud tradition was spilling over into the community. It was the beginning of what the early classes at Westinghouse had worked so hard to establish. They persevered through some very tough years and they will always be remembered for providing such a strong foundation for future classes to build on. Westinghouse was beginning to gain respect with each passing year as Coach Burton was relentless in his efforts to drive his young men to higher levels of achievement. He was scheduling non-league games with some of the bigger and tougher WPIAL schools. Playing schools like New Castle, Greensburg, Altoona, Mt.Lebanon, Jeannette, McKeesport, New Kensington and Penn Hills were challenges, and an opportunity for his teams to gain respect. They were representing the City League and that was an incentive to win. Back then some of the non-league games were played at mid-season as well as early in the season. Traveling outside the city to these away games was a big treat for the city schools as they had an opportunity to play in stadiums that were far superior to what they were accustomed to. For one thing a grass field was non-existent in the City League and playing on one of the W.P.I.A.L. grass fields was a treat. The saying at Westinghouse was "if you do not have it then you will not miss it." Pro Burton preached that to his players. Therefore, the Bulldogs never would let the conditions of a playing field affect their performance. They were always well prepared to challenge those conditions. Coach Burton would never tolerate any excuses or complaints from his players. It was always his way or the highway.

Many of the alumni from the Burton era that I met through the years stated that he was a tough disciplinarian. He controlled his domain with strict regimented measures. He was a no nonsense coach with complete control of his football team. This was his way of gaining respect and it was also the way it was in most households. The father or the mother controlled the behavior at home and this carried over into our school. Teachers did not have to worry about hostile behavior and were able to teach more effectively. Today one would be hard-pressed to find such ideal conditions.

## IN A LEAGUE OF THEIR OWN

Up until 1927 the city schools of Pittsburgh competed in the W.P.I.A.L. and also within the city for local supremacy. In 1927 the city schools departed from the WPIAL and were realigned in the newly formed Pittsburgh City League. There were twelve high schools that made up the new league, and it was divided into two sections. Section 1 contained Allderdice, Peabody, Schenley, South Hills, South Vocational and Westinghouse. Section 2 contained Allegheny, Carrick, Fifth Avenue, Langley, Oliver and Perry. Section 1 was considered by many as the stronger of the two, but that was decided at season's end. Each school played three pre-season games and five section games. The pre-season games were played at the beginning of the season usually against schools from the W.P.I.A.L. At season's end the team with the best record in each section would play each other for the Pittsburgh City League Championship.

In the early years the city schools held their own outside their league, but as time went on they were no match against their W.P.I.A.L. opponents. The W.P.I.A.L. was far superior to their City League counterparts. Westinghouse High School was the only city school that was able to hold their own against the schools from the W.P.I.A.L. During the time period between the years 1916 – 1966 the Bulldogs had a respectable record of 61-55-17 against the WPIAL schools. Apparently there were several reasons for the lopsided games. The City League schools did not have the many luxuries that schools outside the city enjoyed – the best of equipment, facilities, large coaching staffs and lighted stadiums with grass playing fields. One would be hard pressed to find such luxuries in any of the city schools. That's the way it was back then and is still the same today.

On Friday nights during the fall season one could travel along the highways paralleling our three rivers and see the gleaming stadium lights of each of the little towns of Western Pennsylvania. I traveled with my friends many times to see some of the finest of high school football games beyond our city limits. We enjoyed it and it was interesting to see the traditions of the other schools in western Pennsylvania. We found out what we were missing playing in the City League, but we never complained. It was nice to sit in a stadium with lights gleaming down on a green playing field. Those three pre-season games every season were a real treat for the city kids to experience.

In 1967 the pre-season games were discontinued and the two sections were united into one. The two top teams then squared off for the city title. This was fine because it eliminated the lopsided losses to the WPIAL, but it took away the opportunity for the city kids to travel outside of the city. The kids from the city always wanted to challenge their counterparts. While at Westinghouse we felt quite proud to be able to play against the best and pull off an upset. It was gratifying to walk away from one of those stadiums especially Aliquippa with an unexpected victory. We had quite a series of games with them and played them pretty even (5-4-1) in favor of the House. Not bad for a city school.

Today, some fifty years later, all the city schools play their games at Cupples Stadium on the South Side of Pittsburgh. This stadium has lights and an artificial

53

playing surface and is not far from the Pittsburgh Steelers practice complex. There is no longer a home field advantage in the city. All the schools use their home fields for practices and scrimmages. This apparently fits in well for the city school budget. As time marches on commodities improve and provide our youth with the best and latest state of the art facilities. Some of the old photos of years gone by remind us of how far our society has progressed.

54

1921 WESTINGHOUSE HIGH SCHOOL CHAMPION OF CHAMPIONS TEAM

**1921 WESTINGHOUSE H.S. CITY CHAMPIONS AND WPIAL CLASS AA CO-CHAMPIONS**
The following members of the team are in no special order: Ament, Brosie, Rumbaugh (Captain), Dale, W. Brown, McKinney, Mackey, C. Walker, Farmer, Clark, Grunnagle, Lantz, Elward, Wimmer, Reister, Rylands, Gulland, Geilfuss, Swaile, Helquist, Confer, Adams, Ottie (Mgr.), Whipkey (Mgr.), Head Coach O.H. Burton.

55

*Burton • Dimperio • Musilin • Malins • Webb*

THE SKETCHBOOK

At long last the unveiling of our new school in the autumn of 1922

56

## THE NEW GEORGE WESTINGHOUSE HIGH SCHOOL

*WHS Class of June, 1923*

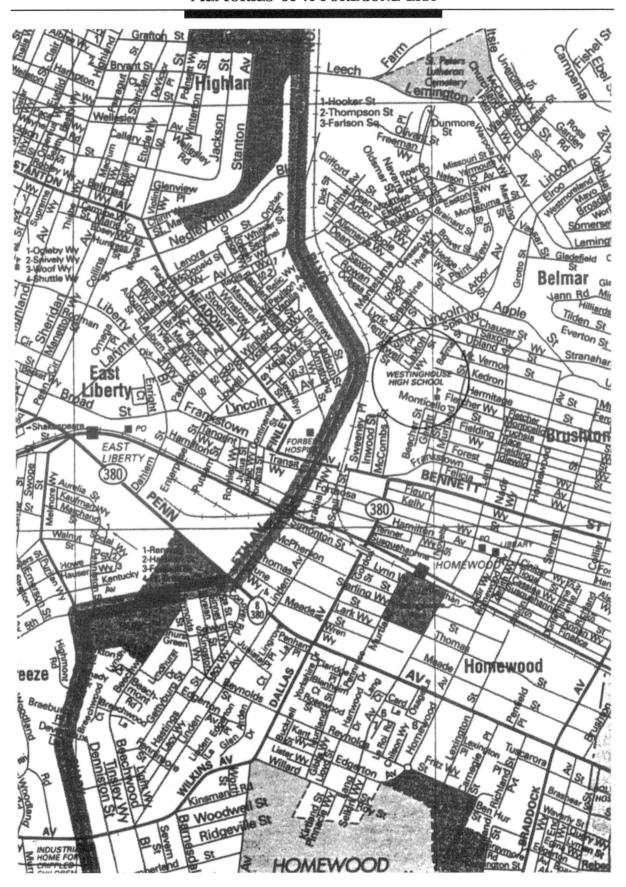

## THE SKETCHBOOK

58

*Burton • Dimperio • Musilin • Malins • Webb*

### SILVER LAKE

Under the apple-green feet of Spring,
You are a smooth jade stone
Lying upon the gentle breast
Of earth, newly young.
Your tremulous whisperings
Melt into clean spaces;
They flutter into shy uneven songs
Seeking the youth of timid leaves.

Under the blazing seal of summer
You are like deep folds of air-stirred silk.
Restless things come to your clear coolness.
Dust-ruffled birds, and trailing tendrils,
And young boys with bodies hard and smooth,
Like pebbles at the sea's edge,
In the stillness of your depths
Echoes the melting beauty of the moon.

How you have grown wise in this autumn
Under the ceaseless dripping of leaves.
They lie upon your body as fragrant wounds.
You are still as the hour before dawn,
And the little winds sigh
At the edge of your mystery.
In the stone-carved arches above you
Pale skeins of smoke tremble at your immortality.

Winter finds you cold, emotionless
In your white impenetrable mask.
You are a candid song of silence
Rising to the grey iron-bound sky,
Your chastity is a burning white pain
In the shelter of your gaunt black arches,
And the bleak naked trees
Etched against the inarticulate hills.

Mary Brown.

59

60

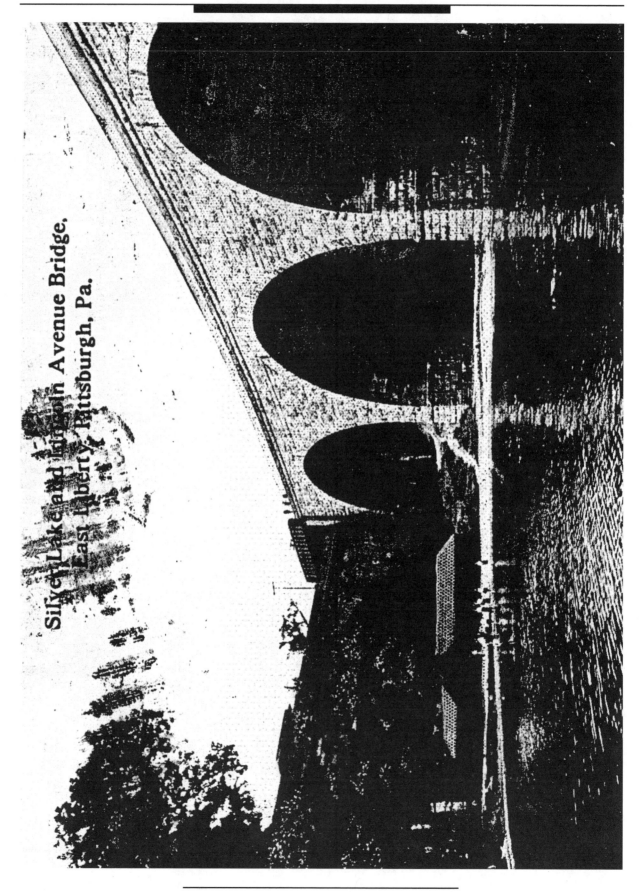

Silver Lake and Lincoln Avenue Bridge,
East Liberty, Pittsburgh, Pa.

Burton • Dimperio • Musilin • Malins • Webb

## THE SKETCHBOOK

62

*Burton • Dimperio • Musilin • Malins • Webb*

THE SKETCHBOOK

63

### THE SKETCHBOOK

64

Yea, Team! Yea, Coach! Here he is — the one and only "Pro" Burton, the miracle man of football. "Pro" will long be remembered by the pupils of Westinghouse (and by the community as well) for his outstanding achievement in developing, year after year, football teams of championship caliber. But far greater and more enduring in its effects is his ability to inspire boys to real sportsmanship — to be "thoroughbreds." Hats off to "Pro"!

*Burton • Dimperio • Musilin • Malins • Webb*

## THE SKETCHBOOK

1927 WESTINGHOUSE HIGH SCHOOL CITY FOOTBALL CHAMPIONS

First Row, left to right: (Assistant Manager), Ayres, Sullivan, Brown (Captain), McQuinn, Hill, Goeddel, Patterson, Will, Ormiston, Grace, Benzie, Campbell (Manager)

Second Row, left to right: McCormick, Dallas, Mayberry, Burkholder, Wilson, English, Davies, Groves, Stroud, Klotz, Carboni

Third Row, left to right: McCabe, O. H. Burton (Coach), Maloney, Ritter, Mathews, Stanford, Conley, (Alumni Assistant), Demarchi, Thompson, Hussey, Rockford, Ficklin, Stanier (Assistant Manager), Ilsley.

65

66

**1928 WESTINGHOUSE HIGH SCHOOL CITY FOOTBALL CHAMPIONS**

The following members of the team are in no special order: DeMarchi, Grove, Jalott, Madine, Martin, Mathews, Nardulli, Ormiston, Patterson, L. Sullivan, Will, Burkholder, Reilly, Hill, Matoney, McCluan, Zollinger, Stanford, Strainer, Benzie, Cooper, Durzo, Gibson, McIllveen, Pacciarelli, Goldman, Beckett, Deremer, Seigler, H. Wadsworth, Drosnes, Dye, Ware, Wendell, Tyson, Wilson, McCabe, Klotz, Woods, Mgr., Ass't. Coach Ralph Zahniser, Head Coach O.H.Pro Burton.

**1929 WESTINGHOUSE HIGH SCHOOL FOOTBALL SQUAD (5-3-0)**

The following members of the team are in no special order: C. Cooper, Dye, Ware, Benzie, Durzo, Scheltenbrand, McIllveen, Rentler, DeMarchi, Deremer, DiSantis, Goldman, Pacciarelli, Dick, Baird, Baker, Beckett, Guardalabene, Harmatta, Penney, Seigler, Wadsworth, Wildman, Pahel, Buchanan, Drosnes, Fields, Harrison, J. Sullivan, Little, Aloe, Palmer, Cotter, Miller, Woods (Mgr.), Coach O.H. Burton.

67

# 3 | THE 1930'S - PRO DRIVES THE BULLDOGS

It was an era that saw very hard times falling upon our country as well as the world over. In 1931, the Great Depression literally bewildered economists and politicians and paralyzed our nation as many families experienced some very trying times that were never to be forgotten. Unfortunately, many economic remedies were not working, and in 1932 a United States presidential change took place. Franklin D. Roosevelt's landslide presidential victory over Herbert Hoover attested to the political bankruptcy of laissez-faire policies. President Roosevelt launched an effective program designed to alleviate the economic depression that gripped our country. He called his program the New Deal which helped to re-establish stability within our economy with government funded programs with widespread social benefits and improvements. It really paid off as our country began to thrive with much determination to regain its prosperity. President Roosevelt displayed dynamic leadership as Americans were able to follow his lead and make great strides toward a successful economic recovery. That generation is to be commended for recovering through a most difficult time. They paved the way through their tireless efforts for the younger generation to live a more comfortable and stable lifestyle. A few years later on St. Patrick's Day in 1936, Pittsburgh found itself under several feet of water. It was a flood that really devastated our city and many surrounding towns. In spite of those troubled times and conditions our city persevered and managed to put this disaster behind them and move on with their lives. They were a proud generation and were more than ready to enjoy some peace and prosperity. The neighborhood schools provided activities that created much interest for each community to get involved and develop a sense of pride and loyalty. High school athletics were really beginning to draw more loyal supporters and a Friday night football game was one of the best bargains in town. Every community along our three rivers (Allegheny, Monongahela and Ohio) had Friday nights under the lights during the fall season to spark the enthusiasm for high school football.

## FINAL YEAR FOR WARE AND DYE

Meanwhile, life back in Homewood began to perk up as Westinghouse and Pro Burton put together a championship team in 1930. The community responded with much support and loyalty in spite of the staggering economy and the Great Depression that was looming ahead. The Bulldogs began to display their winning ways and went 7-2-0 that season; with the two losses coming at the hands of non-league WPIAL opponents – Altoona and Greensburg. They played tough throughout the city league schedule; going undefeated and winning the city title in a hard-fought victory over a tough South Hills team by a 12-6 margin. This was the final year for both Bobby Dye and Joe "Showboat" Ware to play at Westinghouse. They were supported by a strong and dedicated group of teammates – Earl Deremer, Harold Wendell, Lewis Seigler, Harry Harrison, Homer Clark Wadsworth, Duxberry, John Manelli, C. Sullivan, James Hayes and Frank Fields. This was a fine well-coached football team that brought many thrills to their loyal followers. Dye and Ware were two names that I heard the old timers brag about time and time again as I was growing up. I remember my father telling me that they were two of the best to ever play at Westinghouse while he was there. He was their classmate until he had to leave school (junior year) to go to work. Today my dad, at the age of ninety – five, still beams proudly when our conversation is about that 1930 team and Pro Burton.

**1930 SEASON (7-2-0)**

| WHS | 0 | Altoona | 19 |
|---|---|---|---|
| | 13 | Greensburg | 20 |
| | 52 | Allderdice | 7 |
| | 25 | Carrick | 0 |
| | 66 | Fifth Avenue | 0 |
| | 19 | Peabody | 7 |
| | 6 | Schenley | 0 |
| | 20 | South | 6 |

Pittsburgh City League Championship
WHS  12    South Hills   6
Score by periods:

| Westinghouse | 6 | 0 | 0 | 6 — 12 |
|---|---|---|---|---|
| South Hills | 6 | 0 | 0 | 0 — 6 |

Scoring:
Touchdowns — Westinghouse; Fields, Ware; South Hills; Blum
Missed PAT's Westinghouse; Ware and Dye; South Hills; Riggs

## WARE AND DYE LEAVE THEIR MARK

Bobby Dye and Joe "Showboat" Ware were probably two of the finest all around athletes in the history of Westinghouse High School. This may be debated by some who came along in later years, but I will stay with the opinion of many old timers. They were both inducted into the Pennsylvania Sports Hall of Fame for their athletic accomplishments long after their playing days ended. Both were triple threat backs teaming together to give Westinghouse an explosive scoring punch during the 1928, 1929 and 1930 seasons. They were game breakers on both offense and defense and were quite instrumental in helping the Bulldogs win the Pittsburgh City Championship in both 1928 and 1930. They were both excellent all around athletes

69

excelling in other varsity sports such as basketball, baseball, track, soccer and volleyball. Between the two of them they earned twenty-three varsity letters. I have spoken to many local sports enthusiasts through the years and the names of Joe Ware and Bobby Dye were always mentioned with much admiration. In 1977, Joe Ware was selected as the Westinghouse Athlete of the Century by a panel of sports philosophers. This was quite an honor as the school has produced some outstanding athletes through the years. What made Joe Ware and Bobby Dye so special was their ability to perform and dominate at whatever sport was in season. Together they were a coach's dream for Pro Burton and delighted the proud and loyal followers of Westinghouse High School.

After the departure of Dye and Ware the Bulldogs had to rebuild. In 1931, a year of depression, this team was pushed around by multiple scores with little or no scoring power and finished the season with a record of 2-5-1. They were shut out in five of the eight games and Pro Burton turned gray overnight. The returning underclassmen from that 1931 team learned fast and came back with a sectional championship for the following 1932 season. In the city title game that year they lost a thriller to Perry 13-6 at Peabody Field, and they finished the season with a record of 4-4-1. Two of the losses came in non-league play to Wilkinsburg and Mt. Lebanon by identical scores of 7-0. All-City selections by the news media from this 1932 team were Mike Dalfonso, John Mannelli, Sam Barone and Connolly.

The 1933 team started out well until they met Peabody midway through the season and were defeated by the Highlanders 13-7. This knocked the Bulldogs out of title contention. Peabody went on to win their first city championship that year with a 13-0 win over South Hills. Westinghouse finished the season with a record of 4-2-2. That year Bobby Dye assisted Pro Burton with the coaching duties. Members of the team that received All-City selections included Ben Gigliotti, Sam Barone, Mike Monaco, Frank Cupps and Harry McMahon. Others who performed well were Herbie Beckett, Larry Bauer, Rudy Raddick and John Rogan.

## 1934 DEFENSE! DEFENSE!

Defense was the name of the game in 1934 as this team shut out seven out of nine opponents and allowed only thirteen points the entire season. The first team to cross the gold and blue goal line was our neighborhood rival Peabody as they held a 7-0 lead at half time. After a half-time verbal lashing from coach Burton, the Bulldogs came storming back in the second half to win the game 13-7. From what one of the old timers told me, Burton was like a man possessed in that locker room during the half-time break.

All season long this team thrived on defensive efforts game after game. It was a remarkable feat as they compiled a record of 6-0-3 and shared the City Championship with Carrick High School that year. In the city title game they played to a 6-6 tie in a tough defensive struggle. That year they played three tough WPIAL schools and did quite well. They tied Jeannette 0-0; tied Braddock 0-0 and defeated Butler 6-0. No other team in the history of Westinghouse gave up fewer points in one full season. Some of the outstanding members of that team were Vecchiola, Cupps, Speakman,

Deremer, MacCumbee, Monaco, Heh, McHaffley, Rogan, Alfred, Hayes, Moyhan, Huey, Sanden, Esquino, Cervi, Frahle, Page and Duckett. This was probably one of the strongest defensive units ever turned out by Westinghouse.

**1934 SEASON (6-0-3)**

| WHS | 0 | Jeannette | 0 |
|---|---|---|---|
| | 0 | Braddock | 0 |
| | 6 | Butler | 0 |
| | 13 | Allderdice | 0 |
| | 6 | Fifth Avenue | 0 |
| | 13 | Peabody | 7 |
| | 13 | Schenley | 0 |
| | 19 | South | 0 |

Pittsburgh City League Championship

| WHS | 6 | Carrick | | 6 |
|---|---|---|---|---|

Score by periods:

| Westinghouse | 0 | 6 | 0 | 0—6 |
|---|---|---|---|---|
| Carrick | 0 | 0 | 6 | 0—6 |

Scoring:

Touchdowns — Westinghouse; Alford; Carrick; Nath
Missed PAT's Westinghouse and Carrick (placements)

**71**

The 1935 team was City League Section 1 Champions with a record of 4-3-2. By losing to Peabody 3-0 during the regular season they were eliminated from title contention until it was discovered that the Highlanders used an ineligible player. This forced Peabody to forfeit all their games and put Westinghouse in the city title game against South Hills. The Bulldogs were beaten by Section 2 champion South Hills 6-0 at Pitt Stadium before a huge crowd. Rogan was named on every All-City team by the news media, and Byers, Cupps, Heh, Deremer and Esquino also received much recognition.

For the third consecutive year Westinghouse captured the Section 1 title in 1936. They met South Hills again for the city championship and were beaten 12-0. During that season they lost two non-league games to WPIAL powers – Jeannette 6-0 and McKeesport 18-12 and finished the season with a record of 6-3-0. By season's end the Bulldogs reached a milestone of 100 wins. Ed Rogan, Guy Guadagnino, Bud Atchison, Herb Schlegel, Sonny Zimmer, Frank Berardino, Williard Brown, Babe Byers, Joe Fay, Joe Graf and Shorty Hobbs were among the stalwarts of that team. This was the same year on November 19th at 6:30 A.M. that I was born – the third child of my proud parents Joseph and Margaret Pellegrino. Mom and Dad had five children all together as two more were to follow later on.

## LOUIS AND SCHMELING MADE HEADLINES

Earlier in this same year, on June 19th in Madison Square Garden, New York reigning world heavyweight champion Joe Louis was upset by Max Schmeling a German and a huge underdog. Adolph Hitler head of the Nazi regime was delighted and never let our country forget about this during those years before World War II. Two Years later in a propaganda filled rematch at Yankee Stadium Joe Louis encouraged by the support of U.S. President Franklin Roosevelt knocked out Max Schmeling in the first round. Sadly enough we were to realize later that Schmeling was not a supporter of Hitler, but he was portrayed as such by the Nazi Dictator. In later years Louis and Schmeling had developed a sincere and long lasting friendship. In fact Schmeling, even paid for Louis' funeral in 1981 when the former heavyweight champion passed away. Schmeling passed away several years later in February of 2005 at the age of 99.

The 1937 team was built around such standouts as Esquino, Harris, Arrigo, Whittle, Martorelli, Papale and Nigro. For the season they recorded a record of 4-3-1, losing two non-league games and one Section 1 game to Peabody. The 15-13 loss to Peabody eliminated them from title contention. Peabody went on to meet South Hills for the City Championship with South Hills winning in a close game 8-0. During this era South Hills High School had some very strong teams and captured four city titles in six appearances while Westinghouse managed to win four, Peabody and Perry one each during that same time period. The competition back then was quite even as many of the games were low scoring and close. The style of football played was mostly run oriented single-wing offenses, pass when you had to and tough defenses.

After coming up short for the last four seasons the 1938 Bulldogs came storming back. It was a solid team that got better with each game after opening the season with a tough loss at Altoona 14-0. This championship team was led by Childs, Conway, Billy Pringle, Chase, Granata, Castelli, Terry, Schrott, Collaizzi, Woolslare, Klein, Sullivan, Semple, Tappe, Gibson, Abbruzzese, Mango, Warfield, Messner, Rogan, Hockenberger, and Yalenty. The only team to defeat the Silver Lakers was Altoona in non-league play in the first game of the season as they went 7-1-0 for the year. There was no play-off that season as Westinghouse won the city title outright. The yearbook that year left much to be desired as it did not contain a photo of this fine team and had very little in the way of coverage. Much to my regret the hunt for a photo of this team fell short.

72

**1938 SEASON (7-1-0)**

| WHS | 0 | Altoona | 14 |
|---|---|---|---|
| | 14 | Allegheny | 7 |
| | 12 | Fifth Avenue | 6 |
| | 25 | Oliver | 0 |
| | 7 | Peabody | 0 |
| | 20 | Perry | 0 |
| | 4 | South | 0 |
| | 13 | South Hills | 0 |

Westinghouse wins City Championship (No playoff)

## FIRST PERFECT SEASON

The Bulldogs were on a winning streak of seven in a row after the Altoona loss in 1938 and were looking forward to adding to it as the 1939 season began. The 1939 team responded by going undefeated and ran the winning streak up to fifteen straight wins, and a record of 8-0-0. They opened the season with always tough Altoona and this time around it was the Bulldogs who were victorious 12-7. They were challenged throughout the season, but kept the winning steak alive and were the City Champions again for the seventh time without a play-off. The nucleus of that team consisted of Hockenberger, Semple, Rogan, Colaizzi, Sullivan, Miletti, McLaughlin, Castelli, Mango, Gibson (Captain), Abbruzzese, Burton, Latronica, Santora and Cimadora. Joseph (Red) Sullivan made All-City and All-State and later went on to star with the Naval Academy.

73

The Bulldogs were beginning to emerge as a City Champion contender every year and coach Pro Burton was earning the reputation as "Builder of Champions" in all athletics at Westinghouse. As I reviewed some of the yearbooks of the early years, I was impressed with the many championships they had won in other sports such as gymnastics, volleyball, swimming, baseball, basketball and track and field. Especially noteworthy was the success of both the gymnastics and volleyball teams in city and state competition; they were phenomenal. This book is dealing strictly with football, but I would feel remiss if I did not mention that Westinghouse High School also excelled far beyond the gridiron. It would take another dedicated book to cover the other accomplishments with deserving accolades. Let us stay on track and continue on with the football history.

## BULLDOGS GO BACK TO BACK AGAIN

Winning was beginning to really catch on in Homewood as the Bulldogs for the second time in their short history won back-to-back city titles. It was a clear indication of how far coach Burton had brought the football program at Westinghouse. Up to this point in time the Silver Lakers had laid claim to seven championship seasons and were looking for more. As history bares out it was the beginning of what made the winning tradition at Westinghouse so special. The early years of struggling through some very difficult times by the classes that preceded this era. They are to be commended for having the desire and perseverance to succeed. It makes me feel very proud to have realized what they accomplished as I went through my researching efforts.

**1939 SEASON (8-0-0)**

| WHS | 12 | Altoona | 7 |
|---|---|---|---|
| | 20 | Allderdice | 6 |
| | 13 | Carrick | 0 |
| | 31 | Langley | 0 |
| | 12 | Peabody | 6 |
| | 21 | Schenley | 0 |
| | 25 | South | 0 |
| | 14 | South Hills | 0 |

Westinghouse wins City Championship (No playoff)

## REMEMBERING BURTON AND ORMISTON

Coach Pro Burton was a guard during his playing days (1912 and 1913) at Springfield College in Missouri and so he stressed and developed quality in his linemen every year at the Homewood School. Several went on to college and did very well. The most notable was Ken Ormiston who played fullback at Westinghouse 1926, 27 and 28, and later at the University of Pittsburgh he was selected on the All-American team as a guard in 1934 under legendary coach Jock Sutherland. He went from a high school fullback to a guard in college and that had to make Pro Burton very proud. According to many old timers, and I heard it said, that he was one of the best to ever come out of Westinghouse. He was often called "The General" while at Westinghouse because of his leadership ability. Ken Ormiston passed away at the young age of forty-two on September 1, 1951.

In late 1956 memorial plaques were unveiled and presented to the school in memory of both Ken Ormiston and Pro Burton. They epitomized the early years of success that enabled Westinghouse High School to be one of the finest high school football traditions in Western Pennsylvania. In a memorial tribute let us not forget these two legends that helped to build the foundation of our proud tradition at Westinghouse High School.

**74**

IN FOND MEMORY OF

**Mr. O. H. "Pro" Burton**
**1889-1948**
**"Builder of Champions"**
**Westinghouse High School**
**1916-1946**
• • • • • • • • • • • • • • • • • • • • • •
**Ken Ormiston**
**1909-1951**
**Westinghouse's All-Scholastic**
**1926, 27, 28**
**Pitt's All-American 1934**
**"Homewood's Native Son"**

## ACCOLADES AND MEMORIES ARE COUNTLESS

As we continue through the storied football history of Westinghouse High School I may have omitted naming your favorite player or have not praised your favorite team, and I must apologize for that. Every young man who wore the gold and blue colors deserved to be recognized. Each and every one of them (including the student managers) has contributed in some way to the fine tradition of Westinghouse High School. It took a lot of dedication, pride, sacrifice and much more than most people realize to make the football team. There were demands that would never have been tolerated by today's youth. "If you wanted to play for the Bulldogs there was a tough road to travel with no short-cuts." Many of those who traveled that road who are still with us today and those who have departed this life will always be remembered for upholding the special loyalty of Westinghouse High School. Football was the one sport that brought out the sincere enthusiasm and loyalty for every class to enjoy.

75

I have been to many class reunions, alumni functions and socials and the past experiences of our student life there always seems to surface proud reflections of those special years. A lot of it has to do with Westinghouse High School playing such an important role in the communities of Homewood, Brushton, East Liberty, Paulson, Lemington, Lincoln and Larimer. Back then the school was literally our home away from home. My six years at Westinghouse were very fulfilling and rewarding and have provided opportunities to enjoy the many friendships with former classmates. Many times over we cross paths and recapitulate those memorable years.

I have met so many alumni throughout my lifetime that have exemplified so much in the way of memories of their years at Westinghouse. Much of the materials that I have used to put this book together have come from them. The list of names of those people is endless and the one main attribute expressed by all of them is PRIDE. The one word that can best describe the way they felt about their experiences at Westinghouse High School. It was without a doubt the best way I can describe the feelings of the many generations that passed through the portals of our Big House in Homewood. The time spent there was short but the memories last forever.

# A SHORT HISTORY

## O. H. (Pro) BURTON

"Praise from a Friend, or censure from a Foe,
Are Lost on hearers that our MERITS know"—
—HOMER.

Homage is paid this night to O. H. (Pro) Burton, who has performed faithfully the duties of Director of Athletics at the George Westinghouse High School since 1916.

That Coach Burton has been highly successful is easily understood from the impressive records his teams have made. Not only is he beloved by those with whom he had immediate contact, but by his townspeople and others, who regard him a "man among men".

Hardly ever a smile spreads across his broad face—but there is a warm friendship within Coach Burton that is always apparent.

I—like my newspaper contemporaries—regard "Pro" a true, sincere friend. What finer tribute can be paid anyone?

After two years in Springfield, Missouri, College—his home town—where he played guard on the football teams of 1912 and 1913, "Pro" Burton transferred to and later graduated from Springfield, Massachusetts Y M C A College.

Burton's first athletic position was Director of Athletics at the McKeesport Y M C A in 1915. The following year Burton became affiliated with Westinghouse High School. He has served at the Brushton school since that time. His first basketball championship team was in 1919 with Youngk, Beatty, Bell, Dosey, King and Martin.

In 1921, Burton's first City football championship was achieved and he also tied Rochester for the WPIAL championship. The first City baseball title for Burton was in 1924.

Most notable has Burton been in leading Westinghouse to football prominence. The "Silver Lakers" won the City League football championships in 1927 over Oliver, and in 1928 and 1930 over South Hills.

In the playoff for the 1932 honor, Westinghouse lost to Perry, but in 1934 the "Silver Lakers" came back to windup with a 6-6 deadlock in the title playoff with Carrick. Defeat has come to Westinghouse in the last two championship series matches, in 1935 and 1936, by South Hills High.

Burton—and his Westinghouse teams—can feel proud of having won the Section 1 football honors seven times in thirteen years since the City High School League was divided into two groups.

76

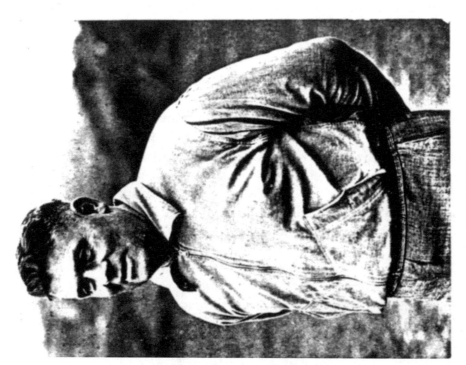

"PRO" BURTON
*The Real Veteran*

*Old friends, old classmates gathered together,*
*To honor a man who's deeds forever*
*We'll greatly cherish and fondly remember,*
*And as a toast before we part*
*An honest blessing from the heart*

**Westinghouse High School Football Team – City Champions – 1930**
Team members in no special order: J. Sullivan, H. Wendell, E. Deremer, Bob Dye, Joe Ware, F. Fields, J. Manella, J. Hayes, C. Sullivan, Duxberry, Seigler, Pritchard, J. Aloe, Paul Penny, Frank Wymard, West, Henry Harrison, R. Little, H. Wadsworth, McNellia, Neubauer, T. Sapienza, Mayberry, Brook, Baily, M. Small, R. Dorsey, G.Miller, Moner, Jackson, Meyer, Boyd, Harmatta, Peak, G. Wadswoth, Fass, Mgr., Head Coach Oliver H. "Pro" Burton.

1930 WESTINGHOUSE BACKFIELD

DYE          DUXBERRY          FIELD          WARE

*Burton • Dimperio • Musilin • Malins • Webb*

77

They were the early pioneers
Of the storied athletic history
Of Westinghouse High School


Classmates and Teammates
WHS Class of 1931
(Courtesy of SKETCHBOOK)
Robert "Bobby" Dye
And
Joseph "Showboat" Ware

Below: Together years later at a Class Reunion (Courtesy of Georgeanne Dye-Stitt)

## BULLDOGS

Westinghouse
Athlete of the Century
**"THE LEGEND"**

*Class of '31*
*Joseph "Showboat" Ware*

*Attended Howard University in Washingto*
*recieved Black All-American award in foo*
*1934 and again in basketball 1934 and 19:*
*While attending Westinghouse H.S., he re*
*12 Varsity Letters, in Football, Baseball,*
*Basketball and Track.*

★ ★ ★

Oct.7, 1977

79

# Greatest Showboat

Time has faded the memories of the accomplishments of many of the potentials. When asked to name an all-time athlete from Westinghouse, curb-side philosophers scratched their heads in puzzlement. Contemporary observers may have immediately offered current sensation Ahmad Shareef as a nominee.

**High Schools**

But the task jarred recollections of one Joseph "Showboat" Ware. A 1931 graduate of Westinghouse, Ware was last week named Westinghouse's Athlete of the Century.

"I was filled up with pride to be back home with the boys I knew," said Ware who now lives in Wilkinsburg. "I was pleased and humbled to get the award. It means something because it came from my roots."

*By Gerry Fraley.*

Ware's roots are more than impressive. During his years at Westinghouse, Ware received 12 varsity letters in football, basketball, baseball, and track. He continued his exploits at Howard University where he was a Black All-America in football and basketball.

A severe illness to his father forced Ware to leave Howard after his third year. Following his return to Pittsburgh, Ware caught on in the Negro National Baseball League and spent time with several teams including the Homestead Grays.

Ware's career is noteworthy, but so is the nickname. Showboat. Very appropriate for a star; unheard of in today's era of drab athletes.

"We went up to Franklin to play basketball one night," said Ware. "They had a good team, but we razzle-dazzled them off the floor. I couldn't miss. Every time I came down the floor, the ball went in. They started yelling 'showboat' every time I got the ball.

"We won the game. Our coach, Coach Burton, though wouldn't let me forget the name. He spread it out and it has stuck through all these years. A lot of people never did know my real first name."

Today, Ware would have enjoyed a lucrative professional career. But times were different 40 years ago. Segregation was the way of the world.

Ware holds no bitterness over his fate.

"It started with my mother and father," he said. "They told me, 'don't let your color hold you back. Do your best no matter how and don't worry.' Those have been my bylines."

• • •

EDITORS NOTE: The article shown above was submitted by Douglas Plaza tenant, Mr Joseph Ware, of F-7-East as an added addition to our Douglas Plaza News.

WKR

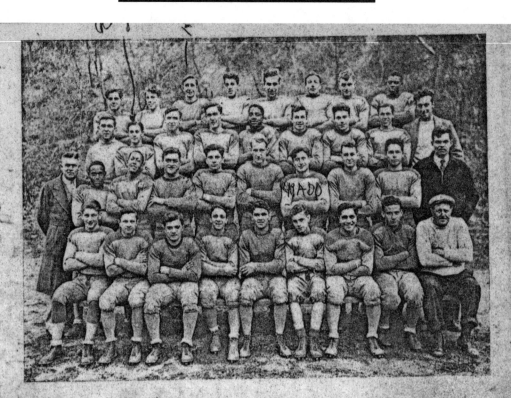

1934

**80**

## THE CHAMPIONSHIP GAME

THE championship of the City High School Football League rests in the hands of co-champions at the conclusion of the title battle between the Westinghouse and Carrick elevens which resulted in a 6-6 deadlock. The Bulldogs, heavy favorites, were clearly the superior team, but after Carrick got the breaks and scored a touchdown in the third period, the Bulldogs lacked the necessary punch to win.

After a poor first quarter in which both teams fumbled consistently, the Bulldogs settled down to serious football, and after a series of first downs, the ball rested on the Carrick four-yard stripe from which Alford plunged it over. McMahon missed the extra point.

Westinghouse showed another scoring threat in the same period when Baumgardner fumbled the kickoff and let it roll behind his goal line, but Nath quickly scooped it up and returned it to the ten-yard line where the suburbanites kicked out of danger. Soon Page gained twenty-one yards around end to put the ball again in a scoring position, but a fumble, resulting from a lateral pass, cost Westinghouse the possession of the ball.

In the third period Carrick with the aid of the breaks got their chance to score; Corace blocked Rogan's punt, but Rogan recovered on the twelve. On the next play Rogan was again swamped, and he elected to run the ball but failed to make the necessary yardage; the ball went to Carrick, that with the aid of an off-side penalty against Westinghouse carried it over.

Mehaffey and Alford contributed some stellar offensive work for Westinghouse; Cupps and Speakman played a great defensive game on the line. Greenwald, Corace, and Nath starred for Carrick.

# OUR FAMILY MATRIARCH

### A Tribute to Aunt Rose Pellegrino Hall

**She was the first one in the Pellegrino Family to graduate from
Westinghouse High School, Class of February 1935**

Rose Marie Pellegrino "Flossy"
Department of Public Safety,
Girl Reserve, Radio, Big Sisters, Volleyball '33,
*Although our Rose is very small
Her pleasing manner captivates us all.*

I will never forget the many football games she took me to see. She had all the spirit and pride of a Westinghouse alumnus who encouraged the rest of us to follow her lead. She took me with her to see her beloved Bulldogs play the game she loved so much whether they were at home or away; an unforgettable journey.

Aunt Rose was truly our family matriarch; always there to help so many of us through life's challenges. She was a single parent who devoted her life to her only daughter, Nora. Later Nora also became a single parent when her young husband, John, passed away from an incurable cancer; leaving her with two beautiful daughters to raise without their father. But, Aunt Rose stepped up, and helped her daughter to raise those two little girls. Perseverance was the attribute that saw such gratifying results. Aunt Rose was very proud of her daughter and two granddaughters as they faced life's challenges without their beloved John.

Not too many years later Aunt Rose's health was declining, and began to limit her life's activities. She faced her health problems with dignity, never complaining. During my last visit with her in the hospital she sat up and sang, "Westinghouse Forever" one last time. She passed away several days later leaving behind a family that will never forget her. She was the rock of her generation. Her love for the Steelers and Pirates was one of heartfelt loyalty.

"God bless you Aunt Rose, and until we meet again in God's heaven save me a seat beside you on the 50 yard line. Once again we will sing together our song "Westinghouse Forever." This book of memories reflects so much of how you introduced to me at a young age the true spirit of Westinghouse High School. May you rest in peace."

81

82

CHAMPIONS

19 39

*Burton • Dimperio • Musilin • Malins • Webb*

SILVER LAKE

84

1939 - GEORGE WESTINGHOUSE HIGH SCHOOL - PITTSBURGH, PA.

# 4 | THE 1940'S AND "PRO" PASSES REINS TO PETE DIMPERIO

This was an era that saw many historical events and developments occur in our country. With the threat of a world war raging on all fronts, more than half of the male graduates entered the armed forces of our country. This was a very tough time as I can remember the effects it had on my family and our neighborhood. This was a time in my young life when I really began to feel a sincere loyalty and love for our country. I was attending Larimer Elementary School at the time when this war our country was fighting was in full force. I can recall the air raid drills that were conducted within our school and the bewilderment as we listened to our teachers instructing us through each one of them. The newspaper drives, the rationing of various goods and services and the patriotic songs that we sang. During the war there was much uncertainty for many of our young men who were still in high school and eligible for military duty. Many left school and joined the service, and many stayed in school long enough to graduate and then left shortly after for military duty.

When we went to the movies we saw the newsreels reflecting all the bombing and fighting that were taking place on all fronts in Europe. I can still hear the voices of all the world leaders, especially our President, Franklin D. Roosevelt, coming across the airwaves. The many night-time air raid sirens blasting away as we sat huddled closely at home waiting for the all clear signals to resume normal activity. It was a very trying time as many of our young men were overseas fighting for the freedom of this country. It was a time when I realized the true value of human life and sacrifice. I can remember when this war finally came to an end. I was awakened by the sounds of horns blowing and people singing in our neighborhood streets in the wee hours of the morning. It was on the day when we got word that the war was finally over. It was a time when you could feel a tremendous pressure being lifted from all of the American people. Now it was time to bring all the members of the armed forces back home so they could rebuild their lives. Unfortunately, many never made it back home and our alma mater remembered them with a huge bronze memorial plaque that still hangs in the main corridor of Westinghouse High School.

## 1940 A SEASON OF HIGHS AND LOWS

During this most trying of times sports activities were not in the hearts of many of us as the threat of war was a major concern. Many of our notable sports figures were leaving their teams to serve our country. This was also the case in many other

85

fields of employment. Men and women were leaving their careers behind to serve our country.

Westinghouse was riding a fifteen game winning streak that began in 1938 and continued through the 1939 season before it came to an abrupt end in the 1940 season opener. The Bulldogs were beaten by Altoona High 20-0. The year 1940 was a season of many highs and lows as everyone wanted to knockoff the defending champions. As the old saying goes "what goes around comes back around" and thus the Bulldogs felt it finishing the season with a record of 4-3-0. Nevertheless, Westinghouse was still a worthy contender for city honors, but did not quite live up to pre-season expectations. The 1940 Pittsburgh City League Championship was shared by South Hills and Oliver without a playoff. World War II was looming and our country was facing some uncertainty as the threat of war was becoming a great concern for our country.

## 1941 BRINGS THE INEVITABLE ON DECEMBER 7TH

Unfortunately, 1941 was a year to be remembered by many of us. It was a year that shocked our country and our community with the bombing of Pearl Harbor on December 7, 1941. One month prior to the Pearl Harbor disaster our Westinghouse Bulldogs completed a successful football season with a record of 5-1-1. This team rebounded from the previous disappointing year and brought the city title back to Homewood. After the opening season loss to always tough Altoona 20-7, they bounced back and defeated Penn High (later renamed Penn Hills) 12-0. In league play they went undefeated with one tie and were crowned city league co-champions with Oliver High School without a playoff. After graduation, several players from this team went on to fight for our country as the war in Europe was escalating on all fronts.

It was a very tough time for many families as the call for military support was taking many boys out of school to help defend our country. One of the members of this 1941 team was from my extended family and that was respectfully Uncle Felix Yannotti, who played guard and wore jersey number 31. After graduating from Westinghouse High School he went to war, and unfortunately, did not make it back home. I remember the impact it had on the family when the sad news came to them. I was only six years old when this happened and I can remember feeling the sadness that surrounded us. He was a fine young man who as a member of the U. S. Marines sacrificed his life defending our country. Later on in years when I was a student at Westinghouse, I would pause at the bronze memorial honor roll plaque in our main corridor. I read his name at the bottom of the alphabetical list and remembered who he was. It was a time for me to reflect and appreciate what he and all of our troops did to protect our country.

This 1941 team had many members who I remember meeting later on in my lifetime as friends or neighbors. One who comes to mind is Paul Mazzei. He was at one time my neighbor and later on one of my teachers at Westinghouse. He was captain and an all-city selection with a full scholarship offer to attend Penn State. He was a two-way performer for Pro Burton – doubling as a single wing quarterback (a blocking back all the way) and middle linebacker on defense. After his playing days at Westinghouse he was drafted into the armed forces in 1942 and never did have an opportunity to play football at Penn State. In the summer of 1944 he was wounded in action – a machine gun bullet ripped through his left knee as his platoon was moving through Orbetello, Italy. Mistaken for dead he was left behind. When finally picked up by American troops three days later, gangrene had set in and his left leg had to be amputated. He later returned home, his left leg amputated below the knee, to learn how to walk with an artificial limb. After this unfortunate experience, Mazzei had to overcome many challenges in his efforts to become a teacher and a coach. With much determination and perseverance he succeeded. He was a man who I respected very much as I was growing up. To me he was a role model for all of us young men to admire and respect. When I see him today I feel very proud to greet him and speak to him. He shared with me some of his memories of his playing days at Westinghouse and his coach Pro Burton. He alluded that old Pro was one tough man to play for. The thing that was impressive was as tough as Pro was his boys were still very loyal to him. Today that would never work. The young men today would not put up with such regimentation. They would walk away and we have seen that happen quite often in today's generation.

Members of that fine 1941 championship team were as follows: Paul Mazzei, Felix Yannotti, Carmen DeStefano, Joe LoPresti, Bill Heilman, Edward Sullivan, Bill Merritt, Howard Weber, Harold Brown, Stan Colcombe, Raymond Brandi, Ralph Anderson, Clarence Tucker, Virgil Cimadore, Howard Caskey, Tom Matthews, Dom Palumbo Oscar Vaughn, John Haunty, John Mylan, John DiLuccio, Louis Biondi, George Watkins, Albert Pitaccio, Bruce Weston, Nick Donatelli, Harold Rogal, John Molinaro, Paul Barbuto, Stuart McConnell, William Richter, Robert Craven and Ira Hockenberger. Carmen DeStefano played a stellar role as a member of this Bulldog team along with co-captains Paul Mazzei and Ran Brandi who were all-city selections. Not to slight anyone whom I did not mention by name, this entire team was to be commended for their outstanding play in bringing back the title to Homewood. Success comes from team work and dedication and this team had both as they stayed together during some very trying times.

**1941 SEASON (5-1-1)**
WHS 7    Altoona    20
12    Penn Hills    0
7    Allderdice    0
19    Peabody    0
6    Schenley    6
32    South    0
19    South Hills    12
Pittsburgh City League Championship
WHS - Oliver Co-Champions (No playoff)

## MANY LEAVE SCHOOL TO JOIN MILITARY

With World War II escalating over in Europe, More than half of the male graduates entered the armed forces of our country. The 1942 team turned in a successful season even though some of the returning lettermen from the 1941 team left school to join the military. It was a very difficult time trying to sort out priorities for many young men as the early part of the season saw the Bulldogs playing pretty ragged football. They defeated Penn High 8-0, but were beaten by both Altoona 27-0 and Mt. Lebanon 14-0 in non-league games. After getting over their early season woes, coach Burton and the boys made the necessary adjustments and posted five shutouts in a row in league play. Early season injuries to star halfbacks Stan Colcombe and Ed Sullivan really hurt them. The boys hit their peak in the Schenley game as they were facing a team that was using the widely acclaimed T-formation. The Bulldogs were ready to challenge the Spartans, and completely out played them winning 18-0.

When the week of the city championship game arrived the Silver Lakers were considered the underdogs as they were preparing to challenge the favored Oliver Bears. Damned fortune then took a hand as big Bill Merritt all-city fullback for the Bulldogs injured a leg early in the title game. He was replaced by Bob Becker who took over and played admirably throughout the rest of the game. Becker's strong play enabled Westinghouse to salvage a share of the city title in a hard fought 6-6 tie with the Oliver Bears.

The members of that courageous team were ends Harold Brown and Ira Hockenberger; tackles Joseph LoPresti and Harold Rogal; guards Al Pitaccio and Paul Barbuto; center Leo Watkins; quarterback Bob Craven; halfbacks Stan Colcombe, Ed Sullivan, Bruce Weston and Harry Borcelli; fullbacks Bill Merritt and Bob Becker and a capable supporting case of Leon Lewis, Joe Chieffo, Joe Ferraro, Louis Sottile, Ray Mazzei, Bob Mason, Regis Heilman, Bill Wiant, Frank McCray, Ricard Muse, Gene Gross, Harold Arrington, James Mason, John Tuttle, Robert Zimmer, and Harry Colcombe.

**1942 SEASON (6-2-1)**

| WHS | 6 | Penn Hills | 0 |
|---|---|---|---|
| | 0 | Altoona | 27 |
| | 0 | Mt. Lebanon | 14 |
| | 19 | Allderdice | 0 |
| | 26 | Peabody | 0 |
| | 18 | Schenley | 0 |
| | 32 | South | 0 |
| | 25 | South Hills | 0 |

Pittsburgh City League Championship

| WHS | 6 | Oliver | 6 |
|---|---|---|---|

## 1943 A REBUILDING YEAR

With the armed forces and graduation claiming several of coach Burton's experienced men, he found it necessary to build an almost entirely new team in 1943. There were only two lettermen returning from the 1942 championship team. They faced a tough schedule in the pre-season games with Penn High, Altoona and Mt. Lebanon. They opened up the season with a close 6-0 victory over Penn followed by a scoreless tie in the next game with Altoona. In the final pre-season game the Bulldogs earned a tough 13-0 decision over Mt. Lebanon. In the city league opener a veteran Schenley team tamed the inexperienced Silver Lakers 23-0 and it affected their title hopes later on. The following week they came back, led by Bob Becker, Robert Lee and Bruce Weston and defeated South Hills 13-0. Then came a 33-0 rout over an outclassed South High team, with Ray Mazzei being the star of the game for Westinghouse. Richard Muse and Bruce Weston combined to bring a 19-13 victory over Allderdice the following week. In the season final the Bulldogs met their neighboring rival Peabody, and prevailed with a hard earned 19-6 victory over the Highlanders. This 1943 team was a masterful job of rebuilding by coach Pro Burton. They had a most successful season finishing with a record of 6-1-1, and much credit went to the stellar play of Bob Craven, Bruce Weston, Robert Lee, Bob Becker, Richard Muse, Bill Nicoletti, Ernest Spina, Ray Mazzei, Louis Sottile, Hugh Smith, James Mason, Louis Biondi, Frank McCray, Regis Heilman and the other members of that team. Their only season loss was to Schenley High School who won the city championship that year with a 21-7 victory over Allegheny High School from the North Side.

Not satisfied with a second place finish in the previous year the 1944 Bulldogs came roaring back into the limelight and brought the city title back to Homewood. They opened the season against North Braddock Scott High School, and lost a heartbreaker 7-6 in the last minute of play after leading most of the way. The following week they took their revenge out on Mt. Lebanon with a 13-0 victory. Then came always tough Altoona and the Mountain Lions defeated the Bulldogs 7-0 in a hard fought game. The Silver Lakers were ready for the league opener as they really took it to Schenley and defeated the defending champions by a lopsided score of 35-0. There were several stars in that game namely Nemo, Richard Muse, Regis Heilman, Bill Nicoletti and BoBo Coles who more than remembered what happened in the 1943 Schenley game. The following week the Bulldogs defeated South Hills 40-7 as Coles, Heilman, Muse and Besley each scored one touchdown and Bill Nicoletti scored twice. The next game was played in a sea of mud as the locals defeated their neighborhood rival Peabody 14-0 in a real battle. Allderdice went down the following week 31-0, but Frankie Garland was injured in the third quarter after playing a stellar game. South High was next on the schedule, and fell victim to the Bulldogs by the score of 20-6.

Then on November 11, 1944, Armistice Day, the Bulldogs met the Perry Commodores for the city championship at Pitt Stadium, and it was covered on radio station WWSW by the legendary sports broadcaster Joe Tucker. I do remember it well as it was the first football game that my father took me to see, and it was a good one. The Bulldogs won in a thriller by the score of 18-13, and left me with a long lasting impression. As I (only eight years of age at the time) sat in Pitt Stadium with all the other Westinghouse faithful I really got caught up in the enthusiasm that surrounded me. Many years later as I reflect back on that game it probably was the

**89**

beginning of my deep seeded loyalty. There was so much for me to absorb that afternoon as I saw what Westinghouse was all about. Obviously it was a very special event in my young life.

Nearly the entire first team had played their last game for Westinghouse in that title game and they were Ends, I. Martin and Heilman; Tackles, Mihm and Brown; Guards Carpenter and Coleman; Center, Mason; Quarterback, Garland; Halfbacks, Muse and Coles; Fullback, Nicoletti. Pro still had a fine group of lettermen and reserves coming back for the following year, and they were: I. Martin, Davies, Valerio, Bell, Hasty, Molinard, McIlwain, Knight, Anderson, Picone, Cushing, Fabrizi, DeMaria, Besley, Cannon, Constantino, Lintelman, Grose, Savio, DeStout, Bisceglia, DeLuca, Johe, Cassidy, Lewis and Villela. The results of that season:

**1944 SEASON (7-2-0)**

| WHS | 6 | N.B. Scott | 7 |
|---|---|---|---|
| | 0 | Altoona | 7 |
| | 13 | Mt. Lebanon | 0 |
| | 35 | Schenley | 0 |
| | 40 | South Hills | 7 |
| | 14 | Peabody | 0 |
| | 31 | Allderdice | 0 |
| | 20 | South | 6 |

Pittsburgh City League Championship

WHS 18     Perry 13

Scoring:

| Westinghouse | 12 | 0 | 6 | 0—18 |
|---|---|---|---|---|
| Perry | 0 | 7 | 0 | 6—13 |

Touchdowns — Westinghouse: Martin, Muse, Heilman; Perry: Buczkowski, Peirish
Point conversion — Perry: Meader (placement)

## PRO'S LAST SEASON AT WESTINGHOUSE

The 1945 team was the last one that Pro Burton would coach at Westinghouse and he produced a champion. It was a team that upheld the reputation established by previous teams through the tireless efforts of coach Burton. They opened the season at North Braddock Scott and came away with a thrilling 27-26 victory. Herb Lintelman was the star of the game with his nifty running ability and speed. The following week the Bulldogs met a Donora team that was loaded with talent with backs Dan Towler, Roscoe Ross, Arnold Galiffa and Lou "Bimbo" Cecconi and an equally talented line led by Rudy Andabaker. The Dragons proved too strong as they defeated the Silver Lakers 27-0. They won the WPIAL title in l944 and l945 and were voted by the newspaper sports writers and readers as the most outstanding high school football team in the last fifty years. Pro really believed in putting his boys against the best and this Donora team was just that. Dan Towler starred at W&J College and later in the NFL for the Los Angeles Rams. Lou "Bimbo" Ciccone later starred at Pitt along with Rudy Andabaker and Arnold Galiffa starred at West Point.

90

After the Donora loss the Bulldogs bounced back the following week and defeated a good Altoona team 12-0. In this game back Tom Tedesco came up with a key interception at a crucial time to snuff out a Lion rally. In the league opener the Bulldogs defeated a South team 34-12 with former Westinghouse star "Honey" Brown playing for South. South Hills was next on the schedule and they were defeated 13-0 with Ateo "Cisco" Bisceglia playing a fine game along with Herbie Lintelman, Marvin Carpenter and James "Dinky" DiMaria. As usual the Peabody game was a dandy one with the Bulldogs winning 14-0. In this one Carpenter, Lintelman, Tedesco, Bisceglia and Lou Fabrizzi played their usual brand of ball. The following week it was a 20-0 victory over Schenley led by John Spinelli playing for the injured Ross Molinaro. He along with Robert Mihm and Marvin Carpenter played a stellar game on defense stopping Schenley's running backs behind the line of scrimmage on numerous occasions. In the final league game Allerdice was beaten by the Silver Lakers 14-7 as Bisceglia and Lintelman each scored to preserve the victory.

The final title appearance for coach Pro Burton was played at Pitt Stadium on November 12, 1945 against Allegheny High School. Bisceglia and Lintelman again showed why they were both All-City as they each scored a touchdown in a 13-0 victory for Westinghouse. They had some fine play from Carpenter and Mihm and backfield support from James Bilotta. This was the last time that Pro Burton would coach a Westinghouse football team and it was surrounded with mixed emotions. The man who devoted his life's work to the many young men in Homewood and East Liberty was now walking away from a school and an athletic program that he had put in the limelight for almost thirty years. The "Builder of Champions" was leaving behind a legacy that was going to be remembered for a long, long time.

**91**

**Pittsburgh City League Championship**

WHS 13     Allegheny     0
Scoring:

| | | | | |
|---|---|---|---|---|
| Westinghouse | 7 | 0 | 6 | 0—13 |
| Allegheny | 0 | 0 | 0 | 0—0 |

Touchdowns – Westinghouse: Bisceglia, Lintleman.
Point conversion – Westinghouse: Bisceglia

This 1945 team was special to him and they would never forget him – Tom Valerio, Herbie Lintelman, DeLuca, Tom Tedesco, Louis Fabrizzi, Robert Mihm, James Green, Marvin Carpenter, Ateo "Cisco" Bisceglia, Ido Martin, Leo Martin, Ross Molinaro, John Spinelli, Sam Picone, Jessie Bell, Constantino, James Bilotta, James DeMaria, Irwin Kramer, Smith, Ralph Gallo, John Nigro, Knight, Matone, Don Hudson, Nick Carlisano, Booker Bledsoe, Bill Baldwin, Ward, Harvey Trilli, Grupe, Dillinger, Paul Becker, Omar Ayoub, James, Cipriano Ciccarelli, J. Medine and Gigliotti, manager.

**1945 SEASON (8-1-0)**

| WHS | | Opponents |
|---|---|---|
| 27 | N.B. Scott | 26 |
| 0 | Donora | 27 |
| 12 | Altoona | 0 |
| 34 | South | 12 |
| 13 | South Hills | 0 |
| 14 | Peabody | 0 |
| 20 | Schenley | 0 |
| 14 | Allderdice | 0 |
| City Championship | | |
| 13 | Allegheny | 0 |

The Pro Burton era was now coming to an end. He had guided the Bulldogs to a record of 149-65-23; eleven Pittsburgh City Legue championships and one WPIAL Class AA co-championship with Rochester High School. The following year on May 28, 1946 O. H. "Pro" Burton resigned as head coach at Westinghouse High School after twenty-nine years. He took over the grid post at Penn High School, but unfortunately he was not able to enjoy his new position for very long. He coached there for two years before passing away in West Penn Hospital on December 20, 1948 at the age of 59 of a heart attack. On that day dark clouds loomed over Westinghouse High School as the man who was a legend to many alumni was gone. Pro had given a life time of service to Westinghouse High School, beginning way back in 1916 when he first arrived there as a young coach and athletic director. He was truly a man among men and the young men who played for him will never forget him. He was the original "Builder of Champions" at Westinghouse.

## THE ARRIVAL OF PETE DIMPERIO

Following the retirement of Pro Burton in 1946, Peter Paul Dimperio arrived at Westinghouse as their new Head Football Coach. He was coming in from Herron Hill Junior High School where he had an outstanding record as a basketball coach. This did not go over very well with members of the 1946 football squad at Westinghouse. They felt with no prior football coaching experience what qualified him to fill the shoes of their former coach Pro Burton. He was on the spot ever since his arrival there. The players were very slow in accepting anyone other than their departed coach. After all, Burton had been a permanent fixture there for some thirty years. Dimperio had his hands full that first year with rebellious attitudes of several of the players. In fact one old timer told me how they refused to run plays that were called in from the sideline by Dimperio. It was not easy for him as several old timers admitted they had difficulty and were slow in accepting anyone but their beloved Pro Burton.

In the 1946 pre-season opener the Bulldogs defeated North Braddock Scott 7-0 in a close one as Fran Rogel former Penn Stater and Pittsburgh Steeler was the fullback on that Scott High team. The following week they played always tough Connellsville

High and defeated them 12-6. Then came Altoona and they were ready for the Bulldogs, avenging for the previous year with a 20-6 win over the Silver Lakers. The city league schedule provided some tough games as Peabody gave the Bulldogs all they could handle in a scoreless tie and South Hills gave the Silver Lakers a scare before losing a close one 15-13. Westinghouse continued to stay undefeated in league play as they defeated Allderdice 27-0, Schenley 19-6 and South 25-7. In spite of the rebellious attitudes of some of his players, Dimperio managed to rise to the challenge, and won his first Pittsburgh City Championship with a 27-7 victory over Allegheny at Pitt Stadium. It was really a pretty good team going 7-1-1 for the season. They were led by Leo Martin, Herb Lintelman and James DiMaria, All-City along with Robert Mihm and Ross Molinaro, All State. Many of the critics were saying that several of the players on this 1946 team were holdovers from the Burton team of the previous year. Dimperio still had to convince the second-guessers that he could coach a team that was strictly one that he put together himself.

The 1946 team members were as follows: Leo Martin, Bob Mihm, John Mallory, Ralph Gallo, Bill Baldwin, Ross Molinaro, Jess Bell, James DeMaria, Herbie Lintelman, James Bilotta, Cipriano Ciccarelli, Nick Carlisano, John Takacs, James Green, Booker Bledsoe, Harry Stokes, Don Hudson, Knight , T. Bailey, Paul Becker, Omar Ayhoub, Irwin Kramer, Harvey Trilli, Marelli, Don Millitary, C. Bennett, Horace Brissett, John Nigro, Fahacs, Frank DiLeo, Jim Robinson, Frank Guadagnino, Tom Vallerio, P. Arrigo, F. Flocarri, Gemperlein, Grupe, R. Modena, J. Pitiacciato, Bill Malroy, and Williams.

**93**

**1946 SEASON (7-1-1)**

| WHS | | Opponents |
|---|---|---|
| 7 | N. B. Scott | 0 |
| 12 | Connellsville | 6 |
| 6 | Altoona | 20 |
| 27 | Allderdice | 0 |
| 0 | Peabody | 0 |
| 19 | Schenley | 6 |
| 25 | South | 7 |
| 15 | South Hills | 13 |
| City Championship | | |
| 27 | Allegheny | 7 |

Pittsburgh City League Championship
WHS 27     Allegheny     7
Scoring:

| | | | | |
|---|---|---|---|---|
| Westinghouse | 0 | 7 | 7 | 13—27 |
| Allegheny | 0 | 0 | 0 | 7—7 |

Touchdowns — Westinghouse: Lintelman 2, Bilotta, Takacs.
　　　　　　　Allegheny: Kirmeyer.
Point conversions — Westinghouse: Bilotta, Lintelman, Cicciarelli.
　　　　　　　Allegheny: Buyna.

## DIMPERIO MAKES SINGLE-WING SPARKLE

By the late forties – 1947, 1948 and 1949 Dimperio managed to win three more city titles. The accolades were beginning to come his way as he was gaining the respect of his peers and most important his players. He brought a ray of sunshine to Westinghouse High School with a high caliber of football and his clever sense of humor. The old timers were dilatory in their acknowledgement of his success. They were reluctant to admit that any man could fill the shoes of the late O. H. "Pro" Burton.

The 1947 championship team went 8-0-1 for the season with a very fine team led by All-State Irvin Kramer and All-City Harry Stokes (older brother of basketball great Maurice Stokes), Cipriano Ciccaarelli, and John Nigro. They opened the pre-season with a hard earned win over North Braddock Scott 14-7. The following week they won another close one 12-6 over Connellsville. Then came always tough Altoona and the Bulldogs battled them to a 0-0 tie. After three tough exhibition games Westinghouse was ready for the city league schedule. After winning the opener over Allderdice 40-0, the Bulldogs had four tough wins over the likes of Peabody 14-13, Schenley 20-0, South Hills 13-12 and finally South 19-0. A week later it was on to Forbes Field to meet the Carrick High School Raiders for the City Championship, and the Silver Lakers prevailed 19-0 after a scoreless first half. It was the fourth title in a row for Westinghouse and they were the first city school to accomplish this in the history of the City League. The Bulldogs were beginning to make their presence known in Western Pennsylvania high school football.

The 1947 team: Frank "Chubby" DiLeo, James Green, Booker Bledsoe, Frank Floccari, Cipriano "Chick" Ciccarelli, Horace Brissett, Chuck Tedesco, James Madine, Andrew Dent, Felix Cutruzulla, Don Hudson, Wesley Demmler, Lou Delaquilla, James Alder, Harry Stokes, Clarence Bennett, Leonard Gallo, Omar Ayoub, M. Morelli, Albert Nigro, Nick Carlisano, Mario Masterberardino, J. Pitacciato, Joe Nicolett, Irwin Kramer, H. Gibbs, Charles Jones, R Arrington. John Cafino, Gene Massaro, Tom Bailey, Bill Hicks, J. Kosmal, Don Maxwell, R. Madamma, Angelo Cuomo, Phil Arrigo, Frank Guadagnino, John Nigro, Mangers Bill Malrey and Tom Tucker.

**1947 SEASON (8-0-1)**

| WHS | | Opponents |
|---|---|---|
| 14 | N. B. Scott | 7 |
| 12 | Connellsville | 6 |
| 0 | Altoona | 0 |
| 40 | Allderdice | 0 |
| 14 | Peabody | 13 |
| 20 | Schenley | 0 |
| 13 | South Hills | 12 |
| 19 | South | 0 |

94

City Championship
19     Carrick     0

Pittsburgh City League Championship
WHS  19     Carrick  0
Scoring:
Westinghouse        0     0     7     12—19
Carrick             0     0     0     0—0
Touchdowns — Westinghouse: Cicciarelli, Green, Gallo.
Point conversions — Westinghouse: Cicciarelli.

The 1948 team was probably the one team that Pete had the most fond memories of, and for that matter myself as well. It was my first year at Westinghouse as a seventh grader and I was in awe of them. I was only twelve years old at the time and I enjoyed football very much. My friends and I would stay after school to watch them practice just about every day. After watching them practice week in and week out I was so impressed with the ball handling of the running backs. They executed the single wing offense to perfection and it was hard to determine which running back ended up with the ball. This team had a season record of 8-1-0 and defeated Carrick 33-12 in the city final. They were led by five All-City players – Felix Cutruzulla, Joe Scalzo, Frank "Chubby" DiLeo, Frank Guadagnino and Mario "Mo" Masterberardino with honorable mention to Leonard Gallo.

In the season opener they showed early on that they had something special with an impressive 26-8 win over a good North Braddock Scott team. The following week several of us from the old neighborhood traveled to Ellwood City and saw a great ballgame as the boys from Homewood won a thriller 12-9. I saw every game this particular season except the one up at Altoona which the Bulldogs lost in a heartbreaker 14-13. They had a good pre-season and now it was time for the City League to begin. The league opener was against Allderdice and it was a good tune-up for the Bulldogs as they won handily 46-0. The following week was at Peabody and it was standing room only as my friends and I were standing behind the end zone facing the school. The Highlanders were leading the Bulldogs 14-13 at the end of three quarters and were looking good until early in the fourth quarter. After the first series of plays in that quarter Peabody elected to punt deep into Westinghouse territory. Joe Scalzo of Westinghouse fielded it one yard deep in the opposite end zone, and he took it all the way (101 yards) for a Bulldog touchdown. The Westinghouse faithful went crazy as the Peabody fans watched in disbelief. It was a run that I will never forget as he was coming from the far end of the field and the closer he came to us the more excited we got. That run took all the fight out of Peabody and ignited the Bulldogs as they scored twice more to win the game 33-14. This was a typical Peabody-Westinghouse game with all the excitement you would expect. It was high school football at its best. The following three games were a breeze as the Silver Lakers defeated Schenley 33-0, South 33-6 and South Hills 41-6. They were the city league, Section 1 winner and would meet the Section 2 winner

**95**

Carrick High School for the city title scheduled for Armistice Day at Forbes Field under the lights.

I can remember the excitement at school during the week of the game. You could feel the electricity in the hallways as the pre-game hype was underway. The day before the game we had a pep rally in the school auditorium as our band led by Mr. Carl McVicker and the cheerleaders led by Mr. Joseph Harsky had the student body at a fever pitch. Coach Dimperio warned the boys to play with the same intensity as they had throughout the regular season. This was a new experience for us seventh graders and we really cut it loose along with the seniors. It was something that we used to hear our older brothers and sisters talk about at the dinner table and now we were able to join them. This is when I really began to feel the effects of the pride, spirit and loyalty that existed at Westinghouse High School.

We were reading in the newspapers that the Carrick Raiders had a big talented team and outweighed the Bulldogs, and Westinghouse was expected to rely on speed and deception to make up the difference. The Silver Lakers were ready and they took control of the game at the outset with the speed and deception of its powerful single wing offense. The Westinghouse line was quicker than the Carrick line and gave our running backs the openings to run through. Our backfield of fullback Frank Guadagnino, halfbacks Lenny Gallo, Charles "Porky" Jones, Tommy Costa and Quarterbacks Joe Nicoletti and Chuck White were superb along with our receivers Felix Cutruzulla and Joe Scalzo. The defense played well as the Silver Lakers defeated Carrick 33-12 for its fifth City Championship in a row.

96

Now the so called critics were beginning to realize that Pete Dimperio was indeed a fine coach and a good fit for the football program at Westinghouse High School. In his first three years the Bulldogs had won seventeen and tied one in city league competition. It was beginning to look as though the road to the City Championship of Pittsburgh was by way of Murtland Avenue in Homewood. Some of the news media were beginning to call Westinghouse – "Championship High". It had a nice ring to it, but every year is a challenge when you have to defend a title, and Pete Dimperio was always cautioning his players to be ready for the challenge. When I was a student there he was constantly reminding the students of the importance of their loyal support at every game. He made us realize how much the team depended upon us for this loyalty. We were beginning to think that the city title was there for the taking, but Dimperio made us realize that it had to be earned. He made us feel like we were all in this together and that was the key to our success. He certainly knew how to motivate the team and the entire student body. We were very fortunate to have him at Westinghouse.

This was Dimperio's team and these boys accepted him as their coach: Frank Guadagnino, F. Moore, Charles Jones, Leonard Gallo, Joe Nicoletti, Joe Scalzo, Frank DiLeo, John Cafino, Mario Masterberardino, Eugene Massaro, Eugene Buccilli, Felix Cutruzulla, Chuck White, Renaldo Modena, H. Gibbs, W. Demmler, Tom Costa, G. Jones, R. Nellis, A Cuomo, L. Ferragonio, E. Twyman, James Alder, J. Kosmal, B. Hallinan, R. Anderson, Chuck Naser, Paul Nelson, Joe Massaro, L. Stabile, Ray Bolena, Bill Antonucci, Harry Shellaby, John Delong, Lou Cuccaro, Joe Harrity, Lou

Dellaquilla, Gene Moore, Tom Pryor, Sal Migliore, Walter Sylvester, and managers, T Tucker, R. Bardelang and R. Gaddie.

**1948 SEASON (8-1-0)**

| WHS | | Opponents |
|---|---|---|
| 26 | N. B. Scott | 7 |
| 12 | Ellwood City | 9 |
| 13 | Altoona | 14 |
| 46 | Allderdice | 0 |
| 33 | Peabody | 14 |
| 33 | Schenley | 0 |
| 33 | South | 6 |
| 41 | South Hills | 6 |

City Championship

| 33 | Carrick | 12 |
|---|---|---|

Pittsburgh City League Championship

| WHS | 33 | Carrick | 12 |
|---|---|---|---|

Scoring:

| | | | | |
|---|---|---|---|---|
| Westinghouse | 13 | 0 | 14 | 6—33 |
| Carrick | 0 | 0 | 6 | 6—12 |

Touchdowns—Westinghouse: Cutruzulla 2, Gallo, Scalzo, Guadagnino.
Carrick: Bredl, Bronder.
Point conversions—Westinghouse: Scalzo 3 (placements).

97

## AN OLD LEGEND DEPARTS

Pro Burton took over the grid post at Penn High School in 1946, but unfortunately he was able to enjoy his new position for only two years. About one month after the1948 football season was over we read in our school newspaper - THE BULLETIN - that legendary coach Pro Burton had passed away on December 20, 1948 in West Penn Hospital of a heart attack at the age of fifty-nine. On that day dark clouds loomed over Westinghouse High School as the man who was a legend to many alumni was gone. Pro had given a lifetime of service to Westinghouse High School, beginning way back in 1916 when he first arrived there as a young coach and athletic director.

He was truly a man among men and the young men who played for him will never forget him. I had never met the man personally, but I felt as though I had known him. His name was mentioned many times over in our household as my father spoke very highly of him. The loyalty for him was always felt by many alumni and this was indeed a sad day for all of those who knew him in the community of Homewood. He was the pioneer of the football fortunes of Westinghouse High School and gave a lifetime of service to our community. He will always be remembered as our "Builder of Champions."

## A NEW LEGEND BEGINS HIS JOURNEY

The 1949 season was looking at four starters and several experienced lettermen returning from the 1948 championship team. The four starters were quarterback Joe Nicoletti, halfback Leonard Gallo, guard Eugene Massaro and tackle Eugene Buccilli, and they were a good nucleus to build around. They opened the season with an impressive 28-6 win over North Braddock Scott as end Richard Anderson scored three touchdowns with his fine pass receiving and speed. It was a costly win for the Bulldogs as star running back Leonard Gallo suffered a severe leg injury in that game. This was a tough break for the senior running back after he played so well in his junior year, and was expected to be a key player for Dimperio. He was replaced by senior Joe Massaro who had plenty of speed and was teaming up with halfback Tommy Costa, fullback Harry Shellaby and quarterback Joe Nicoletti to form a potent backfield for the Bulldogs. The following week they traveled to Altoona and came back home with an impressive 31-14 victory. The Bulldogs must have left that good effort back in Altoona because in the next game they visited the Duquesne Dukes and everything went wrong. Enroute to the game the team bus broke down and the team arrived in Duquesne about an hour late. The bus unloaded the players with their duffel bags at the far end of the stadium and they had to walk past the grandstand to the locker rooms to suit up. The Duquesne team was already on the field warming up and had been for some time. The kickoff was delayed for about forty-five minutes and it was not a good night for the Bulldogs as they were defeated by the Dukes 13-0. It was the first time I had ever seen Westinghouse lose a football game, and my being only thirteen years old at the time did not help me to accept defeat. My dad and uncle were at the game with me and I remember both of them explaining to me that I had to learn to accept defeat graciously when it happens. They were quite right as we all have to learn to take defeat in stride. All good teams bounce back from defeat and adversity and this Westinghouse team did just that the rest of the season.

They breezed through the five game City League schedule, posting four shutouts and gave up only one touchdown and that was to Schenley in a 27-7 Bulldog win. The shutouts were against Allderdice 56-0, Peabody 47-0, South 40-0 and South Hills 28-0. They met Section 2 winner Allegheny in the city championship game, and won their sixth title in a row with a 13-0 victory over the North Side school at Forbes Field under the lights. Guard and linebacker Bill Antonucci was the unsung hero in this game as he intercepted an Allegheny pass late in the game and returned it for a Westinghouse touchdown. This happened with the Bulldogs holding on to a slim 7-0 lead and sealed the win for the boys from Homewood. This fine team ended the season with a record of 8-1-0 and placed five players on the All-City Team. The players selected were Joe Nicoletti, Gene Massaro, Gene Buccilli, and Harry Shellaby. Nicoletti, Bucilli and Shellaby were selected to play in the Jaycee Dapper Dan High School All-Star game. Dimperio had done a fine job again and was being wooed by some of the colleges to leave the high school ranks and coach at the college level.

The 1949 team: James Alder, Eugene Buccilli, Bill Antonucci, Leonard Gallo, Eugene Massaro, Gene Moore, Richard Anderson, Tom Costa, Joe Nicoletti, Harry Shellaby, Ronald Latronica, Edward Buccilli, Earl Twyman, Louis Cuccaro, Lou Ferragonia, Joe Harrity, William Hallinan, E. McClendon, Joe Massaro, Renaldo Modena, Leonard Malley, Alfred Conte, W. Anderson, H. Moore, Hugo Martin, P. Nelson, J. DeLong, Felix Della Valle, J. Colaizzi, R. Renn, R. Green, R. Floyd, W. Hancock, W. Barnes, managers: J. Fanelli and R. Gaddie.

**1949 SEASON (8-1-0)**

| WHS | | Opponents |
|---|---|---|
| 28 | N.B. Scott | 7 |
| 31 | Altoona | 14 |
| 0 | Duquesne | 13 |
| 56 | Allderdice | 0 |
| 47 | Peabody | 0 |
| 27 | Schenley | 7 |
| 40 | South | 0 |
| 28 | South Hills | 0 |

City Championship

| 13 | Allegheny | 0 |
|---|---|---|

Pittsburgh City League Championship
WHS 13    Allegheny    0
Scoring:

| Westinghouse | 0 | 7 | 0 | 6—13 |
|---|---|---|---|---|
| Allegheny | 0 | 0 | 0 | 0—0 |

Touchdowns—Westinghouse: Shellaby, Antonucci.
Point conversions—Westinghouse: Shellaby.

Shortly following the 1949 season the following article by George Kiseda appeared in the Pittsburgh Sun–Telegraph, and it caused quite a stir among the students and faculty at Westinghouse. We were quite upset and concerned and did not want to lose the man who had done so much for all of us. He was our leader and motivator and the mere thought of him possibly leaving was very depressing. In the four years he served at Westinghouse he was considered an icon in our community.

### DIMPERIO WEIGHING OFFERS TO LEAVE WESTINGHOUSE HIGH
### BY GEORGE KISEDA

Pete Dimperio, the City League's only non-losing football coach, is considering the possibility of leaving Westinghouse High School, it was learned yesterday.

The former Thiel College footballer admitted that he has been weighing coaching offers from several colleges and high schools.

99

Dimperio emphasized, however, that he won't accept any offer unless it develops into something that he cannot turn down. He said: **"My heart still belongs at Westinghouse."**

Dimperio did not disclose where the offers originated. All of the colleges are in Western Pennsylvania and three of the high schools are in the WPIAL.

He already has participated in several interviews, he said.

Asked about the current vacancy at Pitt, Dimperio said he would not file an application. Some of his friends have been trying to persuade him to apply.

Dimperio became the Westinghouse coach in 1946 when he replaced the late Pro Burton, who had switched to Penn High School. Pete never had coached football, but he proceeded to win the City League championship four years in a row. He has yet to lose a City League game. Here is his overall record:

|      | W. | L. | T. |
|------|----|----|----|
| 1946 | 7  | 1  | 1  |
| 1947 | 8  | 0  | 1  |
| 1948 | 8  | 1  | 0  |
| 1949 | 8  | 1  | 0  |

**100**

## SENTIMENTAL FAVORITES

The 1948 and 1949 teams are the two teams that were really close at heart to Pete Dimperio. When he arrived at Westinghouse many of them were only freshmen. He molded them together and won them over with his leadership qualities and respect. Long after their school days were over they still came together as a group meeting with Pete socially from time to time. It was this group of men who supported Pete when he called upon them to help in organizing charity benefits for those who were in need of help. They were there for him up until he departed this life. This group still meets once a year for a reunion and I am honored to have been invited to be with them the past several years.

They have showed me a sincere feeling of pride and spirit as I was in awe of them when I was a young seventh grader and now today meeting with them is special. I was really impressed at the way they handled themselves on and off the football field. They showed a lot of class even when they walked the halls of our school. To this day when I see any of them, I still see that image of respect and friendliness. They represented to me the true pride and spirit that existed at Westinghouse High School. They all turned out to be model citizens the way Pete had hoped they would and they never let him down. God bless you guys I look forward to seeing all of you again at your next reunion.

## SPECIAL TIMES WITH PETE

In my last two years at the House I can remember with much satisfaction taking gym classes with Pete Dimperio and how much I enjoyed it. I played basketball for him in the intramural program, and he made me feel like an integral part of the program. He was special to so many of us. I can recall not being able to take swimming (one day a week) with the rest of the class because of a chronic medical problem with my ears. I had two punctured eardrums and while the rest of the class was swimming I would sit by the pool and talk about football and life with Pete. I told Pete "When Uncle Sam comes calling he will draft me and find a place for my bad ears." He nodded and got a chuckle out of my simple humor. And sure enough it turned out that way as I served six years with Uncle Sam. I really enjoyed those talks with him and after I graduated from Westinghouse he was probably the one teacher I missed the most. He was the one who I could relate with and turn to if I had a problem. I realize now that was the beginning of my venture.

## HIS VOICE WAS CAPTIVATING

Many years later at one of my class reunions he remembered me by name which really surprised me. He was our special guest that night and he spoke about **PRIDE**. It was so fitting that he would choose that as his topic. He captivated us with the way he spoke. One could hear a pin drop waiting for each word to flow from his craggy voice. He stressed the pride factor as convincingly as he named many of the career vocations that many of our classmates had pursued. No job, professional or non-professional, should be performed without a sincere sense of pride. He was quite right as he emphasized that every job should be approached and performed to the very best of one's ability. Anything short of that was not acceptable. He truly was a man of his word, and expressed that no challenge was beyond reach. The speech he gave that evening was one that still impresses me when I reflect back. He made us all feel very proud to have had him as our teacher. In fact those who were guests or spouses of our classmates were quite impressed that we were so fortunate to have been associated with him. That was a high compliment for a teacher. We were blessed to have him at Westinghouse. They come around once in a lifetime. Pride was what we inherited during our years of learning at the big House in Homewood.

101

## 1940 WESTINGHOUSE BULLDOGS

## Football Team

**102**

*Head Coach* ...................................................*O.H. "Pro" Burton*
*Co-Captain* ...............................*George Colaizzi, Dick Burton*
*Manager* ..................................................................*Bob Rodden*
*Assistant Manager* ...............................................*Carl Kramer*
*Water Boy*...............................................................*Jim Madden*
*Assistant Coach* .....................................................*A.K. Grupe*
*Faculty Manager* .........................................................*L. Speer*

| | | | | | |
|---|---|---|---|---|---|
| Bill Mihm | L.E | John Sant | R.T. | Carmen DeStafano | G. |
| Ed Dellaquilla | L.T. | John Santora | Q.B. | Frank Gardone | F. |
| Don Dileo | L.Q. | Frank Diamond | L.H. | Ed Sullivan | H.B. |
| Dick Burton | C. | John Henderson | R.H. | Stanley Calcombe | H.B. |
| Lewis Martin | R.Q. | Bill Merritt | F.B. | John DiLucchio | F. |
| Clarence Tucker | R.T. | Harold Brown | L.F. | John Larner | C. |
| Wm. Schrott | R.E. | John Mylan | C. | Ralph Anderson | F. |
| Vic. Santone | Q.B. | James Jordan | R.Q. | Roy Brandi | F.B. |
| Geo. Colzzi | F.B. | Nick Porco | R.T. | Joe LaPresti | T. |
| Virgil Cimador | R.H. | Tom Matthews | Q.B. | John Haunty | T. |
| Vito Latronica | F.B. | John Blackwell | R.H. | Fred Formechella | T. |
| Dan Castleforte | Q.B. | Tom Reghard | F.B. | Harry Davis | F. |
| Paul Mazzei | L.Q. | Harold McClintock | G. | John Mason | G. |
| Bill Heilman | C. | Felix Yannotti | T. | William Brown | H.B. |
| Joe Demase | R.Q. | Boots Garland | T. | Robert O'Brien | C. |

**1941 WESTINGHOUSE HIGH SCHOOL CITY FOOTBALL CHAMPIONS**

The following members of the 1941 team are in no special order: Carmen DeStefano, Joe LoPresti, Bill Heilman, Edward Sullivan, Bill Merritt, Howard Weber, Paul Mazzei, Felix Yannotti, Harold Brown, Stan Colcombe, Raymond Brandi, Ralph Anderson, Clarence Tucker, Virgil Cimadore, Howard Caskey, Tom Mathews, Dom Palombo, Oscar Vaughn, John Haupt, John Mylan, John DiLucchio, Louis Biondi, George Watkins.

103

## 1942 PITTSBURGH CITY LEAGUE CO-CHAMPIONS

**104**

### CHAMPIONSHIP FOOTBALL TEAM OF WESTINGHOUSE HIGH

*Ends*:
Harold Brown
Ira Hockenberger

*Tackles*:
Joseph LoPresti
Harold Rogal

*Guards*:
Al Pitaccio
Paul Barbuto

*Center*:
Leo Watkins

*Quarterback*:
Bob Craven

*Fullback*:
Bill Merritt

*Halfbacks*:
Stan Colcombe
Ed Sullivan
Bruce Weston
Harry Borcelli

*Substitutes*:
Bob Becker
Leon Lewis
Joe Chieffo
Joe Ferrarro

Louis Sottile
Ray Mazzer
Bob Mason

*Other Squad Members*:
Regis Heilman
Bill Wiant
Frank McCray

Richard Muse
Gene Gross
Harold Arrington
James Mason

John Tuttle
Robert Zimmer
Harry Colcombe

The football team of Westinghouse High School turned in a very successful season and finished it by playing a favored Oliver High team and tying for the city championship. Although our team looked ragged in the first three games, the boys threw off their early-season greenness and romped through league competition and permitted Oliver to score only one touchdown.

Our team showed its true Westinghouse spirit by overcoming early-season handicaps in the form of injuries to star halfbacks Stan Colcombe and Ed Sullivan.

The Bulldogs hit their peak in the Schenley game when they were at a disadvantage in playing with the users of the widely acclaimed T-formation and completely defeated their opponents. When the Oliver game came, Pro and his boys were looking hopefully toward the city championship. Dame Fortune then took a hand and Big Bill Merritt, all-city fullback, injured a leg. Although the chances of victory were somewhat decreased, Westinghouse played Oliver for the city championship with Bob Becker capably substituting for Merritt in over half the game. The final score was six for Oliver and six for W. H. S.

*By Robert Craven*

105

*Burton • Dimperio • Musilin • Malins • Webb*

106

1945 PITTSBURGH CITY LEAGUE FOOTBALL CHAMPIONS

WESTINGHOUSE HIGH SQUAD—Front, William Silvio; First row, left to right, J. L. Speer, faculty manager; Picone, Molinaro, Valerio, Mihm, Lintelman, Tedesco, DiMaria, Fabrizi, Carpenter, L. Martin, Bisceglia and Mike Mirone, manager; second row, Demas, Bell, Spinelli, Greene, Cosantino, Savio, Gallo, Smith, Knight, DeStout, DeLuca and Hudson; third row, Bilotto, Bledsoe, Ward, Trilli, Ciccarelli, McLeod, Becker, Nigro, Madine, Little, Kramer and Head Coach O. H. Burton; top row, I. Martin, manager; Austin Grupe, assistant coach; Lioi, Baldwin, Stokes, James, LoPresti, Carlisano, DeSantis, Bennett, Dent, Ayoub, R. Grupe and Dillinger. Westinghouse is the City League defending champion from Sec. 1.

# "Our Beloved Coach"

O. H. "PRO" BURTON - 1946

LAST PICTURE OF PRO BURTON TAKEN AT KENNY-
WOOD PARK, JUNE 1946 AT HOMEWOOD BOARD OF
TRADE SCHOOL PICNIC. C. A. HERMAN, PRESIDENT
OF B. OF T. AND CHAIRMAN OF PICNIC PRESENTED
COACH BURTON WITH A "LORD ELGIN" WATCH.

107

108

THE LEGEND

Pete Dimperio

## 1946 PITTSBURGH CITY LEAGUE FOOTBALL CHAMPIONS

Sun-Telegraph Photo.

**WESTINGHOUSE SQUAD—** Westinghouse High School's football squad, defending champion of the City League, which opposes Scott High School under the lights in North Braddock tonight. Left to right: Back row—Coach Grupe, Williams, Pitacciato, Grupe and Coach Pete Dimperio. Third row—Gemperlein, Robinson, Dileo, Fahacs, Nigro, Birnett, Bennett, Milletary and Marelli. Second row—Trilli, Kramer, Ayoub, Becker, Bailey, Knight, Bledsoe, Hudson, Greene and Carlisano. Front row—Martin, Mihn, Malroy, Gallo, — Baldwin, Molinaro, Bell, DiMaria, Lintelman, Bilotta and Cicarelli. Dimperio succeeded O. H. Burton as coach.

110

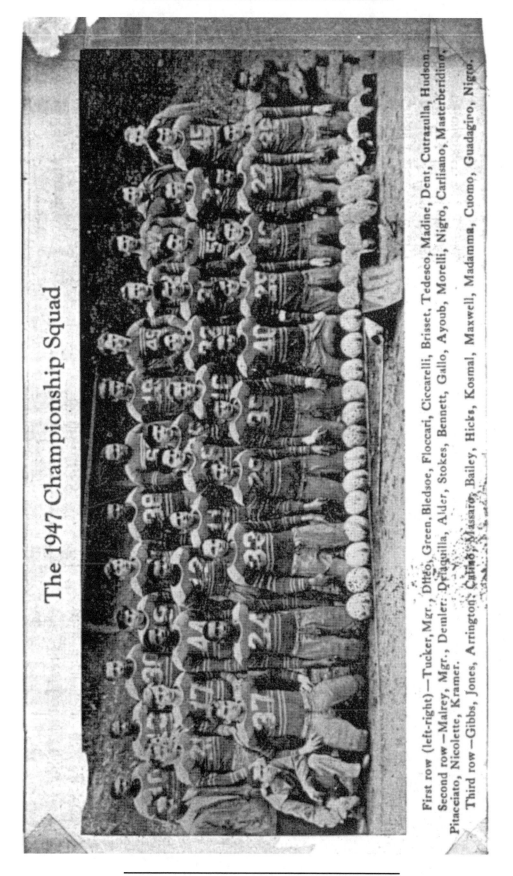

The 1947 Championship Squad

First row (left-right)—Tucker, Mgr., Ditto, Green, Bledsoe, Floccari, Ciccarelli, Brisset, Tedesco, Madine, Dent, Cutrazulla, Hudson. Second row—Malrey, Mgr., Demler, Dellaquilla, Alder, Stokes, Bennett, Gallo, Ayoub, Morelli, Nigro, Carlisano, Masterberidino, Pitacciato, Nicolette, Kramer. Third row—Gibbs, Jones, Arrington, Carino, Massaro, Bailey, Hicks, Kosmal, Maxwell, Madamma, Cuomo, Guadagino, Nigro.

**1948 FOOTBALL TEAM**

First row, left to right:—Gaddie, Manager; Gibbs, Demler, Costa, G. Jones, Nellis, Cuomo, Ferragonia, Twyman, Alder, Kosmal, Hallinan, Anderson, Tucker, Manager.

Second Row:—Bardelang, Manager; F. Moore, C. Jones, Guadagnino, Gallo, Nicoletti, Scalzo, DiLeo, Cafino, Mastroberardino, E. Massaro, Buccilli, Cutruzzula, White, Modena.

Third Row.—Grupe, Assistant Coach; Naser, Nelson, J. Massara, Stabile, Bolena, Antonucci, Shellaby, Delong, Cuccaro, Harrity, Dell'Aquila, G. Moore, Pryor, Dimperio, Coach.

111

112

WESTINGHOUSE . . . The probable starters for Westinghouse High School in tonight's game with Scott at North Braddock. Left to right—Backfield—Jones, Guadagnino, White, Gallo. Line—Scalzo, Dileo, Cafino, Masterberadino, Massaro, Maxwell, Cuttruzulla.

MARIO MASTERBERANDINO

FRANK GUADAGNINO

LEN GALLO

FELIX CUTRUZZULA

113

**BEGIN TITLE DEFENSE**—Champion of the City High League the last two seasons, the Westinghouse Bulldogs will begin their Sec. 1 campaign against the South Orioles at Phillips Park, Carrick, Friday afternoon. The Silver Lakers are coached by Peter Paul Dimperio, who is aided by Austin Grupe. Among first-stringers are Cutruzzula, left end; Masterberandino, center; Gallo, left halfback and er; and Guadagnino, hard-hitting, husky fullback.

Sun-Telegraph Photo

.. DILEO, WESTINGHOUSE LINEMAN ...

... JONES, WESTINGHOUSE HIGH SCHOOL BACKFIELD STARTER ...

## All-City League Team

| Pos. | PLAYER, TEAM | CLASS | HT. | WT. |
|---|---|---|---|---|
| E. | Floyd Keene, Peabody | Sr. | 5-11 | 175 |
| E. | Joe Scalzo, Westinghouse | Sr. | 6-0 | 170 |
| T. | Frank DiLeo, Westinghouse | Sr. | 5-10 | 185 |
| T. | Don Parham, South Hills | Sr. | 5-10 | 205 |
| G. | John Elias, Carrick | Sr. | 5-10 | 185 |
| G. | Louis Iannacchione, Schenley | Sr. | 6-0 | 180 |
| C. | Robert Johnson, Perry | Sr. | 6-1 | 197 |
| B. | Len Gallo, Westinghouse | Jr. | 5-5 | 140 |
| B. | Frank Guadagnino, Westinghouse | Sr. | 6-0 | 180 |
| B. | Don Bredl, Carrick | Sr. | 5-10 | 177 |
| B. | Anthony Simile, Allegheny | Sr. | 5-10 | 180 |

### HONORABLE MENTION

Ends—Bob Salcetti, Carrick; Norman Gant, Fifth Ave.; J. Lewis, South; Felix Cutruzzula, Westinghouse.

Tackles—Edward Schneier, Allderdice; Charles Mason, Fifth Ave.; Max Goldmann, Peabody; Louis Barnes, Schenley; Ed Lighthiser, South Hills.

Guards—Joe Liska, Allegheny; Henry Williams, Fifth Ave.; Richard Lambert, Langley.

Centers—Mario Masterberardino, Westinghouse; Ken Dyer, South; Frank Caracciola, Schenley.

Backs—Jack Brourman, Allderdice; Morry Blummer, Allderdice; Dewey Bryant, Allegheny; George Kerr, Carrick; Sam Rigo, Carrick; John Daley, Langley; Joseph Leone, Langley; William Cosentino, Oliver; Jerry Sweeney, Oliver; Clifford Hargest, Oliver; Russell Kemmerer, Peabody; Sam Ferrainola, Peabody; Thomas Lazoroff, Perry; John Siflck, Perry; Clifford Paige, Schenley; Ralph Voltre, South; Blair Kramer, South Hills; Roy all Flowers, South Hills.

## All-City High School Football Team

Ends—Felix Cutruzzula, Westinghouse, and Richard Heinter, Carrick.

Tackles—Frank DeLeo, Westinghouse, and Richard Kaczmarek, St. George.

Guards—Paul Winters, North Catholic, and Gene Grease, South Hills.

Center—Mario Masterberardino, Westinghouse.

Backs—Allen Braithwaite, St. Wendelin; Anthony Simile, Allegheny; Leonard Gallo, Westinghouse; William Cosentino, Oliver; Jack O'Mahony, North Catholic; Don Bredl, Carrick; Russ Kemmerer, Peabody; Frank Guadagnino, Westinghouse.

### HONORABLE MENTION

Backs—George Kerr, Carrick; John Braun, and James Clair, St. George; Joe Rodgers, North Catholic; Joseph Mannjek, Central Catholic; Blair Kramer, South Hills.

Ends—Don McGann, Carrick; Floyd Keene, Peabody; Norman Gant, Fifth Avenue.

Tackles—Don Parham, South Hills; Richard Lambert, Langley; Lewis Barnes, Schenley.

Guards—James Hopkins, St. Mary of Mount; Louis Iannacchio, Schenley; Henry Williams, Fifth Avenue.

Centers—Robert Johnson, Perry; Al Carinci, Central Catholic; Dave Hilliard, Allegheny; Kenneth Kramer, North Catholic.

Pittsburgh Press, Sun-Telegraph and Post-Gazette honor All-City Football Teams and Most Valuable Players as 1948 football season comes to an end.

HONORED BY PRESS—Twenty-one most valuable football players, selected from City and Catholic High School teams, and Shady Side Academy, were feted by The Press at a dinner in the Pittsburgher Hotel last night. Those honored were: Front row (left to right)—Frank DiLeo, Westinghouse; Donald Parham, South Hills; Floydm Keene, Peabody; Edward Schneier, Taylor Allderdice; Louis Iannacchione, Schenley; Kenneth Dyer, South, and Joseph Rodgers, North. Second row—Donald Bredl, Carrick; Anthony Simile, Allegheny; Charles Mason, Fifth Avenue; William Cosentino, Oliver; Richard Lambert, Langley; Robert Johnston, Perry, and Albert Carinci, Central. Back row— Wilbert Diethorn, St. George; Allan Braithwaite, St. Wendelin; James Hopkins, St. Mary of the Mount; George French, St. Luke; Patrick Brickley, St. Justin; William Woodfill, Sacred Heart, and Hilary Lynch, Shady Side Academy.

116

1949 CHAMPION FOOTBALL SQUAD

First Row, left to right:—Mr. Grupe, J. Alder, E. Buccilli, W. Antonucci, L. Gallo, E. Massaro, G. Moore, R. Anderson, T. Costa, J. Nicoletti, H. Shellaby, Mr. Dimperio.

Second Row:—R. Latronica, E. Buccilli, E. Twyman, L. Cuccaro, L. Ferragonia, J. Harrity, W. Hallinan, E. McClendon, J. Massaro, R. Modena.

Third Row:—R. Gaddie, L. Malley, A. Conte, W. Anderson, H. Moore, H. Martin, P. Nelson, J. DeLong, F. Della Valle, J. Colaizzi, R. Renn.

Fourth Row:—R. Greene, R. Floyd, J. Fanelli, W. Hancock, W. Barnes.

*Burton • Dimperio • Musilin • Malins • Webb*

118

PETE DIMPERIO

Sun-Telegraph

Sun-Telegraph Photo.

**DOUBLE PLAY . . .** Edward (left) and Eugene Bucelli, who should have Westinghouse High School's opponents seeing double this season. They are identical twins. Not only that, both are tackles. Coach Pete Dimperio can't tell 'em apart. They saw action against Scott High last night. Guess which of the twins has the Toni.

**Bulldog Backs Turn On Speed**

Tom Costa
rips off a
long one

119

Len Gallo
turns up field

**Bulldog
fullbacks
Guadagnino
and
Shellaby
were the heart
and soul of the
1948 and 1949
Pittsburgh
City League
Champions.**

120

—Post-Gazette Photo

**DIVES OVER**—Harry Shellaby dives into the end zone with a third-period Westinghouse touchdown—one of seven the Bulldogs scored in notching a 47-0 triumph yesterday over Peabody. Shellaby's touchdown was scored in the third period on a two-yard plunge. The victory was fourth straight in league competition.

**ROOM FOR A BATTLESHIP**—You could have steamed the Missouri through the opening the Westinghouse line pried wide for Fullback Frank Guadagnino through right tackle. Guadagnino, who scored one of Westinghouse's five TD's, picked up 35 yards on this play. Westinghouse defeated Schenley, 33-0, yesterday at Schenley Field for a fourth victory in a row.

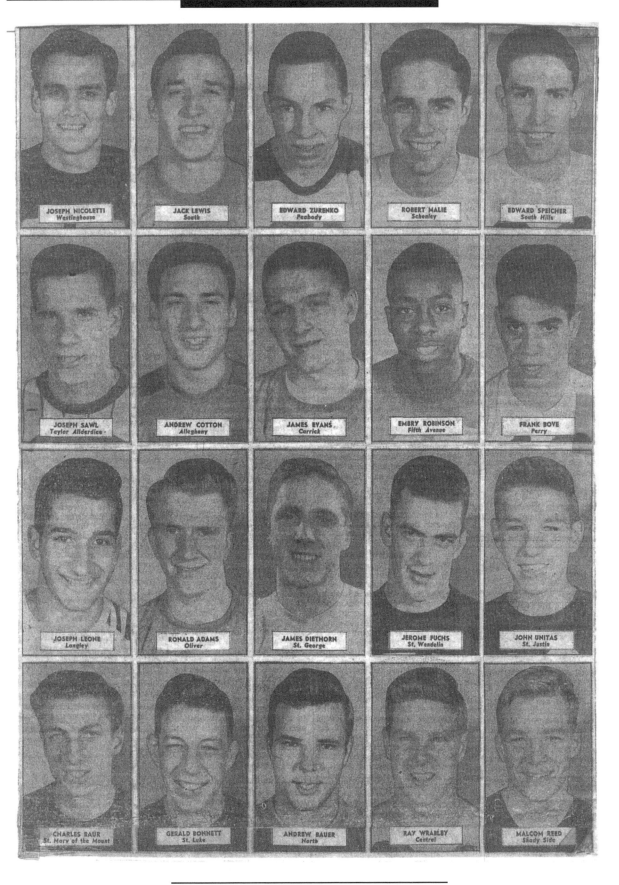

*Burton • Dimperio • Musilin • Malins • Webb*

1948 Miami University of Florida team has several local players

Jack Hackett, 145-pound quarterback star of the Miami University of Florida team who will lead the Hurricane against Pitt at the Stadium day. He is one of five McKeesport players on the invading squad.

LEO Martin, former Westinghouse High School player, star end of the Miami team. He is being oted for All-America.

"PUTTING IT MILDLY OUR FRIENDLY NEIGHBORHOOD RIVAL"

BOB CAMPBELL
*Right Half*

RUSS KEMMERER
*Quarterback*

SAM FERRAINOLA
*Fullback*

DAVE DAVIS
*Left Half*

FLOYD KEENE
*Right End*

MACK GOLDMAN
*Right Tackle*

BOB BAULDING
*Right Guard*

HARVEY KOCHER
*Center*

LOU SHAPIRO
*Left Guard*

PAT SANTELLO
*Left Tackle*

ARTHUR BOYD
*Left End*

—Post-Gazette Photo.

The 1948 Peabody High School Football Team led by Quarterback Russ Kemmerer who made All-City in three sports football, basketball and baseball. After graduating from high school he went on to the University of Pittsburgh. In 1951 he was drafted to pitch for the Boston Red Sox. To know more about Russ Kemmerer you may do so by acquiring the book as quoted by Hall of Famer Ted Williams: "Hey kid, just get it over the plate" written by Russ Kemmerer himself.

123

# PART 2
## A DYNASTY EMERGES

*From the tireless efforts of the legendary coach Pro Burton the Westinghouse winning tradition was well established. His successor Pete Dimperio took over and found an array of talented athletes who were well prepared to continue what Pro Burton had left behind. Dimperio led the Bulldogs to the next level with his own version of the single-wing with much success winning seventeen City Titles in twenty-one years. He made believers out of many of the second guessers who doubted his ability to fill the shoes of Pro Burton. Between Burton and Dimperio the Bulldogs were a dynasty for a better part of the twentieth century.*

# 5 | THE 1950's - BULLDOGS DOMINATE THE CITY

Halfway through the twentieth century Westinghouse was really making headlines in the local sporting news media. By the end of the 1949 season the Bulldogs had won six consecutive Pittsburgh City League titles and were looking more like perennial champions of Pittsburgh. Coach Pete Dimperio was being recognized as one of the best scholastic coaches in Western Pennsylvania and was the recipient of the Dapper Dan Award in 1950.

After dominating the 1940's, winning city titles in 1941, 42, 44, 45, 46, 47, 48 and 49, Westinghouse was looking ahead for more of the same success as the 1950 football season was approaching. The Bulldogs had successfully drawn attention as one of the high school powerhouses in Western Pennsylvania. Up to this point in time the Homewood school was the talk of the town; winning the hearts of many with its winning tradition. The Bulldogs reached a milestone of 200 wins at the halfway mark of the twentieth century and sixteen city titles since the inception of the City League. The Bulldogs were wearing the coveted PA PITT Hat Trophy with much regularity since it's inception in 1945. It was an emblematic trophy that was awarded annually to the Pittsburgh City League Champion in football. This trophy was designed to reflect each year's champion with a brass plate containing the winning school and the year. So far this prestigious trophy had found a home at Westinghouse for the past six years.

At this point in time coach Pete Dimperio was being recognized as a worthy successor to the legendary "Pro" Burton. He was finally receiving the credit he rightfully deserved as he led the Bulldogs to four consecutive championship seasons since he took over at the Homewood school in 1946. He was also receiving offers from other high schools and colleges, but decided that Westinghouse was where his heart belonged. His decision to remain at Westinghouse brought a huge sigh of relief from the entire community. I can remember how concerned many of us were at the mere thought of possibly losing him to another school or university. The many offers that he had to leave were quite attractive. At that point in time there was something special that persuaded Pete to stay at Westinghouse High School – it was the admiration and respect that existed between him, the student body and the entire community. Teachers like him come through and make a difference in one's lifetime. He was just "PETE" and we all loved him. The accolades paid to him were numerous as he became a legend for his many years of service as a teacher, mentor and charitable leader.

## A SEASON OF DISAPPOINTMENTS

Most of the schools were switching from the single-wing offense to the more conventional T-formation. But Coach Dimperio was not going to change his high powered deceptive offense that had brought him and the Bulldogs so much success. His 1950 squad was a talented, but a disappointing one that did not reach the expectations of the pre-season forecasters. In all fairness to this team, a lot of pressure was put on them. For the past six years the student body and the community were spoiled as Westinghouse was riding high and being labeled as perennial champions. We were expecting the city title to be there for the taking and it does not work that way. The 1950 team really gave it all they had, but came up short. They did not repeat as Pittsburgh City league Champions that year as they were bested by a fine Schenley team led by an excellent quarterback named Henry Ford and a running back by the name of Joe Moore. In a key game played at Pitt Stadium they both starred in a hard fought 12-6 win over Westinghouse. Late in that particular game, the Bulldogs had a seventy-five yard touchdown run by halfback Richard Anderson called back for clipping. It would have tied the score at the time with a chance to go ahead with a successful PAT. It was a tough break that seemed to haunt the Bulldogs the rest of the season. Ford and Moore went on to have successful careers following their high school days at Schenley High School. Henry Ford went on to play for the University of Pittsburgh and Joe Moore was quite successful as a coach at a local WPIAL powerhouse Upper St. Clair High School and later as a top assistant coach at the University of Notre Dame.

In the final game of the disappointing 1950 season Westinghouse was upset by arch rival Peabody 7-6 in a sea of mud on the Highlanders home field. The Bulldogs finished the year with a record of 4-4-0, and Schenley went on to capture the Pittsburgh City League Championship with a close 6-0 win over Carrick. It was a year when Pittsburgh's three major newspapers were on strike and we did not have to read about our disappointing season. All was not lost as this team had several talented underclassmen returning the following year anxious to make amends for the disappointing 1950 season. MVP honors that year went to senior tackle and Captain Edward Bucilli. This was the first year since 1944 that the city title trophy did not end up at the Homewood school.

## PETE WINS ONE FOR THE THUMB IN '51

The following year a powerhouse emerged with twenty-two seniors returning from the 1950 squad. Pete had visions of one for the thumb in '51 and he succeeded. This was the fifth title for Dimperio in his first six years at Westinghouse beginning with 1946. The 1951 team was the biggest and strongest of any of the teams that he had coached at Westinghouse High School. They went undefeated that year and received accolades from many of the well respected sports writers in western Pennsylvania. They were considered one of the top ten high school football teams in the WPIAL in the twentieth century. That is a high complement for a Pittsburgh City League school as there were some great teams during that era.

Before the 1951 season began, Dimperio had to make an unexpected major change in his backfield. Starting senior fullback Angelo Aliberti suffered an untimely ankle break before the 1951 summer football camp began. The injury occurred when he was breaking in a new pair of football cleats in a sandlot softball game in late August. While running and attempting to slide home on a bang-bang play at the plate, his cleats caught in the turf and his position as starting fullback went down with him. It was a very unfortunate and foolish injury that he regretted so dearly. Coach Dimperio was quite upset and disappointed, but he had to make a quick decision. He decided to take senior Tom "Butch" Schubert who was one of his starting guards and began working him out at fullback with Aliberti spending all of his time teaching him the new position. They worked together during the summer camp and Schubert was catching on fast. He was ready to go when the season began and excelled so well that at season's end he made the All-City team. By the time Aliberti's broken ankle healed at mid-season the Bulldogs had the luxury of three talented fullbacks – seniors Schubert and Aliberti and junior Charles Inquartano. The following year Inquartano made MVP and All-City while Aliberti was looking back with much regret of his unfortunate fate, but nevertheless thankful for being able to help Schubert to fulfill his role. This was another strength that this top rated 1951 team possessed – team loyalty. Fullback was a key position in Dimperio's version of the single wing as he would handle the ball with regularity play after play in the belly series. Converted fullback Tom Schubert met the challenge. He was the type of competitor that no matter what position he played he was an over-achiever. Dimperio made a wise decision in converting Schubert to fullback after the untimely injury to Aliberti. These two young men worked hard together, supporting Dimperio's decision of turning a bad situation around, and helping the 1951 team develop into one of the best teams to ever come out of Westinghouse. They had twenty-two seniors who were determined to reach the level of play that would make amends for the previous year. They were on a mission playing throughout the year with championship expectations and were never seriously threatened. Without a doubt they were one of the best high school football teams in the nation that year.

129

## A LITTLE CHALK AND NO TALK

The Bulldogs opened the 1951 season with three pre-season games – Allegheny fell victim to the Bulldogs 48-19. The following week a powerful Atoona team was beaten 34-0. This was a surprise as the lopsided victory served notice that Westinghouse was ready to meet the challenge of regaining the Pittsburgh City League Title. The third pre-season game was a tough one against the little Dukes of Duquesne coached by Pete's old friend Angelo "Buff" Donelli.

Dimperio pulled one of his patented locker room strategies. As the team sat in the locker room waiting for Pete's pre-game talk, he wrote on the chalk-board a quote. **"I cannot talk because the Duquesne locker room is right next door and they left our air vent open on purpose. They can hear every word we are saying; therefore I must write our game strategy on the chalkboard."** This infuriated the players as they began to scream and holler - "Pete, we are ready for these guys;

no need for any chalk talk." They were at a fever pitch as they left the locker room making their way to the field. They rode on the vibes of Dimperio's pre-game patented gimmick and defeated the little Dukes 18-7 that night before a packed house. This is a true story as told to me by, Angelo Aliberti who was one of the twenty-two seniors on that 1951 team. Pete sure knew how to motivate his boys with his wit and psychological strategy. I called this a clever case of a little chalk and no talk. With the pre-season over the Bulldogs were ready for the City League competition.

## RECAPTURING THE CITY TITLE

They continued their winning ways and went undefeated in the next five City League games. The Bulldogs averaged forty points per game with its' high powered offense and a defense that was very strong. The next challenge was Carrick High School a worthy contender for the coveted City League title that eluded them in 1950. South Stadium, with a grassless playing field, was the site for this game between two undefeated teams. Carrick had an impressive pre-season tying always tough New Castle 14-14, defeating Brentwood 24-6 and Baldwin 39-0. The Raiders were impressive in the regular season schedule winning all five games handily. They were ready to test the Bulldogs.

Rain had fallen earlier in the day and it made for a slow track for both teams. South Stadium did not have a natural grass playing surface back then, and artificial turf was still in its research stages. This was typical of what the Pittsburgh City School System did not have and most suburbanites did have – a natural grass playing field. The stadium was packed to capacity with 7500 paid admissions while at least 2500 freeloaders watched the game from high above on the McArdle Roadway overlooking the stadium. The first quarter ended scoreless as both teams struggled to get an offense going. The Bulldogs found a way to cope with the soggy playing field in the second quarter. Tom "Butch" Schubert was a workhorse as he repeatedly found running room behind superb Bulldog blocking scoring twice on short plunges. Ernest Jones placekicked two conversions as the Bulldogs led at halftime 14-0. The third quarter was scoreless as neither team could mount any offensive drive. In fact Carrick had only two first downs, and they were made in the first quarter. Schubert continued to roll as he gained 93 yards on 21 carries for the game. Early in the fourth quarter after five consecutive first downs from nifty running by Tom Schubert, Bill Peatross and Francis Griham put the ball on the Carrick one yard line. From there halfback Griham took it in the end zone and the Bulldogs led 20-0.

With less than four minutes left in the game Dimperio sent in the reserves. With one minute left in the game Carrick finally got on the scoreboard on a short pass from Ed Husa to Jack Johnson and Tom Purcell plunged for the conversion. Carrick had finally scored but it was too little too late as Westinghouse regained the Pittsburgh City League Title with a well earned 20-7 victory. The PA PITT HAT was back in the trophy case at Westinghouse.
Score by quarters:

130

| | | | | |
|---|---|---|---|---|
| Westinghouse | 0 | 14 | 0 | 6 – 20 |
| Carrick | 0 | 0 | 0 | 7 – 7 |

Scoring:

Westinghouse – Schubert 2; Griham 1; Extra points – Jones 2 (placements)

Carrick – Johnson; Extra point – Purcell (plunge)

**1951 Season (9-0-0)**
**Pre Season**

| WHS | 48 | Allegheny | 19 |
|---|---|---|---|
| WHS | 34 | Altoona | 0 |
| WHS | 18 | Duquesne | 7 |

City League

| WHS | 64 | South | 8 |
|---|---|---|---|
| WHS | 40 | South Hills | 0 |
| WHS | 53 | Allderdice | 12 |
| WHS | 41 | Peabody | 7 |
| WHS | 41 | Schenley | 7 |

Pittsburgh City League Championship Playoff

| WHS | 20 | Carrick | 7 |
|---|---|---|---|

## MANY HONORS AND ACCOLADES

131

This Westinghouse team possessed power and speed and were voted by the sports writers and readers of the Pittsburgh Post-Gazette as one of the ten best high school teams from Western Pennsylvania in the last fifty years. The first High School All-American to come out of Westinghouse was two way tackle Ronald Latronica who was a member of this team. He was MVP and received a scholarship to Michigan State. To the best of my knowledge All-American status was not in the mix for high school athletes prior to the 1950's era. I am sure Westinghouse would have had a few more worthy of this status in prior years.

This team was loaded with twenty-two seniors and it really showed throughout the season as the second unit played about as much as the first unit. I'd be remised if I did not identify the first team. They were ends Wilbur Mack and Russell Green, tackles Ronald Latronica and Wilbert Anderson, guards Willie Hancock and Jim Costello and center Felix Della Valle leading the way for halfbacks Billy Peatross and Francis "NuNu" Griham, fullback Tom "Butch" Schubert and quarterback Lucio Martin.

## RECOGNIZING CENTER FELIX DELLA VALLE

While there was so much concern over the fullback situation I did not overlook how important the center position was to make this all work. In the single wing offense, the center was the one who was counted on to do his job flawlessly. Every play was started with an accurate snap of the ball, and it was not a simple exchange between him and the quarterback. That would be the case if a team was operating out of the T-formation. Not so with the single wing, the quarterback was the signal caller and was positioned behind the offensive line at a dedicated position to suit the called play. It was a well disguised formation with the center snapping the ball to either the fullback or the tailback to start the play in motion. Felix Della Valle was the talented center who made this all come together. His uncanny accuracy earned him the recognition of an All-City Center and in my estimation the best at that position to come out of Westinghouse High School.

All-City honors were extended to Latronica, Della Valle, Schubert, Peatross, Griham and Mack by the three major newspapers in Pittsburgh. All-State honors went to Latronica and Peatross.

This team would have been a big challenge for both the 1951 WPIAL Class AA Champion Farrell High School and the Pittsburgh Catholic League Champion Central Catholic High School. An effort to match either of these schools in a charity game against Westinghouse was discussed, but never did happen. Farrell was led by two outstanding players – Julius McCoy and Bob Hoffman while Central had the likes of Don Schaeffer, Ray DiPasquale and Ed Vereb along with a strong line.This game would have packed them in at old Forbes Field. All three schools were loaded with talent and were rated as three of the best in the state of Pennsylvania in 1951. Coach Dimperio called his 1951 team the strongest and one of the best to come out of Westinghouse during his long coaching career at the Homewood school. By the end of the 1951 season the overall record for Westinghouse dating back to the 1913 season was 201-82-29 for a winning percentage of 0.710. By that time the Bulldogs had won sixteen Pittsburgh City League Championships and shared one WPIAL Class AA title along the way.

Members of that entire 1951 team were as follows: C. Garland, T. Schubert, F. Della Valle, F.Griham, R. Green, W. Peatross, W. Mack, L. Martin, W. Hancock, W. Anderson, J. Costello, R. Latronica, R. Renn, A. DeLuca, A.Aliberti, J. Ruffa, P. Signore, A. Silvio, A. Ferragonia, C. Hefflin, R. Marsalese, R.Coles, T. Bailey, J. Ricciardelli, A. McGuigan, F. Federeci, W.Walker, J. Ebbitt, E. Jones, C. Paschal, M. Jackson, J. Blattenberger, W. Fink, J. LaMarca, J. Pinson, J. Williams, R. Inquartano, M. Porro, R. Kirk, R. Daniels, E. Haley, R. Steele, R. Lombard, J. Pronio.

## TIME TO REBUILD AND FILL SOME EMPTY SHOES

After the twenty-two seniors from the 1951 team graduated, Coach Dimperio had a huge rebuilding year facing him in 1952. The only returning lettermen left were kicker Ernie Jones and guard Albert "Bo" Silvio. His hopeful starters for 1952 were very young with limited playing experience. Juniors Joe Pronio (265lbs.) and David Jeter (225lbs.) were the starting tackles with good size. Pronio was only fifteen years old with a lot of potential. The pulling guards were senior captain Albert "Bo" Silvio and junior Patsy "Bronco" Signore – both were only 5'6" and 190lbs. with plenty of speed. The center was senior Art McGuigan a tough and heady competitor. The ends were seniors Ricardo Coles and Cody Paschal and junior Joe Ricciardelli. The backfield was led by All-City senior fullback Charles Inquartano; halfbacks were junior Ernie Jones and seniors Russell Steele and James Pinson and the quarterback was junior Ronald Marsalese. This was an inexperienced, but very competitive team that ended the season with a record of 5-3-0. This was probably the best rebuilding job Dimperio had done in his twenty-one years at Westinghouse. Two of those losses were to WPIAL schools – Donora 13-6 and Duquesne 14-0. The lone city league defeat was to Peabody 7-0 on a late touchdown pass from All-City quarterback Al Jacks to Sherman Gardin. Peabody went on to play in the City title game against Carrick at South Stadium. Carrick had a very strong team that year and defeated Peabody 27-6 to win the city championship. All-City honors went to Westinghouse fullback Charles Inquartano with honorable mention going to guards Albert "Bo" Silvio and Patsy "Bronco" Signore and halfbacks Ernie Jones and Russell Steele who all had a fine season for the Bulldogs.

The following year the 1953 team (my senior year) had the talent to challenge for championship honors, but had to settle for second best again with a 6-2-0 record. The two losses were to the WPIAL Class AA Co-Championship Donora 12-6 and to City League Champion Peabody 14-6. The Bulldogs had a chance to win both of these games, but came up short in both efforts. Al Jacks was a fine quarterback for Peabody and led the Highlanders that year to the city title with a 21-0 win over Allegheny. For Westinghouse All-City honors went to halfback Ernie Jones and guard Patsy "Bronco" Signore.

## RATED IN TOP 25 OF WESTERN PENNSYLVANIA

The 1953 team was ranked by the sports writers as one of the top teams in Western Pennsylvania that year. Of the twenty-five teams that were ranked, Peabody (city champions) and Westinghouse were the only Pittsburgh City League schools listed. The rest were from the WPIAL led by Class AA co-champions Donora and Har-Brack. This was quite a tribute to the football team and coach Pete Dimperio. Since they did not win the city title that year, the sports writers were obviously impressed with the effort put forth by the Bulldogs. It was a team that came so close to having an undefeated season – losing only to Donora (WPIAL Champion) and Peabody (Pittsburgh City Champion) in two heart breakers.

Members of that 1953 team were as follows: R. Marsalese, D. Jeter, J. Pronio, P. Signore, J. LaMarca, C. Hefflin, R. Lombard, E. Haley, J. Ricciardelli, C. Smith, W. Walker, E. Jones, P. Galiano, P. Villani, F. Graves, H. Poole, J. Girdano, D. Gruber, G. Brown, G. Depew, H. Nelson, C. Gant, M. Paschal, G. Sproat, F. Schubert, J. Parillo, F. Baglio, J. Cerneglia, A. Fornaser, J. Scott, C. Martin, R. Frederick, J. Kelly, S. Brown, A. Floyd, student managers R. Harris and C. DeLuca.

The 1952 and 1953 teams were not Pittsburgh City League Champions, but they were typical of all Westinghouse teams as they displayed the desire and spirit and played the game with the pride of a champion.

## CHAMPIONSHIP RESURGENCE

Following the 1953 season, Westinghouse came back and regained championship form with an impressive string of titles in 1954, 55, 56, 57, 58, 59, 60, and 61. During this time span the Bulldogs won fifty-eight games, lost twelve and tied two. They did not lose a city league conference game and captured the city championship in each of those eight years. This was a time period that reflected the superiority of the Westinghouse Bulldogs and Coach Pete Dimperio.

During this time period the Bulldogs were facing challenges and changes that reflected the value of how well Pete Dimperio was handling them. When he took over in 1946 Westinghouse was a 75/25 white-black student-body ratio with the football team having a significant number of Italians. By 1954 a change in the student-body enrollment was taking place as the white/black ratio was slowly changing to a more balanced racial mix. Then by 1960 it was becoming a more predominant Afro-American enrollment. With these three major enrollment changes, Westinghouse was still winning. They never lost the proud tradition that the early classes worked so hard to establish. Pete Dimperio was to be commended for his efforts of being fair and recognizing the adjustments that his students had to endure.

He once was asked this question – "Pete, how many black players are on your squad?" His response was merely, "I really do not care what color my players are - black, white, red, purple, or whatever as long as they respect each other and play the game with a high level of sportsmanship. They must play together as a team and refrain from any negative behavior." This was the way Pete expected all of his players to conduct themselves. When they walked the halls at school they were to blend in with the rest of the student body with respect and poise. There was never going to be a superior complex among any of his players. They were well aware that Dimperio expected a mutual respect between any of his players and the rest of the student body. Westinghouse High School was a close knit community during my six years there and was much admired by many of the outsiders. We won together and we lost together, and it carried over many years later when we crossed paths from time to time. It was called **PRIDE**.

Westinghouse opened the 1954 season with a convincing 28-0 win over Donora after a scoreless first half. The Bulldogs came out for the second half with fire in their eyes as Pete lit them up with a fire of his own at halftime. Halfback, Horace Nelson, scored the first touchdown for Westinghouse on a short plunge before the second half was two minutes old. He followed with his second score on a 28 yard scamper five minutes later. Halfback, Bob Merletti, and fullback, Harold Poole, each scored to cap off the second half rally. This was a sweet taste of victory and now it was something to build on. The following week a tough Altoona team was waiting for the cocky Bulldogs and gave them a surprise with a 19-7 loss. It was the first and only defeat for Westinghouse and came early enough in the season to send a message. Aliquippa was the next opponent and the Bulldogs prevailed 7-0 in a real backyard brawl. The Westinghouse team bus left the town of Aliquippa after the game under a heavy barrage of stone throwing and cat calls from the fans of the proud Quips.

134

Next came the City League schedule as the Bulldogs opened up with a convincing win over Allderdice 39-0. The next opponent was Peabody who had bested the Bulldogs in the two previous seasons with Al Jacks at the helm. But this time the Highlanders no longer had Al Jacks as he was now at Penn State. They were still strong with Jim Thompson at quarterback, Chuck Scafuri at halfback and Dominic Grande, at tackle anchoring a big line. The Bulldogs were ready for the Highlanders this time as many of this current Westinghouse team was reserves when Peabody had the best of 1952 and 1953. South Stadium was packed for this one as the Bulldogs rolled with Horace Nelson breaking one for 70 yards to open up the scoring and later added one from twenty yards out to take a 13-0 lead at halftime. The second half saw two more scores by Bill Tibbs and Walter Walker as the Bulldogs bested the Highlanders 25-0. I was a spectator that night and one of the many alumni who along with the student body enjoyed this sweet victory by Westinghouse. This game had all the hype of two neighboring rivals playing for bragging rights on a cool October evening. Having survived the biggest hurdle the Bulldogs rolled over the next three opponents; South, South Hills and Schenley.

They were now the Section I champions and would play the Section 2 champions, Carrick at South Stadium for the Pittsburgh City Championship. The long awaited championship jacket was within their reach, and Carrick High School was going to be a tough challenger. On game day, a few of us alumni visited the school and had lunch with some of the team members. Shortly after lunch we went to the auditorium for the pre-game pep rally. The spirited atmosphere led by the Bulldog marching band and cheerleaders made us feel like we were still part of the student body. We had a great time and were looking forward to the big game that evening.

135

## PREP MAGAZINE GAME OF THE YEAR

South Stadium was packed to capacity along with hundreds of spectators standing on the bridge overlooking the brightly lighted stadium. Carrick was ready to put the Bulldogs to the test led by halfback, Virgil Boccella. He gave Westinghouse all they could handle that night. The Bulldogs got the first break that night and took advantage of it when a high snap to punter Virgil Boccella sailed over his head. The Bulldogs recovered on the Carrick 45 yard line with good field position. Three running plays by Nelson, Merletti and Poole put the ball on the Carrick two yard line. Poole who was shifted from halfback to fullback took a direct snap on a keeper and dove over the pile into the end zone. Poole kicked the extra point to give the Bulldogs a 7-0 lead. The Raiders came back to score a touchdown late in the first half with a chance to tie the score, but the Bulldogs stellar defense, led by John Cerniglia, blocked the try for the extra point (back then there was no option for a two point conversion following a touchdown). Carrick was now very much in the ballgame trailing by a slim 7-6 margin at halftime.

Both teams played scoreless football during the entire second half. Both defenses dug in and played tough. It was a very tense half of football as each team was looking for a break to gain momentum. Both offenses had the speed to break a long one. Late in the fourth quarter the Bulldogs fumbled on their own 17 yard line and Carrick took over with a chance to pull off a victory. The Westinghouse defense dug in and on the first play Curtis Hefflin sacked the Carrick quarterback for a twelve-yard loss. There was now less than two minutes left in the game and on the very next play halfback, Virgil Boccella broke loose and was headed for an apparent touchdown. But coming on strong was Bulldog line-backer Curtis Hefflin who chased him down from behind knocking the ball loose, causing a fumble and miraculously making the recovery. It was a game saving play by Hefflin. The Westinghouse faithful breathed a sigh of relief. The Bulldogs took over and ran out the clock to preserve a hard-fought 7-6 victory. Dimperio was hoisted by his players across the field in one of the greatest of Westinghouse victories. Carrick had given the Bulldogs all they could handle, and were highly praised by Dimperio in an interview following the game. He felt they were by far the best team Westinghouse played all year – even better than Altoona who had defeated the Bulldogs in a pre-season game earlier in the year. .This game was rated by Prep Magazine as the "game of the year" in high school football. A long-awaited championship jacket was now theirs, and the "PA Pitt" Trophy emblematic of Pittsburgh City Champions was returned to the big house in Homewood. All City honors went to Richard Lombard, Curtis Hefflin, Horace Nelson, John Girdano, Ray Gorman and Skip Langford. Coach Dimperio received the National Prep Coaches of Merit Award. The 1954 season was a huge success following two years of disappointment. The Westinghouse Bulldogs were back.

**136**

Score by quarters:
Westinghouse     7 0 0 0 – 7
Carrick          0 6 0 0 – 6
Scoring:
Westinghouse – Poole 1 yard plunge; Poole point after placement
Carrick – Brehm 1.yard plunge; Bocella missed placement blocked by Cerniglia

1954 squad: A. Floyd, J. Cerniglia, H. Nelson, J. Girdano, R. Lombard, C. Hefflin, W. Tibbs, E. Harris, F. Graves, R. Merletti, G. Brown, H. Poole, R. Fredericks, C. DeLuca (Manager), R. McNulty, R. Maurizio, E. Nelson, G. DePew, A. Fornaser, J. Parillo, R. Harris, M. Paschal, C. Martin, J. Scott, F. Baglio, C. Gant, J. Graves, R. Russell, J. Shropshire, T. Williams, J. Hartman, J. Irwin, F.Schubert, J.Johnson, S. Brown, C. Langford, P. Villani, L. Slaughter, E. Woodell, L.Guinn, R. Gorman, R. Ecoff, E. Lodovico, M.Antonucci.

This team was rated as one of the top high school teams in Pennsylvania, by National Prep Magazine in 1954.

**1954 Season (8-1-0)**
**Pre Season**

| WHS | 28 | Donora | 0 |
|---|---|---|---|
| WHS | 7 | Aliquippa | 0 |
| WHS | 7 | Altoona | 19 |

City League

| WHS | 39 | Allderdice | 0 |
|---|---|---|---|
| WHS | 25 | Peabody | 0 |
| WHS | 33 | South Hills | 7 |
| WHS | 46 | South | 0 |
| WHS | 27 | Schenley | 12 |

Pittsburgh City League Championship Playoff

| WHS | 7 | Carrick | 6 |
|---|---|---|---|

## SAN BERNARDINO, CALIFORNIA

In late December of 1954 I relocated to San Bernardino, California to stay with my grandparents and look for a job. I was only eighteen years of age and there were no job opportunities for me in Pittsburgh. The opportunity to attend college at that particular time was not in our family budget. I was hoping to work and pay my own way through college, but nobody was hiring a high school graduate without any skilled experience. I realized this and headed west to California where I was able to get work immediately and begin to pay my way through school. The opportunities were there so I started out by taking a job as a welder's helper for Utility Trailer Manufacturing Company in Monterrey Park, California. After six months, there was a work slowdown, and layoffs followed as I was the last one in and the first one out. Shortly thereafter I relocated to El Monte, California and took a job with Shopping Bag Food Chain (a short distance from home) as a Journeyman. The store was located in Arcadia – about three blocks away from Santa Anita Race Track. Many of the jockeys patronized our store and they were a very unique and interesting group to talk with. Most of them spoke Spanish and limited English. It was fun while it lasted. Staying employed while going to school part-time was a lot easier for me to handle in California.

While in California I did manage to see several high school football games and was impressed. Most of the schools out west played on Friday nights in beautifully lighted stadiums with grass. It was a real treat sitting in one of those stadiums under the lights enjoying the mild California climate. I thought about back home and how we played on a dusty gridiron rolled once a year with oil to keep the dust down. Those kids out west had all the luxuries of big time facilities. When I told some of the ones I met about our home field at Westinghouse not having a single blade of grass they were amazed.

Unfortunately, my stay in California was a short one – eighteen months, as my mother became seriously ill. I returned home to Pittsburgh in May of 1956 to help take care of mom.

137

While in California I kept in touch with family members in Pittsburgh, as I was still interested in how Westinghouse was doing. I received weekly updates from news clippings and got a big kick out of some of the preseason predictions from the sports writers. Coach Dimperio gave his customary pre-season prediction in 1955 - "This is the worst team to represent Westinghouse High School and probably will not win a game." I can remember hearing this statement before. Pete knew how to keep the second guessers guessing, and this team had a tall order in defending the city title that the 1954 team had recaptured. It was the season that long time assistant, Austin Grupe retired and was replaced by a Westinghouse alumnus, Bruce Weston. Bruce Weston was a member of the Bulldog teams of 1941, 42, and 43 – coached by the legendary Pro Burton. He would be a fine assistant as he knew the single wing system quite well.

## QUIPS TAME THE DOGS

The first non-league game of the 1955 season was against always tough Donora High School. The Bulldogs displayed an impressive defense in this one as they shut out the Dragons with a big win 12-0. The following week they would meet the Quips of Aliquippa who had a familiar name on its squad – that being Mike Ditka, a junior. The Bulldogs met their match as the Quips rolled over them 35-0. It was the worst defeat for Westinghouse in many a year, and had the second guessers believing Dimperio of his pre-season prediction. It certainly was the worst game in Coach Dimperio's tenure at the Homewood school. Maybe Dimperio was right in his preseason prediction and now what was he going to do to get his team ready for Altoona the following week. You can take it to the bank that clever thinking Pete would have something up his sleeve.

## THE MYSTERIOUS LETTER

Prior to the final non-league game, Dimperio pulled his team together with another one of his patented pre-game classics. He reminded the boys that after losing to Aliquippa 35-0 the Altoona High School athletic department sent a letter to Westinghouse's athletic department stating a concern that the Bulldogs may no longer be a worthy opponent for scheduling in the future. I remember a family member contacting me in California of how Pete pulled this beautiful scenario on his young team. It was one that I would never forget. This was another one of Dimperio's gifted psychological pre-game strategies and it worked again. The Bulldogs traveled to Altoona the following week for the final non-league game thinking of how the folks at Altoona were looking for an easy win. The mysterious letter was just what the doctor ordered and the fired up Bulldogs were more than ready to take on the much bigger Altoona Lions. They stunned Altoona with speed and deception as Sherrill Brown, Skip Langford and Ronald Russell along with the explosive blocking of pulling guard John Girdano and blocking back Ron Ecoff. Altoona was down 14-0, before making a strong comeback with two touchdowns, but missed a crucial point after conversion. The Bulldogs redeemed their pride with a hard fought victory 14-

13. Having gone 2-1 in non-league play it was time to meet the challenge of the city league. The small but potent Bulldogs were ready to defend the "Pa Pitt" Trophy. In the next five league game Westinghouse was victorious with solid wins over Peabody 25-0; South Hills 20-7; South 38-0; Allderdice 28-0; and Schenley 34-6.

The 1955 season was winding down with one more challenge for the Bulldogs – defending the City League Title. Carrick High School was ready to challenge Westinghouse at South Stadium before 7500 fans. It did not take long for the Bulldogs to set the tone of the game. Carrick received the opening kick off and began their first possession and it was a disaster – fumbling on the second play. The Bulldogs recovered and soon after had their first touchdown. It was the beginning of what was to follow – a long night for Carrick. Westinghouse rolled to a 37-6 victory and possession of the "Pa Pitt" trophy for another year. Sherrill Brown, the smallest player on the field, was the big star for the Bulldogs – gaining 134 yards on 25 carries and three touchdowns. Charles (Skippy) Langford accounted for the other two Bulldog touchdowns, gaining 125 yards in 19 carries.

Score by quarters:

| | | | | |
|---|---|---|---|---|
| Westinghouse | 14 | 7 | 2 | 14 – 37 |
| Carrick | 0 | 0 | 0 | 6 – 6 |

Westinghouse scoring: Touchdowns – S. Brown 3, Langford 2. Extra points – S. Brown, Baglio, Russell 2, Johnson. Safety – Brehm tackled in end zone.
Carrick scoring: Touchdown – DiRenna

**139**

Reflecting back to the only loss of the season 35-0 to Aliquippa, the Bulldogs learned a lot. They managed to rebound and have a very fine season as it was a character builder. The experience of such a loss helped the boys to realize what it takes to meet the challenge of a superior team. There was always somebody waiting to dethrone a team like Westinghouse because of its' winning record. Beating Westinghouse was always considered an upset regardless of what the pre-season prognosis was. The reputation of being a past or defending champion always put more pressure on the Bulldogs. They were always expected to win and a loss was considered an upset. This is the way it was year after year regardless of what the so-called pre-season experts predicted.

The members of the 1955 squad were as follows: J. Girdano, R. Frederick, F. Baglio, J. Collie, A. Fornaser, E. Harris, R. Longo, G. Brown, D. Anderson, L. Slaughter. R. Ecoff, J. Johnson, R. Russell, S. Brown, C. Langford, E. Nelson, J. Recupero, R. Maruizio, R. McNulty, E. Lodovico, J. Irwin, J. Golden, J. Hartman, E. Woodell, M. Lopez, H. Tibbs, J. Folgarelli, J. Shropshire, J. Davis, R. Harris, C. Baxter, Managers: C. DeLuca and J. Haines.

All-City honors went to center Art Fornaser, guards, John Girdano and Bob Frederick, tackle, George Brown, backs Sherrill Brown and Charles Langford. Girdano was voted best lineman and Sherrill Brown best back in the City League. Sherrill Brown accepted a scholarship to Lincoln University along with Charles Langford. John Girdano accepted a scholarship to Tulsa University.

**1955 Season (8-1-0)**
**Pre Season**

| | | | |
|---|---|---|---|
| WHS | 12 | Donora | 0 |
| WHS | 0 | Aliquippa | 35 |
| WHS | 14 | Altoona | 13 |

City League

| | | | |
|---|---|---|---|
| WHS | 28 | Allderdice | 0 |
| WHS | 25 | Peabody | 0 |
| WHS | 20 | South Hills | 7 |
| WHS | 38 | South | 0 |
| WHS | 34 | Schenley | 6 |

Pittsburgh City League Championship Playoff

| | | | |
|---|---|---|---|
| WHS | 37 | Carrick | 6 |

## THE EARLY BEGINNING OF A FUTURE DALLAS COWBOY

140

This was a year for the rest of the City League to take advantage of the Bulldogs. The pre-season prediction for 1956 was not looking good for the Homewood gridders. Graduation really hit hard and only two regulars from the 1955 squad were returning -backs Ed Nelson and Ron Ecoff. The team in size was one of the smallest in the city league. Coach Dimperio was making every effort to get a young sophomore with good size to come out for football. He was Tony Liscio – standing 6'5" tall and tipping the scales at 225 – and a member of the basketball team. Dimperio went as far as talking with Liscio's mother expressing to her that son Tony had a lot of potential and size to someday make it to the NFL. The coaches finally convinced Tony that he can play both football and basketball at Westinghouse and excel at both. This would later benefit both the Bulldogs and Liscio as he was only a sophomore with two more years of eligibility remaining. Liscio was a big quiet kid, easy going and enjoyed playing basketball, but to play football at Westinghouse that was another challenge. He would have to develop a more aggressive mindset in order to earn a position within the regimented football program at Westinghouse. It was a mindset that he was not comfortable with. His close friend Joe Folgarelli, a tough junior member of the football team recognized this, and encouraged Tony repeatedly to stick it out through the tough regimentation of being a scrub. Liscio appreciated Folgarelli's encouragement. He worked very hard to develop a mindset that would help him get through the regimentation of The Room. Joe Folgarelli who was a solid 5'8" and weighing only 165 was an inspiration for Liscio. The future was looking good for both Liscio and Folgarelli who together worked hard to reach a common goal. They stuck it out and later it would pay off for them. Little did Liscio know that some day he would make it to the NFL and play for the Dallas Cowboys. I am sure when he thinks back to his days as a scrub he realizes how long a road it was to get from Westinghouse to Dallas. To this day he still keeps in touch with Joe Folgarelli and periodically visits Pittsburgh to visit with family and his former Bulldog teammates.

## RACIAL CHANGES DO NOT STOP THE BULLDOGS

The racial population was rapidly changing within the community and the 1956 team had only four non-blacks on the starting eleven – linemen Joe Miele and Jim Recupero and backs Ron Ecoff and Robert Tedesco. The many loyal followers were beginning to wonder if Dimperio could coach or win with a team predominately made up of black athletes. Pete turned a deaf ear on the second guessers and molded together a team that was ready to challenge those who were wondering.

The pre-season began with a 6-0 win over Donora – a good start – but much too early to determine how well the Bulldogs would fare over a full season. The following game was against Aliquippa and future Pitt All-American, Mike Ditka. The Quips shut down the Bulldogs 13-0. The final pre-season game was at Altoona. The Lions were out to avenge the previous seasons' loss to Westinghouse. This season was a lot different – there was no Sherrill Brown or Skippy Langford to turn loose. Altoona found redemption as they really hung one on the Bulldogs 33-0. This was a real nightmare for Dimperio – he had to find a scoring punch for an offensive unit that was really struggling – scoring only six points in three games.

The first conference game was against South Hills. Westinghouse was the defending City Champion and they were not looking like a worthy defender. South Hills put the Bulldogs to the test as it took a come from behind late touchdown by Howard Tibbs to give the House a 19-14 victory. The second game was at home against Taylor Allerdice and I was a spectator for this one. The Dragons received the opening kickoff and halfback, Bob Fulkus returned it for an 80 yard touchdown. The Bulldogs were immediately behind 7-0, but not for long. Dimperio decided to go to the air in a surprise move as Ed Nelson hooked up with end, Tom Pitts, for three touchdowns. Sophomore, Eugene McClellan, a 5'6", 135 lb. speedster, ended the scoring with a beautiful 50 yard sweep that really excited the crowd. I remember prior to the play, Dimperio was on the sideline with McClellan at his side giving him words of encouragement before sending him into the game. As the Bulldogs broke the huddle, McClellan lined up as the right halfback and I thought here it comes, a power sweep to the wide side. McClellan was in motion – took the hand-off from the fullback and was off to the races. The blocking was excellent as he turned the corner and there was no catching him. He raced down the sideline past the student section and into the end zone at the open end of the field. This was the clincher in a 28-14 Westinghouse victory. Young McClellan made his debut in this game and Dimperio knew he had a diamond in the rough. He was only a sophomore and the best was yet to come.

The Bulldogs next two games were against Schenley and Peabody and I was a spectator for both. Schenley gave Westinghouse all they could handle before losing to the Bulldogs 12-6 at Westinghouse field. The following week the game was at Peabody Field and it was a squeaker. I was standing behind the Westinghouse bench throughout the game and watched closely the coaching efforts of Dimperio. Several times Pete and I made eye contact as we both were shaking our heads as the game was literally up for grabs. It was a case of who made the least number of mistakes

**141**

and Westinghouse managed to prevail 6-0 over Peabody. Pete and I spoke after the game and he expressed how lucky the Bulldogs were to get by the Highlanders. The following week against an inept South High team and it was an opportunity for the House to go back to basics and regroup. They defeated the Orioles 39-12 and captured the Section One Title. It was quite evident that superior coaching, conditioning, determination and believing they could excel were the keys to their success. There were several close calls during the season as it was obvious that the Bulldogs did not have the best talent in the city. The key was the pride factor as they pulled together at crucial times during the season to overcome challenge after challenge.

The Section Two Title was captured by the Carrick Raiders, and it was beginning to look like they would be able to finally handle Westinghouse for city honors. The two teams had met six times for the City title since 1934 (a 6-6 tie) followed by Westinghouse victories in 1947 (19-0), 1948 (33-12), 1951 (20-7), 1954 (7-6), and 1955 (37-6). The Bulldogs were the defending champions and Carrick was looking for revenge after the beating they took in 1955.

## REMEMBERING RALPH ZAHNISER

About two weeks before the end of the regular season, longtime Carrick Coach, Ralph Zahniser had passed away. This was a tough blow for the Raiders as Zahniser was one of the best of coaches in the city. He had been successful at Carrick for a number of years, and in prior years at Westinghouse during the Pro Burton era.

The city title game between Westinghouse and Carrick was played at South Stadium before a crowd in excess of 6000. I was a spectator at this game and it was a good one. Carrick appeared to be super charged as the game got underway - after the crowd had observed a minute of silence in memory of Ralph Zahniser, the departed Raider coach. Carrick proceeded to score on their first possession as emotions were high on the Raiders sideline – they recovered a Bulldog fumble and capitalized on the opportunity. They led after the first quarter 6-0, but the Bulldogs took over from there and it was all Westinghouse. The Carrick lead was short-lived as the Bulldogs were in control the rest of the game – repeating as City Champions with a 20-6 victory over the game Raiders. Westinghouse had captured their nineteenth Pittsburgh League Title as power, speed and deception had turned back Carrick for the third year in a row.

Score by quarters:
Westinghouse      0  13  0  7 – 20
Carrick           6   0  0  0 – 6
Touchdowns:
Westinghouse - Tedesco, Tibbs, Sparrow
Carrick - Heinecke
Extra Points: Baxter (run), Tibbs (run)

Members of the 1956 squad were as follows: T. Pitts, N. Brown, P. Dean, K. DeHonney, M. Antonucci, B.Anderson, J. Miele, J. Golden, T. Liscio, J. Folgarelli, J.

Recupero, R. Graves, R. Harris, R. Hancock, R. Ecoff, R. Tedesco, W. McClellan, J. Sparrow, R. Henderson, C. Baxter, H. Tibbs, E. Nelson, E. McClellan, J. Haines, L. Rawlings, R. Young, A. Calloway, H. Hosbey, R. Warrick, S. Haley, E. Smith, T. Burley, A. McClain, M. Lopez, Manager; J. Odorisio, Manager.


**1956 Season (7-2-0)**
**Pre Season**
WHS  6      Donora         0
WHS  0      Aliquippa      13
WHS  0      Altoona        30
City League
WHS  28     Allderdice     14
WHS  6      Peabody        0
WHS  19     South Hills    14
WHS  39     South          12
WHS  12     Schenley       6
Pittsburgh City League Championship Playoff
WHS  20     Carrick        6

All – City honors went to Joe Golden and Tom Pitts.

143

## THEY CAME A LONG WAY

The 1957 team experienced the challenges of 1955 and 1956 and now they were ready to control their own destiny. Seniors Joe Folgarelli, Joe Miele and Tom Williams were ready to provide running room for senior backs Howard Tibbs and Bill McClellan. A strong group of juniors led by end Frank Battista, tackle Tony Liscio, backs Ron Henderson and Albert Calloway were ready to step up and play key roles for the upcoming season. Lloyd Rawlings and Richard Hancock, both seniors and junior speed demon Eugene McClellan rounded out the starting unit for Coach Dimperio.

Most of these young guys were only ninth graders when I was a senior and to see them leading the way for the Bulldogs was most gratifying. I remember especially Frank Battista from the time when he was knee-high to a grasshopper running around the Larimer club-yard. I was able to see the talent he had as a youngster and I was proud to see how he developed and became such a fine performer for the Bulldogs. He was a fine all around athlete who reminded me a lot like Joe Scalzo who was a three sport performer for Westinghouse back in the late 1940's.

## IF IT WORKS WHY CHANGE IT

Coach Dimperio continued to go with the single-wing offense – considered to be antiquated – as the more modern T-formation was the way to go for all other football programs across the nation at all levels. This did not convince Dimperio to make a change. The quarterback position was key position in the T-formation, but in Dimperio's single-wing offense there was more than one key position. The whole offense required coordination of timing, speed and deception. Every position was geared to move once the ball was snapped to either the fullback or the tailback. Timing and execution was quite critical as hand-offs, pitch-outs and key blocking by the offensive linemen and the blocking back (quarterback) were ready to spring loose with the center snap. The center was a key position in the single wing formation. Every center snap required accuracy and consistency. This system was in existence at Westinghouse since the 1913 season as former Coach Pro Burton ran a power version up through 1945. Then in 1946, Dimperio's first year, he modified the system to a more diversified combination of both speed and power. Both coaches were quite successful and thus it was not easy to change something that was so effective year after year. Dimperio was not about to make a change to satisfy the critics. It was quite obvious that every opponent on the Bulldogs' schedule had to prepare a different game plan for Westinghouse. This was to Dimperio's advantage and he was a wise old owl. In fact, he rated the 1957 team his most deceptive – quite an accolade coming from the legend.

144

The Bulldogs opened the season in fine fashion with a 28-14 victory over WPIAL powerhouse Aliquippa. The following week they defeated a fine McKeesport team 34-13. Not bad for an antiquated single-wing offense. The third pre-season game was against Altoona, a team that was always a challenge for the Bulldogs. This year was no different as the Mountain Lions tamed the Dogs 34-13. A defeat like this was always a blessing in disguise for it was a wake up call. There is always a team out there waiting to bring you down to size, and there are times when such a loss is a reminder of how it feels to get your clock cleaned. The Bulldogs learned a lot from this one as they were preparing to meet the challenge of Section 1 opponents.

Westinghouse raced through the next five conference opponents without too much trouble. The single-wing machine of the Bulldogs mowed down South Hills 40-0; Schenley 33-7; Peabody 31-0; Allderdice 31-14; and South 39-6. This year it was Fifth Avenue (Coach Dimperio's alma mater) from Section 2 ready to challenge the Bulldogs for the city crown. The Archers were no match for Westinghouse, losing to the Bulldogs 39-13. Eugene McClellan and Howard Tibbs led the offense as they accounted for most of the scoring for Westinghouse.

Score by quarters:
Westinghouse        39
Fifth Avenue        13
Scoring:
Westinghouse touchdowns Tibbs (2) , McClellan (2), Henderson (1),
Calloway (1) PATS:
Fifth Avenue touchdowns:

1957 team members: R. Hancock, L. Rawlings, J. Folgarelli, A. Liscio, J. Miele, F. Battista, E. McClellan, A. Calloway, R. Young, H. Tibbs, G. Thomas, T. Williams, B.

McClellan, H. Hosbey, C. Hefflin, W. Taylor, K. DeHoney, G. Sharp, Al Allsberry, M. Bisceglia, R. Marshall, M. Stanton, G. Jackson, R. Henderson, T. Burley, W. Miller. Managers: J. Odorisio, A. Anderson, G. Russell, R. Snider.

**1957 Season (8-1-0)**

| | | | |
|---|---|---|---|
| WHS | 28 | Aliquippa | 12 |
| WHS | 34 | McKeesport | 13 |
| WHS | 13 | Altoona | 34 |
| WHS | 40 | South Hills | 0 |
| WHS | 33 | Schenley | 7 |
| WHS | 31 | Peabody | 0 |
| WHS | 27 | Allderdice | 6 |
| WHS | 38 | South | 6 |

City Championship Playoff
| | | | |
|---|---|---|---|
| WHS | 39 | Fifth Avenue | 13 |

Dimperio was asked to make some comparisons of the teams he coached since taking over in 1946. He named the 1948 team – most brilliant; the 1951 team most powerful; the 1957 team – most deceptive.

## ANOTHER PARADE ALL-AMERICAN

145

End Tom Williams appeared on the Eddie Fisher Show – as a representative of the Parade High School All-American Football Team. This was quite an honor for the young man from Westinghouse. He was a big solid 230 pound senior looking quite impressive wearing the gold and blue of the Bulldogs as he was introduced to the national television audience along with the other All-American team members. Williams was the second Parade All-American chosen from Westinghouse – the first being Ronald Latronica from the 1951 powerhouse team. It was national recognition like this that helped to make Westinghouse one of the success stories of high school football across the U.S.A.

Coach Pete Dimperio was receiving national acclaim as well. "Coaches of the Year Clinic" headed by college coaches Bud Wilkinson of Oklahoma University and Duffy Daugherty of Michigan State University signed Dimperio as one of the five high school coaches in the nation to serve annually as an adviser. This was the beginning of a very successful endeavor that rewarded Pete Dimperio as he eventually ended up being the manager of this clinic and bringing it to downtown Pittsburgh – beginning with the first one at the William Penn Hotel and later at the Hilton Hotel. This was an annual event that brought the best coaches from across the nation at both the high school and collegiate levels. Dimperio's family – his wife Adele, daughter Peggy, and son Peter Junior provided loyal support in helping him to succeed in making this a most successful event. In later years, Peter Junior and Peggy have taken over the event carrying on the legacy of their father.

I attended my first clinic in 2003 along with Joe Pronio and we were very much impressed with the huge contingent of coaches (college and high school) from all over the country. We met up with retired Westinghouse coach George Webb and some of the local high school coaches and spent some time reminiscing with them. Upon our arrival we were greeted by both Peter Junior and Peggy and they were such fine hosts. It was so nice to see the children of Pete Dimperio, Sr. doing such a fine job carrying on the legacy of their father. I felt the pride and the spirit knowing that our former teacher and coach started this huge event several years ago. He touched so many lives while he was here with us and me being a sentimentalist I feel very proud being able to attend this event year after year.

## SINGLE WING ON STAGE

The upcoming expectations predicted by the City of Pittsburgh sports enthusiasts extended an invitation to Pete Dimperio to showcase his majestic single wing offense. The invitation was accepted and presented at Arsenal Field for all to see. The last time such a sneak preview was presented was in 1951 at Homewood Field under the lights. It was a huge success back then and the 1958 display of speed and deception was just as impressive. The single wing was the Bulldog's trademark and really drew a large viewing audience.

The team had a group of seniors ready to lead the Bulldogs – Ends: Tony Liscio (6'5" 230lbs.) and Frank Battista; tackle Howard Hosbey; guard Lyde Evans who came back from a serious leg injury in 1956 wearing a steel pin; center Ken DeHonney; backs Eugene McClellan and Skip "Cab" Calloway. Juniors ready to step up were tackle Robert Marshall; guard Ralph Young; backs Mike Bisceglia and Ron Henderson.

The Bulldogs opened the season with an impressive win over Aliquippa 19-7. The Quips scored first and led 7-0, but Westinghouse came back using the passing game, a surprise to Aliquippa who was primed to stop the Bulldog's running game. End Frank Battista caught two scoring passes, one each from quarterback Ron Henderson and sophomore fullback John Williams. Then on defense it was Battista again – this time intercepting an Aliquippa pass and racing all the way for a Bulldog touchdown. He was a standout that night as the Aliquippa fans saw the offensive and defensive talents of one of the best receivers to come out of Westinghouse.

The following week it was on to Mt. Lebanon where a capacity crowd was waiting to see just how well the Bulldogs could handle the Blue Devils. The first half belonged to Westinghouse as they went to the locker room leading 13-6. The second half was all Mt. Lebanon as they came from behind to beat the Bulldogs 40-19.

In week three, Westinghouse traveled to Altoona and a capacity crowd was there to see the defending city league champions. Again, the Bulldogs took to the air as quarterback Ron Henderson spotted open receiver Frank Battista with a fifteen yard touchdown pass. Altoona battled back to tie the score 6-6 as both teams missed point after touchdown tries. Late in the game Altoona's defense rose up and stopped Bulldog back Cab Calloway in his own end zone for a safety. That was the end of the scoring as Westinghouse lost a tough decision to the Mountain Lions 8-6.

The Bulldogs were ready to defend their City League crown and opened the regular season with a 31-6 victory over Schenley. Eugene McClelland (3 touchdowns),

146

Skip Calloway and Mike Bisceglia all scored for the House. Next was South High going down to defeat 46-19 as John Williams scored a touchdown on a 96 yard burst of speed along with three scores by Eugene McClellan. The following three weeks there were victories over South Hills 48-12, Peabody 39-6 and Allderdice 33-7. The Bulldogs won the Section 1 crown and would meet Allegheny High School, winners of the Section 2 Crown. It was during this season that Joseph Dimperio, father of Pete Dimperio passed away at the age of eighty-two. Fortunately, he was here long enough to see how well his son Pete was excelling as one of the finest high school football coaches in the country.

The scouting report on Allegheny was that the North Side school had a fine offensive machine. It certainly did not faze the Bulldogs as they displayed an all around fine performance of their own that the boys from Allegheny were unable to contain. Westinghouse defended its City League Title with a convincing 38-0 victory.

Score by quarters:
Westinghouse    6    13    13    6    38
Allegheny       0    0     0     0    0
Scoring touchdowns: McClellan 3; Biscseglia 1;Henderson 1; Allsberry 1.
PATs: Calloway, Henderson

1958 Team Members:
F. Battista, T. Liscio, K. DeHonney, H. Hosbey, G. McClellan, B. Marshall, Calloway, R. Young, J. Williams, A. Allsberry, J. Hancock, I. Bailey, R. Miller, G. Sharp, R. Norman, Ted Harris, E. Golden, J. Ramsey, M. Bisceglia, M. Stanton, R. Henderson, L. Evans, R. Fields, Q. Washington, L. Malone,O. Ray, D. Forlastro, M. Broadus, S. Lloyd, E. Buford,P. Anderson, B. Eliott; Managers, N. DeStefano, J. Mathews, D. Bates.

Senior ends Tony Liscio and Frank Battista made the All-City Team along with Lyde Evans MVP Lineman in the City League and Eugene McClellan – Player of the Year. Scholarships were awarded to Ron Henderson (Michigan State University) and Tony Liscio (Tulsa University). Liscio also made the Teen Magazine All-East Team. Both Juniors Mike Bisceglia and Bob Marshall had a good year and would probably lead the Bulldogs for the following 1959 season. They would both become seniors with high expectations.

147

**1958 Season (7- 2- 0)**

| WHS | 19 | Alliquippa | 7 |
|---|---|---|---|
| " | 19 | Mt. Lebanon | 40 |
| " | 6 | Altoona | 8 |
| " | 31 | Schenley | 6 |
| " | 46 | South | 19 |
| " | 48 | South Hills | 12 |
| " | 39 | Peabody | 6 |
| " | 33 | Allderdice | 7 |

City Championship Game
| WHS | 38 | Allegheny | 0 |
|---|---|---|---|

## 1959 – A SPLIT SEASON

The 1959 season was literally a split season for the Bulldogs as they struggled in their first four games. Seniors Mike Bisceglia (fullback) and Bob Marshall (tackle) were the only experienced holdovers from the 1958 team. They were surrounded by inexperienced juniors and sophomores who were going to have to learn quickly while struggling to get into the win column. Several of the former Bulldogs came back to help Dimperio during the summer football camp working with all the inexperienced position players on techniques and basics.

Westinghouse opened the season with Windber as Altoona was dropped from the schedule. Windber proved to be a tough opponent defeating the Bulldogs 31-6. The following week it was Aliquippa and again Westinghouse came out on the short end 13-0. Two games and only one touchdown scored by the offense. Things were not looking good at all. Har-Brack was the next opponent and the Bulldogs offense was clicking, racking up 40 points; but the defense allowed 43 points. This added up to a third loss in a row for the Bulldogs. The last time Westinghouse lost all three pre-season games was in 1917 during World War I.

The regular season began with a muddy scoreless tie against Peabody. Now the Bulldogs were still winless and half the season was over. Dimperio had to do something quickly so he began to make wholesale position changes. Along with those changes the young Bulldogs realized that they had a tradition to uphold. It was not easy to gain experience quickly, and Dimperio was very patient in his wait for this young team to come of age.

The second game in Section play was a 34-6 win over the Orioles of South High. The Bulldogs were beginning to click as they gained their first win of the season. The following week they defeated South Hills 31-0. The final two weeks of the season saw the Bulldogs winning both games against Allderdice 33-13 and Schenley 35-0. The only white boy on offense was fullback Mike Bisceglia. He was surrounded by an array of running mates in speedsters Alvin Allsberry, Arthur Williams and Edgar Golden.

Westinghouse managed to win the Section 1 crown and a place in the championship game with a record of 4-3-1. This was not a typical Westinghouse

148

season, but one that saw a young team come of age at the right time. They literally took the losses at the beginning of the season and realized what they had to do to turn things around with hard work and dedication. In the championship game Westinghouse was to meet Section 2 winner Carrick. Before the largest crowd to see a city league (over 8,000) title game the Bulldogs really came to play as they performed on both offense and defense with the precision of a well-oiled machine. The single wing offense was clicking on all cylinders and the defense was superb. The House peaked at the right time.

Score by quarters:

| | | | | | |
|---|---|---|---|---|---|
| Westinghouse | 7 | 6 | 20 | 2 | 35 |
| Carrick | 6 | 0 | 0 | 6 | 12 |

Scoring touchdowns:
Westinghouse: Williams 4; Bisceglia 1.
Carrick: Voletich 1, Gudenburr .
PATs: Westinghouse – Allsberry 2; Bisceglia 1.
Safety: Vooletich tackled in Carrick end zone.

1959 Team members:
M. Bisceglia, A. Allsberry, E. Golden, R. Marshall, W. Edwards, R. Burgess, G. Webb, J. Martin, A. Jones, R. Carter, M. Myricks, D. Conley, R. Young, T. Harris, C. Harris, Q. Washington, J. Bosco, P. Anderson, M. Broaddus, A. Davis, A. Millions, R. Dean, R. Harrison, L. Campbell, A. Slaughter, O. Ray. J. Bailey, E. Bufford, J. Hancock, J. Ramsey, D. Weathers. A. Hall, B. Elliott, J. McCoy, L. Malone; Managers, G. Parr, R. Snider

Mike Bisceglia was voted MVP, made the All-City Team and was awarded a scholarship to Tulsa University. After college he received an offer to coach football at Hialeah High School in Florida. He was quite successful there and in 1979 was named Coach of the Year. Mike retired from coaching after thirty-seven years.

Time goes by quickly as I can still remember watching Mike playing in his final year at Westinghouse. I wanted to see the Bulldogs play one more time before I left to serve Uncle Sam at Fort Knox, Kentucky. It was in a game against South Hills, and Mike was impressive. He was every bit a typical Bulldog fullback with relentless bursts up the middle gaining yardage and scoring for the victorious Bulldogs. He was a blue collar performer with all the heart to go with it. He was the go to guy when the going got rough. I caught up with Mike in 2001 at Coach George Webb's retirement dinner and we talked about old times. He was a proud Bulldog and a credit to Westinghouse High School.

As the fifties era came to a close, coach Pete Dimperio was being recognized as one of the finest high school coaches across the United States. The Bulldogs had a run of seven city titles during this decade, and were looking more and more like a football program destined to reach historical milestones. The dynasty was well underway and the accolades were coming in from all over Western Pennsylvania. Many of the schools outside the City of Pittsburgh were not anxious to play the Bulldogs for fear of getting embarrassed trying to stop the high powered single wing

149

offense that Pete Dimperio had put together. Conditioning, dedication and speed were the criteria year in, and year out, as Westinghouse strived to win and bring home a title to the Homewood Community.

It had come a long way and was no longer the little forgotten school that opened its' doors for the first time way back in 1912, to a class of 130 freshmen. They were eager to make Westinghouse High School the focal point of that community. As the story goes good things will happen when people take pride and work together. The rest is history as year after year many of the alumni will proudly claim to have been a part of that fine tradition.

**150**

First row, left to right: D. Cratty, J. Ruffa, P. Signore, R. Coles, A. Di Martino, A. De Luca, C. Garland, A. Aliberti, J. Silipo.

Second row: B. Peatross, H. Martin, E. Buccilli, J. DeLong, L. Cuccaro, B. Shubert, R. Latronnica, J. Harrity, R. Renn, S. Guy.

Third row: B. Lankemeyer, R. Green, L. Martin, F. Griham, F. Della Valle, F. Anderson, L. Malley, A. Conte, A. Hancock, R. Floyd.

Fourth row: Coach Dimperio, J. Costella, A. Ferragonia, T. Bailey, R. Beasley, C. Heflin, W. Mack, R. Gaddie, Mr. Grupe.

## Football

The 1950 football season showed our team, the **Westinghouse Bulldogs,** winning four games while losing the same number. The four defeats were at the hands of Johnstown, Altoona, Schenley, and our greatest rival, Peabody.

The opening game at Johnstown had W.H.S. leave the field on the short end of a 21-0 score. It was evident that we did not have an outstanding pass defense. This is one of the prominent reasons for the other defeats.

In the second game Westinghouse went down to defeat at the hands of Altoona 20-13. Every year this game proves to be one of the toughest of the season.

The Bulldogs then outplayed Duquesne and came through with its first victory of the year.

Westinghouse beat South and South Hills in turn, but the deciding game with Schenley was still at hand. Due to the importance of this game, it was played at Pitt Stadium. It was a hard battle, with Schenley coming out on top 12-6.

Our boys really took it out on Allderdice the next week by swamping them 70-0.

The last game of the year was played at Peabody field in a heavy driving rain. The weather balanced up the teams. After a long, cold, wet afternoon, for the first time in ten years, Peabody defeated W.H.S. 7-6.

Edward Buccilli was presented with the most valuable player award given by the Pittsburgh Press.

The season ended with the Westinghouse Bulldogs placing third in the City League.

# Unitas Only Repeater

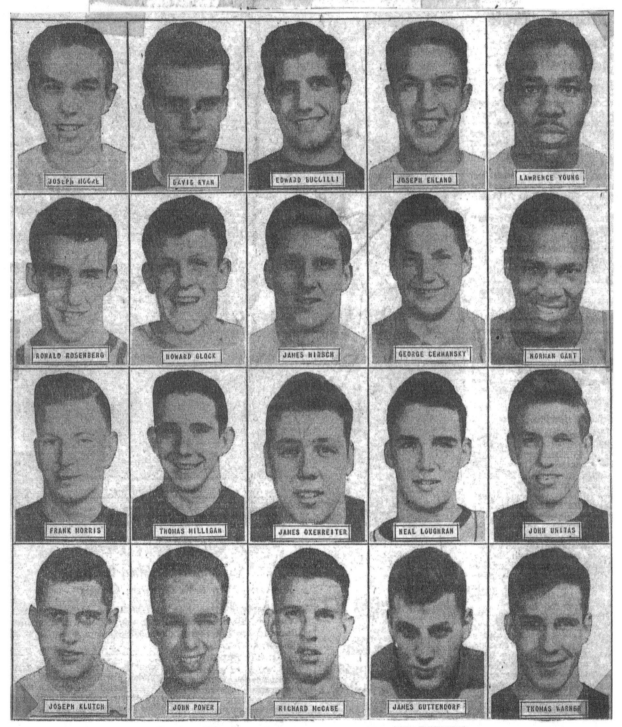

152

## as Most Valuable

Burton • Dimperio • Musilin • Malins • Webb

## Peabody Varsity 1950

First Row—left to right: Allman, Marinaro, Neft, Ryan, Coy, Kieffer, Krotec, Hamilton, Pool, Zikos, W. Kennedy, Barron.

Second Row—Left to Right: Holland, Barthalow, Wright, Shearer, Mandeville, Scott, Berry, DePaolis, Zurenko, Parillo, Kinney. Tolly, H. Johnson, Miller.

Third Row—left to right: Lee, Sumpter, Santonastasi, Smith, Pfahl, Cox Tarr, Painter C. Johnson, D. Kennedy, Hainer, Loefsky, Fogel, Ellery.

Fourth Row—left to right: Erenbaum, Gardin, Swaile, Coach Meyers, Monroe, Edlis, J. Hamilton, Willams, Pow, Morton, Goldstein, Griser, Paul, Blair, Coach Batchelor, Gooding, W. Johnson Berger.

153

154

**1950 Pittsburgh City, Catholic and Prep Schools MVPs**

Front row left to right: Joseph Moore-Schenley; David Ryan-Peabody; Edward Buccilli-Westinghouse; Joseph Ehland-South Hills; Lawrence Young-South High; Ronald Rosenberg-Allderdice. Middle row left to right: Howard Glock-Carrick; James Hirsch-Allegheny; George Cemansky-Oliver; Norman Gant-Fifth Avenue; John Power-St. Mary/Mt.Washington; Thomas Milligan-Langley. Back row left to right: Richard McCabe-North Catholic; James Oxenreiter-St.George; Neal Loughran-St. Wendelin; **John Unitas-St.Justin**; Joseph Klutch-St.Luke; Frank Morris-Perry; Thomas Warner-Shadyside Academy; Not pictured James Guttendorf-Central Catholic. **John Unitas went on to be enshrined in the NFL Hall of Fame.**

1951 Westinghouse Bulldogs rated one of the ten best high school teams in Western PA during the 20th century

**156**

CONTENDERS AGAIN . . . Standout backs on Pete Dimperio's Westinghouse High School football team which is expected to make a strong bid for the City League championship which it lost to Schenley High School last year. Left to right: Lucio Martin, quarterback; Francis Griham, right halfback; Billy Peatross, left halfback; Tom Schubert, fullback; Russell Renn, left halfback. The Bulldogs will be at Altoona for a non-league game tonight.

*Sun-Telegraph Photo*

WESTINGHOUSE GAIN—Halfback Billy Peatross of Westinghouse gains 10 yards around right end in the first quarter of its game with South Hills yesterday at Alliderdice field. Peatross scored a touchdown as Westinghouse, favorite for the City League title, trounced South Hills, 40-7, as league competition opened.

**1951 Westinghouse High School Pittsburgh City League Champions (9-0-0)**

Front Row L/R: C.Garland, T. Shubert, F. DellaValle; F. Griham, R. Green, B. Peatross, W. Mack, L. Martin, W. Hancock, W. Anderson, J. Costello, R. Latronica, R.Renn, R. Lankemeyer (Field Mgr.). Middle Row L/R: J.L.Speer (Faculty Mgr.), Pete Dimperio (Head Coach), A. DeLuca, A. Aliberti, J. Ruffa, P. Signore, A. Silvio, A. Ferragonio, C. Hefflin, R. Marsalese, R. Coles, T. Bailey, J. Ricciardelli, A. McGuigan, F.Federici, W. Walker, A.K. Grupe (Asst. Coach). Back Row L/R: J. Ebbitt, E. Jones, C. Paschal, M. Jackson, J. Blattenberger, W. Fink, J. La Marca, J. Pinson, J. Williams, C. Inquartano, M. Porro, R Kirk, R. Daniels, E. Haley, R. Steele, R. Lombard, Joseph Pronio.

157

158

1951 MOST VALUABLE SCHOLASTIC PLAYERS
Westinghouse MVP Ronald Latronica (middle row 3rd from right)

## EMPTY SHOES!

Westinghouse High School football coach Pete Dimpe is a man with a problem. His entire first team of la season, which won the City League championship, has b graduated, along with seven second-stringers. Practice got der way yesterday to determine their successors.

San-Telegraph Photo by Morris Berm

**1952 TIME TO REBUILD**

Westinghouse High School's probable starting lineup for the opening game at Donora tonight: left to right line, Right End Cody Paschal or Jose Ricciardelli, Right Tackle Joe Bonio, Right Guard Patsy Signora, Center Art McGuigan, Left Guard Al Silvio, Left Tackle Dave Jeters, Left End Ricardo Coles; backfield Right Halfback Ernie Jones, Quarterback Ron Marsalese, Fullback Charles Inquartano, Left Halfback James Pinana, or Russell Steele.

## 1952 - The Best Rebuilding Year By Coach Pete Dimperio

1st row—E. Jones, R. Coles, J. Ricardelli, C. Paschal, D. Jetter, J. Pronio, B. Signore, A. McGuigan, B. Silvio, J. Pinson, C. Inquartano, R. Marsalese, R. Steele, D. DeLuca.

2nd row—F. Tigano, D. Pelligrino, W. Walker, R. Kirk, J. Marino, R. Daniels, J. Blattenberger, R. Nesbitt, P. Galiano, H. Nelson, D. Varlotto, V. Jonnotti, B. Harris, B. Lankmeyer.

3rd row—W. Tibbs, P. Corcoran, H. Poole, D. Gruber, C. Hefflin, G. Sproat, F. Graves, R. Pugh, E. Haley, R. Lombard, G. Depew, C. Longford, E. Harris.

**160**

There never was a group of more gallant warriors than the boys who wore the gold and blue in "52." What they lacked in experience they more than made up for in heart. Every game was a challenge to them, and they met each challenge in the true tradition of a Westinghouse team. With their "never say die" spirit, this squad won the respect and admiration of the entire community, and although they had a very difficult schedule, their ambtiion and drive brought them a winning record.

The W.H.S. gridders opened the season against a Donora Eleven, who took advantage of every opportunity, and although the boys rang up 13 first downs to 6 for their opponents, they came away from the field on the short end of a 13-6 decision.

Their most decisive victory of the season was against Altoona, which provided action for the whole squad. The game was high-lighted by the long runs of Ernie Jone and the hard-charging of the W.H.S. line, which brought a 27-0 victory.

Our Bulldogs were on their way to another crack at the City Title by knocking off their first two opponents, Allderdice and Schenley, but their clash with Peabody provided the fatal blow. Peabody had a big, hard-charging fullback and a good passer in their quarterback, which provided the payoff punch in the final quarter of the game. At the sound of the gun, the score read 7-0.

The scores of the 1952 squad will soon be forgotten, but their spirit, their ambition to be champions, and the philosophy of a great coach, Mr. Dimperio, will live forever in the minds of the students and football fans in the surrounding district.

*Coach*—MR. DIMPERIO

---

*Burton • Dimperio • Musilin • Malins • Webb*

**1953 - Tears flow.
As Bulldogs are
Upset by rival
Peabody 14-6.**

Sun-Telegraph Photo by Tom Tela.

**PEABODY GAIN ...** Fullback Bill Holmes, of Peabody, goes around left end for a seven-yard gain in second quarter of City League football game with Westinghouse yesterday. Coming up to stop him is the Bulldogs' Eugene Haley (57). The Highlanders won the game, 14-6.

Sun-Telegraph Photo.

**BACKS . . .** Iere are the backs Peabody will send against Allegheny in City League championship football game at South High Stadium Friday night. They're Al Jacks, Jim Thompson, John McNamara, Charles Scafuri, T. Hannon.

162

Sun-Telegraph Photo by Charles Bruneck.

**CRASH . . .** Al Jacks, of Peabody (left), is stopped by Allegheny's Willie McCants with a head-to-head tackle in second quarter of City League championship game at South Stadium last night. Jacks starred as Peabody won.

## Rarin' To Go

Peabody brings City Title back to the East End winning over Allegheny 21-0.

**THREATS THROTTLED**

Both quarterbacks had an o night in their passing. Jack tried only 12 and complete four, while Ivey connected o six of 18, including as con pleted two on which Peabod drew interference penalties.

Only twice did Allegheny g inside Peabody's 20. Ivey fum bled on the 19 to end the firs threat in the second period an Tom Peters intercepted an Ive pass on his own 3 to halt th other try in the third quarter

Oddly, Peabody won its se ond league title by followin the pattern Carrick laid out la year. It played an early no league scoreless tie with Ne Castle, then won all of the r maining games on its schedul

PEABODY—21
Ends—Newell, McDaniel, Krotzer.
Tackles—Grande, Hegerty, Paul.
Guards—Rubin, D. Peters, T. Peters, Ewing.
Center—Izenson.
Backs — Jacks, Hannon, Scafuri, M Namara, Holmes, Thompson.
ALLEGHENY—0
Ends—Izydore, Blttner, Lane, Sell.
Tackles—Cirocco, Paolino, Gange.
Guards — Cogsville, Schultz, Sparro Lukenas.
Center—Dietz.
Backs—H. Ivey, Zuger, Lewis, Botl McCants.
Score by quarters:
Peabody         T  T  0  7—
Touchdowns—Thompson, Hannon, Holm
Points after touchdown—Jacks 3 (pla ments)
Officials — Melman, Paterline, Alcm rtner.

**The 1953 Team (my senior year) was one that still impressed the Sports writers even though the Bulldogs fell short of winning a city title berth. Our neighboring rival Peabody took top honors that year bringing the title back to East Liberty. Both Peabody and Westinghouse were rated two of the top 25 teams in Western PA that year.**

Westinghouse was again represented by a well-conditioned, well-trained, and courageous team in the 1953 season. Although the Bulldogs did not win the City Championship this season, only the third time they have failed to do so in twelve years—no team had more spirit.

In the first post-season game with Donora, the Bulldogs outplayed this powerful team but lost 12-6. In the next game, Westinghouse bounced back to defeat Aliquippa 13-6. The Bulldogs ended their stay in the W.P.I.A.L. by downing our traditional rivals Altoona, 20-6.

The Bulldogs opened the City League season in great form by routing Schenley 61-6. The Bulldogs were in there fighting this game, and showed what a great football team looks like. However in the next game fate was really against us, and Peabody came out on top 14-6. After this upset, the Bulldogs raced through the rest of the City League schedule. South was bounced, 32-12. The Bulldogs trounced South Hills 27-12, and ended the season in glory by defeating Allderdice 33-7.

Westinghouse scored 159 points in 5 City League games for an amazing average of 31-4/5 points a game as opposed to 51 points for their rivals, an average of 10-1/5 points.

163

Seated—R. Marsalese, D. Jeters, J. Pronio, P. Signore, J. LaMarca, C. Hefflin, R. Lombard, E. Haley, J. Ricci, ardelli, C. Smith, B. Walden, E. Jones, P. Galiano.

2nd row—Mr. Grupe, R. Harris, P. Villani, F. Graves, H. Poole, J. Blattenberger, D. Gruber, G. Brown, H. Depew, H. Nelson, E. Harris, W. Tibbs, S. Langford, E. Nelson, C. Gant, B. Lankemeyer, C. DeLuca, Coach Dimperio.

3rd row—M. Paschal, G. Sproat, F. Schubert, J. Parillo, F. Baglio, J. Cerneglia, A. Fornaser, J. Scott, C. Martin, R. Frederick, J. Kelly, S. Brown, A. Floyd.

164

JOE PRONIO

BRONCO SIGNORE

WESTINGHOUSE BULLDOGS
1953 CO-CAPTAINS

JOE LA MARCA

JOE RICCIARDELLI

DAVE JETERS

JOE PRONIO

MY 1954 SENIOR CLASSMATES

RON MARSALESE

BRONCO SIGNORE

ERNIE JONES

GENE HALEY

PAUL CALIANO

166

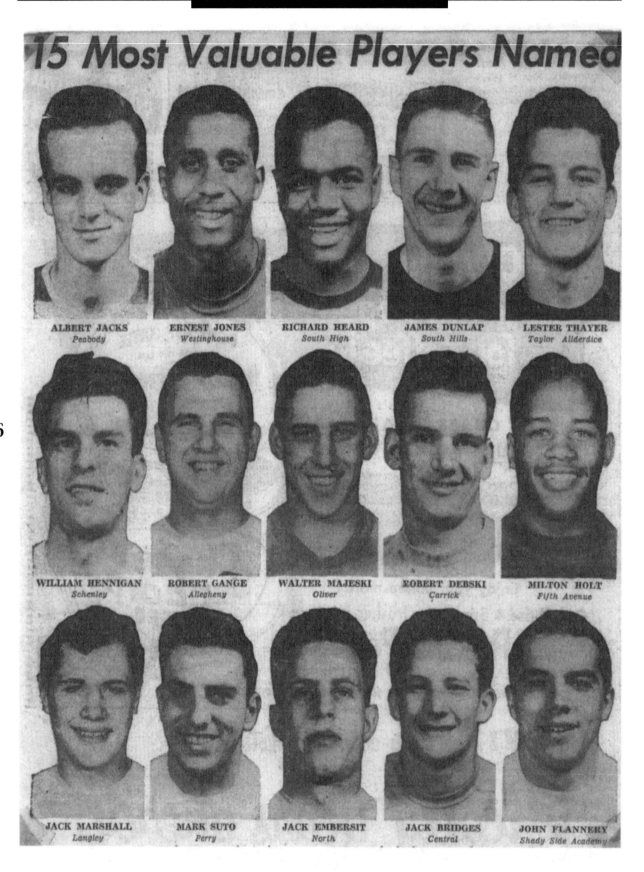

# 15 Most Valuable Players Named

**ALBERT JACKS**
*Peabody*

**ERNEST JONES**
*Westinghouse*

**RICHARD HEARD**
*South High*

**JAMES DUNLAP**
*South Hills*

**LESTER THAYER**
*Taylor Allderdice*

**WILLIAM HENNIGAN**
*Schenley*

**ROBERT GANGE**
*Allegheny*

**WALTER MAJESKI**
*Oliver*

**ROBERT DEBSKI**
*Carrick*

**MILTON HOLT**
*Fifth Avenue*

**JACK MARSHALL**
*Langley*

**MARK SUTO**
*Perry*

**JACK EMBERSIT**
*North*

**JACK BRIDGES**
*Central*

**JOHN FLANNERY**
*Shady Side Academy*

## 1954 CITY CHAMPIONS

PRIMED FOR BATTLE—Westinghouse, after ending Peabody's two-year reign, copped section one honors and meets Carrick, section two winners, for the City League crown Friday night at South Stadium. Both teams posted 5-0 marks for the season. The line, left to right: G. B F. Graves, J. Cerniglia, J. Girdano, R. Lombard, C. H and B. Tibbs. Backfield: H. Nelson, S. Langford, H. and J. Parillo.—Pennywell Photo.

1954                          FOOTBALL TEAM

Coach—P. Dimperio

1st row—Alvin Floyd, John Cerniglia, Horace Nelson, John Girdano, Richard Lombard, Curtis Hefflin, Bill Tibbs, Ernie Harris, Frank Graves, Bob Merietti, George Brown, Harold Poole, Bob Frederick, Charles DeLuca.

2nd row—Bob McNulty, Bob Maurizio, Edward Nelson, Gary Depew, Artie Fornaser, John Parillo, Bobby Harris, Marion Paschal, Charles Martin, James Scott, Frank Baglio, Charles Gant, Ronald Graves, Ronald Russell, John Shropshire.

3rd row—Thomas Williams, Jack Hartman, Jerry Irwin, Fra Schubert, James Johnson, Sherrill Brown, Jack Kelley, Pr Villani, Lynnard Slaughter, Edward Woddell, Louis Guir Bimbo Gorman, Ronald Ecoff, Gene Lodovic, Mike Antonuc

4th row—Peter Dimperio, Bob Lankemeyer, Charles Becke J. Lang Speer.

168

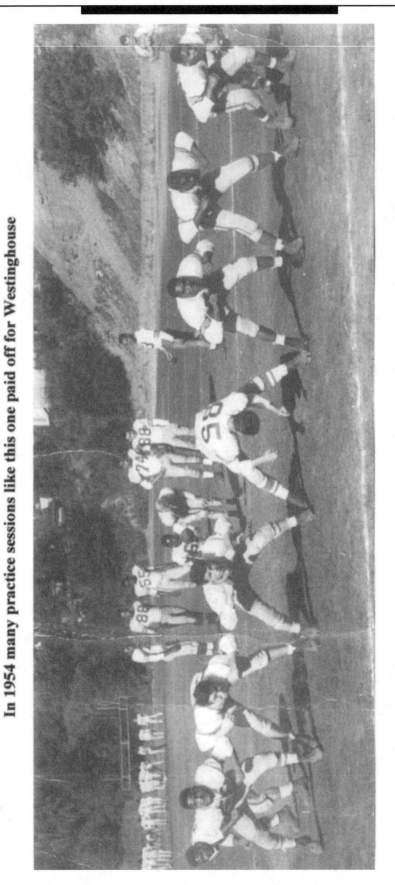

In 1954 many practice sessions like this one paid off for Westinghouse

This is a scene during a practice session the day before the title game, an extra point conversion attempt by Harold Poole. The following night the Bulldogs defeated Carrick 7-6 on a successful PAT by Harold Poole to win the City League Championship.

*Burton • Dimperio • Musilin • Malins • Webb*

**Poole's Boot Decides**

# Bulldogs Win City Title, 7-6

By PAUL A. KURTZ

The scant margin of a point after touchdown, booted expertly by Fullback Harold Poole after his six pointer—lifted Pete Dimperio's hard-driving Westinghouse Bulldogs to another City High League football championship.

Again, Ralph Zahniser and his Carrick Raiders failed. They walked dejectedly to dressing quarters "a brides-maid but not a bride" after dropping a hard-fought 7-6 decision to the Homewooders under ideal weather conditions at the South High Stadium.

Again, Dimperio was carried triumph-

❖ ❖ ❖

antly off the field as the Bulldogs succeeded Peabody as the loop's new titlist. It was the fourth straight time since Dimperio began grid coaching at Westinghouse that he has beaten Zahniser in championship play.

None will deny this was the best played City title game in years. It was enjoyed thoroughly by 6500 fans in the stadium and 1500 more cliff-dwelling, non-paying customers overlooking the field.

The scoring was done in the first two periods. There wasn't a dull moment. Both teams were applauded as play ended virtually in mid-field, sort of an even-stephen affair.

❖ ❖ ❖

An early misplay in the opening quarter paved the way for Westinghouse to pick up its seven points. A high pass from center resulted in Virgil Boccella, a valuable Raider right half, to fumble in the act of punting. He recovered but it was fourth down and Westinghouse took over on the Carrick 44-yard line.

Westinghouse power—and it began exploding—paid off as Eddie Nelson, Bob Merletti and Poole rushed to three straight first downs to the Carrick two.

Merletti stretched to within a foot of the goal. Carrick threw up a defensive wall, but Poole fairly soared over center to make the Westinghouse touchdown with three and a half-minutes left in the period.

Cooly, Poole, with Ray Gorman holding, place-kicked the extra point—that coveted point which was to make the Bulldogs victorious.

Carrick came right back to demonstrate running ability as Sophomore Quarterback Howard Brehm handed-off brilliantly to William Seibel, Virg Boccella and Carl Rueppel. Two first downs carried the Raiders to the Westinghouse three. Seibel slammed at left guard for two as the first quarter ended.

Opening the second quarter, Brehm sneaked for a half-yard and then he feinted nicely to plow through for the Carrick touchdown, even though the Bulldogs were detected offside, of which they were guilty four times in the contest. The dramatic point came as Boccella's attempted placement was blocked by Tackle John Cerniglia. That proved vital in the final reckoning.

Trying to catch-up late in the last quarter, Carrick took to the air. Rueppel heaved a long one toward Seibel at the left corner near the goal line with one minute to play, but Left End Bill Tibbs covered the play successfully.

Both teams had their heroes, particularly in the line where the play was hard but clean. Outstanding was Curtis Hefflin, sturdy Negro left guard for Westinghouse. He was a Gibraltar on defense and repeatedly turned back hard thrusts by Raider backfielders, who had hard-smashers in Boccella and Rueppel.

**WINNING TOUCHDOWN** for Westinghouse is scored from one foot away by Harold Poole against Carrick last night. But it took his extra point to make the touchdown good for a 7-6 victory over the Raiders in the City High League title game.

This was Westinghouse's eighth league grid title in the last 11 years—and its sixth in the last nine campaigns under Dimperio's capable supervision. This was the Bulldogs' seventh hold on the Pa Pitt Hat Trophy, presented by the Chamber of Commerce since 1945.

It also was the Homewooders' 17th City League grid

title. Carrick was beaten by Dimperio - Westinghouse squads in 1947, 1948, 1951 and last night.

Westinghouse made 11 first downs to eight for Carrick. Only two of seven passes were completed by the Bulldogs with the Raiders making two of six. Carrick intercepted one. Westinghouse was penalized 35 yards to 20 for Carrick.

**WESTINGHOUSE**

Ends—Tibbs, Harris.
Tackles—Graves, Cerniglia.
Guards—Hefflin, Gizmado.
Center—Lombard.
Backs—Gorman, Merletti, Nelson, Poole.

**CARRICK**

Ends—Toney, Dillon.
Tackles—Ross, Krut.
Guards—Karcher, Sloan.
Center—Lockard.
Backs—Brehm, Seibel, Boccella, Rueppel.

| | | | | | |
|---|---|---|---|---|---|
| Westinghouse | 7 | 0 | 0 | 0— | 7 |
| Carrick | 0 | 6 | 0 | 0— | 6 |

Touchdowns—Poole, Brehm. Extra Points—Poole (Placement). Mixed Point— Boccella (Placement).
Officials—Rugh, Stegman, Corrigan, Ketchell.

170

**BULLDOGS GET HAT . . . .**
F. Rhodes Henderer (second from right) makes presentation of Pa Pitt's Hat trophy to Westinghouse High School co-captains Richard Lombard (left) and Curtis Hefflin (right) as Pete Dimperio, the Bulldogs' coach, looks on approvingly. Westinghouse was given the trophy for winning the City League football title.

Sun-Telegraph Photo by Charles Bruneck.

1955 CITY CHAMPIONS

171

# Westinghouse dominates with back and lineman of the year

172

Sun-Telegraph Photo by Paul Hunter

John Girdano, City League Lineman of the Year, demonstrating a new way of propeling Sherrill Brown, Player of the Year, over the lines of opposing teams. Girdano is a former "Mr. Pittsburgh" entrant, while Brown was one of the smallest backs in the league the past season, only 5-4 and 152 pounds.

1956 CITY CHAMPIONS

THE STARTING TEAM

First row, left to right: Pierre Dean, End; Joseph Miele, Tackle; Joseph Golden, Tackle; James Recuperio, Guard; Bobbie Harris, Center; Ronald Graves, Guard; Thomas Pitts, End. Second row, left to right: Howard Tibbs, Right Half; Ronald Ecoff, Quarterback; Carl Baxter, Fullback; Robert Tedesco, Left Half.

173

## 1957 CITY CHAMPIONS

**Local Eleven Rounding Into Shap**

An impressive looking armada of first string backs streak down the field together. Westinghouse High School, trying this season for their fourth consecutive city league crown, include H. Tibbs, R. Henderson, W. McLellan, E. McLellan and A. Calloway. The boys are into the full swing of practice sessions at Westinghouse — and looking forward to a lively and victorious season.

**For Upcoming Grid Season**

F. Battista, J. Folgarelli, R. Hancock, L. Rawling, S. Miele, A. Liscio and T. William make up the line of the Westinghouse eleven this year as the team prepares to make its try for the fourth consecutive city league championship.
Westinghouse High School is also Second Division champs. Spirited rivalry with Peabody and with other East End schools is expected this year.

174

Teen Magazine's All-East choice Tony Liscio grabs off a pass.

## The 1958 Season

Victory housed itself at Westinghou again this year. The Bulldog gridders, d scribed by Coach Pete Dimperio as his "spee iest" charges, entered the city league ra in an uncertain role after losing two of thr exhibition games. However, the team r ceived the necessary confidence by winni over Schenley 31-6. The boys had hit th stride.

The first three games brought add strength to title hopes. Peabody, South, a South Hills fell in order. Climaxing the regul season, the Bulldogs defeated Allderdice f the Section I crown. The lads from neighb ing Squirrel Hill were unable to contain t long dashes of Gene McClellan and the p fected pass catching of Frank Battista.

In the finale of this great season, Westin house retained the city title by crushing t Section 2 winner, Allegheny. The Bulldo clicked smoothly to finish the season with 38-0 win. Pete and his boys had done it aga the fifth straight year.

175

**First Row:** A. Liscio, H. Hosbey, K. DeHonney, R. Marshall, E. McClellan, A. Calloway, R. Young, F. Battista. **Second Row:** J. Williams, I. Bailey, A. Allsberry, J. Hancock, R. Miller, G. Sharpe, R. Norman. **Third Row:** N. Destefano mgr., T. Harris, E. Golden, J. Ramsey, M. Bisceglia, M. Stanton, R. Henderson, L. Evans. **Fourth Row:** R. Fields, L. Campbell, L. Malone, Q. Washington, O. Roy, D. Forlastro, M. Broadus. **Fifth Row:** S. Lloyd, E. Bufford, P. Anderson, R. Elliott, D. Bates mgr., J. Matthews mgr.

On page 29 is Pete Dimperio's "fastest" backfield (from top) Al Cal-loway, Mike Bisceglia, Ron Henderson, and Gene McClellan behind an equally fast line of Frank Battista, Ralph Young, Ken DeHonney, Lyde Evans, Bobbie Marshall, Howard Hosbey, and Tony Liscio.

28

Another Bulldog drive is under way.

Offensive Team    DALLAS COWBOYS

MIKE DITKA    LANCE ALWORTH    DUANE THOMAS    ROGER STAUBACH    CALVIN HILL    BOB HAYES

RAYFIELD WRIGHT    BLAINE NYE    DAVE MANDERS    JOHN NILAND    TONY LISCIO

177

To My Friends at
East Liberty
Chamber of Commerce
Best Wishes
Tony Liscio

178

PITTSBURGH SUN-TELEGRAPH    SATURDAY, NOV. 14, 1959

# Roundup of High Scho

**BULLDOZING BULLDOG:** Westinghouse High's powerful full-back, Mike Bisceglia, driving to the Carrick one-yard line in the third period of last night's City League title game. He was halted by Joe Gudenburr (65), Tom Modrak and Nelson F but Art Williams carried over on the next play. W won its sixth straight city title in a romp, 35-12.

Sun-Telegraph Phot

179

180

1959 * Fort Knox, Kentucky * 4th Training Regiment * Company A11 * 4th Platoon

# 6 | THE 1960s AND THE TWENTY-FIVE GAME WINNING STREAK

## 1960 – A Host of Talent Returns

This was the season that student athlete George Webb was waiting for; no more scrubbing and no more mind games. In 1959, he had experienced and survived the regimentation of the Room and now as a sophomore was mentally and physically prepared to exercise his athletic ability as a varsity member of the Westinghouse High School football squad. Little did he know that some day he would be the head coach at the Homewood School. Webb was one of the young upcoming talents waiting for his opportunity to excel for his legendary coach. Let's put this aside for now and realize the 1960 season as it unfolded under the tutelage of Dimperio. New Assistant Coach, Rudy Musilin, took over for the departed Bruce Weston who went on to accept the position as Head Coach at South Hills High School.

The Bulldogs had a City Title to defend and several holdovers from the 1959 season were ready to make another run at the city crown. Three of the four running backs were returning – Edgar Golden, Alvin Allsberry and Art Williams. Departed Fullback Mike Bisceglia was now a freshman at Tulsa University. Replacing him was John Williams as the new Bulldog fullback. Other returning lettermen were center, John Ramsey, ends Earl Bufford and James McCoy, tackles Charles Harris and Ron Fields and All-City guard Ted Harris along with Jim Hancock.

The outlook for 1960 looked promising with plenty of experienced players returning. The opening pre-season game was against always tough Aliquippa. The two teams battled to a 14-14 deadlock. The following week the Bulldogs traveled to meet Har-brack (later renamed Highlands) looking to avenge the 1959 loss. They reversed the results this time defeating the Rams 13-7. The third pre-season encounter was with Mt. Lebanon. The Blue Devils completely outplayed Westinghouse in a 28-0 shutout – capitalizing on several Bulldog miscues. Dimperio was very upset as he verbally called this loss "one of the poorest performances by a Westinghouse team in quite some time". He was not very a happy camper. It was the first and only loss of the season. The pre-season results measured up to a record of 1-1-1, as the Bulldogs were getting prepared for the Section 1 City League schedule.

The opening league game saw Westinghouse bounce back from the lackluster performance at Mt. Lebanon with a 44-13 victory over the South High Orioles. The following week they met former Bulldog assistant coach Bruce Weston and his South Hills team defeating them 44-13. Next on the schedule was Allderdice and Dimperio displayed his second unit for most of the second half after the first unit had scored 33 points. The final score ended by being a 33-0 shutout for the Bulldogs. Schenley was waiting for Westinghouse the following week and proceeded to give them a battle. The Spartans led the Dogs at the half 13-7. Pete was quite upset with the boys and gave them the silent treatment during the halftime break – without entering the locker room. He opened the door to the locker room and called out "OK girls it's time for the second half". The second half was a dandy with the Bulldogs scoring 26 points in the third quarter, but Schenley never gave up. They hung in there and made a game of it before succumbing 39-26. Arch rival Peabody was the final game on the schedule. It was all Westinghouse in this one winning 25-7 and capturing the Section 1 crown. The Section 2 winner was Allegheny High School from the North Side. The two teams were scheduled to meet at South Stadium for the City Championship. The day before the game Coach Dimperio was ill at home and was advised to return home immediately following the game. On game day it had rained steadily and made for very sloppy field conditions. It did not seem to bother the Bulldogs as they received the opening kick-off and on the third play from scrimmage, Art Williams raced 70 yards for a Bulldog touchdown. By the third quarter Westinghouse had a commanding lead of 33-0 and Dimperio sent in his third unit to finish the game. Assistant Coach Rudy Musilin took over as Dimperio was taken back home. The Bulldogs had won their seventh title in a row 39-7 and 23rd in loop grid history for the Homewood school.

**182**

Score by quarters:

| | | | | |
|---|---|---|---|---|
| Westinghouse | 13 | 14 | 6 | 6–39 |
| Allegheny | 0 | 0 | 0 | 7–7 |

Westinghouse scoring – Touchdowns: A. Williams (70-yard run); M. Myricks (3-yard run; 40-yard run); McCoy (recovered Q. Washington fumble in end zone); J. Williams (5-yard run); Q. Washington (4-yard run); Pat's: Allsberry (run), A. Williams (run), Q. Washington (run): Missed Pat's: J. Williams, 2 (runs); Webb (inc. pass).

Allegheny scoring – Touchdowns: L. Williams (7-yard run). Pat: Bourgoin (run).

**1960 Season (7-1-1)**

Pre Season (WPIAL)

| | | |
|---|---|---|
| WHS | 14 | Aliquippa – 14 |
| WHS | 13 | Har-Brack – 7 |
| WHS | 0 | Mt. Lebanon – 28 |

City League

| | | |
|---|---|---|
| WHS | 44 | South – 13 |
| WHS | 41 | South Hills – 13 |
| WHS | 33 | Allderdice – 0 |
| WHS | 39 | Schenley – 26 |
| WHS | 25 | Peabody – 7 |

Pittsburgh City League Championship
WHS – 39    Allegheny – 7

There were several awards received as John Williams was City League MVP and Ted Harris (Bulldog Captain) was Outstanding Lineman of the year. Scholarships were awarded to Ted Harris (Michigan State); James McCoy (Rutgers); Alvin Allsberry (West Texas State); Ron Fields (Dayton) and Edgar Golden (Virginia State). The Williams boys together scored 80% of the Bulldog's points for the season. They were an impressive one-two punch that reminded many of the Joe Ware – Bobby Dye era.

1960 Team Members
J. Martin, A. Allsberry. G. Webb, Frank Bisceglia, L. Berry. S. Saverio, J. Henderson, J. Ramsey, H. Bufford, B. Harrison, A. Davis, C. Harris, D. Conley, P. Anderson, M. Broaddus, J. Brewer, J. Williams, A. Williams, R. Barnes, R. Dean, J. McCoy, R. Fields, Q. Washington, J. Hayes, W. Blanton, C. Slaughter, J. Giles, M. Myricks, T. Harris, E. Goodson, A. Slaughter, E. Golden, L. Malone, J. Hancock, E. Bufford, M. Carpenter; Managers: G. Parry and B. Snider.

## 1961 – THE CITY LEAGUE STREAK CONTINUES

The undefeated streak in city league competition of 45 wins and one scoreless tie beginning back in 1953 was still unblemished and the Bulldogs were determined to add to it in 1961. Westinghouse opened the season at Aliquippa and lost a close 6-0 decision to the Quips. A loss like this to a WPIAL school did not hurt the image of the Bulldogs. Pete Dimperio always felt that in a three game series against WPIAL competition his team would win two out of three games. Nobody could dispute this as he had that kind of success against the bigger schools of the WPIAL. The following week Westinghouse traveled to Mt. Lebanon and surprised the Blue Devils with an upset 12-6 victory. A win like this is a real confidence builder for a city school. Back then Westinghouse more often than not would hold it's own against the bigger WPIAL schools. The final pre-season game was against North Catholic, the remaining Catholic League Champion. The Bulldogs raised some eyebrows in this one defeating the Trojans 26-0. The Westinghouse defense stood tall as they shut down Trojan quarterback Larry Syzkowny.

The new spinning fullback (a key position in Dimperio's single wing offense) was George Webb. He was all of 5'5" at 150 pounds. He was a throwback to little Sherrill Brown the MVP from the 1955 Bulldog team. Webb was thought to be too small when he first "went out" for football as a ninth grader by Dimperio. Now he was a junior with the talent and heart of a Bulldog and ready to make his presence known. Westinghouse, the defending City League champion, was ready to take on the challenge of an eighth consecutive city title – a string that began in 1954.

The Bulldogs opened the 1961 League schedule with a game at Taylor Allderdice. It was a good tune-up as they breezed to a 33-0 half-time lead. Dimperio played every player on the squad as the Bulldogs defeated the Dragons 40-7. The next two games were close ones – Westinghouse had their hands full – as they turned in tough hard-

183

earned wins over Schenley 14-6 and South Hills 20-19.  South Hills Coach Bruce Weston (a former Bulldog and Assistant Coach) came very close to upsetting the boys from Homewood.  After all, he was very familiar with the antiquated Westinghouse single-wing offense.  The following week was a game against winless South High, and every squad member saw playing time in this one in a 55-0 whitewash for the House.  In the Section 1 season finale the Bulldogs defeated neighboring arch rival Peabody 19-0, captured the Section 1 title, and a place in the city championship game against Section 2 winner Langley.

The Section 2 champion Langley was ready to challenge Westinghouse with a strong defensive unit that did not allow an opponent to cross their goal line in league play.  The Bulldogs were accustomed to pre-game challenges and this one was no different.  Westinghouse received the opening kickoff and returned it to mid-field.  On the second play from scrimmage, Bulldog running back John Brewer broke loose and took it all the way for a touchdown.  The House proceeded to shut down the Mustangs 27-0 as Frank McClellan, Melvin Myricks and George Webb all scored for the Bulldogs.  Westinghouse continued to add to their city league winning streak at 51 games, and their eighth consecutive city league championship dating back to the 1954 season.

Score by quarters:
Westinghouse - 14    7    6    0 – 27
Langley -       0    0    0    7 – 7

**184**

Touchdowns – Westinghouse: M. Myricks (15 yd. run); J. Brewer 2 (42 yd. run, 33 yd. run); G. Webb (5 yd. run).  Langley: R. Williams (40 yd. pass from G. Smith).
Points after touchdown – Westinghouse: G. Webb 3 (runs); Langley: E. Becker 1 (run).

**1961 Season (6-2-1)**
Pre Season (WPIAL)
WHS   0    Aliquippa     6
WHS   12   Mt. Lebanon   6
WHS   26   N. Catholic   0
City League
WHS   40   Allderdice    7
WHS   14   Schenley      6
WHS   20   South Hills   19
WHS   55   South         0
WHS   19   Peabody       0
Pittsburgh City League Championship
WHS   27   Langley       0

Enjoying a banner season were Senior George Harrison along with George Webb, Larry Berry, Frank Bisceglia, Donald Hardy – all juniors.  All-City honors went to Melvin Myricks, Larry Malone, Charles Harris , George Webb and Elmer Goodson.

The 1961 Squad:
M. Jones, L. Banks, F. Reed, R. Carter, C. Schatzman, J. Avent, D. Coonahan, R. Williams, M. Peeler, A. Bridges, T. Hilliard, C. Walker, J. Martin, R. Dean, C. Slaughter, L. Malone, E. Goodson, J. Brewer, G. Webb, M. Myricks, R. Harrison, A. Davis, D. Young, C. Harris, H. Bufford, M. Braoddus, L. Rembert, F. McClellan, G. Harris, W. Blanton, L. Loar, R. Bush, K. Lewis, D. Hardy, J. Hayes, L. Berry, F. Bisceglia, V. McClellan, J. Henderson; Managers, F. Taylor, C. Berry, P. Mathis.

Many times Pete was questioned as to how he was able to control the young men that played for him. His reply was – "Motivation with sincerity and honesty as young boys are genuine and look for these attributes from their leader. They recognize the feelings you bestow upon them." Caring for them with respect throughout their high school careers and always ready to help them through tough times was an attribute that Coach Dimperio possessed. I personally can attest to this as he helped me while I was a student and later in life when I was a young adult. Today I am a friend of his son Peter who has carried on his legacy in such an inspirational way. Many of his boys kept in touch with him long after their playing careers were over. The mutual respect of Dimperio and his boys was one that lasted a lifetime.

## 1962-PEABODY ENDS BULLDOG'S CITY LEAGUE WINNING STREAK

The 1962 season was one that I remember quite well. I was, at the time, working at the U. S. Bureau of Mines along with several alumni from Westinghouse High School. We were a close knit group – about seven or eight from different class years and we all had something in common – Westinghouse tradition.

Westinghouse was scheduled to play Mt. Lebanon in a pre-season game that year. Some of our fellow employees were Mt. Lebanon alumni so several of us had decided to attend this game for bragging rights. It was the second game of the season for both schools as each had won their respective season openers (the Bulldogs having defeated Aliquippa 21-6).

The game was played at Mt. Lebanon High School Stadium before a crowd of nine thousand fans. Mt. Lebanon was the WPIAL powerhouse and favored to win, but the Bulldogs (defending City League Champions) were ready and played very well before losing a tough game 21-14. We were quite proud of Westinghouse as they played so well even in defeat. In fact, the Mt. Lebanon fans gave Dimperio and his team a standing ovation as they left the field in appreciation for such a fine effort. I was very proud to see this and it showed me how much respect they had for Westinghouse.

This was George Webb's final season as he was now a senior. This was the year for Peabody to upset and end the longest City League undefeated streak for the Bulldogs that began in 1953 and ended in 1962 at fifty-four games. They played two games, one league game and one playoff game with the Highlanders winning both. Peabody won in regular season play 13-12 after coming back from a 12-0 Westinghouse lead.

The playoff game ended in a 7-7 tie, but the Highlanders had the edge 8-7 in first downs and were awarded the win. They met Langley in the city title game with the

185

Highlanders winning 9-0 at South Stadium – a game that I attended along with my cousin who was a Peabody alumnus. At that game I saw several Westinghouse team members cheering for their arch rival Peabody and it was nice to see the two neighboring schools supporting each other.

This was the year that the Westinghouse City League Champions streak ended at eight years in a row as it had extended from 1954 to 1961. No other school has come close to this. This streak also bested the six years in a row when Bulldogs enjoyed supremacy from 1944 to 1949. These two streaks covered parts of three decades beginning with the later years of the Burton era and carried well into the Dimperio era. Up to this point in time Westinghouse had captured twenty-four city titles and had earned the reputation of perennial city champions of Pittsburgh.

George Webb's senior season was a disappointment for him since the Bulldogs did not win the city title after getting a second chance. But, he had a banner year earning All-City honors and a scholarship to Thiel College. His team mate halfback Jon Henderson went onto play college ball at the University of Colorado. After college he played in the NFL for both the Pittsburgh Steelers and the Washington Redskins.

## 1963 – BULLDOGS BOUNCE BACK

186

The Bulldogs were preparing to redeem themselves after a disappointing 1962 season. It was time to put the disappointments behind them and uphold the tradition and winning spirit that had been the strength of its storied history. Coach Dimperio was making ready to release a lightning quick stable of running backs with the emergence of junior Orin Richburg. He was a record setting 100 yard dash man having been timed at 9.8 seconds. Senior Bill Vassar a co-captain who held down one of the end positions was a tough leader and was looking at several college offers. The Bulldog tackles were big led by Donald "House" Hardy a 6' 4", 240 pounder and Ken Lewis, a 6' 2", 200 pounder. Three Williams' (Nicholson, Hillliard and Williams) were the guards and center respectively. This sizeable array of linemen was ready to spring loose the famous Bulldog single wing. Dimperio was still using this antiquated offense and was not showing any signs of changing over to the T-Formation. The other backs were fullback Bill Givner, quarterback Vann McClellan and halfback Ralph Carter. Teaming up with Vassar at the opposite end was Percy Hanner.

The pre-season opener was at New Castle where, the Bulldogs speed was too much for the bigger Hurricanes to handle. Westinghouse showed how well the single wing is executed as they defeated New Castle 25-0 before 9,500 fans on their home field. The following week they traveled to Mt. Lebanon and this year they reversed the decision from the previous year besting the Blue Devils 13-0 before 5,000 plus spectators. I was still working at the Bureau of Mines and our little Westinghouse alumni group was quite proud of this victory for bragging rights. The Bulldogs did themselves proud with two (shutout) victories in a row over WPIAL powerhouses New Castle and Mt. Lebanon. The final pre-season game was a trip up to Johnstown to do battle against Bishop McCort High School – a top ranked parochial school in Western Pennsylvania – who was on a 27 game winning streak. The Bulldogs came so close to upsetting the Crusaders – outplaying them in all phases of the game before losing 9-7 on a late field goal.

After three well played pre-season games, Westinghouse was ready to bring the City League title back to Homewood. The Bulldogs high powered offense and solid defense rolled through the next five city opponents with impressive wins allowing only 18 total points while averaging 38 points in Section 1 play. The Section 2 winner was Allegheny High School, the next challenge for the Bulldogs at South Stadium for the City League title. Allegheny could not contain the powerful running attack of Westinghouse losing to the Bulldogs 46-6 in one of the most one-sided games in City League history. The PA Pitt Trophy was back in the trophy case at the House.

**Tragedy Strikes**

The morning following the championship game, Coach Dimperio received a tragic phone call. He had learned that his star player, Bill Vassar, and team captain was stabbed to death later on in the evening following the championship game. This was so tragic coming shortly after a championship celebration for the Homewood school. The community was in shock – Billy was a "B" student receiving the Pittsburgh City League Most Valuable Player honor, posthumously. The school retired his number "47" jersey as many college scholarship offers were arriving not realizing that Billy Vassar was dead. Dimperio pulled his squad together explaining to them how the loss of a life is such a painful experience that had devastated a family, a team and a community and how it must be overcome. The 1963 championship season was a bittersweet one that would always remain in the hearts of Billy Vassar's teammates and classmates.

187

The championship game summary:
Score by quarters:

| | | | | | |
|---|---|---|---|---|---|
| Westinghouse | 19 | 13 | 14 | 0 | 46 |
| Allegheny | 0 | 0 | 0 | 6 | 6 |

Scoring:

| | |
|---|---|
| Westinghouse - | E. Henderson, 57 , run (Givner run failed) |
| " | R. Carter, 24 run (Richburg run failed) |
| " | B. Givner, 54, run (Garnett run) |
| " | B. Givner, 97, run (Carter run failed) |
| " | B. Givner, 20, run (Hanner pass from McClellan) |
| " | V. McClellan, 30, run (Banks pass from McClellan) |
| " | L. Banks, 35, run (Richburg run) |
| Allegheny | W. Ripley, 1, run (Owens run failed) |

The 1963 squad:
P. Cappozzoli, R. Maben, C. Austin, S. Henderson, H. Walker, V. Cherry, F. Jackson, R. Carter, R. Young, L. Banks, D. Weston, A. Anderson, W. Garnett, K. Lewis, B. Allen, L. Jones, R. Minter, R. Villani, E. Harrison, W. Williams, R. Hill, C. Phillips, R. Edwards, H. Mosley, H. Conley, W. Vassar, D. Hardy, B. Givner, O. Gaines, O.

Richburg, R. Fields, D. Gilmore, D. Jones, A. Donald, T. Hilliard, W. Nicholson, V. McClellan, J. Avent, C. Schaltzman, F. Reed, E. Henderson, P. Hanner, Rudy Bufford, J. King; Managers – C. Berry, D. Montgomery.

The 1963 Season (8-1-0)
    WPIAL

| WHS | 25 | New Castle | 0 |
| " | 13 | Mt. Lebanon | 0 |
| " | 7 | Bishop McCort | 9 |

    City League

| WHS | 39 | Schenley | 6 |
| " | 33 | Peabody | 0 |
| " | 42 | South | 6 |
| " | 41 | Allderdice | 0 |
| " | 34 | South Hills | 6 |

    City Championship

| WHS | 46 | Allegheny | 6 |

## 1964 – A SEASON DEDICATED TO BILLY VASSAR

188

The 1964 Bulldogs were determined to go undefeated and dedicated the season in honor of their late Captain Billy Vassar. Dimperio continued to get offers to leave Westinghouse, but as he said back in 1951, "My heart still belongs at Westinghouse" was the answer to those who offered him to leave for greener pastures. Pete now in his late 50's was very much the same dedicated teacher and coach as he was during the early years of his career. He was a master at what he did building the character and confidence of young boys into becoming winners and solid citizens.

The 1964 team had a bevy of speedy running backs led by senior Orin Richburg, a high school All-American and state champion sprinter in the 100 and 220 grid junior Wesley Garnett at left and right halfback respectively, seniors Bill Givner back from 1963 at fullback and Eric Henderson at quarterback. This backfield was one of the best and possibly the fastest to play for Dimperio. Sophomore Lloyd Weston 6', 190lbs. emerged as a starting tackle with senior Ronald Villani 6', 225lbs. holding down the other tackle position. Weston was a young talent that was a pleasant surprise for Dimperio as he was maturing quickly and displaying an excellent work ethic. Others earning starting positions were guards Richard Fields, Dave Weston (brother of Lloyd) and Bernie Allen. Others taking over key positions were defensive specialists Perkins Harris, Lloyd Jones, Cephas Austin and Ron Hill.

The Bulldogs opened the season against a tough New Castle team and defeated the Hurricanes 20-6 after trailing 6-0 early in the game. The single wing offense of Westinghouse was still giving their opponents fits as Dimperio refused to change his antiquated system. Why change a well-oiled machine that has worked so well for many years? And so the beat continued on when the Bulldogs traveled to Johnstown to meet Bishop McCort who was still riding an impressive winning streak. Westinghouse ended the Crusaders winning streak in a hard fought 13-12 victory.

The bus ride home from Johnstown was a happy one for the proud Bulldogs. The final pre-season game was against the Catholic League Champions – North Catholic at their home field. The speed of the Bulldogs was too much for the Trojans to handle as Westinghouse extended its pre-season record to 3-0 with a 35-12 victory. The defending City League Champions were ready to challenge the city league schedule.

The Bulldogs continued their winning ways with consecutive victories over five Section 1 opponents: Peabody 27-6, Allderdice 27-0, South 43-6, South Hills 41-6 and Schenley 46-6. The City League Title game was against Section 2 winner Langley at South Stadium. It was all Westinghouse as they defeated the Mustangs 45-6 to win the City Championship and finish a great season undefeated at 9-0. They dedicated the 1964 season to their fallen 1963 team captain William Vassar with an impressive display of determination, respect and dedication. The Bulldogs were now riding a 15 game winning streak and looking forward to extending it the following year.

The championship game summary:
Score by quarters:

| | | | | |
|---|---|---|---|---|
| Westinghouse | 20 | 19 | 6 | 0 – 45 |
| Langley | 0 | 0 | 0 | 6 – 6 |

Scoring:
Westinghouse – B. Givner 6, run (Garnett run) 7-0
"        O. Richburg 64, intercept. Pass (run fails) 13-0
"        E. Henderson 60, run (Garnett run) 20-0
"        W. Garnett, 73, run (Givner run) 27-0
"        W. Garnett 55, run (pass fails) 33-0
"        W. Garnett 52, run/pass play (pass fails) 39-0
"        E. Henderson 40, run (run fails) 45-0
Langley - M. Dudenas 1, run (run fails) 45-6

**189**

Dimperio pulled his starters shortly after the beginning of the second half. The first unit put on a clinic in the first half as they went to the locker room leading 38-0. They watched from the sideline after scoring quickly to put the game out of reach 45-0. The Mustangs managed to avert a shutout scoring a lone touchdown late in the fourth quarter as Westinghouse defended yet another City Title, 45-6.

All-City honors went to MVP Eric Henderson, Bill Givner, Orin Richburg, Wesley Garnett and Lloyd Weston with Honorable Mention going to Ron Hill and Bernie Allen. This All-City team also included Larry Brown from Schenley High School who later played for the Washington Redskins of the NFL after his college career at Kansas State.

This was the year that Coach Pete Dimperio was inducted into the Pennsylvania Sports Hall of Fame joining Westinghouse alumni Joe "Showboat" Ware and Bobby Dye. By this point in time Pete was becoming well known as a public speaker at various local and national sporting events and banquets.

Dimperio made believers of those who doubted him in 1946 – extending the winning tradition of former legendary coach O. H. "Pro" Burton with an impressive run of championship seasons for the Homewood school.

The 1964 Season (9-0-0)
Pre-season (WPIAL)

| WHS | 20 | New Castle | 6 |
|-----|----|-----------|---|
| " | 13 | Bishop McCort | 12 |
| " | 35 | North Catholic | 12 |

City League

| WHS | 27 | Peabody | 6 |
|-----|----|--------|---|
| " | 27 | Allderdice | 0 |
| " | 43 | South | 6 |
| " | 41 | South Hills | 6 |
| " | 46 | Schenley | 6 |

City Championship

| WHS | 45 | Langley | 6 |
|-----|----|--------|---|

This 1964 team worked hard to fulfill a goal of an undefeated season dedicated for the late Billy Vassar. There is no doubt that throughout the 1964 season the memory of Billy Vassar motivated the Bulldogs as they accomplished what they set out to do. It was a special one that had so much spirit and dedication for such a sad ending of a human life.

**190**

The 1964 Squad:
B. Gaines, P. Britton, W. Dudley, E. Tipton, R. Bogus, L. Banks, D. Murray, M. Ellison, R. Cappazolli, D. Vassar, J. King, C. Austin, M. Lipscomb, D. Jones, R. Edward. L. Jones, P. Harris, H. Walker, R. Minter, R. Hill, K. Carter, G. Vassar, Otis Gaines, S. Henderson, H. Conley, E. Whitted, F. Jackson, A. Anderson, G. Sweeney, H. Mosley, Lloyd Weston, R. Villani, D. Gilmore, W. Williams, R. Fields, E. Henderson, B. Allen, O. Richburg, R. Bufford, B. Givner, D. Weston, E. Harrison, W. Garnett, Managers: W. Jordan, E. Haymon, E. Boyd..

This was one of the ten undefeated seasons in the storied history of Westinghouse High School. The attraction of Westinghouse football belonged to a small dedicated clique that attended every Westinghouse game regardless of where it may be. The game at New Castle was a prime example – one of the small dedicated group was an executive from U. S. Steel – he had forgotten that his son was playing in his first football game for Baldwin High School that same evening. Later that evening (about 2:00 A.M.) when he arrived home he found a note from his wife on the vestibule table. It read, "your son played in his first high school game tonight and you were not there." God help this man if Pete had ever gotten wind of such a foolish lapse in memory. You can be sure he would have expressed his displeasure with – "Hells Fire You Big Stoop." This was one of Pete's favorite statements when he was upset with any of us who knew him.

## 1965 – EXTENDING THE 25 GAME WINNING STREAK

The 1965 season was expected to be a challenge for the Bulldogs as they were determined to continue a winning streak that began in 1963. The talented backfield from 1964 was depleted with only one senior, Wesley Garnett returning. Garnett was a superb running back and was considered the best in the state of Pennsylvania. He possessed the speed of a sprinter with the ability to do a 9.9 in the 100 yard dash. The rest of the backfield would come from candidates vying for positions to support Garnett. The other Halfback position would be filled by either Algie Anderson, Ernie Whitted or Donald Murray. Fullback support would come from either Hawthorne Conley or Wade Lipscomb. The signal caller would be either Greg Vassar (brother of the late Bill) or Fred Jackson. The Bulldogs had several lettermen returning to form a very capable offensive line with good size led by juniors Lloyd Weston and Mark Ellison at the tackle positions. The ends were Eugene Harrison and Lloyd Jones and at the guard positions Dave Weston, Richard Fields and Cephas Austin were having a battle. The battle for center was between Dorian Vassar (brother of the late Bill) and Willie Dudley.

The challenge to repeat what the Bulldogs did in 1964 was posing as a tall order with the likes of three tough pre-season opponents waiting to knock them off. The season opened with a trip to always tough New Castle. The Hurricanes had an impressive reputation of having won more football games than any school in Western Pennsylvania. Imagine the thrill of a Westinghouse team taking the field against a team with such a huge reputation. The Bulldogs were literally representing the City League of Pittsburgh and were determined to uphold a proud tradition. The game was a tough defensive struggle for both sides and was scoreless after three quarters. The fourth quarter was more of the same and with only two minutes left in the contest, Westinghouse defensive back Algie Anderson intercepted a New Castle pass deep in Hurricane territory. This was the break the determined Bulldogs needed. A smart call for a trap play by quarterback Greg Vassar enabled the halfback Wesley Garnett to follow an excellent block by Lloyd Weston to score from twenty yards out. It was enough as the Bulldogs upset a tough New Castle team 6-0 before a stunned partisan crowd.

191

The following week it was a trip to Charleroi, PA to do battle with the Cougars, another tough WPIAL opponent. Westinghouse did themselves proud coming away with a 19-7 win on the road. Finding WPIAL opponents to play was getting to be a little scarce as the Bulldogs' reputation for handling some of the WPIAL powerhouses was discouraging many schedulers to avoid playing Westinghouse. They were beginning to realize that playing the Bulldogs for a pre-season game was more than an exhibition. It was an opportunity for Westinghouse to gain respect for the City of Pittsburgh.

Finally, Steubenville Central Catholic High School of Ohio, a nationally ranked football team, agreed to put the Bulldogs to the test. The trip down to Steubenville, Ohio must have given the House some incentive of being the road warriors eager to show the folks in a packed stadium its awesome antiquated single wing attack. After giving up an early touchdown to its worthy opponent, the Bulldogs methodically opened up its offense of speed and deception and by halftime led the Crusaders 22-6. The second half saw Wesley Garnett showing why he was regarded as the best running back in Western Pennsylvania as he scored twice on electrifying dashes to the end zone. The Bulldogs left the folks in Steubenville shaking their heads as they defeated the Crusaders 34-6.

This was the second consecutive season that Westinghouse had won all three of their pre-season games against non-city opponents. Dimperio had to be quite proud as the undefeated streak had reached eighteen games in a row. The City League schedule was next as Westinghouse was ready to defend its title that it had held since 1963. They opened up league play with a rain soaked 40-0 win over South High. The next four games saw the Bulldogs winning over Allderdice 47-7, South Hills 27-0, Schenley 46-7 and 42-12 over Peabody in the season finale. They were the Section 1 champions with little Gladstone High School capturing the Section 2 crown. The Gladstone faithful expressed a no fear statement to Westinghouse, but it was just a weak statement. The Bulldogs rolled over the smaller Gladiators in the City Title game at South Stadium 41-7 before an estimated crowd of 7500. Westinghouse led at halftime 20-0 as the game Gladstone team gave it their best effort. The second half saw the Bulldogs put two more touchdowns and a safety on the scoreboard before Dimperio pulled all his starters. Both teams scored in the fourth quarter and when the gun sounded ending the game it was Westinghouse 41, Langley 7. The Bulldogs captured another city title (number twenty-seven) and extended their undefeated streak to 25 games.

192

The championship game summary:
Score by quarters:

| | | | | | |
|---|---|---|---|---|---|
| Westinghouse | 6 | 14 | 9 | 12 | 41 |
| Langley | 0 | 0 | 0 | 6 | 7 |

Scoring:
Westinghouse – Garnett 33, run; pat (run failed)
  " Whitted 5, run; pat (Conley run)
  " Conley 5, run; pat (Whitted run)
  " Safety, L. Weston blocked punt
  " Garnett, 23, run; pat (Conley run)
  " Garnett, 17, pass from Whitted; pat run failed
  " W. Anderson, 1, run (run failed)
Gladstone – Adams, 8, pass from Hopkins (Adams pass to Lewis)

Wesley Garnett played his final game for Westinghouse and ended his senior year having scored the most touchdowns in a season with twenty-five. This was a school record as he surpassed Eugene McClellan who had scored eighteen during his final season. It was a banner year for Garnett – All-City MVP and PA All-State. Also making the All-City team were seniors Dave Weston, Eugene Harrison, Earnie Whitted and junior Lloyd Weston (brother of Dave). Eugene Harrison and Ernie

Whitted received scholarships to North Carolina A & T University and Bethany College respectively.

The 1965 Season (9-0-0)
Pre-Season (WPIAL)

| WHS | 6 | New Castle | 0 |
|---|---|---|---|
| " | 19 | Charleroi | 0 |
| " | 34 | Steubenville, Ohio | 6 |

City League

| WHS | 40 | South | 0 |
|---|---|---|---|
| " | 41 | Allderdice | 7 |
| " | 27 | South Hills | 0 |
| " | 46 | Schenley | 7 |
| " | 42 | Peabody | 12 |

City Championship

| WHS | 41 | Gladstone | 7 |
|---|---|---|---|

The 1965 Squad:
W. Garnett, L. Weston, D. Weston, R. Fields, H. Conley, G. Vassar,L. Jones, E. Harrison, M. Ellison, W. Dudley, E. Whitted, A. Anderson, R. Hurt, L. Burns, D. Murray, C. Austin, G. Sweeney, E. Allen, D. Vassar, B. Gaines, W. Anderson, W. Lipscomb, R. Bogus, T. Webb, H. Mosley, S. Jones, M. Weston, K. Taylor, J. Chavis, R. Huntley, J. Ross, T. Miller, P. Hopson, R. Allerial, Managers – E. Hayman, W. Jordan.

**193**

This was the first time in the history of Westinghouse High School that the Bulldogs put two back-to-back undefeated football seasons (1964 and 1965). Also, the longest winning streak was now at twenty-four games

## 1966 – Dimperio's Grand Finale

Twenty years had passed as coach Pete Dimperio was now looking at his twenty-first and final year as head football coach at Westinghouse High school. They were years that many of us alumni will never forget as he had done so much to maintain our proud tradition. He went beyond in his efforts to teach all his boys to become proud, respectable citizens. I am one of those boys who will never forget the time he took to help me when I sought out his counsel. Yes, the values that Dimperio taught us about life will always remain in the hearts of those of us who appreciated him.

When he informed the school board of his plans to retire, they were shocked. He was ready to call an end to his teaching career, but the school board was not ready to see him go. He was going to be missed greatly by the student body of Westinghouse as he was leaving a huge pair of shoes to fill.

The 1966 season was a lot different than the 1946 season when he first took over for "Pro" Burton. In 1946, he was not welcomed with open arms, but twenty-one years later it was very different as nobody wanted to see him retire. He gave Westinghouse

MEMORIES OF A FOREGONE ERA

High School so much to be proud of as he was every bit a legend as was his predecessor "Pro" Burton.

The 1966 pre-season had only two games scheduled for the Bulldogs as nobody from the WPIAL wanted to challenge the City Champions who were riding a twenty-four game winning streak. The season opener was at New Castle where the Hurricanes were seeking revenge for three losses in a row to the Bulldogs dating back to the 1963 season.

Westinghouse had two key running backs – speedsters Louis Morgan and Sonny Allen who were both injured in pre-season scrimmage and would not be ready to play for several weeks. This really hurt the Bulldogs chances of staying undefeated. Dimperio would have to rely on fullback Mike Weston, halfbacks Terry Webb and Joel Chavis with Larry Burns at quarterback to carry the load. The Bulldog line was pretty well set with All-City Lloyd Weston anchoring a group of 200 pound veterans – Mark Ellison, Willie Dudley, Wayman Chatman and Jerome Ross. Junior Dorian Vassar (younger brother of the late Bill Vassar) was the center flanked by starting ends Bill Gaines and Reg Balleriel.

There were just under ten thousand fans that turned out at New Castle Stadium to see the team from Pittsburgh with the twenty-four game winning streak. The Bulldogs struck first by going to the airwaves on a touchdown pass from Terry Webb to Reg Balleriel for an early 7-0 lead. This lead was short lived as the Hurricanes struck with three touchdowns and took a 21-7 lead at halftime. This was the first time that a Westinghouse team was so far behind in a game since the 1960 season. Whatever Dimperio said to the boys at halftime must have lit a fire as the Bulldogs came roaring back and regained the lead 25-21 with some fine all around play. It was a lead that they held onto until the determined Hurricanes came back to score on a late touchdown pass to end the Westinghouse winning streak 27-25. It was a fine effort by the Bulldogs, but they sorely missed the services of running backs Lou Morgan and Sonny Allen.

The following week it was another road game, this time in Warren, Ohio just over the Pennsylvania line to meet Warren Harding High School. This game had some pre-game hype as the Warren news media had some impressive articles covering the much respected Westinghouse tradition. The coverage sure reached most of the town folks as well over fifteen thousand fans packed the Harding Stadium to see the Bulldogs battle the hometown boys. It was probably one of the largest crowds to watch Westinghouse play. One of my cousins, a Westinghouse grad living in Warren, attended the game with several of her neighbors, remembered how proud she was of the Bulldogs performance.

Without Morgan and Allen the Bulldogs offense was not clicking on all cylinders. The defense was determined, but were on the field most of game as Harding defeated the Bulldogs 12-0. The Harding fans gave Lloyd Weston a standing ovation when Dimperio took him out of the game with only a couple minutes to play. His name was called out repeatedly as the Bulldogs captain was making plays all over the field. Too bad Morgan and Allen could not play because the offense sorely missed them. Since 1961, the Bulldogs had not lost two games in a row, but nonetheless there was much to be proud of. The fans from both New Castle and Harding appreciated the valiant

194

*Burton • Dimperio • Musilin • Malins • Webb*

effort that the Westinghouse Bulldogs displayed. Since there were only two pre-season games the Bulldogs had a week off before the City League opener. This would give Morgan and Allen another week to get healthy.

Once the City League got underway, the Bulldogs were completely healthy as they marched through the next five opponents. The return of Morgan and Allen had the offense clicking on all cylinders as the Bulldogs mixed in a little bit of a passing attack to support its vaulted running game. To see the single wing in action with a good passing attack supporting the run was a thing of beauty as the Bulldogs won the Section 1 crown with wins over Allderdice 35-14, South Hills 47-7, Schenley 40-0, Peabody 40-14 and South 32-0. The Section 2 winner Gladstone was ready to challenge Westinghouse for the second year in a row. Chuck Adams was the big fullback leading the way for the Gladiators, but the Bulldogs limited him to 30 yards on sixteen carries in the City Championship game. Westinghouse defeated Gladstone in typical Bulldog fashion with a ball-control offense 27-0. It was the last game that Dimperio would coach at Westinghouse. He ended his career with an impressive run of twenty-one years without a losing season that consisted of seventeen City Champions and an overall record of 151-29-5 for a winning percentage of 0.839.

The championship game summary:
Score by quarters

| | | | | | |
|---|---|---|---|---|---|
| Westinghouse | 13 | 7 | 7 | 0 | 27 |
| Gladstone | 0 | 0 | 0 | 0 | 0 |

**195**

Scoring:

| | |
|---|---|
| Westinghouse | M. Weston 6yd run (run failed) 6-0 |
| " | L. Morgan 4yd run (E. Allen run) 13-0 |
| " | T. Webb 70 yd. run (M. Weston run) 20-0 |

Parade High School All-American honors went to Lloyd Weston along with All-State and All-City awards. The University of Pittsburgh offered him a full athletic scholarship that he accepted. It was one of several scholarships that Weston was offered as he decided to stay close to home. Mark Ellison, Willie Gaines and Dorian Vassar were also chosen to the All-City team along with honorable mention awards going to Mike Weston, Louis Morgan and Willie Dudley. Mark Ellison accepted a scholarship to Dayton University and later he was drafted by the New York Giants and became a starting offensive guard. Waymon Chatman was awarded a scholarship to Tuskegee Institute.

The 1966 Season (6-2-0)
Pre-Season (WPIAL)

| | | | |
|---|---|---|---|
| WHS | 25 | New Castle | 27 |
| " | 0 | Warren Harding | 12 |

City League

| | | | |
|---|---|---|---|
| WHS | 35 | Allderdice | 14 |
| " | 47 | South Hills | 7 |

| " | 40 | Schenley | 0 |
|---|----|----------|---|
| " | 40 | Peabody | 14 |
| " | 32 | South | 0 |
| City Championship | | | |
| WHS | 27 | Gladstone | 0 |

The 1966 Squad
L. Weston, M. Weston, B. Gaines, M. Ellison, W. Dudley, R. Ballariel, J. Chavis, A. Simpson, D. Vassar, T. Webb, L. Morgan, A. Turk, W. Chatman, P. Hopson, E. Livingston, J. Miller, L. Burns, K. Taylor, R. Bogus, E. Allen. L. Portis, J. Ross, R. Utley, W. Anderson,G. Williams. J. Turner, L. Dudley, R. Morris, Lance Carter, H. Dorsey, R. Huntley, Terry Young, H. Mosbey, J. Warner, C. Roberson.
Managers: D. Shelton, Curtin Ezell

And so the coaching career of Pete Dimperio came to an end, but not without the most memorable years that Westinghouse High School alumni will always cherish. I arrived at the Homewood school in September of 1948 as a bewildered 12 year old seventh grader and left in June of 1954, a graduating senior with confidence and a winning attitude. A student relationship with Coach Pete Dimperio was priceless. It will always remain in my heart as he showed us how to prepare for life's journey with aspiring determination. Athlete or non-athlete, Pete was always there to help and support.

**196**

## 1960 CITY CHAMPIONS

PITTSBURGH POST-GAZETTE: THURSDAY, NOV. 10, 1960

## Westinghouse Bulldogs Ready for Allegheny in City Title Clash

DEFENDING CHAMPS—This tough football aggregation from Westinghouse will put its city title on the line tonight against Allegheny High. The Westinghouse linemen (left to right) are J. D. McCoy, R. Fields, C. Harris, J. W. Hancock, J. Ramsey, T. Harris and E. Buford. The backs (left to right) are Art Williams, E. Golden, J. Williams, M. Myricks and A. Allsbury. The Bulldogs are undefeated this year in city play and lost one and tied one in exhibition games. Bulldogs will be shooting for thirteenth championship in 16 seasons.

197

198

*Burton • Dimperio • Musilin • Malins • Webb*

# Westinghouse Champ--Again

## Bulldogs Rip Langley—8th Straight Title

### By PAUL A. KURTZ

Never has a Pete Dimperio-coached Westinghouse High football team been defeated in City League championship play.

The husky, all-time Thiel College lineman had his amazing record continued last night by his Homewood "Owls" who struck swiftly and impressively with powerful single-wing operations to defeat the jittery Langley Mustangs of Sheraden, 27-7, at South High Stadium.

The biggest throng, 9200 fans (not including 600 along overhanging McArdle Boulevard) in City League title history saw another Sec. 2 titlist battered down by the Bulldogs' superbly-executed trap plays and effective passing.

Westinghouse won the City loop honor for the eighth consecutive time since Dimperio became the Bulldogs' pilot in 1946. Section 2 hasn't had a City title-winner since Carrick won in 1952 by defeating Peabody.

Westinghouse played at the grassless South Field under ideal grid weather last night, with a burning determination to keep Dimperio's record unblemished.

The Homewooders struck swiftly with two TD's before the first half of the opening quarter had passed.

Jim Harkins' Sheradenites avoided a shutout by tallying on a 40-yard pass play in the final minute against Westinghouse reserves.

Langley suffered deeply from the unusually poor punting by its 6-4, 275-pound right tackle, Pat Buratti. His kicking average was poor and the Mustangs felt this drastically along with the pulverizing line smashes and aerial flings of the Homewooders.

**WESTINGHOUSE HIGH'S** George Webb lands with a bang in Langley's end zone after driving five yards for Bulldog TD in third period at South Stadium. Players up front are Dick Rutkowski (40) and Bob Minech (88) of Langley and McKinley Broadus (46) of Westinghouse. Bulldogs won handily, 27-7, for eighth straight City League championship.

## City Summary

**WESTINGHOUSE**
Ends: McClellan, Goodson, Blanton, Broadus, Loar.
Tackles: C. Harris, Malone, Bush, Hardy, G. Harris, Hayes.
Guards: Davis, Harrison, Biscegia.
Center: Young, Buford.
Backs: Henderson, Myricks, Brewer, Webb, Avent, Berry, Counahan, Slaughter, Carter.

**LANGLEY**
Ends: Clark, Williams, Hearp, Hayes.
Tackles: Minech, Buratti, Wagner, Moore.
Guards: Gillespie, Roth, Reitmeyer, Madia, Locke.
Center: Reed.
Backs: Betts, Smith, Rutkowski, Burnett, Warren, Becker.

| | | | | |
|---|---|---|---|---|
| Westinghouse | 14 | 7 | 6 | 0—27 |
| Langley | 0 | 0 | 0 | 7— 7 |

Westinghouse scoring: Touchdowns — Myricks (15, run); Brewer 2 (42 and 33, run); Webb (5, run).
Points after touchdown — Webb 3 (runs). Missed point—Broadus (pass).
Langley scoring: Touchdowns — Williams (5, run). Point after touchdown—Becker (run).

**PETE DIMPERIO** (left), Westinghouse's winning coach, and Langley Coach Jim Harkins shake after well-played game. In center is Langley's standout quarterback, Booker Betts.

200

### 25 Game Winning Streak

### 1964 Undefeated City Champions

These are the Westinghouse Bulldogs for 1964. From left, front row: W. Gaines, E. Tipton, W. Dudley, M. Ellison, R. Boggus, P. Britton, R. Ballariel, L. Burns, D. Vasser; second row: E. Boyd, F. Jackson, D. Weston, D. Jones, L. Jones, S. Henderson, J. King, W. Lipscomb, D. Murray, E. Whitted, W. Jordan; third row: Assistant Coach Rudy Musulin, A. Anderson, H. Walker, G. Vasser, R. Buford, R. Edwards, H. Conley, C. Alston, H. Mosley, O. Gaines, Head Coach Pete Dimperio; top row: W. Garnett, E. Harrison, L. Weston, R. Villani, P. Harris, B. Allen, O. Richburg, W. Givner, E. Henderson, R. Field, W. Williams, R. Hill, P. Gilmore. They're seeking their 26th City title.

201

### 1965 Undefeated City Champions

*Westinghouse's Bulldogs (from left) on line: Eugene Harrison, Lloyd Weston, Marshall Ellison, Cyphus Alston, Dorian Vasser, Richard Fields, Dave Weston, Lloyd Jones; backfield: Wesley Garnett, Gregory Vasser, Hawthorne Conley, Wade Lipscomb, Ernest Whitted, Donald Murray. They seek 24th City title.*

## Langley Beaten In Playoff, 45-6

# Westinghouse Still King

### Bulldogs Roll In City Playoff

**By PAUL A. KURTZ**

Blinding speed and aggressive line play, a hallmark of Westinghouse High's winning formula, paid off again as the Bulldogs trimmed the Langley High Mustangs, 45-6, before 5000 fans in the South High Stadium yesterday.

Long runs and pass interceptions enabled Pete Dimperio's Sec. 1 champs to retain the Pittsburgh Public School League championship.

Westinghouse scored three touchdowns in the opening quarter.

On the game's third play, Mike Rosso's pass intended for End David Jones was picked off by Westinghouse's defensive end, Lloyd Jones, who was thrown on the Langley 29.

Three plays later, the Homewooders had their first touchdown, Willie Givner going over from the six. Wesley Garnett ran for the seventh point.

Midway in this quarter, Orin Richburg, fleet left half, intercepted a Rosso "look-in" pass and sprinted 60 yards. He missed the point.

With one minute left in the opening period, Quarterback Eric Henderson, a sparkler all season, broke through Langley defensemen and past Richard Jericho for a 60-yard touchdown run. Garnett ran for the 20th point.

Garnett, also a fast-moving right half, scored his first of three straight touchdowns on a 73-yard run at left end behind terrific blocking by Eric Henderson. Givner made it 27-0 on a plunge.

A few minutes later, Eric Henderson intercepted a Rosso pass at the Westinghouse 36. On the third play, Garnett sped around left end again on a 55-yard touchdown jaunt.

The half ended with Westinghouse leading, 39-0, on a 52-yard over-all pass play, Henderson to Garnett.

Henderson ran 40 yards for the Bulldogs' only score in the second half.

Langley was outmaneuvered and overcome by the consistent Westinghouse attack and the Bulldogs' alertness in snaring four of eight passes. The Bulldogs completed four of six

ON 60-YARD TOUCHDOWN RUN—Eric Henderson of Westinghouse eludes Langley High tackler in first quarter and heads for the goal. Westinghouse retained its City League championship yesterday by defeating Langley, 45-6.

Orin Richburg of Westinghouse takes punt and returns it 25 yards.

Pg. 6 Sec. 4—The Pittsburgh Press, Sunday, Nov. 14, 1965

Wesley Garnett of Westinghouse gains seven yards against Gladstone. Garnett scored three TDs as Bulldogs won City title, 41-7.

203

## 1966 – Coach Pete Dimperio's Final Season at Westinghouse

204

—Post-Gazette Photo

*Coach Pete Dimperio (right) and Assistant Rudy Musulin (left) put their hopes in Westinghouse High lettermen: Front (from left)—Dorian Vasser, Sonny Allen. Back — Marc Ellison, Willie Dudley, Lloyd Weston, William Gaines. Bulldogs, carrying 25-game win streak, open 1966 season at New Castle High Friday night.*

**FINE RUNNING JOB** was turned in by End Terry Webb in second quarter of Westinghouse's 27-0 victory over Gladstone when he raced 70 yards for the Bulldogs' third touchdown. Coach Pete Dimperio gives him instructions before sending him on field.

**ON TOP AGAIN** is Westinghouse High's Coach, P Paul Dimperio, as his team boosts him on shoul after capturing City League title for the 16th tim last 20 years. The win was the 14th crown for C perio in 18 years at the Homewood school.

205

206

1966 WESTINGHOUSE HIGH SCHOOL PITTSBURGH CITY FOOTBALL CHAMPIONS

*1st Row:* W. Anderson, G. Williams, J. Turner, L. Budley, R. Morris, L. Carter, H. Dorsey, R. Huntley, T. Younge, H. Mosbey, J. Warner, C. Roberson. *2nd Row:* P. Demperio, H. Ezell, R. Shelton, P. Hopson, W. Chatman, E. Livingston, J. Miller, L. Burns, K. Taylor, R. Bogus, L. Portis, E. Allen, J. Ross, R. Utley, R. Muslin. *2nd Row:* W. Dudley, M. Ellison, L. Weston, M. Weston, W. Gines, D. Vassar, A. Simpson, J. Chavis, R. Ballariel, T. Webb, L. Morgan, A. Turk

*Burton • Dimperio • Musilin • Malins • Webb*

# Football Coach Tired of Winning

## Pete Piloted Bulldogs to 17 City Titles in 21 Campaigns

The Merlin of Murtland Street is hanging up his whistle.

Pete Dimperio, one of the nation's most successful football coaches—and before that a very successful basketball coach—admitted last night that he had sent letters asking a change of assignment to Board of Education officials.

"I feel that I have been coaching long enough," he told the Post-Gazette.

"I want to stay in the teaching profession, perhaps in physical education, and I hope to get another assignment from the Board."

Dimperio, in 21 seasons at Westinghouse, won 17 City League titles, and won 118 City League games while losing five and tying one. Against WPIAL Class AA teams he compiled a 40-21-1 record.

And before transferring to Westinghouse in 1946, his basketball teams at Herron Hill Junior High School compiled a 203-7 record in 12 years.

His resignation from coaching chores was not entirely unexpected. Only recently he had remarked:

"I'm tired of winning."

Reading between the lines, he probably meant that he felt he had coached long enough and wished to get into another educational field not quite so demanding, both physically and psychologically, as that of a football mentor.

"I would like to continue in physical education, but in letters to Ted Abel (director of health and physical education in the city schools) and to Bernard McCormick (deputy superintendent of schools) I told them that I thought this past season was my last as a football coach," he said.

Abel, who had just returned from a business trip, said he had not received Dimperio's letter, but said:

"It would be a darned shame if he did quit coaching.

"He has done so much for those young people at Westinghouse High School, not only those who were on his football squad, but for many others.

**PETE DIMPERIO**
*Through with coaching?*

He set a fine example for the boys out there, and showed them that through hard work they could attain almost any goal."

McCormick, a long-time personal friend of Dimperio, said the two had talked about the possibility of getting a change in assignment from coaching to some other field.

"We discussed various possibilities for the future," McCormick said. "Nothing definite has been decided.

"He just said that he'd prefer not to coach any longer, and wanted an assignment of a different nature."

Then he added: "He had a tremendous way with boys. We hate to see him leave the coaching field."

Dimperio, who captained Fifth Avenue High School's football team in 1924 and Thiel College's gridders in 1929, was also well-known as a humorous after-dinner speaker. Some of his anecdotes on methods of winning football and basketball games have been widely repeated.

While at Thiel, he was named to the Tri-State All-Star team as a tackle four seasons—1926-1929. He received his Masters Degree in education at Springfield College in 1932. He also took courses in administration at Pitt.

In recent years he has been conducting a "Coach of the year" football clinic here in Pittsburgh.

"I will continue with that, whether I coach any more or not," he said last inght.

That clinic has the largest attendance of any similar coaching clinic in the United States.

Over the years he has sent more than 200 of his football players on to colleges and universities on athletic scholarships.

And over the years his work at Westinghouse has received both national and local recognition.

He won the Dapper Dan Award for coach in 1964, and possibly could have won it year after year, but winners are not allowed to repeat. He has been honored as "Man of the Year" in sports in Pittsburgh, has been inducted into the Pennsylvania Sports Hall of Fame, has won the B'nai B'rith Service Award, and has been namd Coach of the Year in Prep National magazine.

His work with youngsters has been outstanding. Among other things, he always insisted that a part of every boy's athletic equipment should be a Holy Bible.

"I have had but one football player who remained on the squad through his high school career who ever got into serious trouble," Dimperio said recently. And many of his boys come from an underprivleged area.

Dimperio went to Westinghouse in 1946. The Bulldogs had won City League titles the two previous seasons. They won four straight for Pete before being tripped by Schenley in 1950.

The Bulldogs won again in 1951, Carrick and Peabody won the next two seasons, but in 1954 Dimperio inaugurated a string of eight consecutive titles.

Peabody broke in to take the 1962 title, but Westinghouse won the next four, including the 1966 crown.

Dimperio looked for a lean year for his Bulldogs last September. Westinghouse had a 25-game winning streak going when the season opened. New Castle snapped it, 27-25, and then Warren (O.) Harding beat the Bulldogs, 12-0.

They came on strong after that, winning the rest of their games and the city title.

That wasn't Pete's biggest string, however. In 1962, Westinghouse had a 52-game winning streak broken by the margin of one first down!

The Bulldogs met Peabody in the City League title game. The game ended in a tie, and the title was decided by first downs—8-7 for Peabody!

Many coaches—most of them, for that matter—scoff at the single wing style of play these days. Dimperio liked it, mixed in a lot of ball-handling wizardry with it, and made most opposing "T-formations," "Slots," "I's" and others look a little bit foolish trying to match it.

Down through the years his teams averaged 33 points per game, and allowed opponents an average of just six.

Who'll succeed him?

"That I couldn't tell you. Rudy Musilin has been my assistant. Whether he will get the job is something only the Board of Education can answer," Pete said.

The Board will not be considering a successor at least not in the immediate future.

207

208

*The Press Box*

11-27-66

# Pete's Tired Of Winning After 21 Years

By ROY McHUGH

As the football coach at Westinghouse High School walked down the hall, a passing student called out, "Beat Gladstone, Pete."

It stopped Pete Dimperio in his tracks.

"Beat Gladstone?" he said. "We beat Gladstone four days ago."

"Did we?" the student answered. "I missed it, Pete."

Winning playoff games for the City championship is routine business at Westinghouse. With 17 titles in 21 years, even Dimperio seems jaded. There are whispers that No. 17 will be his last.

"If Pete quits coaching," he says, not denying them, "it will be because of winning too much. I'm tired of it, and that's a different switch. We're expected to win, and we win. Just like dinner is served and you're not too hungry but it's dinner time, so you eat. When you're through, why, you've done your job."

Championship games or regular-season games, Westinghouse has lost only five times to City opponents since Pete started coaching there.

"If they didn't see us lose in 1950, 1952, 1953 or 1962, they've never seen us lose," he says. "And all the scores were like 7-6 or 13-12—nothing where a coach could say, "Boy, did we give it to Westinghouse!"

Once a big, rough fullback who played for Thiel College when a Thiel or a Geneva or a Washington & Jefferson could recruit a handful of talent and take on all comers, Dimperio never went modern.

At Westinghouse, the football program is stripped down to the essentials—no scouting reports or game films or assistant coaches with head phones running up and down in front of the bench. Just Pete and his one assistant and their single-wing offense on the skinned-dirt field that changes with the weather from a swamp to a dust bowl.

## Romping Through Green Pastures

Westinghouse schedules the big Double-A schools, always away from home. "And when the kids see grass," Dimperio, "they wonder what it is. They jump all over say, "Look, Pete—what's this?""

Lately the Double-A schools have shown little intere: playing Westinghouse.

"They figure this way: If they play us three tim they're going to lose twice," Dimperio reasons.

"New Castle beat us, 27-25, one of the biggest school the state, and 10,000 people went wild. I was happy the cr was so thrilled. We went to Warren, O., and they put up si 'See nationally-known Westinghouse and their famous co They had 17,000 people there and they beat us by 12 p and I told the kids to feel honored. I said, 'Look what we for their morale'."

Pete lacked the one extra running back to make this ye team quite as good as his best, but win or lose, the deep, voice rumbled on.

"We never had the ball, we didn't have the offense keep it, and what a terrible beating the kids took," l says. "I never had a team that played so hard.

"Lloyd Weston was so exhausted after the Warren g he passed out completely in the dressing room. He was over the field that night; the writers in Warren called the greatest high school player they ever saw. And after L came to, what do you think he said? He said, 'Pete, c let you down?'"

## A Garden In Rocky Soil

Lloyd Weston was a product of Dimperio's caste sys Starting out as a rookie, a Westinghouse player is not allc to smile. He must earn that privilege on the field. The year players, until they prove themselves, must walk a side the locker-room walls— never in the middle of the floor.

"The Board of Education frowns on these things," says Pete, "but tell them, 'That's life itself.' You have to learn to crawl before you walk. That's why I'm against Little Leagues. If you plant a seed, you have to watch it and water it and cover it up at night. Then the flower grows.

"In the Little Leagues, they want the flower to grow in a week, but that flower is going to die. Before they're 12 years old, those kids are in full bloom. They go to Mexico to play, and to Florida. They've had all the joys they haven't earned."

At Westinghouse, nothing is unearned.

"We haven't had a banquet in 21 years," says Pete feel it's not normal. When the kids ask, 'Why don't we h a banquet?' I tell them, 'Your banquet is on the field. We you rather eat or have victory?'"

They'd rather have victory and so would Pete, but ea is enough.

# 7 | A TESTIMONY TO PETE DIMPERIO

*TESTIMONIAL  OF  PETE  DIMPERIO*

*TOASTMASTER: HONORABLE  RUGGERIO  ALDISERT*

*COURT  REPORTER:  ANGELO  ALIBERTI*

*PITTSBURGH  HILTON*

*JUNE 4, 1967*

**PETE DIMPERIO**
*Testimonial Dinner Dance*
June 4, 1967
**Pittsburgh Hilton**

**PROGRAM**

INTRODUCTION                                    Dr. Phillip Antonucci

INVOCATION                                      Dean H. N. R. Moor

TOASTMASTER                                     Judge Ruggero Aldisert

**GUESTS OF HONOR**

T. F. (Ted) Abel                    Director of Physical Education, Pittsburgh

Stan Berkman                        Superintendent of Schools, Baltimore, Ohio

Joseph DeFebo                       Coach, Western Reserve University

Carl DePasqua                       Coach, Waynesburg College

Frank DeLeo                         Westinghouse Players Representative

Dave Hart                           Coach, University of Pittsburgh

Tut Melman                          Pennsylvania Sports Hall of Fame

Bernard McCormick       Deputy Superintendent of Schools, Pittsburgh, PA

Harry Singer                        Principal, Westinghouse High School

Nick Skorich                        Assistant Coach, Cleveland Browns

Pie Traynor                         Baseball Hall of Fame

PRESENTATION OF AWARD                           Edward C. Caye

BENEDICTION                         Reverend Charles Ceradini

**COMMITTEE**

Dr. Phillip E. Antonucci, Chairman

Edward J. Caye, Co-Chairman

| | |
|---|---|
| Felix Cutruzzula | Eugene Massaro |
| Chippy DeStout | Rudy Musulin |
| Dave Edgar | Joe Snodgrass |
| Lou Ferragonio | Chuck Tedesco |
| John Foley | Tom Tipe |
| Owen Gormley | Richard Thornton |
| Bill Gormley | John Tumas |
| Frank Guadagnino | Chuck White |
| Frank Gustine | |

## PETE DIMPERIO

Perhaps the easiest and best way of writing a brief biography of Pete would be to take a resume of one of Horatio Alger's success stories and call the hero PETE DIMPERIO; give it the title "BOUND to WIN." Rather than risk the charge of plagiarism we will tell of the real PETE DIMPERIO whose accomplishments are not the figment of the imagination of some author.

Strange as it may seem the successful career of PETE was predicted in the year book of his graduating class at Fifth Avenue High School where Pete was a star in football. The class prophet saw him as a second Knute Rockne. Certainly this has been fulfilled to the fullest extent.

After a year of prep at California Normal where he starred on the greatest of California's football teams, he matriculated at Thiel College. At this school Pete was an outstanding lineman. He was captain of the team and was selected as an All-American on the Small Colleges All-Star Team. His graduate work was done at Springfield College where he received his Masters Degree. Further graduate work was done in administration at the University of Pittsburgh.

The scene of his boyhood was the beginning of his long and successful coaching career. Pete managed and coached independent teams in Hazelwood. During the summer vacation months he conducted very interesting programs on the playgrounds of that district. It was during these sessions that he observed the potential of many local boys that he sent on to college for higher education. Pete's first school assignment was as physical education teacher and basketball coach at Herron Hill Junior High School. His success in the roundball sport was phenomenal. At Herron Hill he won 178 games and lost only 9. When a football coach was needed at Westinghouse High School, Pete was the first choice. His career at Westinghouse has surpassed all expectations and he leaves behind a career that will go down in annals as unequaled for all time. He has an overall record of 151 wins, 29 losses and 5 ties. In City League play he has won 116 games, lost only 5 and tied 3. He has won 17 Pittsburgh City League Championships in 21years.

211

From such fantastic physical achievements it was evident that they would be reflected in the personal lives of the players and their coach. Hundreds of his players were given college scholarships. Today, we find many of his boys as successful men in the professional and business world. They took advantage of the opportunities given to them by their coach. Pete gained fame and renown from his success and it opened up a new field to him, namely as an after dinner speaker. He has appeared at Michigan State, Philadelphia Sportswriters Banquet, Atlantic City National Clinic, University of Pittsburgh and many others. At the present time he is clinic manager of the Eastman Kodak Coach of the Year Clinic. This clinic enjoys the largest attendance of all the national clinics. In addition, we might list some honors as Junior Chamber of Commerce "Man of the Year" in Sports, Dapper Dan Award, National Prep Magazine Coach of the Year in 1954, B'nai Brith Service Award and induction into the Pennsylvania Sports Hall of Fame in 1964.

Though Pete has retired from active coaching, may he continue to be active in the field of sports for many years to come.

## INVOCATION: DEAN MOOR

**DR. PHILLIP ANTONUCCI:** Good evening ladies and gentlemen. I'd like to present your Toastmaster for tonight. He is the National President of the Italian Sons and Daughters of America. He was honored by the proud lawyers of Allegheny County as the "Man in Law." He has lectured on law and medicine in Rome and London. He is a man well known internationally and a lecturer and author. He is a professor of Law at the University of Pittsburgh. Presently, he is a distinguished Judge of Common Pleas Court, and a very good friend of Pete Dimperio. I give you his honor, Judge Ruggerio Aldisert.

**JUDGE ALDISERT:** Thank you very much Dr. Antonucci. Dean Moor, Father Ceradini, distinguished guests in the audience, the family of our guest of honor, and your guest of honor, Pete Dimperio.

First, I want to say that my functions on this program had much to do with my position on the dais. You notice I have been placed next to Dave Hart, the new football coach at Pitt. And he is seated midway between our Guest of Honor, with that great record at Westinghouse, and Carl DePasqua, and Dave Hart is hoping that this will rub off on him tonight.

You know, someone said this is sort of a farewell banquet on the occasion of Pete Dimperio's retirement. Well, I have news for you, from what I have heard from the people coming up to the dais and what he has said to them, he is going to be busier now than he has ever been in his life. He is full of plans for the future. When we think of retirement, it is someone who was wished well on a new journey, and they tell the story about when Pete first broke into the coaching ranks. He was given that chance to see if he had this spirit of charity, and see whether the charity was in his soul. And they gave him a hundred dollars for his first coaching job. And he went out into the street and saw a disreputable character, his shoes needed polished, his clothes were torn, and his trousers were patched. And Pete gave him the one hundred dollars and said, "God speed my son." And the next day he went out on the street saw the same man. It was the same location, and his shoes were still scuffed and his clothes still torn, and his pants still baggy, and he came up to Pete and said, "Here's your 1,100 dollars, God speed came in first and paid 11 to 1."

We are reminded in as much as the namesake of our Guest of Honor is the same as the Honorable, Saint Peter. And one day he received a call in his office of the pearly gates. And he answered the phone and a voice came out and said, "This is Saint Elizabeth, I am waiting to be admitted to heaven." And he said, "Saint Elizabeth, I am filled up right now, call me in a day or two and we'll have room for you. A few days later the phone rang and she said, "I think I'm going to be led astray, for today I smoked my first cigarette." Just remember your tradition, and we'll have room for you in heaven. And Saint Elizabeth relates that on this day she attended a cocktail party and had her first drink. And Saint Peter said, "Have patience, we'll be ready for you in a few days." The next day the phone rang and a voice said, "Forget it, I'm having more fun out here."

Well, Pete, we're here not to forget about it. We're here tonight to join with those, who through the years have been part and partial of your career. Those boys who have played for you and those former friends, those men with whom you have participated in those many years in your athletic endeavor, and those of us who have not had that pleasure, we join with you in this community tribute. It is symbolic that "This Week," and "Time" magazine had an article called, "The Golden Age of Sport." And the article begins with this quotation, that only 13 years ago, after saying himself that there must be some limits on the extent of speed and agility, Brutus Hamilton compiled a list of what we considered to be the ultimate in Track and Field performances. "No one," said Hamilton, "That no one based on long experience would ever run the 100-yard dash in less than 10 seconds." And the article goes on to mention other records that Brutus Hamilton said would never be beaten. And "Time" magazine says that since then, in every case, someone has. Sports records have always been perishable. With you, the spoilage rate is enormous. Athletes have never been so skillful. Competition has never been so tough, and the appetite for sports has never been so insatiable. Well, my friends, tonight, we in Pittsburgh are paying tribute to the greatest spoiler of records in high school competition and in the history of organized athletics in the United States of America.

**213**

*(TREMENDOUS APPLAUSE)*

The man we honor tonight has produced teams that captured 17 City Championships at Westinghouse High School. Of city games, he compiled a record of 116 wins and only 5 losses. And this came after his record at Herron Hill where there was a great record in basketball. And this has been accomplished in this era which has now been called, "The Golden Age of Sport." And for the establishment of this incredible record, Pete should be the subject of athletic tribute and convocation as we have here tonight. But the record of Dimperio is not the bare statistics of successful times. The true measure of success is the personal interest of a lifetime of teaching. For this, there is no measuring boxscore. For this, there is only the personal satisfaction that Pete has in his own heart. The title he cherishes is "The Teacher of Men." And perhaps, after this, we turn to a teacher who can arouse a feeling for one single good action accomplishes more than he who fills our memory with rows and rows of natural form. And the education of Henry Adams tells us that "A teacher affects eternity, he can never tell where his influence stops." For one thing is certain, my friends, the Dimperio saga has touched the lives of all of us. The community of America will always stand in his debt. They will always remember his record. Yes, as a coach, but perhaps more important, the fact that this man sent on to higher education over two hundred men, from what certainly cannot be classed as the best economical district in the City of Pittsburgh. The community honors him tonight. It is not simply the sports community; it is the community of Judges of law, courts, and I see my colleague, the Honorable Ralph Smith. The law of Judges who have the pensions from law and order. It is the community of the social Judges who have seen the values of social sports placed in the formative minds of so many. It is the community of Educators, Clergymen, Businessmen, and Labor Leaders, but most of all the community of mothers and fathers who give shining testimonial that with Dimperio their child received at the Dimperio schools and a bit of Pete's legend would go with them. So that is why we are here tonight. Men and women through all walks of life, representing all phases of the community which you have helped to direct. We are here to pay tribute to you: Their friend, their coach, their teacher. So, on behalf of you Pete, permit me to welcome you to your Testimonial.

**214**

*(GRAND APPLAUSE)*

Sharing the tribute with Pete is his devoted family. Permit me to introduce them to you. Mrs. Pete Dimperio, Pete Dimperio, Jr., and daughter Peggy. And also with us tonight is Pete's brother Mike Dimperio and his sister Rose. Will you please all stand.

*All the men who played with Pete as an athlete and all the boys who played for him stood up and applauded.*

For your first speaker, we have the Director of the section on Physical and Health Education of the Pittsburgh Public Schools. This man has served as teacher and coach of the Health and Education in all phases of the elementary and senior high school level. He is, in addition to his supervisory duties, known to be active in the State and County Associations for the Health and Physical Education and Recreations. Recently, he has been honored by the District Association of this organization. At this time, may I present Theodore F. (better known as Ted) Abel. For a few remarks on behalf of our Guest of Honor, Ted Abel.

**TED ABEL:** Mr. Toastmaster, friends of Pete, good evening. I wonder how many of us can truthfully say, "I'm glad I knew him." Well, I feel that way about the man we are honoring here tonight. He is a leader of men- a tremendous influence on our youth. As a coach, he brought to his boys an expert knowledge of the skills of the game. His principles have been of the highest. He has recognized that coaching is teaching. He insisted on the enforcement of all rules, and he sought no favors for the athletes. He was fair and concerned with his relationship to students. He paid very careful attention to his players at all times and taught them to use only ethical ways to win. He set good examples for his boys to follow. He helped them learn. It is no wonder that these ideals of Pete made such a forceful impact on his students at Westinghouse and Herron Hill.

Pete was always a highly successful coach at Herron Hill. I don't know how many of you remember when he stepped into the coaching spot at Westinghouse. He was left to take over those big shoes to fill. He proved himself right from the start, and has been a winner ever since. Perhaps this is because he taught more than the skill of the game; he built a career. And this desire to excel, many of them are here tonight, he put on the road to higher education. He, as an educator, personally saw to it that deserving boys received scholarships. He contributed to the future of his most promising youngsters. How proud he must be, to know they are fine citizens of their community. It is this coach that we are honoring this evening. The man who has been an inspiration. He is a thoroughbred, the way I feel. A quieter man you will never meet. Among the greats a thoroughbred comes through. And who does it come through most? It is Pete. We are glad that he remains with us as a teacher. It is instilled in the minds of the youth of the Pittsburgh Public Schools, and that is Pete for his honor.

**JUDGE ALDISERT:** Thank you Ted. This committee was making a decision as to whom would come the furthest distance to pay tribute to Pete Dimperio. He, who won this prize, is not in this very room, but he is in the hotel. He is Major Jim Green of the United States Army. He flew all the way from Germany, arriving just 2 hours ago, because he was one of Pete's boys in the class of 1947 at Westinghouse. Let's give a round of applause for Major Jim Green of the United States Army.

The next speaker isn't from Germany, but he is from Ohio. He has the great distinction of having been one of Pete's teammates at Thiel College, and, of course, Stan keeps taking credit for all of his subsequent success. He started his own career at Monaca, and then to Wilkinsburg, and to greener pastures of Ohio. When he was through he turned to the administrative arm of education, having served as Superintendent of the Baltimore, Ohio Public School System. Today, he is at Lafayette pursuing his first love, the educating of young minds. Tonight, however, Stan Berkman is with us and I present him to you.

**STAN BERKMAN:** Thank you your Honor. Present Clergy, friends, our honored guest, Pete, and his family. I feel highly honored this evening that I would be asked to say a few words about my fraternity brother, teammate, and a very good friend since 1926. There are a few things I would like to say, but I feel like a misfit in a nudist colony. I don't know where to begin. When we went to school, times were pretty tough in the late 20's, and it was really a rough road to hoe. Pete, to me, was a fellow who always had the answers. I think in 1928 he made every team we played against, and he wasn't very big. I think the thing that caused him to get through was, never once did he have time out for an injury. And back in those days a small school like Thiel College, we had only 25 to 30 boys on the squad. I could see why Pete turned out to be the finest coach in the United States; he took so many bets then, that he made up his mind to start winning, and he has been doing it ever since. To me, it

215

isn't just the championship teams that made him a wonderful man, but also his regard and concern for others.

I remember he happened to be treasurer of our fraternity one year, and they had a ruling that, if you were a month in arrears in the rent, you had to move out of the fraternity house. This one particular month, I had to give the report, and whose name was first; it was my own. And, of course, when the meeting was over the President said, "Stan, you have to move out." And we thought it was a pretty good fraternity house. In the back lot they had an old 2-story chicken house, and my roommate said we didn't know where the rent was coming from, especially in those days. He said, "Let's take our cots and go to the chicken house." We moved out. It must have hurt Pete, and I don't remember if he was responsible for making this rule or not. He came out and saw what we were putting up with and said, "How dumb can you be. You're the treasurer of the Fraternity; why don't you write out a check." I said, "Write out a check, I don't even know what a check looks like." He told us to write it out and show it to the President, and he'll think the rent is paid up. So, I wrote the check out, and we moved back into the fraternity house.

In 1929 he happened to be the Director of a certain playground, and he called me and said, "Stan, I wish you'd do me a favor." I said, "I'd be glad to." He said, "Our championship team is being awarded trophies, and I'd like you to present them." I said, "all right." I went to Hazelwood, but he didn't tell me that the championship game was being played that evening. I was dumbfounded. If you know Hazelwood, back in those days. I umpired the game and didn't have many friends that night. So, I'm going to stop right now; It's pretty hard to say the things I'd like to say about Pete. I'd like to repay the complement when he said, "Stan, I wish that if I had a son he'd have played under you." Tonight, I wish if I had a son he'd have played under you, because I think you would have taught him to be a good citizen that we are parts of now. Mrs. Berkman and I wish you the best there is to have. "God bless you."

**JUDGE ALDISERT:** To carry on precisely the feeling of Stan Berkman about the desire of a father whose son he taught well, there is a human interest story. A true story associated with our next speaker, because in days past, a father who was ill came to Pete and said, "I am ill, I'm worrying that I will not live much longer. Will you, Pete, take care of my son." His son was named Joseph DeFebo, and Pete saw that this young man received a scholarship at Thiel College. Not only did this boy receive the scholarship and do well at this college, but he went on to become a star of the football team, and later the head coach and also his alma mater's Director. He has acquired an enviable record as a player, and at the present time serves as a football coach at Western Reserve University. Let's welcome Joseph DeFebo.

**JOSEPH DeFEBO:** Your Honor, members of the head table, Pete's family and friends of Pete, It's a real pleasure for me to be here. I'd like to think of Pete as a Dad. He has certainly been more than that to me over the past years. I had an unusual experience a little while ago. Pete and I were talking, and a young lady came by and Pete introduced me to her. The lady asked who I was, and he gave her my name and told her I was a Taylor Allderdice boy, and she said, "What the hell is he doing here."

I remember a story. It was about the way he continued to win. This one day his competitor was giving him a good match on the golf course. And on the 76th hole it was all even. And Pete pared out and said, "I'd give anything to get a birdie out of the next hole." And this little red devil came out of the ground and asked him if he would give up a third of his sex life. And Pete said, "yes, yes." The devil told him to go ahead and hit the ball. Well, sure enough the ball went into the hole. Pete won the match, and on the last hole he asked his competitor what his name was, and he answered, Father O'Connor.

You know Pete for his wonderful humor in football and his well-disciplined teams. We also know him for his well-conditioned teams and his fine winning teams. I am sitting a long way from him. And I am sitting next to Nick Skorich, and maybe a little of his luck will rub off on me. I certainly hope so. I know Pete is making a lot of coaches happy announcing his retirement, because they won't have to face him across the field in the future. One of the finest things that one could say about a football coach is that he has always been willing to help his fellow coaches, and this to me is a legend. I don't know if I have been the very first one that Pete had attend college: I am sure I might have been one of the first. I was on the playground with Pete, and they were some of the most enjoyable years of my life. I know I speak for all of the hundreds of boys who had opportunities as a result of Pete's efforts, when I say this. I am very appreciative, and I am sure that every boy who had this opportunity is appreciative. I'd like to say, and you are all aware of the fact, that Pete is not only a good coach, but a great coach. But more important to me is that he has been a good friend. Congratulations, and the best of luck, health and happiness for you and your entire family.

**217**

**JUDGE ALDISERT:** Thank you Joe. The name of Carl DePasqua is known to all those who have followed football in the Pittsburgh area for the past decade or so. Carl DePasqua is about as Italian as me. And the name Pasqua means Easter. And Easter means the resurrection. It was up to Carl DePasqua to bring about a resurrection of winning football history in the year of 1966. After 10 years at the University of Pittsburgh as an assistant coach, he moved to Waynesburg College and acquired this fantastic record 15 victories and no losses. He became the coach of that team that was given the title of the N.I.A.A. National Champions of the year. His team at Waynesburg College was selected the No.1 team in the United States by the Washington Touchdown Club. Their coach, our friend, Carl DePasqua.

**CARL DePASQUA:** Your Honor, Reverend Clergy, Pete, your lovely family and friends. I kind of feel like luck who has died not too long ago in Green County. And as a result, the preacher went to the dissertation at the funeral. And he went on about his attributes and what a wonderful man he was, and at this time in the audience down in front, his wife turned to his son and said, "Go up there and look in the coffin and see if that's your pa.

I certainly was quite elated when I heard they wanted me to be here this evening to play a small part at Pete's Testimonial Dinner. I was quite thrilled, because I met Pete on the banquet tour many times. He attended the Testimonial they had for me at the Elks Club. I can't help thinking that in the small college level that coaching football was a creative art. I think many educators feel the same way. And they always say that the best taught subject in school is football. And I think this is indicative of Pete. He theorizes what should be done, and then, he puts his theory into practices on the field. And finally, the test comes in the arenas.

We all realize that it is a game of detail and perfection; I think I'd like to bring in Michaelangelo. He once said that little things are trifle, and perfection is no trifle. And to illustrate this further, I'd like to go to a Frenchman and the famous artist in Renoir. And he was noted internationally for his painting of nudes, and it was difficult to obtain such reality. And someone asked him how he achieved it and he said, "I just keep painting and painting until I feel like pinching it." I have been saying it for years, and mind you, he has been telling me this for years. It's fun. This is very true. I think the credentials you have include your predecessors. I have been here 20 years, and I think of the names I can run off, the Ashmans, the Browns, and many many more. I can't recall them all at this time. But I think you are the dean of them all. We know not where our next life will be, but I'm sure that you'll be a thoroughbred there, too.

**JUDGE ALDISERT:** Thank you Carl. Ladies and gentlemen, we have presented to you that group of men who have played football under the Guest of Honor. The committee has selected one of them to represent this group in the speaking program this evening. He is a graduate of Westinghouse High School, class of 1949. He played on Pete's teams in the years 1946,47, and 48. He was chosen the most valuable player of the 1948 team. He received a 4-year scholarship to the University of Pittsburgh. He went on to serve in Korea and is now a Major in the Pennsylvania Air National Guard. He is well known in the insurance business, and a dear friend of all of us, Frank (Chubby) DiLeo.

**218**

**FRANK (CHUBBY) DiLEO:** I stayed up all night to remember this ad-libbed speech. Friends, Pete, Judge, Dean Moor, Father Ceradini, and our manager, Gaddie, wherever you are. (It goes to show you what a $5 bill will do.) Well, I'll tell you, I'm a little nervous. I haven't seen a crowd like this since the Westinghouse — Peabody game. It's an honor to be at the table with Pete; I claim him to be my father, too. I think he's beginning to get a little worried; I'm the 35th guy tonight that claims Pete's his father.

Judge Aldisert, I have been fortunate to know you from the Italian Sons and Daughters. In case you don't know, he is Italian. All I can say for the Judge is, if he ever told you (excuse me girls) to go to hell, you can't wait to get started. He goes down in my books as one of the best—next to Pete. Of course, it's Pete's banquet, that's another story. Father Ceradini, it's no accident that I'm up here tonight; they didn't know anybody else, so I got the job. Not too many of us could afford the $8.50. Father Ceradini has been my Pastor in Brushton since I was born—I guess. But I have learned a lot from him. He has taught me that conscious cannot prevent sin— it only prevents you from enjoying it. I would have to say to Frank Gustine, "It was a privilege meeting you." He is a real gentleman, he keeps his gloves in his glove compartment. The best one I have ever heard is—you have a point here and a point there and a lot of bull in between. This is ad-libbed, of course. I was supposed to be talking about Pete, but everybody else is doing that. Pete often said about coaching at Westinghouse was like running an elevator; you have your ups and downs, but it's the jerks in between that keep you going. He really didn't have much to work with in those days. Of course, I'll have to say we were real lucky fellows. I can still remember the first day he came to Westinghouse. We were 10th graders. I remember the first day he put us through our paces; it was obvious we had a winner. I think it was obvious. How do you get out of this jam? Well we won that year and the year after and the year after. Victory wasn't the only thing with Pete, it wasn't whether you won or lost, just as long as you won. We were a little scarce on brains. I'll never forget the day Pete gave us an oral quiz. He asked how many legs a dog had and Chicarelli said 3, and he was the closest. You don't believe this is ad-libbed? Well, in spite of everything, and all kidding aside, he did produce his share of business and professional men. Engineers and men from all walks of life who came from some meager backgrounds. And if Pete hadn't given us a little knowledge and influence, I don't think we would be here tonight.

There has been a few physical changes in a few of us. Chuck Tedesco used to have beautiful curly hair, but all Chuck can tell us about being bald is that it's always neat. We have another fellow who used to think he was built like a Greek God. He was so well built that it looks like he has doubled it. Pete used to tell us we had to be good students as well as football players. One day after practice he asked us fellows how we liked school, and everyone said, "Closed." We have another fellow here this evening who flew in from New Jersey - Joe Scalzo. Stand up Joe. We haven't seen Joe for many years. He was one of our ends. He was a natural born end. As a matter of fact, when he was born his father said, "This is the end." I don't know how much influence Pete has had on our habits, but John Traficante is hiding over there, and he is still afraid to smoke in front of Pete. Well, again, we are lucky to have had contact with Pete in our lives. In fact, there are more folks here tonight who didn't play for him, and it just proves how much he has influenced many people. I'm going to finish with a little story that I think boils down to the moral. He designed teaching us football, as well as teaching us about life. His ulterior motive was to make good citizens out of us and contribute something to society. Now for the story. It's about a little black boy at a circus. He was watching a man filling up balloons with gas and letting them go up into the air. He filled up a red one and let it go up into the air. He filled up a blue one and let it go up into the air. And finally, as he was filling up a black balloon, the little boy asked the man if the black balloon would go up, too. The man answered, "Boy, it's not the color of the balloon that counts, it's the stuff inside that counts. It's the stuff inside that makes it go up."

**JUDGE ALDISERT:** Thank you "Chubby" DeLeo, insurance and businessman, of Penn Hills. As National President of the Sons and Daughters of America, we have lodges numbering I think about 280 from Long Island to Long Beach to Coral Gables, and for years we had a lodge by the name of Penn Hills Lodge. Lou Cardamone came in one day and said, "We have a new dynamic leader," and I said, "Fine. What's his name?" And he told me Chubby DeLeo. Six months later the name of the lodge was changed from Penn Hills Lodge to DeLeo Lodge. He is a very good friend of mine, and it was a pleasure introducing him.

At this time Leonard Staisey and Tom Forrester were presented and took a bow. Also, Andy McGraw and David B. Roberts, Prothonotary, took a bow.

I have a telegram from Puerto Rico, "Sorry to miss such an event." Neany Campbell, McKeesport.

**219**

I want to say at this time that David Hart, a dynamic man, full of boundless energy was brought to the University of Pittsburgh to rebuild it's football image. He brought to this University the immense desire and capacity to work hard. What did he tell his first squad? We'll work together. And during the first 4 months of his new position, he made over 70 appearances at banquets, dinners, and meetings in the Tri-State area. He visited the homes of his boys, talked to their parents, and attended their high school games. For he was determined that football would be brought back to the University in the way that we in the Pittsburgh area traditionally wanted Pitt to be. His first team last year did as everyone expected it would, it did not win. And, although, he was bitterly disappointed in his first season, he said, "It'll be different the second time around." Let us support our new coach and give him a Pittsburgh welcome, Dave Hart, coach at the University of Pittsburgh.

**DAVE HART:**  Reverend Clergy, gentlemen, honored guest, Pete Dimperio, family of Pete, honored friends of Pete. You know a lot has been said about this banquet. I have heard numerous people talk about it. A week or so ago, Pete told me he was sorry he could not attend his own banquet. You know, he's a witty guy. And there are a lot of people that are sorry they could not be here tonight. I'm sorry that it was mentioned that I'd like the winning ingredients to brush off. We have been on the rostrum together many times. We went over to Cumberland together and we sort of entertained. Very seriously, we are honoring Pete, and praising him as a successful high school coach. He, in my opinion, possesses the ingredients of a winner; with discipline, sacrifice, and pride. I know I speak for all coaches on how fortunate we were able to work with the young people of America - it's a great feeling. And I try to list undefeated teams and there isn't a greater one than Pete Dimperio. I know, being in the business 16 years and fortunate to be with 6 undefeated teams myself. When I think of Pete, I think of discipline, sacrifice, and pride. I made it my business to visit with this great individual. And I took it upon myself to go to Westinghouse. I came back so enthused that every member of my staff went down to watch this individual work. And on the occasion I was fortunate enough to go down there, they were practicing off season. Not illegitimately, but he led the captains of the squad, Weston and Marshall. I watched them working out. They worked wonders without sleds and machines and did not have all the apparatus and equipment that you would expect to see. It's true. The fact that you saw these young men working with dedication and guidance for Pete Dimperio. And discipline, when he spoke they jumped. I watched boys standing at attention. I said, Pete, who are these guys? They are non-lettermen. There's a strong feeling of pride in being an upper classman or letterman here.

Pete has had the opportunity time and time again to go on to greater heights, but he stayed dedicated to the City of Pittsburgh and Westinghouse High School. I have been with Pete and watched the third ingredient, that of pride. I have heard people say, "Boy is he lucky." Luck is the residue of design. Pete made the opportunity and prepared himself for it. I'm honored just to be here tonight to pay tribute to a guy like this. And I want to say on behalf of the University of Pittsburgh that Pete and his family will always have a free ticket to watch Lloyd Weston represent him and Westinghouse High School at the University of Pittsburgh.

220

**JUDGE ALDISERT:** Thank you very much Dave. *(Telegrams read)*

*Congratulations, Pete, to a swell guy - Francis Rooney*

Regret unable to pay tribute to your success. The flu hit me. We at the Post-Gazette hope you continue to visit our department where you never fail to ease our job tensions with your wit. We wish you and your family the best of luck. Congratulations to a swell guy. —Dan McGidney, Sports Editor, Pittsburgh Post-Gazette.

Next, the past president of the Eastern Collegiate Athletic Association, past President of the Collegiate Basketball Association, the Vice President of the Sports Hall of Fame, dear friend of Pete, well known and beloved by all, let's welcome Tut Melman.

**TUT MELMAN:** Thank you judge. I have to get serious now, because there are a number of members here in the audience, a number of officials, old-timers, and old-time officials. Just hearing Pete's name, they wanted to be here on behalf of this occasion. Namely, Buck Snyder and Dan Snyder, and they are here tonight. The thing they liked about Pete was working with him. Some of us and most of the old-timers, will remember the occasions when we worked with Pete as an Official. Did you know Pete was a Football Official at one time? It'll be a surprise to you, but it's an actual fact. We had a lot of fun with Pete. I wouldn't try to tell you he was the best official; I won't attempt that, but after the game was over you had a lot of fun with him. He would laugh about certain situations that occurred and how some of us officials handled them. I think some of us are guilty of taking the game too seriously. Not only we officials, but we coaches as well, might take it a little too seriously at times. He would always add a little humor into the situation. Pete would smile or laugh at different things and I don't think it was a sin. I believe it was a virtue. I think it's something we should practice more of in order to bring about better relations with one another as we progress through the years.

In honoring Pete, the real purpose here, on my behalf, is representing the Pennsylvania Sports Hall of Fame. I don't know how many people here are aware of the fact that Coach Pete Dimperio is a recipient of the Pennsylvania Sports Hall of Fame. I think it occurred in 1964 at a banquet here in Pittsburgh. I hope you will excuse me if I'm a little bit off. The amazing part of this award to Pete is the fact that he alone, mind you, is the only High School Coach to my knowledge that has been inducted into the Pennsylvania Sports Hall of Fame. And, another thing that is impressive about this, is the fact that he tallied one of the highest vote counts in the history of the balloting. To refresh your memories, I would like to recall by name some of the recipients who are part of this organization. This is a page out of the past, and I'm sure you will appreciate such a sentimental honor. Listen to this. Connie Mack, Stan Musial, Jim Thorpe, Arnold Palmer, Barney Ewell, Pie Traynor, Steve Van Buren, Paul Waner, Rip Engle, Burt Bell, Christy Mathewson, Chick Davies, Lefty Grove, Roy Campanella. I was there for Roy Campanella's banquet. He came up in his wheel chair to receive his award; it was an emotional time for all. Clark

**221**

Hinkle, Johnny Lujack, Pop Warner, Jock Sutherland, Art Rooney, Johnny Woodruff, Honus Wagner. How about that! What an illustrious family for Pete to belong to. So, in signing off, and trying to cut the program time down a little; on behalf of the Southwest Chapter here in Pittsburgh, it's really a thrill to be honoring one of our boys. We are happy that some of us were able to give Pete this honor, and thank you all very much.

**JUDGE ALDISERT:** Thank you very much Tut for your illuminating description of the Hall of Fame. **One thing is certain, if all of the others deserved it, Pete Dimperio deserved it too.**

In addition to Mrs. Dimperio, Pete has had a boss at Westinghouse. He is with us tonight. He has served in the Pittsburgh School System for most of his adult life. He was the Principal at the Fifth Avenue High School, and now, serves as the Principal of Westinghouse High School. Like many great educators, he is a staunch believer that athletics is an important part of education. Let's welcome Harry Singer.

**HARRY SINGER:** Mr. Toastmaster, and friends of Pete. About 3 or 4 days before Pete announced his retirement, he and I talked. He told me he planned to retire from active coaching. I had mixed feelings at the time. I was happy and I was sad. I was happy because he solved a problem for me, and that was, what to do with all the trophies. We had four areas in front of our building, and I was counting the mass number of years he coached. I was figuring on the additional room needed. There was no additional space, and I was going to ask him to get rid of the older ones. The sad part of it is the passing of Pete from the coaching scene.

About four years ago, exactly, when I came to Westinghouse, they were playing one of the powerhouses of the Ohio Valley. There was a question about the superiority of Westinghouse. This gentleman turned to me and asked where Pete's assistants were, and I hadn't thought about it. I said, I didn't understand. Did you look across the field? You will see that we have five assistants to the head coach. And I said, "Pete has an assistant coach; he's out scouting, and Pete's taking care of everything on the field." He couldn't get over that. He couldn't understand how one man could direct the plays of the team, take care of the injuries, and tape up ankles and whatever else they're supposed to do. And he won that game handily. There was a four year series of games with this team. The last game was played this year, and this team beat Pete. The next day as Pete and I were reading the newspaper of this local town, we noticed that the story of events were a full page, with bold headlines that this team had beaten Westinghouse. Here was real happiness. It was great that another team found such joy in beating a team that Pete coached. And I was happy for them, Pete, even though we lost. I guess this is a real definition of happiness—beating Pete. It was nice working with you for the last four years.

**JUDGE ALDISERT:** Thank you very much Mr. Singer. Ladies and gentlemen, in my capacity as a judge, I am active in many civil organizations. And I have met people who have impressed me very much. A most able and competent person has given yeoman service to this committee. Greet him and give him the tribute he deserves—EDWARD CAYE. He is a former teacher in the Public School System, and he is one of Pittsburgh's great people.

The next speaker started his illustrious career at Shaler High School. He went to the University of Cincinnati and earned honorable mention in his senior year. After the service in the United States Navy, he came to Pittsburgh and joined the Steelers as a guard. He served as head coach for the Pittsburgh Central Catholic High School for the years 1949 through 1952. And in1958 he joined the Green Bay Packers as an assistant coach. He has served as head football coach of the Philadelphia Eagles, and is now an assistant coach of the Cleveland Browns. Nick Skorich.

**NICK SKORICH:** Thank you very much Mr. Toastmaster. Dean Moor, Pete's family, most honored Guest of Honor, Pete, and honored guests. This is, of course, an unusual pleasure for me; and when most people stepping to the podium say it's a pleasure, 99 times out of 100, it is. It is for me.

I visited the Westinghouse program that coach Hart is talking about. I saw the conditioning program these boys went through, and realized the type of dedication they had and what the competition might be. I was smart enough not to play Westinghouse, McKeesport, and those others. Smart enough because I made the mistake of following the pressures. I would have been another losing coach. It's a pleasure to be here for that reason and the respect I have for Pete Dimperio. You know, among the super athletes, ultimate athletes, whatever it might be, football, basketball, or track, among the teams that he plays on, and I have had the pleasure, there is one thing. The ultimate complement. It is a players player. Of course, it says many things. It implies to super ability, dedication, accomplishment, and hard work. He has all these things. May God give all to participate in this sport, but when he gets the complement — the players player — which of course is the road to championships — this is the ultimate complement. And among the coaching of men, and this is hard, far less and far more rare, the ultimate complement is the coaches coach. And I am talking about Pete Dimperio. I am talking about the confidence that all people that might coach this game would want to think of Pete Dimperio. He is the super producer of any sport; plus that, an unusual educator and a super coach. When he has these qualities, then he is the coaches coach. And this to me is Pete Dimperio.

You know, there is an old cliché that says something about the Italians built this world. And they say the Irish run the world, because they produce the politicians. And they say everybody owns it but the Italians. I speak of a builder tonight, an Italian builder. The toastmaster mentioned earlier, but he touched on the thing that I think is so crucial and important. The dedicated teacher, the dedicated coach, the one that wants to take the formative individual, the young men of 13 or 14, and maybe younger, for these are the formative years you mold and form. Pete, of course, has been in the position over the years to handle thousands of young men that have come under his influence, and as the Toastmaster said, "The mark that he made on them and the mark they will carry is the mark that cannot be made." I pay tribute to that. I pay tribute to the things Pete has done for other people. The dedication, the hard work, the pains his family has lived with in helping him do this. I pay tribute to that. I conclude, I hope that all of us in this room might in some way make this world , a little bit of this world, a better place to live as Pete Dimperio has done.

223

**JUDGE ALDISERT:** Thank you, Nick, for your most eloquent observations. You know the story of the banquet speaker who was talking and talking and talking for some time. He looked up and saw part of his audience go. Then, he went on for another half-hour and was getting into the real climax of the presentation. And about one fourth of the original audience remained and he went on for another half-hour and started coming down to the gait of the speech when he saw only one person remaining in the audience. And he concluded by saying, "And you sir are a gentleman." And the man replied, "Gentleman hell, I'm the next speaker."

Now, we have our last speaker. And I ask you all to continue with the patience and respect that you have extended to all of our speakers this evening. It is greatly appreciated. We have purposely taken him out of turn and saved him for the end, because he has a message for us. Bernard J. McCormick, Deputy Superintendent of the Board of Education. This means he is second in command of America's dynamic Metropolitan School System. He shares the extreme burden of a Public School Administrator in an area of most sensitive relations with an alert, brilliant, young generation sitting in the seats with a populous sensitive to changing trend in the sociological conditions of our Community. It can be said, that the office of Superintendent in Pittsburgh has met the challenge ably with courage and with great tolerance. We have with us the man who has served as Principal of Schenley High School and as Principal of Allderdice High School. He is a gadget of both Indiana State College and the University of Pittsburgh. Not only does he stand in augmented position in the school system, but he bears a warm admiration for our Guest of Honor. Ladies and gentlemen, the featured speaker of the evening, Bernard McCormick.

**BERNARD McCORMICK:** Gentlemen, Clergy, Pete and your family, ladies and gentlemen. I came really to speak for the Board of Education, but having been surrounded by Pete's Mafia, I think I'm the only Irishman on the platform. The Irish, too, love Pete. This one does, certainly. I am grateful to the committee for giving me the position to honor a cherished, old friend. In honoring Pete tonight, I think we honor all teachers who choose to invest their talents and their lives in the education of youth, and who in rare occasions bring that very extra special pleasure of devotion that makes them stand apart from their fellows as this lad has from his. Pete and I were first associated at Herron Hill Jr. High School. This is before he began his public career at Westinghouse. His record as a basketball coach was more phenomenal than his football record at Westinghouse. He resented the ruling that forbid from putting shoulder pads on the basketball team.

Then and now, is his intuited skill in working with boys. Pete would have been a great teacher of any subject. It doesn't matter, because he has always taught boys, not subjects, not only football, but the uncanny understanding he had with boys in teaching them to do the precise thing at the right time. This, I think, makes him the success that he is. His drollness, his sternest, a pat on the shoulder, on the head or sometimes on the rear end. His encouragement always seemed to bring out the best in the boys. Coaching football was his life, because it gave him the opportunity of any teaching career to make digestive in the lives of boys.

As some of us know, Pete could have left Westinghouse on more than one occasion for a number of coaching offers. I have never told the story I will tell tonight. I have not told it to Pete. It's been a while back, 10 or 12 years ago, as I recall that I had a long distance phone call very late at night. It suggested that some people had been talking in the West pretty late. I remember Chet Smith and Al Abrams as I had been an athletic buff all my life. The caller asked if I was the McCormick on the Board of Control of the PIAA in Harrisburg, and I said, "I was." He asked me if I ever coached football, and I said, "No." He asked me if I ever played football. I said, "No." I went out for it just one day, and as I tried to put the shoulder pads on, a leg at a time, the coach suggested I show up for baseball in the spring. And my caller said, "Good," because he didn't want to talk to anyone who was knowledgeable about football or winning or losing but he wanted to talk to someone who could tell him about Pete Dimperio. And he wanted to talk to him man to man. It has been some years ago, but I do remember it quite well. I was impressed with my caller and his reputation. Well, I answered him like this. I told him that if Pete wanted to be a football coach in college, he would be a winning coach, whether my caller wanted him to be or not. He would be a winning coach, because his team would be well prepared, especially in the fundamentals of the game. More than that, Pete's boys would give him one hundred percent every second they were on the field. I told him the parents, of the boys, would be confident and proud to have Pete as their coach. He would never in any way exploit them or let them play if they were not physically fit. He would not report to the press or blame a boy publicly for a missed assignment on the field. When the team won, the credit would go to the boys.

225

Pete was in a class with Duffy Daugherty and Bud Wilkinson as a coach, and a sweet talker to the Alumni. I told him the Administration of any college would quickly accept him because of his competency in his field and respect him for his system of values. I concluded by telling him the college would be richer for having Pete, his lovely wife, daughter Peggy and son Pete, Jr. I was asked to keep the call confidential, and to this day, I will not tell from whom the call came. And by recalling this incident from about a decade ago, I have tried to express my regard for a distinguished teacher, coach, and friend whose professional and unique personality has served well the Pittsburgh Board of Education which has employed him all these years. And more important, the thousands at Westinghouse High School who have been priviledged to be under his influence. I was going to tell you a joke, but it's late. It was to lead to my closing remark.

Pete is only retiring from coaching football; he is not retiring from service with the Board of Education. Pete will stay busy. And this week or next week, before the end of the school term, we will talk again as we have every other year. We will look for Pete, a role in which he can serve and extend the qualities he has to offer to young people, as long as he chooses to work for me. My warm personal congratulations to Pete for a job well done. I think you may have much more wealth than most men in your bank of memories. Tonight, we have tried to make another deposit. Thank you.

**JUDGE ALDISERT:** Thank you very much Mr. McCormick on behalf of the Italian Mafia sitting up here. And if I may be personable, I want you to know that I was in Dublin just three weeks ago. And to my astonishment, and to your dismay, and an obvious pleasure of Dean Moor, when I went to visit St. Patrick's Cathedral I found out it was a Protestant Church.

Ladies and gentlemen, for the presentation of the award, Dr. Antonucci has asked the committee to be represented by the man who worked so hard, who has given his all for the success of this evening's dinner, Frank Gustine.

**FRANK GUSTINE:** Thank you judge. I am going to be very short and brief. I do want to pay special tribute to you people out there. I have never been on a committee that worked so hard and loves Pete Dimperio. I have never met a man more loved and respected. Ed Caye was supposed to make this presentation, but Pete I guess you know how we feel. And we just love you, and of course, we want you to remember this night as long as you live. We wish you and your family the best of health.

*(Presentation of Plaque) — It says here:*

**TO PETE DIMPERIO, EDUCATOR AND COACH, WHO HAS SERVED MANY YEARS IN THE PITTSBURGH SCHOOL SYSTEM AT HERRON HILL JUNIOR HIGH SCHOOL AS BASKETBALL COACH AND AS FOOTBALL COACH AT WESTINGHOUSE HIGH SCHOOL WHERE HE GAINED NATIONAL FAME WINNING SEVENTEEN CITY CHAMPIONSHIPS IN TWENTY-ONE YEARS OF COACHING. AS A UNIQUE GRASP OF HUMAN PROUDNESS, ESTEEM, AND AFFECTIONS OF ALL, AND ON BEHALF OF YOUR MANY FRIENDS, WE EXTEND OUR SENSE OF LOSS IN YOUR RETIREMENT.**

226

And I want you to know this from the deepest part of my heart, that we are here because we love you. *(STANDING OVATION)*

**PETE DIMPERIO:** Thank you Frank. Reverend Clergy, you know I'm not a violet, but I'm loved to death. I know this banquet represents my players, for without them I would not be here. I am so grateful; they were tremendous. I think I was the luckiest man in the world to be coaching those type of men. And as you saw this evening, they are all something and sound citizens. I am going to make an analogy. It is an example of what Westinghouse has done.

I am going to describe a boy's life. I had a little boy, this is typical of all my players. I had a little boy playing for me. He was 5 foot 3, and he was small. He had tremendous desire and speed. I loved this kid. And I loved them a hell of a lot better if they could run. I put him on the squad. A year later he was my regular, and we won with him. I know we beat Altoona. It is because of their size; you get good publicity for beating a big team. He beat them single handedly. He said, "Pete, I'd like to go to college." I told him he was a good boy and he was smart. I think you can give something to a University with your speed and determination. I sent this boy to Lincoln University. He went for four years and joined the ROTC and came out as a Second Lieutenant. After he came out of school, he went right into the Army. And about eight months ago, he came to visit me. He had double bars on his shoulders, and he was a Captain. He was being sent to Vietnam. And the thrill I got when Jim

Lucas wrote a story about a hero, a Captain of a Platoon. He said they were pinned down in the hill, but they were pinned down before. You could hear this voice all over the place. He was tremendous. And naturally the name was Sherrill Brown. That 5 foot 3 boy. The newspapers called and said they thought he played for me. I said, "He certainly did." And four months later Sherrill Brown was killed. He was really significant in every way an athlete of Westinghouse High School. **"All my athletes to me are Sherrill Brown."**

I never saw a boy at Westinghouse High School that ever disappointed me. They really did their job. They were a service to life. They respected authority and they respected themselves. They had pride. And I know people you are here tonight because of winning. You know, certain things sometimes remind me of this; It's not the lamppost that sheds a little light, it's just the lamppost. The real significance is that these young men live a life of service. Live a life that America is going to be greater and greater. There is so much greatness in America. You know, with all the racial problems; you should see the type of boys coming out of High Schools. If they are anything like the Westinghouse boys, I'm the luckiest guy in the world, to think I had the opportunity of associating with them. And today, they're going to be greater men and I am proud of them. And again, I want to thank you all for coming here tonight. Thank you from me. Thank you for coming.

### *(GRAND OVATION)*

**JUDGE ALDISERT:** So, my friends, we end as we began. That the story of Pete Dimperio is not the story of statistics, but it is the story of the "Molder of Men." May Pete have the health and the continued energy to be a builder in this community in the future as he has done so long and ably in the past. Ladies and gentlemen, on behalf of the committee, may I thank you for coming here this evening to do honor to this great man. May I thank you the members of the committee whose names appeared on the program, and may I direct your attention to a proclamation which has been signed by his Honor, Joseph M. Barr which says, **"BY VIRTUE OF THE AUTHORITY VESTED IN ME, I HEREBY PROCLAIM THE PERIOD OF JUNE 4 THROUGH JUNE 10 TO BE PETE DIMPERIO WEEK IN PITTSBURGH. AND I ASK OUR CITIZENS TO JOIN IN A TRIBUTE TO A GREAT TEACHER AND A GREAT COACH."**

Now, for the benediction, great athlete in his own right, dear friend of our Guest of Honor, and known to us all, Reverend Charles Ceradini.

**By Angelo Aliberti, Court Reporter**
**WHS Class of 1952**

227

228

## PETE DIMPERIO

### *Testimonial Dinner Dance*

**June 4, 1967**

**Pittsburgh Hilton**

## PROGRAM

INTRODUCTION..................................................................................Dr. Phillip Antonucci

INVOCATION...................................................................................... Dean H. N. R. Moor

TOASTMASTER................................................................................ Judge Ruggero Aldisert

## GUESTS OF HONOR

T. F. (Ted) Abel................................................Director of Physical Education, Pittsburgh

Stan Berkman..................................................Superintendent of Schools, Baltic, Ohio

Joseph DeFebo.................................................Coach, Western Reserve University

Carl DePasqua.................................................Coach, Waynesburg College

Frank DeLeo....................................................Westinghouse Players Representative

Dave Hart........................................................Coach, University of Pittsburgh

Tut Melman......................................................Pennsylvania Sports Hall of Fame

Bernard McCormick........................................Deputy Superintendent of Schools, Pittsburgh

Harry Singer....................................................Principal, Westinghouse High School

Nick Skorich.................................................... Assistant Coach, Cleveland Browns

Pie Traynor......................................................Baseball Hall of Fame

PRESENTATION OF AWARD............................................................Edward C. Caye

BENEDICTION.................................................................................Reverend Charles Ceradini

229

## COMMITTEE

Dr. Phillip E. Antonucci, Chairman
Edward J. Caye, Co-Chairman

| | |
|---|---|
| Felix Cutruzzula | Eugene Massaro |
| Chippy DeStout | Rudy Musulin |
| Dave Edgar | Joe Snodgrass |
| Lou Ferragonio | Chuck Tedesco |
| John Foley | Tom Tipe |
| Owen Gormley | Richard Thornton |
| Bill Gormley | John Tumas |
| Frank Guadagnino | Chuck White |
| Frank Gustine | |

PETE DIMPERIO

TESTIMONIAL DINNER-DANCE

SUNDAY EVENING 7:00 PM

JUNE 4TH

PITTSBURGH HILTON BALLROOM

TICKETS $8.50

BEING HELD BY FRIENDS AND

ASSOCIATES OF WESTINGHOUSE

HIGH SCHOOLS RETIRING

FOOTBALL COACH

*DINNER ------- *DANCING

*CELEBRITIES

MAKE UP A TABLE AND CALL

FOR TICKETS - 621 - 4100

OR: STOP IN AT

FRANKIE GUSTINES
3911 FORBES AVENUE
OAKLAND, PGH. 15213

**230**

# A soldier's story

PITTSBURGH POST-GAZETTE * MONDAY, MAY 29, 2000

Images of Sherrill Vance Brown fill a scrapbook assembled by his wife, Lelia, who is in the photo at left with Brown and his father, Hoffman. The other picture is of Brown with Vietnamese children. Also shown is a certificate he received for completing Ranger training.

By Jonathan D. Silver
Post-Gazette Staff Writer

*Several days before this article appeared in the Pittsburgh Post-Gazette I received a phone call from Staff Writer Jonathan Silver, asking me if I remember Sherrill Brown from our years at Westinghouse High School. I proudly replied yes and shared my memories of Sherrill with this writer. I was deeply moved and honored. I will always remember him as the heart and soul of the 1955 Bulldogs. God bless you Captain Brown for sacrificing your life for America.*

As a football coach, or anyone else for that matter, you could be forgiven for overlooking Sherrill Vance Brown. After all, there wasn't much to him.

Standing only 5 feet 5 inches, Brown was an unlikely candidate for the Westinghouse Bulldogs, Homewood's storied football team.

He was stocky but short. His first name sounded like a girl's. And he kept to his East Liberty family, acting more like a bookish student than a posturing jock.

From the beginning, though, the Bulldogs' coach, local legend Pete Dimperio, saw only promise. Small or not, Dimperio wanted him for the team.

It turned out to be a prescient move. By his senior year in 1956, Brown had carved out a reputation that easily eclipsed his size. Wearing number 60, the running back flummoxed his foes, delighted his fans, and carried the ball over and over again, making Pittsburgh's all-city team.

It was Brown's crowning achievement. Before him, the future must have seemed wide open. He was college-bound, recruited by the football team at predominantly black Lincoln University in Missouri. And although he didn't know it yet, a wife, a beautiful baby girl and a military career lay ahead of him.

Something else was waiting for him, though, something sinister and deadly. It lurked 10 years and thousands of miles away, buried in the soil of a far-away

231

## "A Tribute to Sherrill Brown"
### June 4, 1967

The following are the heartfelt spoken words of Coach Pete Dimperio as he spoke to those of us who had gathered to honor him at his Retirement Testimonial.

I am going to make an analogy. It is an example of what Westinghouse has done. I am going to describe a boy's life. I had a little boy, this is typical of all my players. I had a little boy playing for me. He was 5 foot 3, and he was small. He had tremendous desire and speed. I loved this kid. And I loved them a hell of a lot better if they could run. I put him on the squad. A year later he was my regular, and we won with him. I know we beat Altoona. It is because of their size; you get good publicity for beating a big team. He beat them single handedly. He said, "Pete, I'd like to go to college." I told him he was a good boy and he was smart. I think you can give something to a University with your speed and determination. I sent this boy to Lincoln University. He went for four years and joined the ROTC and came out as a Second Lieutenant. After he came out of school, he went right into the Army. And about eight months ago, he came to visit me. He had double bars on his shoulders, and he was a Captain. He was being sent to Vietnam. And the thrill I got when Jim Lucas wrote a story about a hero, a Captain of a Platoon. He said they were pinned down in the hill, but they were pinned down before. You could hear this voice all over the place. He was tremendous. And naturally the name was Sherrill Brown.... that 5 foot 3 boy. The newspapers called and said they thought he played for me. I said, "He certainly did." And four months later Sherrill Brown was killed. He was really significant in every way an athlete of Westinghouse High School. **"All my athletes to me are Sherrill Brown."**

**WEDNESDAY, JULY 13, 1966**

## Ex-Westinghouse Football Star

# *Viet Cong Mine Kills Wilkinsburg Captain*

Army Capt. Sherrill Brown, of Wilkinsburg, a former all-city fullback at Westinghouse High School, has been killed in action in Viet Nam, his family was notified yesterday.

A telegram received by his wife, Lelia, said Captain Brown, an infantry officer, was killed July 10 "as a result of a metal fragment wound received when the vehicle in which he was a passenger detonated a hostile mine."

**High Praise From Coach**

Pete Dimperio, Captain Brown's high school coach, described him as "an asset to us, to his country and to his race. He had tremendous ability and was one of the best and smartest players I I ever coached," Dimperio said.

Captain Brown, 27, lived at 1418 Clark St., and was the father of a daughter, Paris, 4.

Captain Brown was five

**CAPT. SHERRILL BROWN**
*Killed in action.*

feet, five inches tall and weighed only 145 pounds

when he played high school football in 1954 and 1955. He was captain of the team in his senior year.

Captain Brown also was president of the Varsity Club and was a dash man on the Westinghouse track team. He graduated in 1960 from Lincoln University, Jefferson City, Mo., where he took Reserve Officers Training Corps courses.

**Varied Assignments**

Captain Brown was assigned to Fort Benning, Ga., Fort Knox, Ky., Fort Bragg, N.C., and Germany before being assigned to Viet Nam, where he arrived Feb. 4, 1966, for a 13-months tour. He had re-enlisted after his first two-year tour of duty ended.

In addition to his wife and daughter, Captain Brown is survived by his father, Hoffman Brown; two brothers, Hoffman Brown Jr., and Robert Brown; and a sister, Mrs. Valre Tipton, all of the Clark Street address.

*Burton • Dimperio • Musilin • Malins • Webb*

# 8 | THE 1970s - WORTHY SUCCESSORS MUSILIN AND MALINS

## 1967 - RUDY'S FIRST SEASON

In 1967 the City League made a major change in football going to an eight game schedule consisting of Pittsburgh city schools only. In prior years each school in the city played three pre-season games against WPIAL schools prior to the five games against City League competition in both Sections 1 and 2. This change was made to enable the Pittsburgh schools to play at a competitive level that was better suited for the league. The pre-season games were proving to be so one-sided that it was best to discontinue the embarrassment. Westinghouse was the only city school, during that time period, that was able to challenge the WPIAL with any consistency. When Pete Dimperio was there he always felt that no matter whom the WPIAL opponents were the Bulldogs would win the best of a three game series. His record proved him to be right on.

It was going to be somewhat strange to look across the field and not see Pete Dimperio standing with his players waiting to take the field at the sound of the band playing "Westinghouse Forever". From 1946 to 1966 Coach Dimperio was the leader of the Bulldogs, but the 1967 season was the beginning of a new era for his successor Rudy Musilin. Rudy knew he had huge shoes to fill, but his main objective was to continue the winning tradition of the Westinghouse Bulldogs with much of the same system as his predecessor. Why change something that was so successful in past years – "If its not broken, then why fix it?" The single wing though considered an antique system was still alive and well at Westinghouse. Muslin was Pete's assistant coach for eight years before taking over the controls in 1967. "I was J. V. coach, trainer, scout – it was four years before I saw Westinghouse play". Musilin said, "and that was an exhibition game". Rudy was looking at a full closet left over from Dimperio's 1966 City Champions. Several lettermen led by running backs Mike Weston, Sonny Allen and center Dorian Vassar were ready to defend their city title. This year Rudy had two very able assistants – Paul Mazzie and Gus Catanese supporting him. Mazzie was an All-City performer at Westinghouse in 1940 and 1941 and a member of the class of 1942 and a decorated World War II veteran. Catanese was also a local talent from Peabody High School who later became head coach at Perry Traditional Academy and guided the Commodores to several Pittsburgh City Titles.

Rudy led the Bulldogs to an undefeated regular season, before being upset in the City Championship game by Allderdice 20-13. It made headlines in our local media as it was the first City League Title for the Dragons from Squirrel Hill. At the time several of us alumni were tuned into our office radios as the game was being carried over a local station. We were all working at the time for Swindell-Dressler Engineering Company on Smithfield Street in downtown Pittsburgh. There were also a group of alumni from Allderdice working there as well and as expected they were quite happy over the upset win. Our Westinghouse pride never wavered as we took the loss graciously and extended the alumni from Allderdice their dues. At the time it was the first Pittsburgh City title ever for the Dragons compared to the numerous titles that the Bulldogs had claimed over the years. In fact, one of the Allderdice alumni announced the final score over the company PA system – "House of David 20, The House 13". Our response was, "The Lord helped Allderdice gain their first city title in its history." I was kidding with one of the guys from Allderdice and said, "Look how happy you are, if it wasn't for the proud reputation of Westinghouse you would not be savoring such an honorable feat. When you beat the best you have a right to brag, but look out next year there will be hell to pay." It was all about good sportsmanship.

The following two years Westinghouse struggled somewhat missing the playoffs in 1968 with a record of 5-3-0, and yes they did not forget about defending 1967 champion Allderdice as they defeated the Dragons 34-13. In 1969 the Bulldogs managed to reach the city playoffs, but lost in the first round to South High School 14-12. They finished the season 6-3-0 and Carrick defeated Peabody in the city final that year 30-6.

**234**

## 1970 – THE HOUSE BOUNCES BACK

The Bulldogs were back in a big way in 1970 as they went undefeated and went on to capture the city title. The last time they claimed the PA Pitt Trophy was in 1966 – the final year of Pete Dimperio's illustrious coaching career.

The old single wing was still being employed by Coach Musilin, but the Bulldogs offense was not clicking to satisfy him. Early in the season he made some position changes and shifted Bobby Hadnot a superior end to tailback to take advantage of his speed and passing ability. This change proved to be a good one as Hadnot was now teamed with fullback Lovie Venson and wingback John Sims to form an explosive backfield along with quarterback Morrow. Musilin felt this trio of backs – Venson, Sims and Hadnot were as good as any that he had ever seen at Westinghouse.

The Bulldogs opened the season with a 26-6 win over the Raiders of Carrick High School – a team that was rated to contend for the Pittsburgh City Championship that year. Both teams did not perform as expected in this season opener – the famed Westinghouse deception was a bumbling, stumbling mess. Carrick's starting quarterback Tom Loadman was a nervous sophomore playing his first varsity game that day – throwing five interceptions. He progressed rapidly throughout the season and became one of the premier passing threats in the City League. By season's end, Carrick had developed a potent passing attack with Loadman leading the way. The Raiders went undefeated after the season opening loss to Westinghouse and developed a strong defensive unit to support its potent offense. Meanwhile, the House was improving as well with the early season position changes made by Coach

Musilin. The timing displayed by Hadnot, Venson, and Sims was being compared to some of the outstanding teams from the Dimperio era. The Bulldog offense was really clicking now and the defense was solid in leading the House to an undefeated season of 8-0-0.

The City title was a rematch between Westinghouse and Carrick to be played for the first time on the artificial turf of Three Rivers Stadium, home of the Pittsburgh Steelers. It was covered locally for the first time on television and Carrick was the defending city champions having won the title in 1969.

This was a new season and the 1970 Bulldogs were determined to bring the title back to Homewood – the last one being in 1966. Game day was a chilly, damp one with steady rain showers falling throughout the entire game, and made the artificial surface of Three Rivers Stadium both wet and slick. The Westinghouse huddle called Lovie Vensen's number forty-one times and the fleet 5'7", 165 pound junior responded with 258 yards and three touchdowns. He also had a thirty yard touchdown called back. The score at halftime was 12-6 Westinghouse and Carrick was still in the game. With Sims being hampered by an ankle injury and the slick field conditions cutting down on Hadnot's wide sweeps, it was up to fullback Vensen to carry the load for the Bulldogs. The Westinghouse defense held Carrick to 42 yards rushing and 106 yards passing on 23 attempts. The line play of Bulldog performers Deacon Jones and Andre Staton was superb. Carrick coach Cass Blair commented after the game how impressed he was of Lovie Vensen and the overall performance of the Bulldogs. The final score was Westinghouse 26, Carrick 6 as the House stormed back scoring 14 points in the fourth quarter and regained the City Title that had eluded them for three years.

235

The Championship game summary:

Score by quarters:

| Westinghouse | 6 | 6 | 0 | 14 | 26 |
|---|---|---|---|---|---|
| Carrick | 0 | 6 | 0 | 0 | 6 |

Scoring:

| Westinghouse | L. Vensen 16 yd. run (Extra point failed) |
|---|---|
| Westinghouse | L. Vensen 1 yd. run (Extra point failed) |
| Carrick | Reggie Ash 9 yd. run (Extra point failed) |
| Westinghouse | L. Vensen 1 yd. run (Extra point Jackson run) |
| Westinghouse | E. Taylor 56yd. interception runback |

The 1970 squad:

L. Vensen, J. Sims, B. Hadnot, D. Vassar, D. Jones, A. Staton, E Taylor, M. Taylor, G. Sims, E. Lane, Morrow, J. Charley, R. Jackson, Tyler, White, J. Thomas, L Kyser, B. Martin, L. Green, B. Gray, R. Baltimore, K. Young, Milliones, R. Freeman, Bey, Brown, D. Weston, Jones, Stribling, Gaines, Drake, McMillan.

**The 1970 Season (9-0-0)**

| | | | |
|---|---|---|---|
| WHS | 26 | Carrick | 6 |
| WHS | 26 | Allderdice | 6 |
| WHS | 44 | Allegheny | 6 |
| WHS | 40 | Gladstone | 0 |
| WHS | 26 | Langley | 0 |
| WHS | 44 | Peabody | 20 |
| WHS | 22 | Perry | 0 |
| WHS | 28 | South Hills | 6 |
| City Championship Playoff | | | |
| WHS | 26 | Carrick | 6 |

The 1970 season was the last one for Rudy Musilin at Westinghouse when he resigned after four years of service as head coach and several as Dimperio's assistant at the Homewood school. His record at Westinghouse was an impressive 28-7-0, winning one City title in 1970 and was runner-up to Allderdice in 1967.

## FROM AMBRIDGE TO HOMEWOOD

Fred Malins was appointed to succeed Rudy Musilin as the new head football coach at Westinghouse beginning with the 1971 season. Malins was an alumnus of Ambridge High School in Beaver County. Since 1913, this was only the fifth time that a head football coaching change was made at Westinghouse. Malins, was traveling daily from Ambridge, PA to Homewood an hour's drive each way. He was a white man now coaching an all-black football team in the shadows of a legend, Pete Dimperio. He was in a no-win situation at the Homewood school.

The first change he made was a significant one as he decided to discontinue the antiquated single-wing and go with the more widely used T-formation. After many years of success with the single-wing it was going to be interesting to see how well the Bulldogs would adjust to this offensive change. Enrollment was declining and even coming four years after the departure of Dimperio there was bound to be comparisons. Nevertheless, Malins in his seven years at the House produced a fine record of 44-10-2 and led the Bulldogs into two City Championship games. In his first season 1971, they were 7-1-0 losing only to Peabody 32-28, and finished in a tie for second place in the City League. The Bulldogs were eliminated from the playoffs by the league's tie-breaking formula that had not been a favorable solution and was subjected to change in the near future.

The 1972 season was being considered a "Question Mark" according to Malins. He was faced with a rebuilding job having lost eleven starters from the 1971 team. The Bulldogs were adjusting to Malin's power – I formation, and it was taking time and patience. They no longer had the advantage of forcing other teams to make special adjustments in preparation to stop their potent single-wing. Malins was beginning to see some progress as he guided the Bulldogs to a respectable 5-2-1 season.

236

## THE MEAN THIRTEEN

"This is going to be a tough year for us" Malins said of his youthful squad in 1973. "This isn't anything like the teams we've had here". He was right in more ways than one. Times were changing at Westinghouse, where the single-wing and winning football were once traditions – along with hazing, mind games, fear and a belief that grades and football did not mix.

Malins greeted 45 players at the beginning of fall practice and it quickly dwindled down to twenty. Malins explained, "We lost a lot on eligibility." "The kids just don't want to play any more. It's not like it used to be. We're dealing with a different type of kid."

In an effort to upgrade its program, the Westinghouse administration raised the eligibility rule from 1.0 to 1.8 out of 4.0. The rest of the city was governed by a 1.0 standard (D average). To be eligible a student was required to pass four subjects and gym.

By mid-season Malins had the thinnest squad in years, a group he called, "The Mean Thirteen". He told them it took eleven to be on the field, so the other two would have to be ready at all times to spell relief. It was quite obvious that there would be times when an injury would have to be ignored. Those thirteen boys played hurt throughout the season and finished with a record of 4-4-0. They were truly a dedicated group of gridiron warriors that persevered through some very difficult times. The last time a Westinghouse squad was that short on players was 1916 when coach "Pro" Burton suited up seventeen boys – it was his first year at the Homewood school. The "Mean Thirteen" will always be remembered in the folklore of Westinghouse football.

237

## INELIGIBILITY BRINGS DOWN THE HOUSE IN 1974

The 1974 season was a confusing one as the Bulldogs came back strong posting a record of 7-1-0 only to have it reduced to 4-4-0 due to an ineligible player. The cited player was not a starter, but he had appeared in the first three games of the season before his school record discrepancy was discovered. The only game loss that Westinghouse had suffered was to Allegheny High School 18-14. They were still receiving accolades as the best team at season's end. Peabody and Perry ended up playing for the coveted City Championship that year with Peabody winning 20-0. During the regular season Westinghouse had defeated both playoff teams – Peabody by 32-6 and Perry by 8-6. It was a tough break for Coach Malins and the Bulldogs.

## BULLDOGS REBOUND FROM ADVERSITIES

The following year, 1975, Westinghouse came back to have a fine year making it to the playoffs, but losing to Carrick 20-12 in the semi-finals. Carrick then advanced to the City Championship game to face Perry with the Commodores winning 14-0. Westinghouse finished the season with a respectable record of 7-2-0. Malins had to be pleased as the Bulldogs continued to contend year after year in spite of the declining enrollment and the many adversities they faced along the way. Having come from a WPIAL football program and seeing for himself how much less the City League had to work with, Coach Malins realized the dedication and determination his boys possessed. There was no home field with plush grass, no meals at a training table, no elaborate weight-lifting program, no projection room to watch game films and no deep coaching staff large enough to provide special support for all positions on both offense and defense. Football at Westinghouse was all about dedication, hard work, spirit and loyalty with a strong will to be a winner. These conditions always existed at the Homewood school as every Westinghouse team since the Burton Era never let this affect their desire to play like a champion. They learned that the game of football was so much like life.

## NEIGHBORING RIVALS ARE CO-CHAMPIONS

Bicentennial year 1976 was a celebration that spread across our great country. The Pittsburgh Steelers were Super Bowl X champions having defeated the Dallas Cowboys in Miami 21-17. I made the trip to Miami for that one as it was a great victory for the Steelers. It was a game that was one of the highlights of my life. Getting caught up in a Super Bowl weekend was truly a memory that I will never forget. Our Pittsburgh Steelers had defeated America's Team in one of the greatest games in Super Bowl history, and having been there to see it all in person was most gratifying. It was the second half of the back-to-back Super Bowl wins for our proud city. Later in the year in Pittsburgh two neighboring rivals, Westinghouse High School and Peabody High School battled for the City League Championship and bragging rights for another year. This was like a football Civil War as the two schools were located on opposite ends of East Liberty. The game was moved to Mt. Lebanon Stadium and was played November 8 on a Saturday afternoon under a cool sunny sky before a packed house. It was an opportunity for both schools to showcase City League football. Obviously, the behavior of both schools was being put to the test in an area where student behavior was never a problem at football games. The reputation of this intense rivalry between Westinghouse and Peabody at a neutral stadium was really going to be watched by the experimental game planners. After all in years past there were incidents that occurred before and after a Westinghouse vs Peabody game that turned a truly great neighborhood rivalry into an ugly mess. On this day it was a victory for the City League. The two neighboring rivals battled to a 20-20 stalemate; sharing the City Title as Co-Champions. It was one that ranked up there with some of the great games in City League history. The fact that the game ended in a tie may have been a blessing in disguise as no incidents were reported. It was only the fourth time in sixty years that the two schools had battled to a tie – 1946, 0-0; 1962, 7-7; 1976, 20-20.

The Highlanders led at halftime 20-6 and throughout most of the game. The Bulldogs came back to tie the score 20-20 with only two minutes left to play when quarterback Ahmad Shareef connected with halfback Sam Morris racing down the left sideline for the tying touchdown. The Bulldogs lined up for the extra point try, but a bad center snap sealed the games' fate. Back then there was no overtime to break a tie so Westinghouse and Peabody had to settle for a share of the 1976

Pittsburgh City-League Championship. Up to this point in time it was title number 30 for Westinghouse and number 6 for Peabody.

The City Co-Champs also tied with five players each for the **City-League All-Star Team: Westinghouse** was represented by End – Don Arrington; Guard – Lovett Bailey; QB – Ahmad Shareef; RB – Terry Mitchem; LB – James Wilson. **Peabody** was represented by T – Barry McCreary; C – Rodney Allen; RB – Lareese Ashley; LB – Craig Walls; DB – Cephus Bell.

**MVP:** Lareese Ashley, Peabody, and Ahmad Shareef, Westinghouse, tie.

**Coach of the Year:** Joe Hnath, Peabody, and Fred Malins, Westinghouse, tie.

### The 1976 Season (7-0-2)

| | | | |
|---|---|---|---|
| WHS | 26 | Carrick | 14 |
| WHS | 45 | Allderdice | 0 |
| WHS | 33 | Allegheny | 0 |
| WHS | 27 | Brashear | 0 |
| WHS | 50 | Oliver | 0 |
| WHS | 30 | South | 6 |
| WHS | 14 | Perry | 0 |
| WHS | 12 | South Hills | 12 |
| City Championship Playoff | | | |
| WHS | 20 | Peabody | 20 |

**239**

# SOUTH HIGH WINS FIRST CITY TITLE

South High School was still looking for its first football city championship in 1977. Westinghouse was the defending co-champion from 1976, and the Orioles of South High School were working hard to end a long drought that had haunted the South Side school for many years. Since the inception of crowning a Pittsburgh City League Champion in 1919, South High School had never taken home the coveted crown. They made it to the City final game in 1973, but they were defeated in the title game by Perry High School (later renamed Perry Traditional Academy) 38-6.

South Coach Glenn Miller had a group of dedicated boys who were determined to put an end to the long awaited city crown. They put together a fine season going 7-1-0 losing only to Brashear 14-6 in the final game of the season. That loss to Brashear really was a blessing in disguise. Coach Miller was disappointed as the Oriole's went into the season final quite big headed and were beaten. They had already defeated Westinghouse early in the season 14-10 and were headed for the coveted City Crown by season's end. In the meantime, Westinghouse finished its season 7-1-0 defeating arch rival Peabody 20-18 in the season's final game.

The 1977 city final was going to be a rematch between Westinghouse and South High as they had met earlier in the season with South winning a close 14-10 decision. This was going to be Coach Miller's final game as he was retiring after thirty years of coaching. His boys were well aware of this and they shut down Westinghouse 22-0 for its first City Championship in the school's history. It was a great win for South

High and a storybook finish to Coach Glenn Miller's coaching career.

Ironically ten years earlier in 1967, Taylor Allderdice won its first city championship defeating Westinghouse 20-13. So historically Westinghouse High School had brought the best out of their challengers when the Pittsburgh City Title was on the line. Allderdice and South can both claim that distinction as each defeated Westinghouse to win their first city titles in their school's history.

Respect for Westinghouse High School's gridiron record was widely acclaimed throughout Western Pennsylvania during much of the twentieth century. From 1913 up through 1977, the Bulldogs had compiled a record of 377 wins, 115 losses, and 35 ties for a winning percentage of 0.766. The milestone to win 500 games was well within their reach.

This was the last season for Coach Fred Malins as head football coach at Westinghouse. He endured many challenges during his seven years at the House and in spite of some less than ideal conditions he was able to compile a record of 41-15-3. He managed to guide the Bulldogs to a share of one City Championship with Peabody in 1976 and runner-up to South in 1977. He was leaving with a lasting impression that playing football at Westinghouse was painful and pride was the best medicine.

## A WESTINGHOUSE ALUMNUS TAKES OVER

240

For the sixth time in school history Westinghouse was getting a new head football coach for the 1978 season. He was George Webb, a 1963 graduate of Westinghouse and a Thiel College Alumnus. Webb was an All-City performer during his playing days at Westinghouse and served on the faculty at his alma mater since 1969. He was an excellent choice to take over the head coaching duties at the Homewood school. He played his football under the tutelage of the legendary Pete Dimperio.

Webb was quite familiar with the proud tradition of the Bulldogs as he had experienced it first hand as a student athlete. Now it was time for him to lead the House to further glory. He knew all too well the sacrifices and dedication it took to wear the gold and blue of Westinghouse. But times had changed since his playing days as this generation of boys had to be handled with a more delicate approach. The elements out on the streets were so overwhelming that it threatened to destroy a young boy who was unable to avoid such painful temptations and distractions. Coach Webb was well aware of what he was facing and he knew it wasn't going to be an easy ride. He realized that he had to be more than a coach, and he had all the attributes to get the job done. His dedication and loyalty was soon to be realized and appreciated by the community of Homewood.

The 1978 season was a real struggle as the Bulldogs posted a record of 3-5-0. It was the first losing season at Westinghouse since the 1931 season when the Bulldogs finished with a record of 2-5-1 under legendary coach "Pro" Burton. Webb knew he had to be patient and he was working hard to rekindle and maintain the winning spirit at Westinghouse. Peabody won the City Championship that year by defeating Perry 13-8.

## MAGNET PROGRAM AFFECTS THE HOUSE

The following year, 1979, the Pittsburgh Public School System introduced the open enrollment or Magnet Program. Now a student would have a choice of school to attend that offered a special program he or she desired to pursue. This certainly created both good and bad situations for several of the city schools. The old tradition of staying at home and attending the high school in your school district was being challenged. The community spirit was being challenged – especially the athletic programs.

This new enrollment system seemed to be benefiting two schools – Brashear High School and Perry Traditional Academy. Homewood was losing its community loyalty that it held for so many years. Both Brashear and Perry were reaping the harvest as they were attracting many of the fine student athletes across the City of Pittsburgh. Coach Webb continued to work hard trying to convince his student athletes to stay at Westinghouse and continue to maintain the values that made the Homewood school so special. This was not an easy task as the student peer pressure was having a lot to do with the temptation of leaving one school district to enroll in another. There were many reasons why this was taking place as many of the students were searching for what was best suited for them. Educational choices were the most important concern for the students, but before long it was developing into an athletic lottery. I could see that coming during my travels to and from work in downtown Pittsburgh.

It was common to see students traveling cross-town on buses wearing their school colors. I can remember back when the Pittsburgh Public School System watched closely for enrollment violations, but now it was a whole new plan. It was attend the school where you lived or else lose your eligibility status to play varsity sports. Times were changing and the Homewood community was losing a lot of quality student athletes as they were attending other schools of choice. Westinghouse High School was one of the hardest hit when this new enrollment program was put into the Pittsburgh Public School System. Realistically the magnet plan was a good opportunity for students to attend programs that were best suited for their educational needs, but it appeared to go beyond those limits. Westinghouse was seeing too many of their students leaving to go elsewhere. I was really concerned to see this happen; it appeared that the traditional value of a neighborhood was no longer a priority to our young people. It was like leaving your family behind for better choices. Maybe I am too much of a sentimentalist, but this is what Westinghouse High School had done for me.

I was proud of the six years that I spent there; of course that was fifty years ago and we did not have to contend with any of the elements that have put the wrath of fear into those who remain there today. Obviously, this is something that has to change before we lose more innocent lives. These elements of destruction are appearing everywhere and until our society wakes up and regroups it will continue. It all has to start at home with respect and parental guidance. I do not envy any parents or single parents that are trying to raise children today. It has to be a

241

monumental challenge with all the distractions that have surrounded our society. There are so many discouraging elements that can literally bring down a human being. With all the latest state of the art conveniences that have made life much easier we still have too many people who are suffering, and that is so hard to imagine.

It is a tough world out there and it will take the strength of our leaders to right the ship of life. Promises come and go with every administration, but we have so many issues that have to be addressed here in our own country. Helping the overseas countries is fine, but we have so many concerns here in our country that must be resolved. We need leadership in our country that must strive to solve our own problems before we try to help those countries abroad.

242

A WINNING TRADITION

**Rudy Musilin and Pete Dimperio**

243

**Fred Malins, D. Simone, Phyllis Jones, E. Karpa, Leon Dillard**

244

—Press Photo by Albert M. Herrmann Jr.

Westinghouse's Lovie Venson on his way to 10 of the 258 yards he gained in a 26-6 win over Carrick for the City League title.

1976 City League Co-Champions:  Westinghouse 20 Peabody 20

Westinghouse's Don Arrington has pass batted away by Peabody's Kevin Wells (34) and Donell Creighton.

Press Photos by Anthony Kaminski

245

246

*This is what happens when small minds take over and ruin the fun of watching a high school football game like normal people would.*

—Post-Gazette Photo by BILL LEVIS

## Standees

Carrick High students and fans who were banned from attending yesterday's Carrick-Fifth Avenue football game at South High Stadium by city school rules watch the game from a walkway outside the stadium while an adult sits in the grandstands. Carrick won the game, 36-22. The ban was imposed to prevent possible fighting among students and fans from rival schools.

*Football Squad:* H. Dorsey, E. Livingston, J. Ellison, A. Simpson, R. Duck, D. Warner, D. Mosley, T. Young, J. Gordon, A. Young, C. Ezell, Manager. FOURTH ROW: R. Huntley, D. Emanuel, R. Morris, R. Bogus, L. Carter, K. Taylor, D. Shelton, S. Allen, M. Weston, W. Anderson, D. Vasser, J. Miller, M. Hill, H. Hopson.

*Football Squad.* FRONT ROW: N. Givens, Manager, C. Haywood, E. Lane, J. Ward, S. Smith, W. Porter, R. Wright, A. Young, E. Venson, C. Jackson, Manager. SECOND ROW: Coach A. Catanese, G. Anderson, E. McKenzie, E. Sharpley, L. Hammond, J. Pearson, D. Anderson, T. Myles, W. Dennis, A. Vasser, A. Currie, Coach P. Mazzei. THIRD ROW: Coach R. Musulin, D. Hawthorne, L. Dudley.

## FOOTBALL

The fabled Westinghouse Bulldogs began their season with a shattering romp over Oliver High. Under the direction of Coach Rudy Musulin, the Bulldogs marched all the way to the championship game. Spirited by the explosive assaults of senior fullback, Mike Weston, and the fleet-footed jaunts of senior halfbacks, Sonny Allen and Willie Anderson, the "House" rolled over eight teams in the newly combined City League. In their only loss of the season, the Bulldogs competed with honor. For it is defeat rather than victory that is the true test of a champion. The 1967 WHS Football Squad exhibited the qualities of school spirit and fair play that are vital allies of sportmanship, the Westinghouse tradition.

| 1967 FOOTBALL RECORD | | |
|---|---|---|
| Westinghouse | | Opponent |
| 67 | Oliver | 0 |
| 35 | Fifth Avenue | 19 |
| 41 | Langley | 0 |
| 40 | Peabody | 27 |
| 25 | Schenley | 0 |
| 13 | South Hills | 12 |
| 26 | Carrick | 19 |
| 33 | Gladstone | 6 |
| | Championship Game | |
| 13 | Allderdice | 20 |

The "House" in meditation.

Coach Rudy Musulin

247

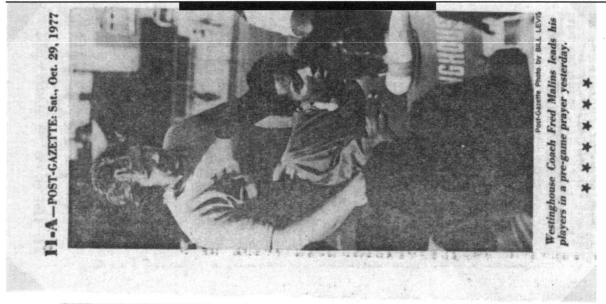

F1-A—POST-GAZETTE: Sat., Oct. 29, 1977

Post-Gazette Photo by BILL LEVIS

Westinghouse Coach Fred Malins leads his players in a pre-game prayer yesterday.

★★★★★

248

1976

Post-Gazette Photo by BILL LEVIS

Ahmad Shareef, fleet Westinghouse quarterback, en route to 59-yard TD. The House beat South, 30-6.

*Burton • Dimperio • Musilin • Malins • Webb*

# PART 3
## CHANGES AND CHALLENGES

*George Webb the student athlete who played for the legendary Pete Dimperio, was now the Head Coach of the Westinghouse Bulldogs. The challenges he faced were numerous as the generation he tutored were troubled with many outside pressures. Webb was to be commended for his gifted leadership as he guided many of those young men to the pinnacle of their high school football careers. Those young men followed his lead and reached a milestone that many high schools across the country are striving to reach. That milestone was garnering the 500th win in history of the proud Westinghouse Bulldogs. In spite of those many changes and challenges the Bulldogs rose to the top one more time before the end of a memorable twentieth century. Coach Webb will long be remembered along with Pro Burton and Pete Dimperio for guiding Westinghouse High School for so many successful years.*

# 9 | THE 1980s AND THE PASSING OF A LEGEND

For the first time since 1966, Pittsburgh's City League football teams were leaving their oil soaked concrete fields traveling out to meet the big bad boys of the WPIAL. City schools stopped playing outside competition for the past fourteen years mainly because they were getting beat badly. Too many games were so one sided that the city coaches had to ask the opposition to let the clock run in the second half during timeouts. Westinghouse's Pete Dimperio was one city coach who never had to ask for mercy in the 1950's and 1960's, his Bulldogs played the best of the WPIAL and elsewhere, and more often than not, they would return home a winner. During that time period his record against those outside opponents was a respectable 43-18-2. Coincidentally, after the 1966 season (the year Dimperio retired) the City League discontinued playing outside competition.

"For Westinghouse, going out to play the WPIAL teams on grass fields, under the lights in front of 12,000 fans was the biggest thrill of them all," lamented the 75 year old Dimperio. In fact, in 1966, the Bulldogs were unable to find an outside opponent to complete its pre-season schedule of three games. Nobody wanted to play Westinghouse back then.

But 1980 was a different era and the experiment of playing one outside opponent was going to be interesting. Westinghouse was scheduled to play Punxsutawney in its season opener. The Bulldogs returned home disappointed after a 42-14 beating. Coach Webb had his work cut out for him. The Bulldogs battled back and finished the season with a respectable record of 5-3-1.

## WEBB CAPTURES FIRST CITY TITLE

The following year, 1981, was one that Coach George Webb would never forget. It was one that saw his Bulldogs led by All-City quarterback Fred Marshall compile a fine season record of 10-1-0. Marshall was running the T-formation with all the attributes of a field general. When he was a junior in 1980, Webb called all his plays, but this year was different. Webb said, "He really came into his own – calling his own plays at the line of scrimmage, it was like having another coach on the field." He was the real deal – passing with uncanny accuracy and running with the football when he had to. Marshall was also the team's punter along with handling all the place kicking duties. He was probably the best passing quarterback in Westinghouse history since 1971 when the house abandoned the famed single-wing offense. The last time a Westinghouse quarterback made All-City was 1976 and 1977 and he was Ahmad Shareef.

The Bulldogs opened the 1981 season with a familiar outside opponent, Punxsutawney. This time around the House reversed the results defeating the Groundhogs 13-0. The following week, it was the City League opener against South Hills. The Bulldogs prevailed 24-0. By the eighth week of the season Westinghouse was undefeated and the next game was against neighboring rival Peabody who was also undefeated in league play. This was the big game as it always had been in the history of City League football. It was going to be Westinghouse's high powered offense against a strong Peabody defense. The game was played at Westinghouse Field and it rained throughout causing field conditions to become a sea of mud. Westinghouse led throughout most of the game 6-0 on a Fred Marshall to Sheridan Arrington pass and run play that covered 47 yards. Marshall missed the all-important placement kick that would come back to haunt them later. Peabody took advantage of a Westinghouse miscue in the fourth quarter and capitalized on it. The Highlanders gained good field position when the Bulldogs failed to get a fourth down punt away from their own twenty-four yard line. Peabody took over and after two running plays put the ball on the Westinghouse eight yard line. From there Highlander running back Larry Eleam took it in for the touchdown. The try for extra point was good as kicker and quarterback Chris Olive split the uprights and Peabody went back home with a hard earned 7-6 victory. The Bulldogs out-gained the Highlanders almost two to one but still lost the game.

As the season schedule came to an end, Peabody was on top with a record of 7-0-1 followed by Westinghouse and Carrick each with records of 7-1-0 in City League play. By virtue of this final finish Peabody qualified to play in the Pittsburgh City Championship game against the winner of the Westinghouse-Carrick playoff. Carrick was led by Kevin Hanlon who was All-City quarterback in 1980 as a junior. This season he was considered as one of the best to come out of Carrick High School. Metro Index College Scouting Service listed Hanlon as the No. 1 Sleeper (or most underrated player) in the WPIAL and City League. I was quite familiar with Kevin as his older brother Chip worked with me at a small company (Deci Corporation) in Bridgeville. In fact, I attended this playoff game with Chip and his family at South Stadium on November 7, 1981. It had all the pre-game hype of a showdown between two good quarterbacks. Chip knew I was a Westinghouse grad, and I realized that the Hanlon family had high hopes for Kevin and his Carrick teammates. I sat through the entire game with mixed emotions and applauded both teams. Carrick scored first on an 80 yard drive capped off with a 21 yard scoring pass from Hanlon to Joe Reddy. Hanlon's extra point kick failed and the Raiders led 6-0 after one quarter of play. In the second quarter the Bulldogs executed a nine-minute, eighteen play drive covering 80 yards. Tim Anderson plunged over from the one yard line for the tying touchdown. Westinghouse stayed on the ground for the entire drive as Carrick gambled that Marshall was going to go to the air. He did not as Webb took advantage of the prevent defense that the Raiders were willing to go with. This enabled Westinghouse to stay on the ground as they piled up the yardage and used the clock to its advantage. The score was tied 6-6 at halftime – a surprise to all the experts as they expected an air show between Hanlon and Marshall. They were half right – Carrick passed, but Westinghouse stayed with the ground game knowing that Marshall could air it out if needed.

On the first play from scrimmage after the intermission, Bulldog speedster, Rick Diggs rambled 75 yards untouched for the go-ahead touchdown. Hanlon continued to move the ball through the air, but could not get near the end zone. An interception by Darvin Randolph and a continually tight defense by the House held the Raiders at bay. With a little over two minutes left in the game the Bulldog's Tim Anderson scored his second touchdown on a thirteen yard scamper. This sealed the win for the House. Carrick scored with fifty-two seconds left on a beautiful 55-yard pass from Hanlon to Dan Higgins, but it was too late for the Raiders. Westinghouse prevailed 19-12 and would meet Peabody the following week for the City Championship. As I was leaving South Stadium I looked across the field and saw that familiar wave of gold and blue and heard the sound of the Westinghouse band playing "Westinghouse Forever" – I felt the goose bumps as that old school spirit never goes away.

## PEABODY VERSES WESTINGHOUSE ENOUGH SAID!

For as long as anyone can remember this has been the game in the City League; a neighborhood rivalry with bragging rights to the winner. The sight was South Stadium on November 14, 1981 at 10:00 A.M. – a Saturday morning slugfest. On paper it was Westinghouse's offensive machine to be tested by a solid Peabody defense.

They had played earlier in the season on a muddy field and Peabody came away with a close 7-6 win. This time it was on the artificial turf of South Stadium before an overflow crowd of 10,000 loyal fans from both East Liberty and Homewood and many curious outsiders to see these two old rivals square off again.

The House drew first blood on a thirty yard pass play from Fred Marshall to Jonathan Bailey. The try for point after failed. Westinghouse led 6-0 after the first quarter. Early in the second quarter Westinghouse took advantage of a blocked punt that came to rest on the Peabody 11. Three plays later Marshall hit Bailey again in the corner of the end zone and the Bulldogs led 12-0. The try for point after again failed.

Peabody came back on their next possession scoring on a 31 yard run by Ted Nelson and a perfect extra point kick by quarterback Chris Olive closed the gap to 12-7. On the ensuing kickoff Peabody recovered a Bulldog fumble on the Westinghouse 27 yard line. But the House defense stood its ground and held. The score at the half was still 12-7 in favor of Westinghouse. Both teams battled hard in the second half with no further scoring. Peabody gained only one first down the entire second half as the Bulldog defense was relentless. George Webb had captured his first City title as Head Coach at Westinghouse. His mentor former Bulldog coach Pete Dimperio, Sr. was there in attendance and a proud spectator. This is what made coaching so rewarding; seeing one of your former pupils winning a championship. Dimperio's son Pete, Jr. was Faculty Manager at the time and a strong supporter for George Webb.

253

Score by quarters:

| | | | | |
|---|---|---|---|---|
| Peabody | 0 | 7 | 0 | 0 – 7 |
| Westinghouse | 6 | 6 | 0 | 0 – 12 |

Scoring:

Westinghouse – Bailey 30 pass from Marshall (Pass failed)

Westinghouse – Bailey 6 pass from Marshall (Kick failed)

Peabody – Nelson 31 run (Olive Kick)

All three playoff teams placed players on the 1981 City League All-Star Team.

Westinghouse – Fred Marshall, QB, Mark Walker, LB

Peabody – Larry Eleam, HB-OLB.

Carrick – Kevin Hanlon, QB; Joe Reddy, E-DB

Schenley: Miles Brandon, DE; Anthony Williams, DE-DT

Brashear; Daryle Faulk, DLB-OT

Perry: Brain Miller, C-G-DT

Langley: Bob Howard, TB-DHB

South Hills: Brian Renk, OT-DT

City Player of the Year: Kevin Hanlon, Carrick

City Coach of Year: George Webb, Westinghouse

1981 Westinghouse Squad:

J. Evins, R. Fitzpatrick, P. Smith, F. Marshall, D. Poindexter, J. Bailey,
D. Jackson, D. Hall, D. Pollard, T. Anderson, V. Givner, R. Rose, J. Strowder,
D. Randolph, G. Jackson, P. Lindo, R. Diggs, B. Shealy, G. Harper, A. Wright,
J. McNeil, A. Lane, G. Branch, D. Holmes, I. Syhmms, R. Olivis, L. Jackson,
M. Walker, D. Segers, G. Simmons, B. Manison, S. Ellies, K. Wilbon,
R. Tillman, G. Smith, M. Washington, C. Jackson, D. Ware, W. Best,
C. Patterson, O. Felix, S. Arrington, K. Jackson, P. Harris, K. Henry, D. Braxton.

Head Coach – George Webb

Assistant Coaches – John Barnes, Leroy Dillard, John Tarke

Principal – William L. Nicholson

Faculty Manager – Peter Dimperio, Jr.

Student Managers – T. Patterson, W. Wheaton, D. Webb, S. Martin, C. Evins

**1981 Season Record**

| | | | |
|---|---|---|---|
| WHS | 13 | Punxsutawney | 0 |
| WHS | 24 | South Hills | 0 |
| WHS | 7 | Schenley | 0 |
| WHS | 26 | Oliver | 0 |
| WHS | 58 | Allegheny | 7 |
| WHS | 38 | South | 6 |
| WHS | 17 | Perry | 13 |
| WHS | 6 | Peabody | 7 |
| WHS | 18 | Langley | 14 |

Playoff

WHS  19     Carrick      12
    City Championship
WHS  12     Peabody       7

The following year, 1982, the Bulldogs were the defending champions and returned to South Stadium to defend their title. They completed the regular season with a record of 8-2-0. Brashear was a worthy challenger and defeated the House 13-6 and were crowned City Champions for 1982. It was Brashear Coach Ron Wabby's first season as Head Coach and winning his first City League title was quite an honor.

He had served as an Assistant on the Brashear coaching staff for five years under Jim Thompson (a Peabody graduate). Two weeks earlier Westinghouse had defeated Brashear 21-8 at home during the regular season, but Wabby had his team well prepared for the return match as they took the title away from the House.

During the early 80's, several years after he retired, Pete Dimperio was quite proud of his former players who were still involved with Westinghouse. Head Coach, George "Spider" Webb and his assistant, Joe Golden, both played for Pete in the early 60's. So did Dr. Bill Nicholson, the school's principal. "I sent Spider to Thiel, where I had played my college ball," said Dimperio. "My son, Pete, Jr., is the Activities Director and Faculty Manager at Westinghouse so I am still close to the Homewood school." Dimperio would always remain a huge part of Westinghouse High School. The mere mention of the school or the former coach was synonymous.

The mid 80's saw the Bulldogs having just average success as Brashear and Perry were the schools that dominated.

**255**

## WESTINGHOUSE MOURNS THE LOSS OF A LEGEND

On July 14, 1986 dark clouds loomed over Pittsburgh when a news bulletin broke that legendary Westinghouse coach Pete Dimperio had passed away.

I remember boarding a bus in Oakmont the following morning heading for work. I sat in my seat and began to read my newspaper when I came across the obituary of our former teacher and coach. I must have read the article of his passing several times until I arrived at my workplace in downtown Pittsburgh. As I pondered over a cup of coffee, my phone rang and it was Chuck White a Westinghouse alumnus. We spoke and made plans to pay our last respects. I felt like I lost a family member as he came into my life several times long after my school days. I'd like to share this article with you as it so much reflects the feelings of many of us who were fortunate to have had him as our coach, teacher and friend.

## DIMPERIO DIES, BUT HIS LESSONS LIVE
*By Bill Utterback – The Pittsburgh Press*
*July 15, 1986*

The glow from the movie screen at the Silver Lake Drive-in Theater cast a vague light on the football field at Westinghouse High School. It was just enough light for

Coach Pete Dimperio to conduct practice.

"Sometimes we'd be down there until 8 or 9 at night," said Rudy Musulin, Dimperios' assistant for seven years.

We'd be down there in the dark going over a single play 50 or100 times; going over it until everybody got it right; until everybody was perfect. That's the way Pete coached, nobody ever complained. The kids understood. You don't quit working until the job is done."

On those dark nights, and every other time he walked onto a field, Dimperio was coaching football. And he was coaching life. And he was successful at both.

Dimperio, 81, died of cancer yesterday in Shadyside Hospital. The lessons he taught on the football field have not perished.

"Pete's philosophy was that you could accomplish anything you wanted if you worked hard enough." Dr. Sal Migliore, a Penn Hills' orthodontist and a 1950 graduate of Westinghouse. "I've carried that philosophy wherever I've gone, whatever I've done. It's ingrained in me. It's tattooed on me. I think everybody who played for him feels that way."

Dimperio coached at Westinghouse for 21 seasons and won 17 City League titles before retiring in 1966. His overall record was 158-26-1, including a 118-5-1 record and a 59 game winning streak in City League competition. He won 12 titles in his last 13 seasons.

"Pete Dimperio and his teams at Westinghouse in the 40's and 50's and 60's personified excellence," said Westinghouse Coach George Webb who played for Dimperio from 1959-1962.

"I can remember many nights we were on the field well after it was dark, going over plays. On the nights before championship games, we'd be down there in the dark going over the same plays we'd used all year. We'd run them until he was sure we knew everything perfectly."

A 1926 graduate of Fifth Avenue High School, Dimperio played four years of football at Thiel College and coached junior high basketball at Herron Hill for 12 years – his record was 203-7 – before being appointed head football coach at Westinghouse.

Westinghouse had won City League titles under Coach O. H. "Pro" Burton in 1944 and 1945. Dimperio took over in 1946.

"Pro Burton was king in the community and everybody was saying 'Pete Who?,' but they found out who he was very quickly," Migliore said.

Dimperio led Westinghouse to City League titles in his first three seasons.

Through the years, Dimperio never changed from his single-wing offense.

"Everybody in the city of Pittsburgh knew our plays. We never changed the plays, but nobody could ever stop us," Migliore said.

The key was hard work.

"He believed in repetition," Webb said. "We'd run a play over and over and over in practice, then we'd run it some more."

He didn't give us a lot to learn," said Lenny Gallo, who played at Westinghouse from 1947-1949. 'We had only a few plays, but he made sure we knew them perfectly. That's all it takes to win."

Conditioning was important.

"We'd do 100 sit-ups and 100 pushups every day. We'd do neck bridges and he'd come around and sit on your chest," Migliore said. "And we ran. We'd run through the obstacle course, through the drive-in and down Washington Boulevard to the river. It was a 5 to 8 mile run every day after practice."

The football field at Westinghouse is surrounded by hills. Dimperio would stand at the top of a hill with his whistle.

"We'd run up and down the hills 10 or12 times before and after practice," Webb said. "We were the best-conditioned team in the city."

"He was a motivator and a master of psychology," said Frank Guadagnino, of Penn Hills, a 1948 graduate. "One time, we were playing a team that was very much an underdog to us. Pete benched the first team in practice and didn't let them start the game. He said we weren't working hard enough. By the time we got into game, we were ready to tear that team apart to get our first-team jobs back."

Sometimes Dimperio would use fiery speeches. Sometimes he would hardly say anything at all.

"We were losing to Schenley in 1961," Webb said, "Pete walked in at halftime and said, "I don't want anything to do with this team: you don't care about winning. Then he walked away. That's when the pride factor kicked in. We weren't going to let him down. We won the game."

Winning was not Dimperio's primary objective. It was a tool. It made it easier for him to teach.

"Everybody feels good about winning . . . but winning doesn't help you if you don't learn something." Dimperio said in a 1985 interview with The Pittsburgh Press.

And they all learned from Dimperio.

"He told us that whatever we chose to do in life, do the best job we could. If you're going to be a doctor, be the best doctor. If you're going to be a garbage man, be the best garbage man in the city," Guadagnino said.

"If you want to be a lawyer, be the best lawyer. If you want to be a bum, be the best bum," Webb said.

Guadagnino and Webb attended Westinghouse 15 years apart, but they learned the same lessons from Dimperio. He touched a lot of people in two decades, including the 250 athletes who earned college scholarships after playing for him.

"He was more than a football coach to those kids, said Musulin, the coach at South Vo-Tech. He gave them direction. He gave them a sense of pride."

Dimperio is survived by his wife, Adeline Villella, a son Peter P. Jr. of Oakmont, a daughter, Mary Margaret at home, a brother John of West Homestead and a sister Rose Fiorilli of Monessen.

Visitation will be from 2 to 4 and 7 to 9 p.m. today and tomorrow at John A. Freyvogel and Sons Inc., 4900 Center Avenue, Oakland.

Funeral services will be at 10 a.m. at St. Philomena's Church, 2740 Beechwood Boulevard, Squirrel Hill. Burial will be at Calvary Cemetery Hazelwood.

**257**

## SO CLOSE YET SO FAR

As the 80's decade was coming to an end the 1989 season was one that saw the House make such a strong showing in an effort to win the Pittsburgh City League Championship and possibly the PIAA State Championship.

Coach Webb guided his team to a fine season record of 9-3-0. The Bulldogs qualified for the City Title game losing a tough 7-6 decision to Perry Traditional Academy. The Commodores went on to the state playoffs and won the PIAA State AAA Final with a well earned victory over perennial Pennsylvania powerhouse Berwick High School 20-8. Perry coached by Gus Catanese had accomplished a City League first by capturing the coveted P.I.A.A. State Title. This victory was one for the entire City League of Pittsburgh and the only one to this date. Winning a state title in football by a Pittsburgh City League High School is definitely one for the ages. Perry High School had become a strong contender for state honors during the later part of the twentieth Century. Coach Gus Catanese, an old friend of mine from Morningside and a former assistant coach at Westinghouse High School, did a fine job at Perry High School winning several Pittsburgh City Titles at the North side school. He was awarded Coach of the Year honors in 1989 and 2000 by the NIASHF Chapter before retiring in 2001.

This fine 1989 Bulldog team showed signs of what was coming later in the 90's. The House was beginning to make strides, and regain some of the glory that had slipped away. In spite of losing so many talented athletes who chose to attend school elsewhere Westinghouse continued to contend for top honors. Years ago the opportunity to play football for Westinghouse High School was the desire of many who regarded it as an honor to have donned the gold and blue of the Bulldogs. Times have changed as it is no longer a mystique to play football at Westinghouse. The young men of today have a different mindset that sometimes goes far beyond what we considered to be worthwhile.

258

# Dimperio taught the game of life to his players

**By Dan Donovan**
The Pittsburgh Press

Friday, January 25, 1985

Lots of X's and lots of O's will be drawn, and trap blocks and sweeps and blitzes will dominate the annual Coach of the Year clinic this weekend at the Green Tree Marriott. But Pete Dimperio, who conducts the clinic, knows football plays are the mechanism of high school football, not its heart.

"Lots of coaches think the X's and O's are what's valuable." But it's not. The kids are. You've got to get close to the kids and tell them you're the greatest coach in the world. They'll believe you because everything else you tell them is right."

A coach must earn the kids' heart by caring, Dimperio said, not just by winning.

The coach who depends on winning for respect is going to lose. Next year he will lose — everybody does eventually — and when he does he will lose all his respect."

Dimperio likes to draw X's and O's. By the end of the conversation, he is drawing the single wing and showing how deception, not power, made it succeed enough for Westinghouse High School to win 17 City League championships in 21 years, 1946-66.

"We spent more time on deception than blocking," Dimperio said. The same principle holds true today, Dimperio said. The San Francisco 49ers won the Super Bowl because quarterback Joe Montana was a master of deception and play-action passes.

Dimperio was 118-5-1 in the City League, which means a loss about every four years, and 40-21-1 against the better teams in the WPIAL — Aliquippa, New Castle, Altoona, Mt. Lebanon.

Dimperio is 79, his face craggy but his wit sharp enough to realize it's more difficult to get close to high school kids today.

"The trouble with high school football today is they have placed four or five schools into one. Loyalty to that school takes time to develop and the kids don't get a sense of playing for the community. The schools are so big, they get lost in the shuffle.

"You have to teach the kids to care about each other, care about their school. I told them if they don't care about Westinghouse more than life itself, to get out of here. If they tell me they don't like an English teacher, I tell them to get out of here. They have to like it all Westinghouse, the English teacher, all of it."

Dimperio said it's difficult for a coach teaching at a different school than the one he's coaching to motivate the students that way.

"A lot of the coaches don't teach in the same school. I think that's bad. My success was my closeness with the players. I knew their brothers, their parents, where they lived, what they ate. I was not their coach, I was their leader, showing them the way to success in life."

To be a good coach, Dimperio said, you must develop a cult.

"I know people think that is a bad word, that a cult is a bad thing. But that's not always true. I had 50 kids who saw me in the halls every day and who spent an hour with me after school. And every day they heard me talk for 10 minutes about life, about money, about girls."

Dimperio always coached in an economically depressed area, but he told players he hoped they didn't make any easy money.

"If you make easy money, it's the worst thing that can happen to you. You'll waste it. If you earn money the hard way, you'll watch it more carefully, be careful how it is spent, because it was so hard to get."

And Dimperio taught "respect for womanhood."

"I told them to treat every girl like a lady."

Rarely, Dimperio said, does a day go by when he doesn't run into a former player who says his words helped him to a better life. He ticks off a list of lawyers, doctors, coaches, and educators who played for him, still calling them "kids," even though admitting "they are all 40 or 50 now.

The thrill of coaching is not winning. Winning is a thrill for a moment. The real thrill is looking back at kids 40 years and finding out what they are doing today. In business, you don't have the neat things that happen to you in high school football. The human element is missing. In football, you're dealing with human beings every day, with their emotions and tragedies."

"I always tried to give my kids some direction. If you don't have a direction in football, and it doesn't have a follow-through in real life, what good is football?

"Everybody feels good about winning. I always said winning was easy — you need good athletes, lots of luck, some breaks and you can win. But winning doesn't help you if you don't learn something."

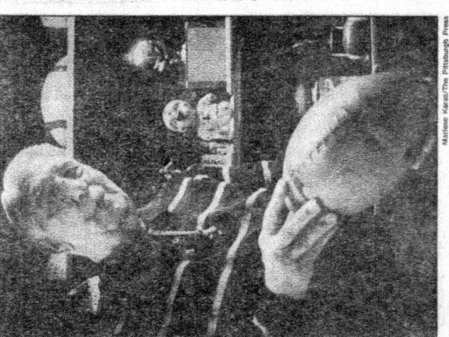

*Marlene Karas/The Pittsburgh Press*

Pete Dimperio displays his football memorabilia

259

260

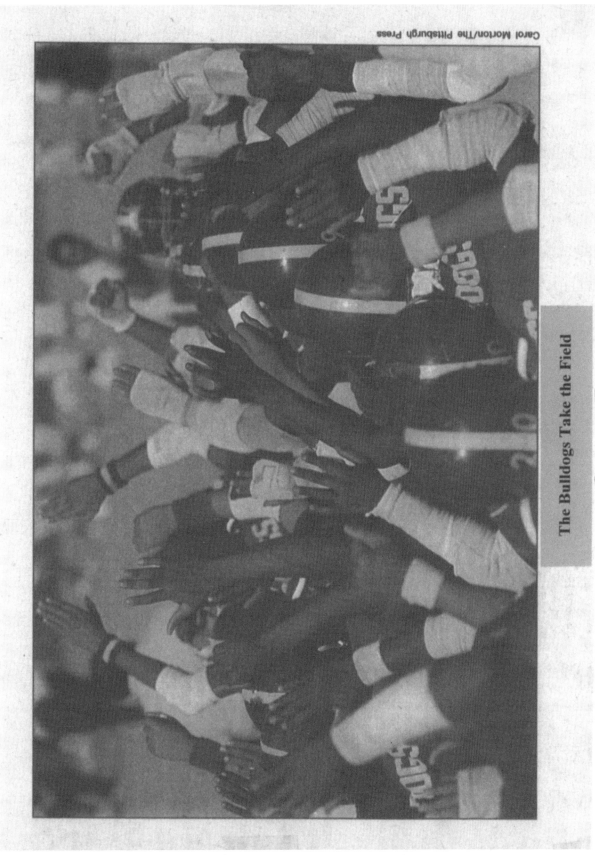

Carol Morton/The Pittsburgh Press

The Bulldogs Take the Field

261

*Burton • Dimperio • Musilin • Malins • Webb*

**Pittsburgh Post-Gazette**　　　　　　　　SATURDAY, OCTOBER 23, 1982

262

Albert French/Post-Gazette

Westinghouse Coach George Webb and his team celebrate after clinching a berth in the city championship football game with a 34-6 victory over Allderdice yesterday. Westinghouse meets Brashear, a 15-8 winner over Schenley, for the city title Saturday, Nov. 13. Today's high school coverage, Pages 11-12.

*Burton • Dimperio • Musilin • Malins • Webb*

# 10 | THE 1990s - WEBB LEADS HOUSE TO A MILESTONE

The last decade of the 20th century saw Westinghouse High School continue its quest to stay on top and challenge Perry Traditional Academy for the coveted city title. This generation of young people was facing so many negative challenges that were affecting their lives. They were the kind of challenges that past generations never had to deal with. These young people were facing many disturbing distractions that were so bizarre and were far reaching across the country. Much of this behavior was beginning to surface shortly after the Vietnam War. This was a war that was so devastating to our young men that many of them were not able to overcome the mental and physical anguish they experienced while defending our homeland. Our country paid a high price as many families were suffering losses that would affect them forever.

The Post-Vietnam era was one that reflected so many changes in our society. Many families were experiencing trying times stemming from the aftermath of such a senseless war. Many of our veterans came home facing a thankless society, and a government that was not doing such a good job of helping them to get their lives back together. This was very discouraging after having sacrificed their lives only to return home to find the lack of appreciation among so many of our small minded protesters. How sad.

Much bitterness among our young people began to surface and thus our society was subjected to negative behavior. Drug trafficking, gang related turf wars and drive by shootings were literally destroying our young people. Westinghouse High School was suffering greatly from this out of control behavior pattern. Other schools in the city of Pittsburgh were also experiencing this widespread dilemma. Much fear was developing among the youth as they were literally afraid to attend school due to the dangers that existed in the streets and in the schools. This kind of behavior was literally affecting the lives and ambitions of the young people who were trying get an education and take part in school activities. The pressures that were inflicted upon these young people by the unruly and disrespectful hoodlums were unbelievable. I cannot imagine my youthful years being subjected to this kind of pressure. Respect for each other was a virtue that we learned at home and it was always the heart and soul of our behavior.

There is no quick fix to remedy this most discouraging behavior. It all begins at home, but more often than not the home life is non-existent – meaning both parents are working or only one parent is shouldering the burden. Many households are dysfunctional as there is a lack of respect and family unity. If family values are not respected at home then unfortunately they are carried over into the schools. This is such an injustice for the teaching profession to have to face day in and day out. It creates such an unhealthy situation. Until our society wakes up and faces up to these challenges with sensible solutions we are doomed.

Whatever happened to the old-fashioned family values that were the heart and soul of our society? They should not be considered old-fashioned values as many of our youth of today think they are. One word, **RESPECT** epitomizes what is lacking in our society today. Look around and realize where we are coming up short. More often than not it will be the lack of self respect and respect of others. The younger generation is struggling in many ways, and for some they refuse to see the trees for the forest. This statement is as clear as a ringing bell. There seems to be a lot of hatred and anger among them. Respect and compassion for others are values that the entire world needs to develop.

Westinghouse High School was no different than any other school across this great land of ours, feeling the affects of much of this unfortunate behavior pattern. It was creating so much hatred and fear that it was overflowing into senseless turf wars between neighboring schools. How sad to think that past generations used the turf of mother nature to play football games, but this generation has been using the city streets as their turf to make warfare within our neighborhoods. The value for human life is being challenged by small minds that have no respect for each other. We were proud to wear our school colors, but today many of the youth proudly wear various colors of bandanas or shirts to represent their gang allegiance. Much of this eventually leads to destruction of human lives. Only God can help these poor souls because they will never experience the full value of life.

One of the most discouraging trends that I have seen happening in recent years is the movie industry producing films of a violent nature. Our young people are viewing such films day in and day out. Even some of the cartoons are displaying aggressive behavior that our preschoolers are watching from time to time. Something is wrong here and it does not take a psychologist to sort out the potential consequences that are developing. Until our society wakes up and realizes that good sound entertainment does not have to contain violent behavior. The old proverb – "Plant good seeds and harvest healthy crops." This goes beyond the farmers' almanac. It really does apply to every family throughout the world. Raise good children and they will blossom.

Many times over I have said "I may have left Westinghouse, but Westinghouse never left me." I wonder how many of our younger generation would echo those sentiments today. We thank our parents for providing us with the quality of life that can be summarized with one word – **RESPECT.** Many of us did not have much, but there was always that one value of self respect and respect for others.

Enough for the venting of my frustrations; and let me close out this final decade of football at Westinghouse as it turned out to be a special one in many ways. Through the determined efforts of Coach George Webb and his staff the Bulldogs were able to climb to one more glorious and victorious level; a level that was so much

264

a part of the rich tradition of Westinghouse High School.

Coach George Webb was every bit a believer of respect, pride and loyalty. I had the pleasure of meeting him personally in 1992 and I was really impressed. I saw a man who was dedicated to his profession in every sense of the word. When he told me how he felt every time he heard our school song, "Westinghouse Forever" I knew where he was coming from. And win he did as in the 90's Webb reached a level of coaching that so many of his peers applauded. He made many of us alumni quite proud as he was so well respected by his players. Throughout most of his 25 years as head coach, Webb had to deal with many of the problems that challenged his players. He spent as much time dealing with their personal problems as he did with coaching and leading them to successful football careers. He learned some valuable lessons from his former high school coach, Pete Dimperio, and one of them was coaching the game of football much like facing the challenges in life. They are quite similar in nature with many setbacks and challenges that required perseverance and determination.

His dedication to the football program at Westinghouse was beginning to pay dividends. The early 90's saw the House battle Perry for city league supremacy, as the Commodores continued to draw talented athletes from the Homewood area. It had to be quite frustrating for Coach Webb; he never knew from season to season what to expect from the underclassmen as far as who was staying at the House; or who was transferring to attend another city school. The 1990 season saw the Bulldogs finish the season at 6-5-0 as Perry won the City Championship that year edging Oliver in the title game 6-0. The Bulldogs came back in 1991 to post a fine season record of 8-4-0. They battled Perry for the City Championship before losing a tough 14-11 decision to the Commodores.

265

## HOMEWOOD WINS TWO MIDGET FOOTBALL CROWNS

There was a horn of plenty waiting to feed into the future Westinghouse Bulldogs football program. It was good news when the Homewood - Brushton Stingers won the Allegheny County Midget League championship with a 7-0 victory over the Penn Hills Midgets. Also in the Termite Division the Homewood –Brushton Termites defeated Wilkinsburg 19-0 for the title after posting a perfect 12-0 season. Thanks to the Pittsburgh Courier for covering this as I would not have known there was still a keen interest for football looming in Homewood and Brushton. Now there was the question of how much of this talent would end up playing for the Westinghouse Bulldogs. The open enrollment in the Pittsburgh Public School System would continue to provide students with choices of transferring to other schools. This really affected Westinghouse in many ways as I alluded to this fact many times over.

## PARENTS THINK WESTINGHOUSE IS UNSAFE

Some residents in the Westinghouse school district were refusing to let their children attend classes at the high school, fearing the children would be attacked by unruly youths from Homewood. This was revealed in a feature article of the

Pittsburgh Press newspaper dated May 7, 1992. How in the world can such street behavior not affect the desire of students to attend Westinghouse? I was so disappointed when I read this article. After having experienced six years (1948-1954) of total pride and loyalty at this same school I am lost for the choice of words that I have for those trouble makers. Words that cannot be printed in this book express how I feel as I do not wish to go any further with this paragraph. Small minds of today become smaller by tomorrow. How sad it was to see Westinghouse High School suffer because of those senseless trouble makers. "I say, get a life and move on to a more respectable way of living. Let these young people fulfill their dreams with a good education so they can pursue their endeavors."

## A BANNER YEAR FOR THE HOUSE

Finally, after over ten years of frustration the City League Championship Trophy returned to Homewood in 1992. Not since the 1981 season had the Bulldogs won the coveted title. It was a long time coming and the House did it in a big way compiling a season record of 11-1-0 losing only to Lock Haven 20-19 in the PIAA State Playoffs.

The Bulldogs scored 484 points while giving up only 42 points to the opposition in twelve games. Seven of the wins that year were shutouts. It was one of the finest teams to represent Westinghouse in recent years as they performed with all the qualities of a champion. I managed to follow them throughout the season by radio on Pittsburgh Station WYJZ with Tony Girdano and Eddie Jeffries calling the action. Several of their games were carried on this radio station, and it brought back the old school spirit. Several of the former Bulldogs were visitors in the broadcast booth week after week sharing their memories of former coach Pete Dimperio and their glory days at the House with the broadcast team from WYJZ.

During the 1992 season the Pittsburgh Press and Post-Gazette newspapers were on strike and thus the news coverage shifted to other sources. Fortunately the Pittsburgh Courier was still working and did a fine job enabling us to keep tract of what was going on in the news world.

## CITY LEAGUE OPENS WITH A SHOWDOWN

The opening night of high school football began at South Stadium on September 4th with an afternoon game between defending City-League Champion Perry and worthy challenger Westinghouse. The two had met the previous year and it was a dandy with Perry coached by Gus Catanese besting the Bulldogs in a thriller 14-11. Both teams were returning several experienced lettermen promising another good match-up. Westinghouse was led by senior Shawn Yancey, 6-3, 250, a two-way stalwart at both center and defensive tackle. The Bulldogs were rebuilding their backfield as graduation had depleted the entire group led by quarterback Aaron Justice who had gone on to the University of Akron. Perry was returning several key veterans that were sure to make the Commodores an early favorite to challenge again for the title. Coach Webb managed to find enough talent to rebuild his backfield and behind a solid veteran line the Bulldogs upset the Commodores 17-3. The

266

Bulldogs proceeded to play the caliber of football that was a long time coming. The coaching staff led by George Webb worked hard to mold a championship contender. The big win over Perry was a real confidence builder.

## YANCEY TAKES CHARGE

Senior Shawn Yancey at 6' 4", 250 lbs. proved to be a strong leader for the Bulldogs with his outstanding athletic ability. Offensively his blocking ability created huge holes for backs, Hudhaifa Ismaeli, Elrades Wright, Wally Goldston, Anthony Williams and Shannon Campbell. Yancey along with Andre Nunley formed a line that give the Bulldogs room to break free and break free they did. The House was finally back. Yancey was arguably the best player in the City League, as Coach Webb alluded to this compliment. Joe Butler of Metro Index Scouting Service said the following of Yancey, "He's athletic with long arms and big hands, and is light on his feet for a player his size. He has a basketball body, but football size. When in full pads, Yancey looks quite intimidating. The dark plastic visor he wears on his face mask adds to his Darth Vader image."

## HOUSE ROLLS

The news media quoted – *"The only team that can beat Westinghouse is Westinghouse."* The coaching staff of the Bulldogs was fearful of this happening. There was one big echo – "If the heads stay on straight, and the work ethic during practice continues, the Too Live Crew on Murtland Avenue will challenge for the state title." The talent was there, but the biggest issue was whether they would be able to match up with the sophistication of suburban schools.

267

The Bulldogs began to roll after the big win over Perry winning the next eight games handily with six shut-outs. They were ready to challenge for the City Title along with Perry, Allderdice and Schenley – all qualifying for a playoff spot. The semi-final pairings pitted Westinghouse against Schenley and Perry opposing Allderdice. The Bulldogs rose to the fore with a lopsided 56-0 victory over Schenley while Perry bested Allderdice 14-0. Both games were broadcast over WYJZ radio with Tony Girdano and Eddie Jefferies calling the action.

## IT'S SHOWTIME PERRY VERSES WESTINGHOUSE

After winning the third semi-final City League playoff game in the past four years, Westinghouse Head Coach George Webb was preparing his team to meet the Commodores of Perry Traditional Academy for a fourth time in playoff competition. Perry had won the previous playoff meetings, twice in championship games. The Bulldogs defeated Perry in the season opener, but the Commodores were hoping to avenge that loss with a revamped offensive line and the addition of Lewis Waters who did not play in that game. The Bulldogs also won last year's regular season game only to come up short in the championship game. It was time for the House to bring the title back to Homewood and end Perry's three year reign.

The Bulldog faithful were not to be denied, as Westinghouse found a way to stop Perry's three year hold on the title with a solid 15-6 victory. The Bulldogs dominated the first half of the game scoring first on a 42 –yard field goal by Shawn Yancey early in the first quarter. Later in the quarter halfback Hudhaifa Ismaeli scored the first Bulldog touchdown on a beautiful 27-yard run to put the House on top 9-0 as Yancey's extra point attempt was blocked. The second quarter see-sawed back and forth with both teams having opportunities, but stout defenses prevailed on both sides. Perry had a field goal attempt blocked by the Bulldog's Taibu Wright. The House scored late in the second quarter on a 32-yard play by Wright putting the Bulldogs up 15-0 at half time. The third quarter saw a Bulldog field goal attempt from 19-yards blocked by Perry's Marcus Buford as the quarter ended. The Commodores began a comeback in the fourth quarter as Buford scored on a 15-yard pass reception to make the score 15-6 as the extra point attempt was not good. Perry soon got the ball back and began another series against the Bulldogs, but Westinghouse thwarted the effort with an interception by Ismaeli who played an outstanding game on both sides of the ball. The PA Pitt Hat, emblematic of the Pittsburgh City Title, was back in Homewood as the Bulldogs prevailed 15-6. It was a long time coming and the House did it in a big way compiling a season record of 11-1-0 losing only to Lock Haven 20-19 in the PIAA State Playoffs in a heartbreaker.

I called Coach Webb at the school the following week after the heartbreaking loss to Lock Haven and expressed to him how proud I was of him and the team for such an outstanding season. He appreciated my being such a loyal alumnus and since then we have become good friends. I told him how I had been tracking the football history of Westinghouse for a number of years and he was quite surprised that I had devoted so much to this endeavor. We continued to keep in touch with visits and phone calls. Needless to say we had a lot of memories to reminisce about.

## HEARTBREAKING LOSS IN STATE PLAYOFFS

Next game for Westinghouse was a trip to Altoona's Mansion Park in hopes of bringing the AAA State Title back home. The worthy opponent was Lock Haven High School from District 6 in Clinton County. The Bobcats were known to have unprecedented quickness, an aggressive defense led by 6-4, 265-pound nose guard Mahingus Silver and the disruptive Dustin Flook, and a diversified offense.

The Bulldogs found out early in the game that they were well scouted as some untimely mistakes and turnovers hurt the Bulldogs. Before they could settle down they were trailing 13-0. The Bobcats were able to neutralize the Bulldog's counter play because their nose guard was driving our center back into our pulling guard and tackle. This disrupted the execution of this misdirection play that worked all season by running backs Anthony Williams and Hudhaifa Ismaeli. Williams was the City's only 1000 yard rusher, but Lock Haven had him well scouted. This prompted Webb to call upon quarterback Wally Goldston to opt for more passing plays. He responded to the challenge and hit Taibu Wright on a beautiful 47-yard scoring play that put the Bulldogs back in the game 13-6.

There were times in the game when the officiating was too quick on the whistles as the Bulldogs were popping leather forcing the Bobcats to fumble the ball on several occasions. The quick whistles enabled Lock Haven to maintain possession. At times it was disturbing for Westinghouse, but they continued fighting to overcome their early game deficit.

Late in the game Westinghouse came back after trailing 13-6 at the half and scored twice to lead for the first time 19-13. The shocker came soon after the House gained the short lived lead. Lock Haven had one more big play left in its arsenal stunning the Bulldogs with a 56-yard scoring strike to tie the game 19-19. Then freshman kicker Travis Forney's extra point made it 20-19. Westinghouse came storming back, but time was running out with only three minutes left in the game. The Bulldogs drove from its own six yard line to the Lock Haven 30 yard line as time expired. And with it expired the hopes and dreams of this once in a lifetime Bulldog team. They came so close to winning an opportunity to bring the first Class AAA State Title to Homewood.

I listened to the entire game by radio and came away feeling very proud of this team that Coach George Webb put together. They played Westinghouse football that will always be remembered by the Bulldog faithful. Sometimes the best does not always win and it has often been said that it is better to be lucky than good. This was one game that had all the luck going against the Bulldogs.

## BULLDOGS CONTINUE ON THE HIGH ROAD IN 1993

269

Good fortune continued in 1993 as Coach George Webb molded together another title contender. Several holdovers from the '92 team were again to make another run for the City League Title. Coming so close to a state title was a positive experience for those returning veterans. They were part of a team that amassed 482 points wile limiting their opponents to a mere 42 points with seven shutouts in a twelve game schedule. It was one of the most impressive years in the history of Westinghouse football.

But that was last year and now it was time to get ready to defend the coveted PA Pitt Trophy. The House opened the 1993 season with a shutout win over neighboring Peabody. The following week it was Perry Traditional Academy waiting to get revenge from the two losses to the Bulldogs the previous year. Westinghouse was ready for the challenge and defeated the Commodores 35-13. Then came the lone defeat of the season as Schenley upset Westinghouse 28-20 and taught the Bulldogs that taking the high road was going to require a "stay focused mindset" in order to continue their winning ways. Coach Webb kept his charges on a solid path as the House won the next six games, but not without a close 14-12 win against a tough Brashear team midway through the season.

The playoffs were the next hurdle for the defending champs. The semi-final pairings were Westinghouse facing arch rival Peabody and Perry going up against Schenley. Junior quarterback Ramon Robinson was the offensive leader for the Bulldogs with his impressive all-around play. He was a solid performer with the ability to break away every time he touched the ball. Being an option type quarterback he kept defenses on their heels with his clever option techniques.

In the semi-finals the Bulldogs defeated Peabody in a tough rematch 22-13 while Perry topped Schenley 20-13 in the other rematch. Both games were excellent and well attended. The following week it was Westinghouse the defending champion against Perry who had been a nemesis for the Bulldogs more often than not. This time around Robinson and the House were ready, turning back the Commodores 40-0. The following week it was another shot at states against Lock Haven again in a quarter-final rematch. The Bulldog and Ramon Robinson played their hearts out before losing again to the Bobcats 13-8. The coaching staff for Lock Haven commended Robinson for his outstanding play.

Freshman linebacker, Robert Dixon, made All-City. This is the first time a freshman has received such an honor. The Bulldogs finished the season with an impressive record of 10-2-0. Ramon Robinson received All-City honors and was returning for his senior year in 1994.

## IT WAS PEABODY AND SCHENLEY IN 1994

Both Peabody and Schenley bounced back from 1993 with strong teams. Westinghouse did not make the playoffs for the first time since 1987. Senior Ramon Robinson made Fab."22" team. Peabody, our neighboring rival, had a great year posting a regular season record of 10-0. The Highlanders had team speed experience and were well balanced. They had all the attributes of a championship caliber team under Coach Bob Flaus. Schenley Coach, Jim Trent, worked hard to build a contender after seven seasons at the Oakland school. The Spartans were a solid team with a seven season record of 9-1. The Highlanders defeated Schenley in the City League Championship game of 8-7 for its eighth City title in school history. It was a tough game with both teams having opportunities to win. Darnell Dinkins scored first for Schenley on a 50-yard run with a recovered fumble in the first quarter and a Will Hargrove pass to wide receiver Ron Beck that covered 36 yards. Sophomore Kevin Barton ran for the winning two point conversion. Peabody senior center/defensive end Emanuel DiNatali (6-2-225) played a strong game on both sides of the ball. "Manny" is a member of my extended family through marriage. Westinghouse senior, Ramon Robinson made Fabulous 22. Sophomore linebacker – fullback Robert Dixon, made All-City for the second year in a row.

## IT WAS BRICK BY BRICK IN '95

The Post-Gazette pre-season rankings were: 1. Perry, 2. Schenley, 3. Peabody. Perry was considered a heavy favorite with seventeen starters back from 1994 to win the City Title. With only five seniors returning the Bulldogs were still expected to contend for a playoff spot based on potential talent. A lot depended on how well this inexperienced tem would come together. Junior linebacker-fullback, Robert Dixon, was one of the top players returning. He was an All-City selection in 1994. Webb was also counting on senior receiver, Julian Bennett and senior wingback-defensive end Ayo Young.

This was the year that the PIAA decided to use the overtime period to break all ties in all regular season games. This was already in place for all play-off games and championship games.

After a slow start the Bulldogs came around to win its final five games. Coach Webb was applauded by Joe Butler of Metro Index Scouting saying, "He's a tremendous coach". Webb alluded he was no miracle worker, but indicated that success comes from hard work, conditioning and discipline with a dash of flexibility thrown in for good measure. "I ask the kids to listen and do the things we ask them to do." His assistant coach, Leroy Dillard, once called the Bulldogs, "the meanest junkyard dogs around". According to Webb, Coach Dillard deserves much of the credit for the teams' ability to persevere despite their smallish stature and numbers. "He does a superb job of conditioning the team," said Webb of Dillard. He does outstanding work."

Offensively Webb used a scheme that was something of an anachronism. The Bulldogs turned to the Delaware Wing-T-offensive, which relied on counter plays, adept ball-handling and quick, elusive running backs, in 1986. This was done after the Bulldogs had used variations of the single wing formation since 1970. Webb felt it was a more suitable system for the personnel he had to work with. He was a believer that you had to be more adaptable or else you were not going to win.

Athletic Director, Lance Carter, expressed "Coach Webb takes marginal kids and makes them into great ballplayers." The program is intended to enable the kids to overcome a lot of more talented teams. I echo his sentiments as this is the way it was whenever I was a student at Westinghouse. I can recall how our team togetherness led by Coach Dimperio was the key to beating teams with more talented athletes. It was very tough to beat the Bulldogs when the entire team was molded together to overcome the opposition. Coach Webb, one of Dimperio's spark plugs, instilled the same values in his players.

271

The first four games of the 1995 season saw the Bulldogs winning the opener over Langley 22-16 followed by a 22-16 loss to Oliver; then later a tough win over Peabody 6-2. Perry defeated Westinghouse 7-6 after forcing the Bulldogs into poor field position throughout the game. Week five was the beginning of the turn around for the House. Schenley was beaten 35-0 with a performance by the Bulldogs that really surprised Webb. This was the beginning of better things to come. The following four games saw the Bulldogs gaining the valuable experience that Coach Webb was hoping for. South, Allderdice, Brashear and Carrick were all beaten as the House qualified for the playoffs with a record of 7-2. The other playoff teams were Peabody, Perry and Schenley. In one semi-final Westinghouse defeated Schenley 14-0 gaining a berth in the final against Peabody who had upset Perry in the other semi-final 20-12.

## BULLDOGS MEET DEFENDING CHAMPS

It was billed as another typical Peabody versus Westinghouse game. This time it was for the Pittsburgh City League Championship. Peabody was the 1994 defending champions and was looking to repeat in 1995. The two teams had met early in the season with the Bulldogs winning 6-2, but both teams improved along the way.

The game was played in a cold driving rain. Peabody fumbled deep in Highlander territory. The Bulldogs Shanti Ford recovered the ball on the 14-yard line of Peabody. On the next play, Ayo Young ran through the Peabody defense for a touchdown. Lamaas Bey went in for the two-point conversion. On the ensuing kick-off, Westinghouse did not kick the ball deep. Peabody failed to cover the ball, but the Bulldogs didn't. Westinghouse took over at the 30-yard line and scored on a 20-yard keeper by quarterback Andy Blackwell. Young ran in the two-point conversion and the House led 16-0 after the first quarter. Peabody struck back on a 45-yard run by Alan Parker, but the two-point conversion try failed, making the score 16-6. The Highlanders scored again as they were determined to close the gap. Austin Jones hit William Hargrove on a 23-yard touchdown strike. The two-point conversion failed and the Bulldogs now led 16-12. On the ensuing kick-off the Bulldogs gained good field position. They drove downfield and scored again on a 19-yard pass from Andy Blackwell to Julian Bennett. The two-point conversion was good and the House led 24-12 at the half. The second half was played in a downpour with no further scoring as both teams battled on even terms. It was the best game of the year. Westinghouse quarterback, Andy Blackwell, said it best, "Brick by brick is how we built this house". The House was the new City League Champions with a hard-fought victory. Webb said, "We started from ashes this year and built this team up. We just kept coming and coming." Peabody Coach, Bob Flaus alluded that his team couldn't quite get in gear as the Highlanders talented halfback, Kevin Barlow, was held to twenty yards on seven carries. Bulldog standout, Robert Dixon, shadowed the elusive Barlow the entire game and it worked.

The next game for the Bulldogs was a trip to the State playoffs to meet District 10, Sharon High School. A team that significantly outweighed the smaller Bulldogs and it showed in the final score, a 35-0 defeat. There was no need to hang their heads as it was a typical David versus Goliath match, but this time Goliath prevailed. Sharon was the runner-up in last year's PIAA State AAA game, losing to a powerhouse Berwick team 27-7.

## 1996 A YEAR OF MILESTONES

Webb saw a host of seniors returning from the 1995 championship team led by four time All-City performer, Robert Dixon. Dixon was the only player to make All-City all four years of his high school career at Westinghouse High School. I cannot recall anyone receiving such an honor in either the City League or the WPIAL. I can remember in 1993 (Dixon's freshman year) listening to a play-by-play game and hearing his name being called repeatedly making a play after play from his linebacker position. The broadcast team was impressed since he was only a ninth grader with such poise and talent. He was now a senior and the Bulldogs had a fine group of seniors to make another run at the city title.

This team averaged a hefty 235 lbs. from tackle to tackle with an all senior set of backs led by quarterback Andrew Blackwell and halfbacks Robert Dixon and Lamas Bey. There was overall team speed and it reminded me so much of the old Bulldog powerhouses. There were 45 players that showed up for the first practice. Usually

Webb was lucky to get thirty players, but this year it seemed to attract more kids after a fine l995 season.

The season opener saw the Bulldogs defeating Carrick 30-6, followed by a 54-0 win over Langley. Oliver played the House tough in game three before losing by 23-14. The Bears were a team that could surprise, but Robert Dixon of Westinghouse did a yeoman job to avoid an upset by the Bears.

Peabody was next for the Bulldogs and they were a real challenge. Kevin Barlow was expected to lead the Highlanders with all the ability to be one of the best to come out of the City League. Westinghouse found out in week four as Barlow rushed for 110 yards and helped the Highlanders defeat the Bulldogs 27-18. Peabody Coach, Bob Flaus, had to be pleased with the effort his team showed against a good Bulldog team.

## CLOSING IN ON 500 WINS

The Bulldogs rebounded the following week with big a win over always tough Perry 22-12. This victory was the halfway mark of the regular season. It gave Westinghouse its' 498th win in the school's storied history. I was well aware that the Bulldogs were closing in on the milestone of 500 wins. Only six WPIAL schools had won 500 games. They were New Castle, Greensburg Salem, Johnstown, Jeanette, Washington and Monessen.

I made a phone call to the Pittsburgh Post-Gazette Sports Department and informed Mike White, the high school sports correspondent, that Westinghouse was very close to reaching this milestone. He asked me to send him confirmation of this being factual and to call him the week of this scheduled historic game. I agreed to do that with great pleasure. The next game was a close 17-13 win for the Bulldogs over a determined Schenley team; it was win number 499 for Westinghouse.

273

Early in the week of this historic game the Pittsburgh Post-Gazette printed that Westinghouse would be seeking its 500th win against South High School. Coach Webb called me at home to tell me he was leaving a pass at the main stadium gate for me to see the game. I was looking forward to seeing Westinghouse play after having been away for so many years. The House was victorious over South 21-0 and thus making it the first City League School to win 500 games. It was a proud time for the school and added much to the rich history of Westinghouse.

The following week the Bulldogs defeated Allderdice 33-6 and ended the regular season with a 44-0 win over Brashear. Westinghouse finished with a record of 8-1 and qualified for the city playoffs along with Peabody, Perry and Schenley. This was the second consecutive year that the same four schools made the playoffs, and it was expected to be no different than the previous one as any one of the four teams was capable of taking the city title. The playoff games were played at South Stadium and the fans were treated to two fine football games. Peabody defeated Schenley 14-12 and gained the right to meet Westinghouse in the city final as the the Bulldogs beat Perry 19-3 for the second time this season in the other semi-final.

The two neighboring rivals separated by the Meadow Street Bridge were ready to do battle again for the Pittsburgh City League Championship. Early in the season Peabody defeated Westinghouse 27-18 and was looking to repeat the decision. This was a typical grudge match for bragging rights. Years ago, the bridge that separated the two school districts was no longer the norm as open enrollment gave one a choice. There were two next door neighbors with one family attending Peabody and the other family attending Westinghouse. This was a known fact and oh how I wish I could have had this choice back in 1952; so much for my wishful thinking that kept me off the Westinghouse varsity. It still hurts me to this day.

Let us get back to the title game. It was a day of nasty inclement weather. The game was delayed for 28 minutes in the first half because of thunder and lightening as both teams were sent back to their locker rooms. Later after the storm delay the Bulldogs offense ripped through South Stadium and propelled for two quick touchdowns before the half ended to take a 21-6 lead to the locker room. Coach Webb reminded his boys that the job was not done and there was still another half of football to play. The Bulldogs came out the second half and never let up scoring three more times to win going away 40-12. It is tough to beat a full house in poker and Westinghouse had a full house backfield with Andy Blackwell, Lamaas Bey, Robert Dixon and Ezra Coles. This was title number thirty-five in the storied history of Westinghouse High School and over 500 wins. I am proud to say it was a pleasure to rewrite the history of such a proud tradition. "Thanks for the Memories Westinghouse Forever".

### 1996 City League Championship Summary
### Westinghouse 40    Peabody 12

274

Scoring:

Westinghouse – Andy Blackwell 11 yd. run (Ezra Coles run)
Peabody – Kevin Barlow 28 yd. pass from Austin Jones (pass failed)
Westinghouse – Lamaas Bey  48 yd. run (pass failed)
Westinghouse – Jason Freeman 10 yd. pass from Blackwell (Khalil Arter kick)
Westinghouse – Robert Cash 7 yd. pass from Blackwell (Arter kick)
Westinghouse – Robert Dixon 10 yd. run (pass failed)
Peabody – Kevin Barlow 79 yd. kickoff return (run failed)
Westinghouse – Lammas Bey 15 yd. run (kick failed)

### PIAA Class AAA Playoff (First round)
### Greenville (Dist. 10) 29    Westinghouse (Dist. 8) 6

This was a game that saw the Bulldogs score first on a flawless 11-play, 80 yard drive late in the first quarter. On a 3 yard pass from Andy Blackwell to Robert Cash the House took the lead 6-0. It was a short lived lead as Greenville came back to score to give the Trojans a 7-6 lead. The Bulldogs wheels began to spin in the sloppy turf of Sharon High Stadium. Three critical mistakes by the House proved costly as every time they mounted a drive they self-destructed. Even most of the press box pundits from the Greenville area speculated that it would have been a different game if the Bulldogs had not self-destructed. All in all, there was nothing to hang their heads as the fans did see a good football team not playing up to its potential. As Coach Webb alluded to that you cannot make costly mistakes and expect to win. It was a great year for Coach Webb and his Westinghouse Bulldogs and I will always treasure my memories of this fine team.

## MORE ACCOLADES FOR THE 500 WINS

As the 20th century was coming to a close, much in the way of recognition by the news media was given to the Bulldogs for having reached the 500 wins milestone. Westinghouse was being applauded for its outstanding winning percentage of 0.726. Being ranked high across the state of Pennsylvania (No. 3) as well as the nation (No. 5) was huge. In October of 1997, according to the National Association of High Schools in Kansas City, Missouri, Westinghouse High School was ranked 5th among the top 12 high schools in the nation in the percentage of wins across the nation. Considering what I have read of the many successful football programs across America, Westinghouse High School can be proud of what it accomplished during this historic time period. This will be a tough act to follow, but I can see Perry High School accomplishing this feat in the not too distant future. The way the enrollment policy is structured within the city of Pittsburgh, Perry is destined to achieve this goal sooner or later.

Westinghouse always had a loyal student body and needs this kind of support to continue in order to follow what the early classes have so proudly accomplished. As a proud alumnus I have this say to the future classes at Westinghouse; "When you walk through that corridor of the Hall of Fame, pause to realize, that the alumni you see gracing those walls were proud to have graduated from Westinghouse High School." Our winning ways in football was a morale booster and a form of motivation that was the heart and soul of Westinghouse High School, and it lasted for almost 90 years. It was something special that will continue to be remembered by so many of us that benefited from the pride and spirit that it gave to us. That pride and spirit had a lot to do with the Bulldogs winning over 500 games and 35 championships. Today I extend my best wishes to those students at Westinghouse and sincerely hope that they will achieve their goals and be proud of having passed through those hallowed halls.

275

# THE END OF AN ERA

## GEORGE WEBB

# Rivals battle for City title

**By Steve Hecht**
Post-Gazette Sports Writer

Peabody versus Westinghouse. Enough said!

For as long as anyone can remember, this has been *the* game in City League football. An intense neighborhood rivalry. Lots of pagentry. As hard hitting a game as there is in Western Pennsylvania.

This morning at 10, when the two teams battle for the city championship at South Stadium, most expect the game to turn into another classic. But, this year's game could have a few different twists.

"We're going to have a little different wrinkle in our offense," Peabody Coach Bob Werl said yesterday. "I hope it works."

Said Westinghouse Coach George Webb on Thursday, "I have a few new ideas. But I don't think I'm going to tell you what they are."

Hmmm. A couple of flea flickers? The old Statue-of-Liberty play? Westinghouse bringing back the single wing?

When Westinghouse plays Pea-

body, anything can happen. But, there are two things that almost always occur. The games are close and very exciting.

The last four games between the two squads lend credence to that.

• In 1976, Westinghouse and Peabody met in the city championship and battled to a 20-20 tie.

• In 1977, Westinghouse won on a touchdown run by quarterback Ahmad Shareef with no time left on the clock.

• In 1979, Peabody won on a field goal by Dave Vento in the final minute of play.

• Three weeks ago, Peabody beat Westinghouse, 7-6, in the mud.

On paper, this morning's game shapes up as a confrontation between an excellent Westinghouse offense and a very good Peabody defense.

Westinghouse (9-1) is averaging 22.5 points per game and giving up 5.9 points. Peabody (7-1-1) is averaging just 11.7 points on offense, but is yielding just 3.6 a game.

The most well-known player in

this morning's game, Westinghouse quarterback Fred Marshall, has passed for 1,104 yards this season and has scored 81 points. By contrast, Peabody's leading scorer, quarterback-placekicker Chris Olive, has scored 26 points.

"I'm really looking for our offense to score more points against Westinghouse," Werl said. "That's going to be the key to the game.

"The more that Marshall has his hands on the ball, the more they have a shot to score. We have to play ball control."

The Post-Gazette's pick in this game is Westinghouse by 7.

**City championship lineups**
**Westinghouse offense** — Fred Marshall, QB, 6-1, 185; Robert Fitzpatrick, HB, 5-8, 165; Tim Anderson, FB, 5-7, 170; Rick Diggs, WB, 5-7, 155, Sheriden Arrington, E, 6-0, 150; Keith Jackson, E, 5-9, 150; Allen Lane, OT, 6-0, 195; Deramus Ware, OT, 6-4, 195; Steve McMillan, OG, 6-0, 170; Shawn Ellies, OG, 6-0, 170; Gus Branch, C, 6-1, 170.
**Peabody defense** — Paul Moore, DE, 6-0, 178; DeValle Dorsey, DE, 5-10, 165; Chris Finn, DT, 5-10, 198; Charles Wallace, DT, 5-11, 198; Jim Harris, LB, 5-10, 176; Larry Eleam, LB, 5-9, 158; Fred Brown, LB, 5-11, 175; Jerome Ray, LB, 5-7, 164; Ted Nelson, DB, 6-0, 162; Ray Williams, DB, 6-0, 150; Rich Sheffey, DB, 5-7, 155.

Fred Marshall

POST-GAZETTE: Sat., Nov. 14, 1981 —

*Burton • Dimperio • Musilin • Malins • Webb*

**D-2** Pittsburgh Press, Sun., Nov. 15, 1981

# Westinghouse Prevails In City Title Test, 12-7

### By TOM McMILLAN

Half the city was there, or at least it seemed that way. But then, Peabody and Westinghouse could attract a crowd for a game of checkers at midnight, so marvelously intense is their ancient rivalry.

This one was 10 in the morning, which is an ungodly hour for a football game. But it was still Peabody and Westinghouse, for the City League championship and the exclusive right to wave index fingers in the East End, and South Stadium was besieged with a sea of humanity.

And the players *knew* the reason.

"I live with these guys. If we would've lost, I would've been hearing it all my life," said Fred Marshall, the quarterback who provides Westinghouse with its pulse rate. "Now, I can remember it the rest of my life. I'll remember it forever."

He should. Marshall, who passed for more than 1,000 yards during a brilliant regular season, rifled a pair of touchdown passes to Jonathan Bailey to lift the 'House to a 12-7 victory and its first outright City title since 1970. The win, before a crowd estimated at 10,000, avenged the Bulldogs' 7-6 loss to Peabody three weeks earlier, their only blemish in 11 games.

"Westinghouse hadn't won the City since '70, and we had to bring it back for the class of '82," said Robert Rose, a defensive back who swiped three Peabody passes.

And the significance of dispatching the Highlanders (7-2-1) to claim the title wasn't lost on Rose or his teammates. "People from Peabody live right next door to people from Westinghouse," Rose said. "We grew up together. We played little league together. I played football with half the Peabody team when I was a little kid. That's why this was so big."

Peabody was making its fourth straight appearance in the City final — the Highlanders won the title in 1978, and lost to Brashear the last two seasons — but in the beginning, Westinghouse was the team playing with the poise of a veteran of these proceedings. Seven minutes into the game, Marshall dropped back and lofted a 30-yard pass to Bailey over the middle, and the Bulldogs erected a 6-0 lead they would never relinquish. Marshall's pass on the conversion attempt was knocked away.

The 'House doubled its lead early in the second quarter, taking advantage of a blocked punt that came

## City League Champions

Here's a year-by-year list of City League football champions:

| | |
|---|---|
| 1919 — Allegheny | 1949 — Westinghouse |
| 1920 — Fifth Ave. | 1950 — Schenley |
| 1921 — Westinghouse | 1951 — Westinghouse |
| 1922 — Allegheny | 1952 — Carrick |
| 1923 — Allegheny | 1953 — Peabody |
| 1924 — Schenley | 1954 — Westinghouse |
| 1925 — Schenley | 1955 — Westinghouse |
| 1926 — Schenley | 1956 — Westinghouse |
| 1927 — Westinghouse | 1957 — Westinghouse |
| 1928 — Westinghouse | 1958 — Westinghouse |
| 1929 — Schenley | 1959 — Westinghouse |
| 1930 — Westinghouse | 1960 — Westinghouse |
| 1931 — South Hills | 1961 — Westinghouse |
| 1932 — Perry | 1962 — Peabody |
| 1933 — Peabody | 1963 — Westinghouse |
| 1934 — Carrick | 1964 — Westinghouse |
| — Westinghouse | 1965 — Westinghouse |
| 1935 — South Hills | 1966 — Westinghouse |
| 1936 — South Hills | 1967 — Allderdice |
| 1937 — South Hills | 1968 — South Hills |
| 1938 — Westinghouse | 1969 — Carrick |
| 1939 — Westinghouse | 1970 — Westinghouse |
| 1940 — Oliver | 1971 — Peabody |
| — South Hills | 1972 — Carrick |
| 1941 — Oliver | 1973 — Perry |
| — Westinghouse | 1974 — Peabody |
| 1942 — Oliver | 1975 — Perry |
| — Westinghouse | 1976 — Peabody |
| 1943 — Schenley | — Westinghouse |
| 1944 — Westinghouse | 1977 — South |
| 1945 — Westinghouse | 1978 — Peabody |
| 1946 — Westinghouse | 1979 — Brashear |
| 1947 — Westinghouse | 1980 — Brashear |
| 1948 — Westinghouse | 1981 — Westinghouse |

to rest on the Peabody 11. Three plays later, Marshall whipped a 6-yard pass to Bailey in the corner of the end zone, and the Bulldogs' advantage had swelled to 12-0.

There were to be some anxious moments for Westinghouse later in the half, including a 31-yard touchdown jaunt by the Highlanders' Ted Nelson, a perfect kick by Chris Olive, and a fumble on the ensuing kickoff that Peabody recovered at the Bulldogs' 27. But the defense stood its ground, and in the overflowing Westinghouse

278

279

Press Photo by John Sale

*Jonathon Bailey of Westinghouse catches 30-yard touchdown pass against Peabody.*

stands, they were already beginning to chant "We . . . are . . . the 'House."

In the second half, the Bulldogs simply choked Peabody to death, limiting the Highlanders to one first down.

"Our defense did an excellent job, and Freddie Marshall did an excellent job," said Westinghouse Coach George Webb. "We had a lot of injuries — Marshall and Pappy Fitzpatrick were the only healthy guys in the backfield — but the kids came through. They worked for it. They earned it.

"Freddie's a great leader. He kept the guys together."

And together, they staked their claim to the football championship of the city. Not to mention the East End.

| | | | | |
|---|---|---|---|---|
| Peabody | 0 | 7 | 0 | 0 — 7 |
| Westinghouse | 6 | 6 | 0 | 0 — 12 |

WEST — Bailey 30 pass from Marshall (pass failed)
WEST — Bailey 6 pass from Marshall (kick failed)
PEA — Nelson 31 run (Olive kick)

280

1981 CITY CHAMPIONS

Burton • Dimperio • Musilin • Malins • Webb

1992 – Bulldogs end Perry's three-year hold on City Title 15-6.

PHOTO BY DEBRA-ANN BRABAZON

**ALL DAY**—Westinghouse senior quarterback Wally Goldston gets excellent line blocking as he drops back to pass in the Bulldogs' 15-6 City League championship win over Perry Traditional Academy.

PHOTO BY DEBRA-ANN BRABAZON

**SMASH MOUTH**—It was smash-mouth football in the truest sense, as Perry and Westinghouse went at it again in their City League playoff showdown won this time by Westinghouse. Perry had won three consecutive City League titles and four in the last six years.

281

### By ERIC KIMBEL
#### Courier Staff Writer

The house rocked last Saturday when the Westinghouse Bulldogs defeated Perry to win the City League football championship, ending Perry's three-year hold on the title.

The Bulldogs dominated the first half of the game. They scored first on a 42-yard field goal by Shawn Yancey early in the first quarter.

Hudhaifa Ismaeli then scored the first touchdown of the game early in the first quarter on a beautiful 27-yard-run to put the Bulldogs on top 9-0. Yancey's extra point attempt was blocked.

The second quarter started better for the Commodores. Rahsene Hill forced a fumble which was picked up by Dorian Couzzens, but the Bulldog defense held strong as Darlon Smith intercepted a Perry pass to give the Bulldogs the ball at their own 16-yard-line. The Bulldogs were unable to score on that possession, and Perry took control of the ball.

Perry mounted a drive that put them in the red zone, but the Westinghouse curtain came down and Perry, forced to try a field goal, had it blocked by Taibu Wright.

The Bulldogs turned the ball over on another fumble forced by Hill. But again they couldn't take advantage as Wright blocked a Perry pass, and then sacked Hill on consecutive plays to force a Perry punt.

Wright scored a touchdown on a 32-yard play late in the second quarter, putting Bulldogs up 15-0 at half.

The third quarter was a defensive showdown. Westinghouse mounted an impressive drive to get into the Perry red zone, but the drive was stopped. The Bulldogs attempted a field goal from the 19-yard line that was blocked by Marcus Buford. The third quarter ended without a score, and the Bulldogs were still on top 15-0.

The Commodores began a comeback in the fourth quarter. Buford traveled in a 15-yard touchdown reception to make the score 15-6 early in the fourth. Perry soon got the ball back and began another series against the Bulldogs, but Westinghouse thwarted the effort with an interception by Ismaeli.

Westinghouse will face Lock Haven Friday at 7 p.m. continuing their bid for a AAA state championship. The game will be played at Altoona High School.

PHOTO BY DEBRA-ANN BRABAZON

**HOUSE ROCKS**—When Homewood-Brushton senses a City League title, it means standing room only at South Stadium where the Bulldogs treated their fans to a City League championship. The Bulldogs now move on to make a run at the state title playing Lock Haven Friday night in Altoona. Westinghouse is hoping fans will also show up there.

283

*Burton • Dimperio • Musilin • Malins • Webb*

284

1993 CITY CHAMPS

*Burton • Dimperio • Musilin • Malins • Webb*

# Bulldogs chew off No. 500

## Westinghouse is first in City to reach mark

By Mike White
Post-Gazette Sports Writer

There was nothing overly spectacular about Westinghouse's 21-0 victory over South yesterday at South Stadium. Unless you consider it from a historical perspective.

The win was the 500th in Westinghouse history. The Bulldogs are the first City League team to reach the milestone.

"It's nothing to go overboard about, but it's still nice to have because not many schools have done it," said Westinghouse Coach George Webb.

Only seven WPIAL teams have won 500 games. They are New Castle, Greensburg Salem, Johnstown, Jeannette, Washington, Monessen and Beaver.

"There are so many guys I know who have played and been a part of the tradition at Westinghouse High School," said Webb. "But this should be something that all Westinghouse people should take pride in."

Westinghouse (6-1 overall, 6-1 in City League) didn't need much offense to gain its 500th victory. The

SEE **BULLDOGS**, PAGE D-3

Westinghouse 21, South 0

South .............. 0  0 0 0— 0
Westinghouse .......... 0 13 8 0—21
W — Leron Harper 57 interception return (Khalis Arter kick)
W — Antoine Mitchell 14 blocked punt return (kick failed)
W — Robert Dixon 37 run (Lamaas Bey run)

## FOOTBALL

### BEST FOOTBALL TEAMS IN WPIAL-CITY LEAGUE HISTORY
(Active teams only)

| SCHOOL | YRS | G | W | L | T | PCT. |
|---|---|---|---|---|---|---|
| Westinghouse | 84 | 728 | 500 | 188 | 40 | .714 |
| Upper St. Clair | 38 | 387 | 271 | 108 | 8 | .711 |
| Mt. Lebanon | 69 | 654 | 441 | 183 | 30 | .697 |
| Greensburg Salem | 96 | 898 | 585 | 271 | 42 | .675 |
| Jeannette | 93 | 832 | 539 | 255 | 38 | .671 |
| Blackhawk | 24 | 258 | 169 | 81 | 8 | .671 |
| New Castle | 100 | 977 | 612 | 296 | 69 | .662 |
| Gateway | 39 | 393 | 254 | 127 | 12 | .662 |
| Kiski Area | 35 | 356 | 223 | 126 | 7 | .636 |
| Freeport | 75 | 713 | 429 | 238 | 46 | .635 |
| Monessen | 92 | 842 | 510 | 284 | 48 | .634 |
| Johnstown | 97 | 901 | 535 | 310 | 56 | .625 |
| Washington | 96 | 863 | 507 | 300 | 56 | .620 |
| Beth-Center | 39 | 374 | 224 | 135 | 15 | .619 |
| Aliquippa | 85 | 778 | 460 | 279 | 39 | .616 |
| Penn Hills | 60 | 589 | 352 | 215 | 22 | .616 |
| North Hills | 60 | 580 | 343 | 210 | 27 | .615 |

Source: David Batchelor

## The House wins 500th

**BULLDOGS** FROM PAGE D-1

Bulldogs struck in the second quarter on a 57-yard interception return by Leron Harper and Antoine Mitchell's 14-yard return after a blocked punt.

Robert Dixon's 37-yard run in the third quarter wrapped up the scoring for Westinghouse, which outgained winless South (0-7, 0-7) by only 53 yards (193 to 140).

Webb has been part of 41 percent of the wins. He played for Westinghouse from 1959-62, was an assistant coach from 1969 through 1977 and has been head coach since 1978. All told, he's been involved in 206 wins as a coach and player. His record as a head coach is 124-61-5.

But what may be more impressive than the 500 wins is Westinghouse's all-time winning percen-

tage. The Bulldogs have the be winning percentage of all activ schools in the WPIAL and Ci League. In 84 seasons, Westin house is 500-188-40, which is go for a .713 mark. Upper St. Clair second at .711.

●

In other City League action, A derdice defeated Oliver, 34-14, b hind Chuck Jacobs' 258 yards ar three touchdowns on 19 carrie Jacobs, a senior who now has 1,0 yards on 140 carries, became tl first City League player to surpa 1,000 rushing yards this season.

Allderdice (4-3 overall, 4-3 in Ci League) took a 16-0 halftime lea Oliver (3-4, 3-4) cut the lead to 1( in the third quarter, but Jacobs' : yard touchdown run, his second the game, extended the Dragor lead to 22-8.

285

Lake Fong/Post-Gazette
Westinghouse players celebrate their City League championship yesterday at South Stadium.

## FOOTBALL PLAYOFFS

### CITY LEAGUE
**SEMIFINALS**

Peabody 14 ..................................... Schenley 12
Westinghouse 19 .................................. Perry 3

**CHAMPIONSHIP**

Westinghouse 40 .............................. Peabody 12

### SATURDAY'S SUMMARIES

### CITY LEAGUE CHAMPIONSHIP
**Westinghouse 40, Peabody 12**

| | | | | | |
|---|---|---|---|---|---|
| Westinghouse | 0 | 21 | 7 | 12 | — 40 |
| Peabody | 0 | 6 | 0 | 6 | — 12 |

W — Andy Blackwell 11 run (Ezra Coles run)
P — Kevan Barlow 28 pass from Austin Jones (pass failed)
W — Lamaas Bey 48 run (pass failed)
W — Jason Freeman 10 pass from Blackwell (Khalil Arter kick)
W — Robert Cash 7 pass from Blackwell (Arter kick)
W — Robert Dixon 10 run (pass failed)
P — Barlow 79 kickoff return (run failed)
W — Bey 15 run (kick failed)

### TEAM STATISTICS

| Westinghouse | | Peabody |
|---|---|---|
| 20 | First downs | 12 |
| 345 | Rushing yards | 74 |
| 65 | Passing yards | 81 |
| 410 | Total yards | 155 |
| 6-14-0 | Comp-Att-Int | 4-14-1 |
| 3-1 | Fumbles-Lost | 7-5 |
| 8-81 | Penalties-Yards | 5-64 |
| 4-20 | Punts-Average | 2-22 |

### INDIVIDUAL STATISTICS

RUSHING—Westinghouse: Lamaas Bey 18-164, Robert Dixon 19-107; Andy Blackwell 9-46; Ezra Coles 5-31; Jason Freeman 2-minus 3; Peabody: Kevan Barlow 11-51; Rocky Thomas 5-35; Larry Bell 4-18; Austin Jones 7-minus 13; Omar Henderson 1-minus 17.

PASSING—Westinghouse: Andy Blackwell 6-14-0-65; Peabody: Austin Jones 3-13-1-69; Kevan Barlow 1-1-0-12.

RECEIVING—Westinghouse: Jason Freeman 3-44, Robert Cash 2-16, Lamaas Bey 1-5; Peabody: Kevan Barlow 2-55, Rocky Thomas 1-14, Von Stevenson 1-12.

### CITY LEAGUE CHAMPIONSHIPS IN THE 1990s

1995 — Westinghouse 24 ................ Peabody 12
1994 — Peabody 8 ........................ Schenley 7
1993 — Westinghouse 40 ..................... Perry 0
1992 — Westinghouse 15 ..................... Perry 6
1991 — Perry 14 ................... Westinghouse 11
1990 — Perry 6 ............................. Oliver 0

## WPIAL CLASS A QUARTERFINALS
**Farrell 14, Duquesne 0**

| | | | | | |
|---|---|---|---|---|---|
| Duquesne | 0 | 0 | 0 | 0 | — 0 |
| Farrell | 0 | 6 | 0 | 8 | — 14 |

F — Rennie Gash Gash 1 run (kick failed)
F — Gash 1 run (Chico Pinkins run)

# FULL HOUSE
## Westinghouse beats Peabody, 40-12

By Mike White
Post-Gazette Sports Writer

Yesterday's City League championship game was delayed for about 20 minutes in the first quarter because of lightning. Both teams were sent to the locker rooms.

Later in the first half, a Westinghouse offensive storm ripped through South Stadium. This time, Peabody couldn't run for cover.

Westinghouse (10-1) scored twice in the final minute of the first half and it propelled the Bulldogs to a 40-12 victory over Peabody (9-2). It is the second straight championship for Westinghouse, fourth in five years and 39th overall, including four co-championships.

"The two scores [near halftime] came close to breaking our backs," said Peabody Coach Bob Flaus.

Maybe the scores didn't break Peabody's back, but the Highlanders couldn't straighten themselves the rest of the game.

"When this team gets on you and gets you down, they put their foot on your throat and that's it. You can't get up." Flaus said.

Peabody had cut Westinghouse's lead to 8-6 with 2:56 left in the first half when Kevan Barlow caught a pass out of the backfield, broke two tackles and raced for a 28-yard touchdown.

But after the ensuing kickoff, Westinghouse marched 90 yards in only five plays for a score. Ezra Coles ran 23 yards to the Peabody 48. On the next play, halfback Lamaas Bey broke into the secondary, shook off Peabody's Rocky Thomas at the 20 and sprinted into the end zone with 58 seconds left.

On the first play after the kickoff, Bey intercepted Peabody's Austin Jones, and Westinghouse took over at its own 33 with 42 seconds left.

"We didn't want to sit on the ball. We were trying to score," Flaus said.

A personal foul penalty and a 29-yard pass from Andy Blackwell to Jason Freeman helped Westinghouse move to the Peabody 16 with 26 seconds left. Then on second-and-4, Blackwell hit Freeman with a 10-yard TD pass with 16 seconds left in the half.

"When they scored their touchdown, they thought they were riding high. They thought they were going to stay in the game with us," Blackwell said. "But we just told ourselves we had to step it up."

Westinghouse dominated the second half, holding Peabody to three first downs. Westinghouse held Barlow, Peabody's star running back, to 51 yards on 11 carries for the game. He rushed for more than 100 yards in every game but two this year. And Peabody lost both.

"We knew they were a one-dimensional team and we knew we had to shut him down," said Blackwell.

Westinghouse used linebacker Robert Dixon to shadow Barlow. The strategy worked.

"We felt if we could negate Barlow with Dixon, our other 10 players were better than their 10 players," Westinghouse Coach George Webb said.

Although Barlow caught the 28-yard touchdown pass, the only other time he hurt Westinghouse was a 79-yard kickoff return when Westinghouse already had a 34-6 lead.

Peabody also had six turnovers.

Meanwhile, Westinghouse hurt Peabody with Blackwell, Bey and Dixon. Bey finished with 164 yards on 18 carries and Dixon had 107 on 19 attempts. Blackwell completed 6 of 10 for 65 yards and also rushed for 46 yards on nine carries.

"Everybody was worried about us stopping Barlow, but I said they have to stop three of our guys — Blackwell, Bey and Dixon," said Webb, whose team lost to Peabody earlier this season.

In the second half, Blackwell threw a 7-yard touchdown pass to Robert Cash, Dixon scored on a 10-yard run and Bey a 15-yard run.

"Our offensive line was just firing off today. They were great," Blackwell said.

It was only the sixth time in City League championship history that a team scored 40 points. Westinghouse has done it five times.

"Winning is never old hat," Webb said. "It's just something that, year after year, you want to see kids succeed."

Westinghouse will play in the PIAA Class AAA playoffs next weekend.

### WESTINGHOUSE 1996 SEASON (10-2-0)

| | | | |
|---|---|---|---|
| WHS | 30 | CARRICK | 6 |
| WHS | 54 | LANGLEY | 6 |
| WHS | 24 | OLIVER | 13 |
| WHS | 18 | PEABODY | 27 |
| WHS | 22 | PERRY | 12 |
| WHS | 17 | SCHENLEY | 13 |
| WHS | 21 | SOUTH (500th win) | 0 |
| WHS | 33 | ALLDERDICE | 6 |
| WHS | 48 | BRASHEAR | 0 |

### PLAYOFFS

### CITY LEAGUE SEMI-FINALS

| | | | |
|---|---|---|---|
| WHS | 19 | **PERRY** | 3 |
| PEABODY 14 | | SCHENLEY | 12 |

### CITY LEAGUE FINAL

| | | | |
|---|---|---|---|
| WHS | 40 | **PEABODY** | 12 |

### PIAA STATE AAA (1st ROUND)

| | | |
|---|---|---|
| **GREENVILLE 29** | WHS | 6 |

### PIAA STATE AAAA (1st ROUND)

| | | |
|---|---|---|
| ERIE McDOWELL 25 | SCHENLEY | 6 |

287

## CITY LEAGUE FOOTBALL

# Great coaching key to Westinghouse success

**By Rege Behe**
FOR THE TRIBUNE-REVIEW

Most high school football teams keep track of statistics from year to year, detailing a program's leading rushers, passers and tacklers.

Not so at Westinghouse High School.

"As far as I know, we don't have anything like that," said coach George Webb.

"The only records the team was concerned about were winning and losing," said Pete Dimperio Jr., son of the late legendary Westinghouse Bulldogs coach Pete Dimperio Sr. and athletic director at Peabody High School.

That perhaps is one of the secrets of Westinghouse's football program that has faced innumerable changes through the years, but consistently managed to stay atop the victory column in the City League.

With last Thursday's victory over South, Westinghouse upped its overall record to 500-188-40 and became the 26th high school in Pennsylvania to reach the 500-victory plateau.

The Bulldogs' winning percentage of .681 is the best among those schools, and their 34 City League championships are unmatched in western Pennsylvania when it comes to league play.

If there's any common thread running through Westinghouse's teams, it's great coaching. Beginning with Pro Burton (1919-45) to Dimperio (1946-1966) to Rudy Musulin (1967-70) to Fred Malins (1971-77) to Webb (1978-present), the Bulldogs have always been known for their conditioning and discipline.

"When I was coaching, they were always known as the most disciplined team anyone could play against," said Chuck Klausing, who coached at Braddock High School, IUP and Carnegie Mellon University.

"Pete (Dimperio Sr.) was a great motivator. The offense they ran, the single wing, is outmoded today, but then it was one of the most deceptive you would see."

According to Dimperio Jr., his father's predecessor, Pro Burton, had a lot to do with instilling the tradition of discipline at Westinghouse.

"He was an instructor in the Marine Corps," Dimperio Jr. said of Burton, whose career record was 17-60-6. "He was the one who began the tradition at the school."

When Dimperio Sr. came to Westinghouse in 1946, he was not met with open arms, according to his son. Burton had taken a position at Penn Hills High School to begin its football program and many of the players either didn't want to play for Dimperio Sr. or decided to transfer. After all, Dimperio Sr., who studied at Springfield College in Massachusetts, was only a junior high school basketball coach at Herron Hill (currently Milliones) Middle School.

"The students didn't like the fact that he had no experience," said John Wilborn, author of 'Fundamentally Yours — Pete Dimperio'. "But he made the players realize if they were going to be on the team, they had to work with him and do it his way."

Once students got to know Dimperio Sr., Wilborn added, the adjustment from Burton to Dimperio Sr. became much easier.

"He was very much a people person," said Wilborn. "When he went to Westinghouse in 1946 he could relate to a lot of the kids because they were Italian-Americans like himself."

## NOBODY DOES IT BETTER

Westinghouse leads all City League schools with 34 league championships. A look at the past champions:

| Year | Champion | Year | Champion |
|---|---|---|---|
| 1919 | Allegheny | 1959 | Westinghouse |
| 1920 | Fifth Avenue | 1960 | Westinghouse |
| 1921 | Westinghouse | 1961 | Westinghouse |
| 1922 | Allegheny | 1962 | Peabody |
| 1923 | Allegheny | 1963 | Westinghouse |
| 1924 | Schenley | 1964 | Westinghouse |
| 1925 | Schenley | 1965 | Westinghouse |
| 1926 | Schenley | 1966 | Westinghouse |
| 1927 | Westinghouse | 1967 | Allderdice |
| 1928 | Westinghouse | 1968 | South Hills |
| 1929 | Schenley | 1969 | Carrick |
| 1930 | Westinghouse | 1970 | Westinghouse |
| 1931 | South Hills | 1971 | Peabody |
| 1932 | Perry | 1972 | Carrick |
| 1933 | Peabody | 1973 | Perry |
| 1934 | Carrick, Westinghouse | 1974 | Peabody |
| 1935 | South Hills | 1975 | Perry |
| 1936 | South Hills | 1976 | Peabody, Westinghouse |
| 1937 | South Hills | 1977 | South |
| 1938 | Westinghouse | 1978 | Peabody |
| 1939 | Westinghouse | 1979 | Brashear |
| 1940 | Oliver, South Hills | 1980 | Brashear |
| 1941 | Oliver, Westinghouse | 1981 | Westinghouse |
| 1942 | Oliver, Westinghouse | 1982 | Brashear |
| 1943 | Schenley | 1983 | Carrick |
| 1944 | Westinghouse | 1984 | Brashear |
| 1945 | Westinghouse | 1985 | Brashear |
| 1946 | Westinghouse | 1986 | Perry |
| 1947 | Westinghouse | 1987 | Brashear |
| 1948 | Westinghouse | 1988 | Brashear |
| 1949 | Westinghouse | 1989 | Perry |
| 1950 | Schenley | 1990 | Perry |
| 1951 | Westinghouse | 1991 | Perry |
| 1952 | Carrick | 1992 | Westinghouse |
| 1953 | Peabody | 1993 | Westinghouse |
| 1954 | Westinghouse | 1994 | Peabody |
| 1955 | Westinghouse | 1995 | Westinghouse |
| 1956 | Westinghouse | | |
| 1957 | Westinghouse | | |
| 1958 | Westinghouse | | |

"He also instilled a close-knit feeling among the players through discipline, and that's very unlike what you see now with celebrations after every play. Things like that weren't tolerated."

Coaching against Dimperio Sr. was tough for many reasons. One of them was the Bulldogs never seemed to get tired.

"They were well-disciplined and trained hard year round," said George Cupples, former City League athletic director and football coach at Fifth Avenue High School.

He matched wits against Dimperio on a number of occasions. "The kids were dedicated to the school and the team," he added.

The single wing offense Dimperio cherished relied on deception, coordination and great skill.

"With the single wing you had to have discipline," said Webb, who played fullback for Dimperio from 1959-62. "There was a short pass on every play."

"For 22 years he used the same offense, and was always successful," said Dimperio Jr. of his father's offensive scheme.

"Spider (Webb) still runs some of his plays and even numbers them the same."

Westinghouse's record isn't a paper tiger built on wins against inferior competition. Up until a few years ago, City League schools scheduled games against WPIAL teams and other opponents. Westinghouse was always more than competitive.

"They'd go out and beat North Catholic or Mt. Lebanon and the kids were amazed they were able to do it," Cupples said. "And it was because they worked and trained so hard."

"Westinghouse was always able to compete against teams such as Har-Brack (now Highlands), Aliquippa, Charleroi, Mt. Lebanon and New Castle," Dimperio Jr. said.

In the late 1950s, the demographics of the Homewood-Brushton area began to change from a composition of Italians and Scotch-Irish to the present day where the community is predominately African-American. Dimperio kept on winning.

"He was a force that kept the winning tradition going through the changes," said Dimperio Jr. "The whole composition of the school changed, but Pete kept on winning."

So names of former great Bulldogs players such as Joe Nicoletti, Len Gallo, Frank DiLeo, Tony Liscio, Phil Cutruzzella, Eugene Massaro, Ron Latronica and John Giordano gave way to Wesley Garnett, Mark Ellison, Orin Richburg, Lloyd Weston, Darnell Rankin, Keino Fitzpatrick, Hudaifa Ismaeli and Ayo Young. They have passed the baton to current stars Andy Blackwell, Lamaas Bey, Robert Dixon, Ed Patterson and Omar Smith.

Webb keeps the team on the same path as his predecessors — winning games, sometimes winning championships, but always upholding the tradition of hard-working teams.

With such tradition comes high expectations despite changing times and changing attitudes, not only among youth, but also in the community.

"I think people expect you to have a winning team year in and year out," Webb said. "They've been spoiled. But in recent years its been harder with the open enrollment (available to students in Pittsburgh public school system) and the young people going to other schools.

"People in the district still expect us to win, and I tell them we can if you just keep the kids here."

*Burton • Dimperio • Musilin • Malins • Webb*

288

289

Burton • Dimperio • Musilin • Malins • Webb

1996 CHAMPIONS

# 1994 Many Souls, One Body

## CITY LEAGUE CHAMPIONSHIP

### TODAY, 1 P.M., SOUTH STADIUM

### Peabody Highlanders (10-0)

**HEAD COACH — BOB FLAUS**

**REGULAR SEASON RESULTS**

| | | |
|---|---|---|
| 52 | South | 0 |
| 26 | Westinghouse | 12 |
| 40 | Brashear | 7 |
| 35 | Carrick | 0 |
| 24 | Langley | 0 |
| 36 | Oliver | 0 |
| 45 | Allderdice | 0 |
| 28 | Perry | 0 |
| 34 | Schenley | 7 |

**CITY LEAGUE PLAYOFFS**

| | | |
|---|---|---|
| 40 | Allderdice | 8 |

**Totals**

| | | |
|---|---|---|
| 360 | Opponents | 41 |

**TEAM LEADERS**

| Scoring | TD | XP | Tot |
|---|---|---|---|
| Dorion Reid | 10 | 8 | 68 |
| Lynel Barlow | 9 | 10 | 64 |
| Anthony Jetter | 9 | 6 | 60 |
| Kevan Barlow | 8 | 4 | 52 |
| Byron Morant | 4 | 4 | 28 |

**PROBABLE STARTERS — OFFENSE**

| Name | Pos | Ht. | Wt. | Yr. |
|---|---|---|---|---|
| Will Hargrove | QB | 6-1 | 160 | Jr. |
| Lynel Barlow | RB | 6-0 | 215 | Sr. |
| Anthony Jetter | RB | 6-0 | 175 | Sr. |
| Dorion Reid | RB | 5-8 | 165 | Jr. |
| Ron Beck | WR | 5-10 | 150 | Sr. |
| Byron Morant | WR | 5-8 | 150 | Sr. |
| Josh Jones | OT | 6-2 | 245 | Sr. |
| Marty Kane | OT | 6-2 | 240 | Jr. |
| George Sly | OG | 5-6 | 225 | Jr. |
| Michael Hale | OG | 5-11 | 195 | Sr. |
| Emanuel DiNatale | C | 6-2 | 225 | Sr. |

**PROBABLE STARTERS — DEFENSE**

| Name | Pos | Ht. | Wt. | Yr. |
|---|---|---|---|---|
| Larry Bell | NG | 5-10 | 190 | So. |
| Jaamyil Dean | DE | 5-8 | 235 | Sr. |
| Emanuel DiNatale | DE | 6-2 | 225 | Sr. |
| Anthony Jetter | LB | 6-0 | 175 | Sr. |
| Dorion Reid | LB | 5-8 | 165 | Jr. |
| Lynel Barlow | LB | 6-0 | 215 | Sr. |
| Maurice Cissell | LB | 6-0 | 190 | Sr. |
| Jeff Foreman | DB | 5-10 | 160 | Sr. |
| Allen Parker | DB | 5-10 | 165 | Jr. |
| Ron Beck | DB | 5-10 | 150 | Sr. |
| Byron Morant | DB | 5-8 | 150 | Sr. |

### Schenley Spartans (9-1)

**HEAD COACH — JIM TRENT**

**REGULAR SEASON RESULTS**

| | | |
|---|---|---|
| 49 | Perry | 21 |
| 34 | Allderdice | 12 |
| 40 | South | 8 |
| 19 | Westinghouse | 14 |
| 19 | Brashear | 12 |
| 26 | Carrick | 8 |
| 32 | Langley | 13 |
| 27 | Oliver | 0 |
| 7 | Peabody | 34 |

**CITY LEAGUE PLAYOFFS**

| | | |
|---|---|---|
| 21 | Perry | 14 |

**Totals**

| | | |
|---|---|---|
| 274 | Opponents | 136 |

**TEAM LEADERS**

| Rushing | Att | Yds | Avg |
|---|---|---|---|
| Troy Davidson | 104 | 1061 | 10.4 |
| Tim Duhart | 76 | 780 | 10.3 |
| Darnell Dinkins | 26 | 402 | 15.5 |

| Scoring | TD | XP | Tot |
|---|---|---|---|
| Troy Davidson | 17 | 8 | 110 |

| Passing | Att | Cp | Yds |
|---|---|---|---|
| Darnell Dinkins | 87 | 43 | 1056 |

| Receiving | Rec | Yds | Avg |
|---|---|---|---|
| Lou Smith | 17 | 422 | 24.5 |

**PROBABLE STARTERS — OFFENSE**

| Name | Pos | Ht. | Wt. | Yr. |
|---|---|---|---|---|
| Darnell Dinkins | QB | 6-4 | 210 | Sr. |
| Troy Davidson | RB | 6-0 | 180 | Sr. |
| Tim Duhart | RB | 5-9 | 180 | Sr. |
| Don Harris | RB | 6-0 | 225 | Sr. |
| Lee Smith | WR | 6-0 | 180 | Sr. |
| Tom Podgorski | TE | 6-1 | 180 | Jr. |
| James Snowden | OT | 5-11 | 265 | Jr. |
| James Porco | OT | 6-0 | 220 | Jr. |
| Corey McGough | C | 5-10 | 170 | Jr. |
| Dwayne Moore | OG | 6-1 | 240 | Sr. |
| Steve Dubinion | OG | 6-1 | 225 | So. |

**PROBABLE STARTERS — DEFENSE**

| Name | Pos | Ht. | Wt. | Yr. |
|---|---|---|---|---|
| Will Reynolds | DL | 5-9 | 220 | Jr. |
| Damon Marsh | DL | 6-0 | 245 | Jr. |
| Dwayne Moore | DL | 6-1 | 240 | Sr. |
| Ron Wiafe | DL | 6-0 | 190 | Jr. |
| Tim Duhart | LB | 5-9 | 180 | Sr. |
| Don Harris | LB | 6-0 | 225 | Sr. |
| Sean Farr | LB | 5-9 | 180 | So. |
| Darnell Dinkins | LB | 6-4 | 210 | Sr. |
| Phet Vongsavnh | DB | 5-7 | 150 | So. |
| Troy Davidson | DB | 6-0 | 180 | Sr. |
| Lee Smith | DB | 6-0 | 180 | Sr. |

PITTSBURGH POST-GAZETTE * SUNDAY NOVEMBER 13, 1994

# NO. 1 AT LAST

## Peabody beats Schenley, 8-7, to win City title

**By Mike White**
Post-Gazette Sports Writer

Peabody Coach Bob Flaus isn't one for finger pointing. Although his team had won its first 10 games, Flaus had a team rule — no pointing of index fingers signifying No. 1.

"That's showboating. You don't need to do that," Flaus said.

But after yesterday's game, Flaus let his players break the rule. There was ample reason.

Peabody (11-0) won the City League championship for the first time since 1978 with an 8-7 victory over Schenley (9-2) at South Stadium. Both teams will play in the PIAA playoffs next weekend.

"I didn't want them pointing until they really were No. 1," Flaus said.

After the win, the Peabody players gathered around defensive coordinator Leonard Carter and raised their index fingers into the sky. Then Carter got into the rhythm with a song.

"It's time . . . for a championship rap."

"We are the Bruise Brothers," the players chimed back.

"I told you so . . . that we'd go 11-0."

"We are the Bruise Brothers," the players echoed.

"And now we'll have some fun."

"We are the Bruise Brothers."

"Because we're No. 1."

While Peabody celebrated, tears flowed from a number of Schenley's players. The Spartans came close to winning the first City title for the school since 1950. They led, 7-0, at halftime, but Peabody scored with 6:13 left in the third quarter, and Kevan Barlow ran for the two-point conversion that proved to be the difference.

"It hurts because we really weren't expected to be here this year. Yet we came so close," said Schenley Coach Jim Trent.

Schenley drove to the Peabody 15-yard line on its first two possessions but ended up turning the ball over on downs both times. Then in the fourth quarter, Schenley moved to the 18 before quarterback Darnell Dinkins was intercepted in the end zone.

Peabody has given up only 48 points all year, but only two opposing offenses have scored touchdowns. One team scored on a kickoff return, one on a blocked punt and two on returns of fumbles.

Schenley's only touchdown came late in the first quarter when Dinkins, who plays outside linebacker, picked up a fumble and returned it 50 yards for a touchdown. Phet Vongsavnh kicked the extra point.

Peabody took the second-half kickoff and drove 65 yards in 11 plays for a score. Facing a second-and-27 at the Schenley 36, quarterback Will Hargrove dropped back and hit Ron Beck behind the secondary for a touchdown pass. Barlow then ran for the conversion to make it 8-7 with 6:13 left.

"Normally we kick it," Flaus said. "But the way things were going, I thought that might be all the scoring."

In the fourth quarter, Schenley had moved to the Peabody 18, but Dinkins' pass to Lee Smith was underthrown, and Allen Parker intercepted for Peabody with 7:45 left in the game.

For the day, Dinkins completed only 3 of 10 passes for 34 yards.

Peabody gave Schenley one last chance, though, as Barlow fumbled the ball away and Dinkins recovered at the Peabody 32 with 5:17 left. It was one of the few things that Barlow did wrong. The sophomore running back had 120 yards on 17 carries.

But two plays after the fumble, Dinkins' pass over the middle was picked off by Ron Beck. Peabody then ran out the clock.

Peabody plays Sharon in the state Class AAA playoffs next weekend while Schenley plays Erie Central in Class AAAA Saturday afternoon at South.

"I don't know if this [championship] has hit me yet," Flaus said. "I'll probably be lying in bed tonight, wake up at 3 o'clock and it'll hit me. But then I'll probably get smacked by my wife and go right back to sleep."

# 1996 A MILESTONE YEAR
# BULLDOGS REACH 500 WINS

----

## WESTINGHOUSE VERSES PEABODY
## REGULAR SEASON
## PEABODY 27 WESTINGHOUSE 18
## CITY LEAGUE PLAYOFF
## WESTINGHOUSE 40 PEABODY 12

293

----

Highlanders Kevin Barlow,
Bulldogs Lamas Bey,
Andy Blackwell, and Robert Dixon
displayed a wealth of talent as neighborhood rivals
clashed for bragging rights.

PITTSBURGH POST-GAZETTE ■ THURSDAY, SEPTEMBER 26, 1996

*Kevan Barlow revels in his role as leader for the Highlanders.*

294

V.W.H. Campbell Jr./Post-Gazette photos

Peabody's Kevin Barlow rushed for 114 yards in last week's big 27-18 win over defending City League champion Westinghouse.

*Wednesday, Nov. 6, 1996*

# o the City gritty

Chaz Palla photo

Westinghouse running back Lamaas Bey is part of a potent three-pronged rushing attack

*Burton • Dimperio • Musilin • Malins • Webb*

296

PITTSBURGH POST-GAZETTE ■ THURSDAY, SEPTEMBER 12, 1996

*Westinghouse guy has legs for running, arm for throwing and he**d for t—*

Peter Diana/Post-Gazette

Andy Blackwell quarterbacked Westinghouse to the City League championship last season.

# Mr. Blackwell one spiffy QB

**By Rick Shrum**
Post-Gazette Sports Writer

occasionally.

**Backfield in motion**

His football accomplishments are im-

D 10 ★★  SUNDAY, NOV. 10, 1996

J.C. Schisler ph

Westinghouse's Robert Dixon (left) makes play for the ball against Peabody QB Austin Jones

# Westinghouse races to city crown

By Rege Behe
FOR THE TRIBUNE-REVIEW

Much like the proverbial mail carrier, neither rain nor snow nor hail nor thunder and lightning kept Westinghouse from its appointment with destiny Saturday.

The Bulldogs (10-1) amassed 364 yards rushing, took advantage of six Peabody turnovers and overcame a 28-minute delay in the first quarter due to hazardous weather conditions to beat the Highlanders (9-2), 40-12, for the City League championship at South Stadium.

"I told the guys yesterday I didn't care if it rained, snowed, hailed, whatever, we were going to play some football," said Westinghouse coach George Webb.

The Bulldogs not only gained a spot in the PIAA Class AAA playoffs against Greenville from District 10, but avenged a 27-18 regular season loss to garner their fourth championship in five years.

"The first time we played, we weren't fired up," said quarterback Andy Blackwell, who passed for two touchdowns and ran for another score. "Today we came out and played like we know how."

After Blackwell scored on a four-yard run with five minutes left in the first half, Peabody answered with a 28-yard touchdown pass from Austin Jones to Kevan Barlow to pull within two at 8-6.

Freeman after a Bey interception.

"That almost broke our backs," said Peabody coa Bob Flaus. "You can't let that happen, because wh this team gets on you, when they get you down li that, they put their foot on your throat and you ca get up."

"That was the turning point," said Blackwell of I team's two lightning quick scores at the end of the h: "Peabody knew they were done."

Webb had a slightly different perspective.

"I told them at halftime the game was still tight," said. "We had a couple of kids celebrating, but they young kids."

Fortunately for the Bulldogs, Robert Dixon was one who felt the game was in hand. Not only did Dix rush for 105 yards, but he also shadowed Barlow, lin ing him to 52 yards on 11 carries.

"That was my job, to shadow Barlow from the m ster position," Dixon said.

The Bulldogs salted away the win with a 7-yard p: from Blackwell to Robert Cash late in the third quar and Dixon's 10-yard run with 5:56 left in the game.

"It just wasn't meant to be this year," said Fla after the game. His team was playing its final ga regardless of yesterday's outcome due to a PIAA rul that made it ineligible for the state playoffs for us

297

**298**

PITTSBURGH POST-GAZETTE ■ FRIDAY, NOVEMBER 11, 1994

Braddock High School had a 56-game
unbeaten streak from 1953-1960,
including six straight WPIAL titles

# THE SPIRIT OF 56

Braddock's players, shown huddling around Chuck Klausing, had a streak that broke Paul Brown's national record at Massillon, Ohio.

Post-Gazette Library

Chuck Klausing has a veritable warehouse full of trophies, including five WPIAL championship trophies (a sixth was stolen).

# Klausing's Braddock teams to huddle again

299

Darrell Sapp/Post-Gazette

**Football players at Westinghouse High School contend with the sea of mud that their all-dirt field becomes when it rains.**

300

Unlike years ago when all of the Pittsburgh city schools played on home fields that did not have grass, today Cupples Stadium pictured above, serves as the common playing field for all of the schools. It has an artificial playing surface. Therefore the muddy field conditions of years ago are gone. Flexible scheduling enables all of the schools to benefit from the luxury of playing in a first class stadium.

301

# 11 | BEYOND THE 20TH CENTURY

Westinghouse High School began to struggle late in the last decade of the 20th century. After the fine 1996 season the Bulldogs were losing many talented athletes to other city schools. The exodus of so many of its students was really sad to see. Football was so much a part of the school tradition and was complimented by a loyal student body that spilled over into the surrounding communities.

The years of 1997 through 1999 saw the Bulldogs struggling to remain competitive. They were unable to reach the championship levels of the past. In retrospect, as we look back some 50 years ago it reflects how times have changed:

| | |
|---|---|
| 1947 – (8-0-1) (City Champions) | 1997 – (7-3-0) |
| 1948 – (8-1-0) (City Champions) | 1998 – (5-4-0) |
| 1949 – (8-1-0) (City Champions) | 1999 – (2-7-0) |
| 24-2-1 | 14-14-0 |

Since the storied history of football at Westinghouse High School is the focal point of my book, I began to realize how difficult it was going to be for that storied history to continue into the 21st Century. So many significant changes have taken place within that school district. So many of the original families have moved away and a new generation has taken over. The changes made in the Pittsburgh Public School System have been way beyond what we were accustomed to in past years. Will the big house in Homewood ever again experience what the early classes worked so hard to accomplish? True, there is much more to high school than athletics, but nobody will ever deny how it builds character and pride for our young people. We are talking about a sport that is so much like life itself, with ups and downs that will control the outcome of a game or the destiny of one's life.

School spirit and community spirit together spelled pride at Westinghouse. It was a school district that was second to none when it came time to excel. The pride factor was as strong as ever and guided so many of our alumni to the next level of life. Therein lies the true catalyst that brought respect and success to so many who walked those hallowed halls of Westinghouse High School.

Several years ago (1979) the Pittsburgh Public School System instituted an opportunity for students to pick and choose a curriculum that was best suited for his or her future. It was basically an open enrollment policy to attend a magnet school of choice that offered a course of study that was best suited for their endeavor. This appeared to be a pretty good system for our young people, but this would require much travel time; from home to school on the other side of the city and back home. Traveling away from home every day was a sense of freedom to roam and for some that spelled trouble. When you take a young student out of their neighborhood and expect them to travel into another school district without incident is wishful thinking. Even though we expect civil behavior it is not going to happen. Some of our youth do not respect civil behavior and therein lies a very serious problem. A solution to this problem must start at home, but unfortunately many of our youth do not have a stable home life.

School spirit and community spirit was the strength of every school district before the powers to be decided to make changes that our youth were not ready to handle. The underlying facts are published daily by the news media; acts of violence that has affected so many young lives. In the case of Westinghouse High School there have been too many violent events within that school district that have driven many students away from attending the school.

## ENROLLMENT HAS DWINDLED

The school enrollment is at its lowest enrollment level (415) since 1922, the year it moved from Baxter Street in Brushton, to Murtland Avenue in Homewood. When I left there in 1954 the enrollment was 1200. Since the enrollment is so low, sizeable floor space is now being occupied by the Pittsburgh Board of Education Administrative Staff. This has all taken place recently after a sizeable amount of over 30 million dollars was spent to upgrade this historic landmark. My class of 1954 had an opportunity to visit the school during the weekend of our 50th Class Reunion back in June of 2004. We came away quite impressed with all the changes and improvements that were made.

303

We were told by our tour guide that there was enough space to accommodate at least 2000 students. Featuring the latest state of the art facilities it was a visit that made us all proud – Olympic size swimming pool with balcony bleachers for spectators, a huge gymnasium with the bulldog logo at center circle, cafeteria with a culinary department, music departments for band, orchestra and chorus, library and computer department, beauty and cosmetology department and last but not least the athletic field has a natural grass playing surface. We were blown away after seeing all of this, and were shocked when told how much the enrollment has dropped. Years ago we were happy with so much less, but it was the way of life and we were proud of what little we had.

---

There has been a steady exodus of students leaving what was once one of the proudest of any high school in America. How sad it is for many of us to realize what has happened to our once proud football program.

***Pittsburgh Post – Gazette sports writer Rick Shrum said it best in the following article dated September 22, 2005:***

## "HOUSE IN NEED OF REPAIRS"

Since taking City silver in 2001 (George Webb's final year as Head Coach), Westinghouse has declined precipitously. The Bulldogs are in a 6-22 depression: 0-2 this year, 1-7 last year, 1-8 in 2003 and 4-5 in 2002.

The 'House's rivalry with Peabody (its East End neighbor), likewise has lost its edge. Peabody has won the past four, including a 30-0 score Saturday. It was 40-8 last year, 47-0 in 2003, and 32-8 in 2002.

Still this is a storied series, dating back to 1915, and will likely be great again. The Bulldogs and Highlanders have met 91 times, and despite Peabody's recent dominance, the House still leads the all-time series, 58-28-5.

---

A losing trend has surfaced within the boys' athletic programs at Westinghouse since the turn of the century. No matter what competitive sport it is the results have been discouraging. I pick up a newspaper and read the high school sports page and see the Bulldogs on the short end of a final score. Something is wrong here as the Westinghouse alumni are not accustomed to losing. It is really hard to believe this is happening to what was once a proud and competitive athletic program. In 2005 the Bulldogs were 0-8 in football the first winless season in its history and came up short in basketball with a record of 1-23 – two high profile sports in most high school programs. I liken it to a brilliant piece of gold being tarnished through neglect and thus losing its luster.

I can recall reading this essay in the WHS Class of 1923 Yearbook and it is worth repeating again. Therein are some heartfelt words of how the students back then felt about Westinghouse High School. We may never see the likes of this kind of loyalty again as most of our young people would respond with **"SO WHAT... NO BIG DEAL."** Times have changed and that everlasting value *"RESPECT"* is non-existent in the souls of so many of our young people.

---

## "WESTINGHOUSISM"

There is Patriotism, there is Americanism, and there is *"Westinghousism."* Patriotism usually means loyalty to the ideals of the patriot in time of war: Americanism, loyalty to the welfare of America at all times: *Westinghousism,* loyalty to the welfare of Westinghouse. America is more than an expanse of territory. Westinghouse High School is more than a mass of brick, clay and mortar. Westinghouse is what her students are. What they become, she will be. They can write her name on the clouds or drag it in the dust. Her name can appear at the top only when they put it there. She can claim only as many silver cups as they win for her. In short, they determine her pulse beat of success.

*WHS Class of January 1923*

## THE GIRLS STEP UP

Thank goodness the girls' basketball program has shouldered the pride and loyalty that was always the strength at Westinghouse. Coach Phyllis Jones has done a marvelous job guiding the girls to the playoffs year after year. There have been a few of the girls who have excelled in helping the football team with kicking and special teams duty. I was shocked when this came to light in the news media in recent years. Times have really changed as this would have never happened during the glory years of Westinghouse football. Back then football was for the boys as the girls proudly cheered them on.

When I think back in time and remember some of the stalwarts we had at the House a girl would never think of venturing into the football arena. It would have been a cold day in hell. The Bulldogs were never hurting for support from the girls other than the marching band and the cheerleaders. All I can say to the boys of today is this *"Put on a helmet and play some good old fashioned Bulldog football."* Make a wise choice and stay away from turf wars in the streets and find your way back to the good old turf of a football stadium. You will find respect and glory when you make your presence known under the lights at South Stadium. There is nothing more gratifying than hearing the roar of the crowd chanting *"We are Westinghouse forever."* To this day I can still feel the thrill of winning at the House; it never goes away.

How sad it is to see how tough it is for this generation of young people to avoid some of the threats that have literally plagued those who want to excel. Those who threaten our youth have small minds and must be avoided at all costs. Cast the bad apple aside before it ruins the entire bushel. Young people have to stand tall and say no to those who threaten to do them mental and bodily harm. There is nothing worse than seeing young talent wasting away to a foolish group of losers who have no respect for human life.

**305**

## FOOTBALL AND MORE FOOTBALL

High school football is so much a part of the tradition that exists within the city of Pittsburgh and the outlying areas known as the WPIAL. With the Pittsburgh Steelers, the University of Pittsburgh, Penn State University and so many of the smaller colleges carrying on the gridiron tradition we have a plethora of football history that is second to none. It has been the heart and soul of Western Pennsylvania year after year since the early days of Jock Sutherland at Pitt and the legendary Art Rooney of the Pittsburgh Steelers. There is football in the air when autumn arrives in Western Pennsylvania as every weekend brings the thrills of gridiron glory. Friday nights is high school football in every town along the three river valleys followed by college football on Saturdays and then our Pittsburgh Steelers on Sundays. It does not get any better than that.

The fact that Western Pennsylvania was at one time the iron and steel capital of the world along with a rich coal industry it was a natural for the young men who grew up in that environment to play the brand of football that has produced so many outstanding athletes. It has become known as the area that produced several outstanding quarterbacks. The Pro Football Hall of Fame in Canton, Ohio and the College Football Hall of Fame in South Bend, Indiana are graced with so many Western Pennsylvania legends. They are remembered year after year when the topic of football is discussed.

## GOING OUT A WINNER

Two of the most successful high school football coaches in western Pennsylvania retired after the turn of the century – Gus Catanese from Perry Traditional Academy and George Webb from Westinghouse High School; both from the City of Pittsburgh Public School System. I knew Gus Catanese from our early years of growing up in the community of Morningside, and in later years I met George Webb personally at one of my class reunions. Both men served for many years at their respective high schools with much success and accolades, and left behind a legacy that will long be remembered.

Coach Gus Catanese retired after the 2000 football season compiling an impressive record of 183-58-4 and led Perry to seven Pittsburgh City League Titles and one PIAA State Title in 1989. He played for the Morningside Bulldogs coached by Joe Natoli, Peabody High School and later at Slippery Rock University.

Coach George Webb retired after the 2001 football season; a season that saw him lead the Bulldogs (9-2-0) to the play-offs one more time before losing the city title game to Perry 14-6. After compiling an impressive record of 156-82-5 and leading the House to five Pittsburgh City League Titles it was time to hang it up. Considering some of the challenges that he endured Webb was still able to have an outstanding career that earned him a place in the Pennsylvania Football Coaches Hall of Fame. Webb played four years at Westinghouse High School for the legendary Pete Dimperio, and later at Thiel College. My wife Pat and I attended his retirement celebration that was held at the Ramada Inn in Penn Hills, PA on June 14, 2002. I had an opportunity to speak at this event and would like to share it with my readers.

## TRIBUTE TO GEORGE WEBB
(June 14, 2002)

Let me begin with a short phrase –"Westinghouse Forever, Loyal and True". This is a phrase that fits so many of us who have passed through Westinghouse High School. It epitomizes the dedication and loyalty of our honoree, George Webb. As a fine coach and teacher he has had to face the many challenges of his profession that did not exist in past generations. He did it by overcoming adversities that have challenged his patience and expertise. He truly represents a profession that prepares young people for life and lifes work and should be regarded as one of the most valuable resources of our country.

I first spoke with Coach Webb in the fall of 1992 shortly after he had guided Westinghouse to a 15-6 win over Perry High School for the City title. I called him at the school to congratulate him and the team for a fine season, and at that time I identified myself as a proud 1954 graduate from Westinghouse. He appreciated that someone so far removed in years could still have the interest and loyalty for the school. I expressed to him why and how I maintained such a spirited interest in our rich tradition, and he really appreciated that. As I told him — I may have left Westinghouse, but Westinghouse never left me. We have kept in touch ever since that first telephone conversation.

He graciously accepted an invitation to be our guest of honor as my class of 1954 celebrated our Millennium Reunion in the year 2000 at the Churchill Country Club. He was an excellent speaker and related to our class with such enthusiasm and sincerity. We thoroughly enjoyed his presence and how he brought us up to date of the many changes that have taken place since our school days at Westinghouse. Many of my classmates remember when his mentor, Pete Dimperio, was also one of our special guests several years ago. I mention Pete Dimperio tonight because I know how proud he must be of you, Coach Webb, and of your accomplishments as a successful coach, teacher and most importantly, a fine human being. You are a legend of our generation who joins our Westinghouse legends of yesteryear, "Pro" Burton and Pete Dimperio. Westinghouse High School was quite fortunate to have you as you carried on our proud tradition with such class and dedication. As I read your biography it states that your family moved up here to Pittsburgh, PA from Virginia in 1954, the same year that I left Westinghouse. Where did the time go? Here we are fifty years later proudly claiming you as one of our own. You will always be remembered as the student athlete, teacher and coach of Westinghouse High School who worked very hard to help so many students realize their dreams and goals.

Coach, my wife, Pat, and I want to wish you a well deserved happy and healthy retirement. Also on behalf of my classmates of 1954, thank you for being there for us. Tonight it was an honor for us to share this memorable milestone of your life. May God bless you and reward you with the best that he can offer.

Best Wishes,
Carmen and Pat Pellegrino

307

The last time that I can recall a Pittsburgh City high school football coach retiring with such high acclaim was in 1967, when the legendary Pete Dimperio decided it was time to call it a career. Catanese and Webb reminded me a lot of Dimperio in the way they were able to motivate young men at the high school level. True there was a difference of several years between the two eras, but the bottom line is having the patience and gaining the respect and trust of your players. They both put a lot of time and effort into the football programs at both schools.

As a student I will always remember the sincerity and concern that Coach Dimperio so effectively possessed. He was able to single out the trouble makers as he excluded them from his team. He ran a tight ship and expected mutual respect among his players. He was a builder of young men who would never forget the House where they learned how to be a winner.

As each generation emerged there were social trends that were more challenging for our young people. The city of Pittsburgh was no different than any other city across America. Webb and Catanese were able to bring the best out of the young men they tutored and at a time when there were so many distractions to cope with. They met the challenges and those young men who followed their lead were all the better for it. Since both coaches came out of the City League of Pittsburgh they were able to understand where our youth were coming from. They knew what it was like to live and play in the city and not have the luxuries that some of the suburbanites enjoyed. Whether it was yesterday, today or tomorrow that's the way life is growing up in the city. I have been there and it did not hinder my desire to go on and make it to the next level.

The youth of today have got to realize that life is what you make it. There are several ways to travel and there are several ways to succeed, but there is only one way to be honest and that is to have respect. Respect is something that starts at home and gains momentum with each passing year of our lives. It is one attribute that separates the good from the bad. It's your choice and here's hoping you are wise enough to make the right one. Self respect and respect for others will always prevail over the small minds that continue to create chaos throughout the world. Until the people of this universe learn how to get along and respect one another we will always be challenged by those who have no regard for the value of life. God will always be there to help us to appreciate the gift of life.

## FINDING PEACE OF MIND

308

Somewhere between my ambitions and my limitations I have learned to find peace of mind. Today after many years of resentment I have come to the realization that what happened in the past is over with and life goes on. God has blessed me with other accomplishments that go far beyond those that I had longed for. He has given me the ambition and ability to write and reflect upon those memories of a foregone era that gave me so much to be thankful for. It was an era that I am so proud to have lived through. As I finalize this chapter I want to thank all those who I had the opportunity to share this journey with. You know who you are. Some have gone to the other side and some our still with us, as I will always treasure this priceless era. Westinghouse High School and its' surrounding communities will always have a place in my heart forever and a day. It was truly Americana with all the values that made our country a treasure of life.

PITTSBURGH POST-GAZETTE ▪ FRIDAY, NOVEMBER 10, 2000

## HIGH SCHOOLS

After 22 seasons at Perry Traditional Academy, Coach Gus Catanese goes out a winner.

Bob Donaldson/Post-G

309

Burton • Dimperio • Musilin • Malins • Webb

310

PITTSBURGH POST-GAZETTE * FRIDAY JUNE 7, 2002

# Longtime coach to leave Bulldogs

## Webb to retire after 24 years at Westinghouse

By Mike White
Post-Gazette Sports Writer

The Westinghouse Bulldogs are losing their top dog.

George Webb, the football coach at Westinghouse High School for 24 seasons, has decided to retire. He leaves as one of the most successful coaches in City League history, winning 155 games and leading the Bulldogs to five City League championships. He lost in the championship game four times.

"I wish I could coach forever, but I can't," said Webb, who had a 155-80-5 record. "It's going to be hard. After so many years, coaching just becomes part of your routine. It's going to be tough for me and different to be without it."

Westinghouse is losing more than a football coach. Webb also is retiring as an art teacher at the school. He was the head coach of the school's boys' track team and an assistant coach with the girls' basketball team. At one time, he was the girls' basketball head coach. He has been coaching and teaching at Westinghouse since 1969, and his retirement from all of the jobs becomes effective at the end of the school year.

He was an elementary school teacher for two years before coming to Westinghouse. "It's been from

one sport to another. It's just time to spend more time with my wife and do some of the things we haven't had a chance to do."

Webb, 57, and his wife, Pat, have three children. Although Webb wore many coaching hats at Westinghouse, he was known mostly for football.

"When you think of City League football coaches, one of the names that comes to mind right away is George Webb," said Bob Pajak, manager of athletics in the City League. "I think he's going to be a tough act to follow and replace."

If you cut Webb, he might bleed the blue and gold of Westinghouse. He is a 1963 Westinghouse graduate who played for legendary coach Pete Dimperio. He became a Westinghouse assistant coach under Rudy Musulin in 1969 and became head coach in 1978.

"George's teams were always very disciplined, and they were always the type of team that got better as the year went on," Pajak said.

Webb watched Westinghouse football change drastically over the decades. The school used to get all of the students in the Homewood area. But when the Pittsburgh Public Schools changed their enrollment policy two decades ago, many Homewood students chose to attend other schools in the City League.

Darrell Sapp/Post-Gazette

As coach of the Westinghouse football team, George Webb won five City League championships in nine appearances.

Webb sometimes had only 25 or 30 players on his team, but Westinghouse thrived in the '90s with four titles in five consecutive years.

"I don't think kids have changed as much as society changed," Webb said. "Kids have so many more things to do nowadays than play football. They have so many more things pulling at them, like the streets or music. A lot of them feel like they don't need sports anymore. It's tough to be an athlete today, because there are so many distractions."

Don't ask Webb to name the best player he has ever coached, or the best one his teams have faced. He

said it's too hard to choose. But Webb will go down as one of the best coaches.

His successor has not been selected, but Webb said it most likely will be one of his assistants — Darryl Moore or Leroy Dillard.

In City League annals, Webb will always be remembered for walking up and down the sideline carrying a staff with the head of a bulldog carved into the top. What will happen to that staff?

"It will still be with me," he said. "And don't be surprised if you still see me on the sideline just helping out. Football is a passion of mine."

**George A. Webb, Sr.**

**Retirement Celebration**

**Ramada Inn & Conference Center**
699 Rodi Road
Pittsburgh, PA 15235-4588
(412) 244-1600

**Friday, June 14, 2002**

Reception: 6:00 p.m. – 7:00 p.m.
Dinner Buffet: 7:00 p.m. – 8:00 p.m.
Program: 8:00 p.m. – 9:00 p.m.
Dancing: 9:00 p.m. – Until

311

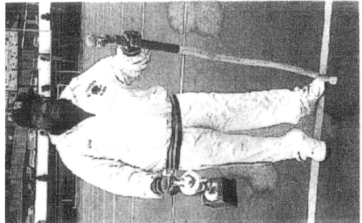

Carterman Graphics, Ltd.
Lance H. Carter, Sr.
Design Consultant
116 Urban Drive
Verona, PA 15147
Phone: (412) 247-3990
Fax: (412) 247-4440
Email: CarGraLTD@aol.com

## Program

Welcome...........................Ms. Gwen Missouri

Master of Ceremonies...............Mr. Robert L. Burley

Invocation........................Ms. Gwen Missouri

**Dinner Buffet**

Musical Selection...Mrs. Linda Ross Brown & Mr. Calvin M. Stemley

**Guest Speakers**

Remarks.........................Mr. Lawrence E. Berry

Remarks.............................Mr. Edward Ray

Remarks...........................Dr. Gloria Spencer

Remarks............................Mr. Keith Gardner

Musical Selection................Mr. George A. Webb, Jr.

**Guest Speakers**

Remarks.........................Dr. William Nicholson

Remarks............................Ms. Olivia Jones

Remarks.............................Mr. Leroy Dillard

Musical Selection...Mrs. Linda Ross Brown & Mr. Calvin M. Stemley

**Special Presentations**

Remarks..........................Mr. Myron Watzman

Remarks..........Dawn R. Webb Turner & Mr. Damon Webb

**Honoree**

Remarks...............Retiree Mr. George A. Webb, Sr.

Closing Remarks...................Mr. Robert L. Burley

Benediction.......................Ms. Gwen Missouri

## Acknowledgements

A most special thank you is afforded to the following. Without the support, cooperation and unselfish commitment of them this event would not have been successful.

Sol's Store of Ambridge
Pittsburgh Trophy Company
Manchester Craftsman's Guild
Master Marketing International
Ramada Inn & Conference Center
Westinghouse High School Parent Football Association
The DJ's
Mrs. Linda Ross Brown
Mr. George A. Webb, Jr.
Mr. Damon Webb
Mr. Lawrence E. Berry
Mr. Edward Ray
Dr. Gloria Spencer
Mr. Keith Gardner
Dr. William Nicholson
Ms. Olivia Jones
Mr. Myron Watzman
Mr. Dennis Boyce

The George A. Webb, Sr. Retirement Committee:

Mr. Leroy Dillard
Mr. Richard Scott
Mrs. Phyllis A. Jones
Mr. Calvin M. Stemley
Mr. Donald Conley
Ms. Gwen Missouri
Mrs. Dawn R. Webb Turner
Mrs. Patricia Roberts Webb
Mr. Robert L. Burley
Mr. Lance H. Carter, Sr.

## Webb, May The Life You Live, Speak For You

George Webb, husband, father, son, brother, friend, teacher, coach, gentleman. You, George, are all of these things and more. In each of us are desires to learn, but teachers like you help to bring out that desire You, George, were truly blessed by God with a personality and charm that radiates wherever you are. I can truthfully say: "You are a great person to know and anyone who knows you knows this!"

George, you have touched so many lives during your teaching and coaching career. You have taught parents, their children and in some cases, their grandchildren. You have been a household name at Westinghouse for many, many years. You, Webb, are right there with BC (**Before Christ**). They call you BW (**Before Webb**). When people speak of different activities and events, they often say, "**Was that before Webb?**"

George, may your mind and your heart continue to grow and prosper. May the many young lives you've touched never forget "**Mr. Webb**". May your teaching help to provide a **thirst** to never stop learning in all your students.

To your children and wife Pat, who has stood with you through all the trials and tribulation, I quote, "It doesn't always matter where you go in life, but who you have beside you." May God continue to bless and keep you and your family wrapped in his loving arms.

To teach is to never stop learning, to learn is wise, to be wise is to be able to reach a person's heart and soul as well as their mind. To be able to accomplish these goals as you have is **Divine!**

### We All Love You!

-- Mrs. Clemmie Hampton Roberts

313

## GWHS Championship Football History

Congratulations to George Westinghouse High School, home of the City League Championship Bulldogs, with the best winning percentage of all active WPIAL and City League schools from 1921 - 1996!

◆ Best percentage of all active schools in the WPIAL & City League (.714%)
◆ 84 seasons of public league play with 504 wins, 188 losses, & 40 ties
◆ 35 Independent Championship and 4 Co-championships
◆ Program flourished under the tutelage of Head Coaches:
Oro H. "Pro" Burton, Pete Dimperio, Rudy Musilin, Fred Malins & George A. Webb

### Westinghouse: The Early Years

Players toiled on an oil dirt field in equipment comprised of Red Grange helmets and very little padding. Fans and community support was overwhelming. Spectators were everywhere. The bleachers, sidelines, and hillsides were a sea of people. Financial support from the Board of Education and city administration funded the annual awarding of titles and trophies at player recognition banquets.

### Westinghouse: Now

Players wearing high tech equipment battle on a neutral field of Astroturf and practice on a cushion of grass. Social and economic conditions limit student and community fan support. The lack of funds from the Board of Education and city administration limit necessary recognition for players.

### Westinghouse: School Spirit

One thing that has been dominant in Westinghouse's athletics is its school spirit. There is no other school in the city to compare with us when it comes to supporting our teams. This has always been an established fact and we hope in the future it will become even more so. When a team goes on the field and finds that it has the school behind it, it is in them to give the very best it has. Probably no spectator realizes this, but it is true. There are, and will be, hundreds of instances in the annals of our school when a little cheer from the sidelines will put new life into a worn-out player. And so we appeal to the students returning to school next fall to support their teams, and uphold the Westinghouse School Spirit.

——excerpt from W.H.S. Sketchbook 1921

*Burton • Dimperio • Musilin • Malins • Webb*

**314**

## George A. Webb, Sr.

I, George A. Webb was born on March 30, 1944, in a small town near Norfolk, VA, called Portsmouth, VA. In 1954 my family moved to Pittsburgh, PA. I attended Crescent Elementary School in Homewood where I was raised. I began Westinghouse Jr. H.S. in 1957 and it was there I met my mentor and African-American teacher Mr. Edward Ray. Mr. Ray later took me under his wing and helped mold me through motivation and counseling. This ultimately gave me the drive I needed to succeed which later lead to many honor roll achievements and participation in Jr. High sports like basketball and track.

As time moved on my interest in school grew stronger and by 1959, I joined the football and baseball teams and several school activities in High School. I was a member of the Biology Club, Art Club, Spanish Club, Student Council President and the National Honor Society. In 1961, I was a member of the Post-Gazette All-City team and in 1962 received an Honorable mention for my accomplishments. Throughout my years as a student, I have received several awards in 1961 and 1962 including the AAA Safety Poster Contest and eventually graduating with honors in January of 1963.

From 1963 through 1967 I attended Thiel College, where I continued to play football and participate in track and field. Many of my college achievements include Dormitory advisor, yearbook staff and artist/illustrator for all school publications. I competed in many art contests and won numerous awards and certificates. I was a proud member of Who's Who among Students in American Colleges and Universities in 1965 and 1966. My fraternity days began when I joined PHI-THETA-PHI Fraternity and Phi Delta Epsilon, a National Honorary Journalism Fraternity.

I married **Patricia Roberts** in 1965 and as a result of this most perfect union helped to bring into this world three remarkable and loving children: **George Jr., Dawn and Damon.**

After college graduation in 1967, I was hired by the Pittsburgh Public School District where my first job was teaching at Crescent Elementary School. Later in 1969, I started at Westinghouse High School where I began coaching Jr. High Basketball, Track and Varsity Football. It wasn't until 1978 that I became the Head Football Coach. Receiving

Coach of the Year in 1981was very special, because that same year were also the City Champions. By 1989, we were so fired up that a string of Championships followed in 1992, 1993, 1995, 1996, and again in 2001. During these years I was Coach of the Year and we were either City Champions or runner-ups.

## A History of the GWHS Athletic Program

Athletics at George Westinghouse High School is rich in history, pride and tradition. This legacy has been honed by the many generations of student athletes that have passed through these hallowed halls respectfully known as "The House". Many of these athletes have gone on to distinguish themselves in various fields of endeavors, such as, doctors, lawyers, politicians, educators, business executives, etc, and many have gone on to become professional athletes. To name any of these legendary athletes here would be a disservice to so many others whose numbers are legion.

The athletic teams at George Westinghouse High School have had unparalleled success, winning championships in all major sports. Discipline, sportsmanship and a burning desire to win have always been trademarks of a typical bulldog team and the standard for other teams to follow. This success has given George Westinghouse athletic teams a national following fueled by admirers and alumni who have said, " You can be sure if it's Westinghouse".

– George A. Webb, Sr.

## Alma Mater

**Westinghouse forever loyal and true.**
**Nothing can ever change our love for you.**

**Rah!    Rah!    Rah!**

**Westinghouse forever we're true to you.**
**We love our colors of GOLD and BLUE.**

# 12 | MY PERSONAL REFLECTIONS

Through the many years that I have been following the fortunes of football at Westinghouse High School I have experienced so many rewarding memories. The six years that I spent there as a student were very much a vital part of my life as I have many times over reflected on some of those special times. The school's faculty prepared me well for life's work, and my loyalty for Westinghouse has been a long lasting one. *"Everybody's Letterman"* is a caption that appeared in my high school yearbook next to my senior photo, but I never really gave it much thought until many years later. Our Yearbook Editor, Marge Hooper Shellaby, must have seen something that was characteristically a part of my personality. I was one who always found a common ground with all my classmates. We were all together under one roof preparing for our life's journey. Our school was our home away from home. Thank God we came along at a time when our society and values showed us how to respect each other.

A desire to play football for the Bulldogs was in my heart, but circumstances beyond my control took it away. I managed to do the next best thing – track it and write about it. It was quite difficult for me to accept the next best thing, but I am glad that I was able to maintain a keen interest in the history of such a storied tradition. As a young student I thought the football fortunes of Westinghouse would last forever, but forever has gone away and it is hard to say goodbye to yesterday. I found an alternative way of pulling together my memories of a sport that I truly enjoyed. I learned to find peace of mind somewhere between my ambitions and my limitations.

Here I am fifty years later continuing my life's journey. Life has many twists and turns, and I truly believe that what goes around comes back around – meaning I have found my old comfort zone again… reflecting on events and experiences that have lingered within my bank of memories. The feelings, sentiments, opinions and personal experiences from the many alumni that I have spoken with in recent years have been priceless. The one thing that impressed me the most was the sincerity of the many people who shared with me their thoughts and memories of Westinghouse High School. Many expressed how special it was to have been a part of such a proud tradition. To me that really is a tribute to the fine faculty and school board that we had during that time period. It was a very special time for so many of us.

I have lived my life striving to accomplish whatever goals I may have set for myself. The most challenging one was going back to college to get my degree. It was a time in my life that I had to dig down deep into my arsenal of resources to find the right mindset I needed to accomplish what I had desired for so many years. It was quite evident to me that Westinghouse High School had prepared me well to take on this challenge after having been out of high school for nearly twenty years. It was a public school, and yes it was well staffed to prepare so many of us to further our education and get on with life's challenges. We did not have to go across town in search of a better suited curriculum as we had it all at Westinghouse. There were excellent vocational schools (Connelly Trade, Washington Vocational and Arsenal Trade) for those who desired to learn a skilled trade. I am appalled at the way the public school system in Pittsburgh has tried to fix a system that really never needed to be fixed. Every one of the Pittsburgh city high schools (there were twelve back then) had the same curriculum and there was no need to transfer unless it was due to a family relocating to another area of the city. Every neighborhood in the city had a dedicated school district with which to claim a special pride and loyalty. Today that no longer exists and there are problems that have developed because the School Board decided to change a system that worked so well for a better part of the twentieth century. Some will say it was time for a change, but I firmly disagree. All one has to do is listen to the news each day and read the newspaper to realize what it has done to our young people. It took away our neighborhood pride and loyalty; two values that are so critical in making our society a better place to live. Violence among our youth was non-existent back when we were in school. Those two values of pride and loyalty helped to make us respect one another, and thus we were able to learn how to deal with life's challenges.

## BEHIND CLOSED DOORS

This is a topic that I have hesitated to reflect upon, but after much consideration I decided to sort out how I perceived its value. My main reason is two-fold – **First**: The mystique that was so much a part of the success story of the Westinghouse Bulldogs, and how it was respected by those who survived the pain and gain of its' code of silence . **Second**: How it has remained a vivid memory in the minds of those who had experienced its many challenges, and still believe it was a rewarding experience that they would never forget. Never would such a fraternity have existed had those who pledged revealed its' sanctifying secrets. This was a powerful allegiance of young men who were not to be denied on or off the field. It was not like pledging to join a college fraternity as that would have been a cakewalk. This was not the case as anyone who experienced the rigors of **"The Room"** would have jumped through hoops at the thought of anything less demanding than what they had to experience in order to make the Bulldog varsity. What happened behind those closed doors; stayed behind those closed doors.

It is not my intention in any way to tarnish or question a sensitive yet a big part of the proud Bulldog football tradition. Many revelations (both positive and negative) have been told by those who have experienced the many challenges of **"The Room."** I perceived it as a proud family of Bulldogs tenaciously preparing to play like champions, but sometimes that tenacity went a little too far. It was to some a metaphysical *"Survival of the Fittest."* In fact when reminiscing with many of the

316

former Bulldogs, they were more so anxious to talk about their experiences regarding **"The Room"** than the many championships they had won for their big house in Homewood. It was obvious to me that only a loyal Bulldog could appreciate those experiences. The following is how I perceived the many hours of reminiscing with many of the former players who either agreed or disagreed with what **"The Room"** philosophy was all about. Most of them were willing to go the long haul in order to don the gold and blue of the Westinghouse Bulldogs. I respect their loyalty, pride and allegiance, and it no doubt was a very big part of the winning tradition at Westinghouse back then.

To the best of my recollections after reminiscing with many of the old timers, the so-called **Room** tradition originated when "Pro" Burton retired after the l945 football season. It seemed evident to me that the old timers during the Burton era never had control of the locker room. Burton had complete control of the entire athletic program at Westinghouse and the locker room was part of his domain. Then in 1946 Burton's successor, Pete Dimperio took over for the upcoming season. This was a very tough time for Coach Dimperio as "Pro" Burton had many loyal supporters at Westinghouse, and they were quite disappointed when he left the Homewood School to take a similar position at Penn High School (later known as Penn Hills). Many of the holdovers from Coach Burton's 1945 championship team were still there at Westinghouse, and they were not waiting for Pete Dimperio with open arms. Inspite of Burton's reputation of being a tough disciplinarian his players were still very loyal to him.   For thirty years Burton had complete control of the situation at Westinghouse as he was the Athletic Director as well as the coach of several other varsity sports as well as football.   He was regarded as the *"The Builder of Champions"*.

317

It was a very difficult transition for Dimperio to make – coming from Herron Hill Jr. High to Westinghouse High School.  He was very successful at Herron Hill as a basketball coach, but the boys at Westinghouse were not impressed.  Upon his arrival, they decided, as a team, to organize a strike against him during the seventh period gym class. Apparently they felt they did not need a coach to lead them.  They were, in his eyes, the cockiest and most aggressive group of young men he had ever met in his career.  Dimperio retaliated by rising to the occasion and kicking all the seniors off the team.  This did not last very long as those cocky seniors realized they no longer had a team and apologized to Dimperio.  He believed in giving a young man every opportunity to excel.  He was a sincere and clever psychologist who had a knack for developing young men into becoming good citizens.

This generation of players took advantage of an opportunity to form a **fraternity** within their seventh period gym class, and it soon became known as **The Room**.  It was a place for the football team members to have some time to themselves all year round.  It was quality time for them to bond together a camaraderie that others respected.  The control of **The Room** behavior was left to those individuals who Dimperio felt had mature minds and leadership qualities.  Any out of control behavior I feel was because those who he trusted let him down. Dimperio was very fair and concerned about all of his boys and there was no reason whatsoever to let him down. He was an advocator of respect and responsibility. When his predecessor

"Pro" Burton was at Westinghouse he controlled everything that associated with the football program including the locker room. One of "Pro's" former players and a personal friend of mine told me that it was "Pro's" way or the highway. He was in control of the situation at all times and handled his players with a firm hand and would not accept anything less than his expectations. "Pro" Burton did it his way and his players respected his wishes. Sure there were team leaders, but "Pro" set the tone of control his way. I spoke with many who played for "Pro" and it was he who controlled that locker room not the veterans. Those veterans were scrubs at one time, and it was "Pro" who molded them. Therefore, there was no call for a veteran to take advantage of a new scrub. If discipline was in order, it was "Pro" who dished it out. He was not about to lose a talented scrub because a veteran felt like lashing out his frustrations. "Pro" demanded respect from the entire team and he got it.

Dimperio came to Westinghouse to teach young men how to win with pride and respect; giving them every opportunity to excel. He was an excellent motivator. Those who took over leadership roles were expected to lead by example and accept full responsibility for their actions. They knew Dimperio was under pressure to follow the success that retired coach "Pro" Burton had enjoyed. It wasn't until the holdovers from Burton's 1944 and 1945 championship teams were graduated before Dimperio felt that he had gained the respect he deserved. After leading the 1946 and 1947 teams to championship seasons the critics finally began to believe in him. The mystique of **The Room** was in place and it lasted throughout the entire Dimperio era. Once a young man completed his final season of football eligibility he was no longer permitted to enter the football locker room. Dimperio trusted the leadership quality of certain individuals who in some cases were not worthy of his trust, and this haunted quite a few of the candidates who left the squad. In all likelihood to those who got carried away it was a way of gaining control of the new football candidates or **scrubs** (as they were called back then).

*The Sports dictionary definition for* **scrub: n.** a substitute player – ***adj.*** small, stunted, inferior, etc. or *in Thesaurus terms for* **scrub: a – second-rate, unimportant, mediocre.** The meaning of scrub (as I perceived it) according to Bulldog tradition is a newcomer who is determined to meet the challenges of making the football team. The new candidates faced many challenges and demands and persevered through sheer desire and dedication. They were determined to shed the so-called scrub label and go that extra mile to make the Westinghouse varsity and be a part of the proud Bulldog fraternity. The mystique of **The Room** was part of that winning tradition because to this day those who were part of it are still quite proud to reminisce about what it meant to them.

The behavior pattern within **The Room** was more of a regimented nature somewhat like basic training in a military platoon with all the pranks and mind games. There was never talk about any sadistic or inhumane behavior inflicted upon the scrubs. Control by the veterans was inevitable – as they seized the opportunity to gain control with tough aggressive tactics. It was their way of instilling that no fear instinct within the minds of the new scrubs that would someday take the field for Westinghouse High School. It was up to the team leader or leaders to use good judgement by recognizing when to call off the dogs. In some cases it was too late for

318

some of those individuals who are probably still somewhat bitter today. They kept the code of silence and merely quit the team, walked away, and never reported such behavior to the school administrators. Personally I blame the team leaders for the loss of any promising candidates because of foolish inhumane behavior being inflicted. Mature judgment was not always orchestrated and as a result there was always a price to pay.

The sport of football by nature is an aggressive game that is bound to create havoc when the participants are constantly making bodily contact play after play for sixty minutes. Injuries are bound to occur when heads are knocking and bodies are flying all over the field of play. The practice sessions are sometimes even tougher than the game itself as the level of competition accelerates. Starting positions are up for grabs and those who impress the coaching staff will move up the depth chart. This is no game for the timid minds to pursue. There is only one way to play the game of football and that is with reckless abandon and a hard nose for the ball. The **Room** was without a doubt the heart and soul of football at Westinghouse High School. You either accept the challenges or pack your bag and try another sport.

Today many years later, I wonder how many of those former jocks would feel if their sons or grandsons were being subjected to some of the aggressive behavior that they dished out. Times have changed through the years and fortunately most team leaders of today are expected to exercise a more civil way of bonding a team together. Our society has changed and would never allow such regimentation along with that code of silence. Back then we were inclined to keep certain activities concealed for the sake of loyalty to the football fraternity. The student body thrived on our winning tradition and those who left the football program because of any personal reasons did so without causing any further hard feelings or resentment. There was no reason to take it any further. I personally was a friend of many who walked away and I respected their exodus.

**319**

In recent years our society has had to deal with hazing and out of control behavior across the country at the high school level. To me this kind of behavior can literally destroy an athletic program. In 2001 an incident occurred at Westinghouse that went a little too far and it made the news. It played out as follows: A long standing tradition that no player shall walk under the goal posts before the first game of the season — a member of the team had forgotten this much respected tradition and walked under the goal post at a practice session. He was beaten by several teammates and was hospitalized overnight requiring medical attention. This incident raised much concern and was dealt with immediately with suspensions and sincere apologies from the out of control players. Upon the return to the team of the attacked player a heartfelt reunion was held. Led by the young boy's mother and his teammates they walked together under those goal posts prayerfully vowing to have a new beginning. This shall never happen again as the power of prayer will reinforce the strength of a teams' loyalty and respect for each other.

This kind of behavior has no place in the development of a successful football program and individuals who execute such behavior are of no value to a football team. Today this type of behavior can only cause dissention among team members and is of no value for team bonding. In fact a high school in New York (Mepham High

School) cancelled its' entire 2003 football season because three players were accused of sodomizing three other players during that schools' pre-season football camp. This type of behavior is unacceptable and causes dissention and disrespect to an entire football team. This is a sad situation that affects many innocent young men who are willing to work hard in an effort to play football and enjoy the game. We have a sad society out there when a few disrespectful individuals can literally ruin an entire football program. They should be dismissed immediately as they have no respect for human dignity and the sport of football.

Football is a team sport that requires much dedication and unity in order to be successful. Apparently the cases reported today across the land lacked the unique respect and harmony that **"The Room"** of yesteryear at Westinghouse High School possessed. The main ingredient that the Westinghouse football program had was **PRIDE**, and today that key value is missing from many of those troubled schools across the land. **"Bulldog Pride,"** is still being displayed at Westinghouse to this very day. All those present day students have to do is walk the main corridor of the "Wall of Fame" to realize that opportunity is there for each and every one of them. Each one of those who appear on those walls is a product of the pride that motivated them to succeed. It is a value that is so much needed in our society today.

A team cannot afford unnecessary injuries caused by out of control and inhumane behavior. A healthy football team goes a long way in having a successful season. Extra curricular rough housing is bound to happen since the game of football is an aggressive sport. Only the strong willed individuals with a lot of savvy are successful and survive. It certainly gave those who survived **The Room** something to tell their sons and grandsons of what it was like to prepare and play for the Westinghouse Bulldogs. The football program was a tough one to survive as it was a proud fraternity that was well prepared to carry on the fine winning tradition of Westinghouse High School. The one question many of aspiring scrubs would ask themselves – "How much am I willing to sacrifice in order to play football for a winning tradition?" Success goes to those who work hard to reach a desired goal. Ask any proud US Marine who experienced Paris Island. I mention Paris Island because **The ROOM** reminded me so much of the regimented challenge that each of the scrubs experienced in order to wear the gold and blue of Westinghouse.

It was a miracle that of all the rough house activity that took place there were no reported injuries or serious accidents. I am sure if such were the case the team leader would have had a lot of explaining to do. Dimperio would not have appreciated losing one of his players because of foolish behavior. There was a lot to lose if out of control behavior took place. The team leader had to be one with common sense and a sound mindset. Mature and sensible teenagers are what a coach has to develop in order to maintain a solid football program. Sometimes the most aggressive player is not the one you want in a leadership role unless he is able to control himself at all times. When the game is on the line a sound leader is what you want on that field. That leader will motivate the aggressive ones with a strong convincing demeanor.

What follows now is a description of **The Room** as I remember it. In general a room can be defined as a space for various needs, but the room I am going to describe was one that echoed personal experiences that only a true bulldog can appreciate. It

320

was located in the rear of Westinghouse High School, adjacent to the laundry room, and was off limits to any outsider. It was a locker room where only the proud and the privileged dared to enter and walk through. Sacrifice, dedication, perseverance, loyalty, pride and the will to win are some of the attributes that were developed within the confines of this room. It was a unique looking geometric shaped locker room with two solid steel doors (one interior and one exterior). The **interior door** came from an interior corridor within the school and when entering through that door there was a set of steps (5 or 6) descending down to the floor of the locker room. When standing in the corridor at the top of those steps and looking into **The Room** you somehow got a compelled feeling that you were not to go any further. It was likened to a huge pitlike setting with the floor being located at the bottom of those descending steps. On the left side of the room was the shower room and around the interior walls of the room were several wooden benches. Above the benches were wall mounted clothes hooks. Directly across the room on the exterior wall were tall frosted, drab looking, steel casement windows and in the far left corner was the **exterior door** leading outside to the courtyard area situated high above the football field.

The only time I was in a position to view **The Room** was during a visit with one of my very close friends, "Bronco" Signore, who was co-captain of the football team. It was a setting that I still remember to this day as he held open the door to the room while we spoke at the top of those steps. Yes, he was proud to let me observe the room from that doorway and I respected him for that. It gave me somewhat of a chilled feeling to stand there, but nevertheless I was impressed. I knew what this locker room meant to our football team. **The mere sight of watching a team member entering The Room through either one of those steel doors and hearing them slamming shut was mystifying to the other students.** It created a sense of pride and respect for each team member to live by.

A newly initiated candidate (scrub) was compelled to honor the code of silence and to develop a strong mindset as quickly as possible in order to meet the forthcoming challenges. Many of those individuals who were quiet and passive and wanted to play football realized they had to make a behavior adjustment – meaning they would have to adjust from that passive demeanor to a more aggressive one. The shower room had several shower heads for use, but only one was dedicated for the scrubs to use – naturally it did not spray water very well.

A scrub never knew the luxury of a long hot shower as it was wise for him to get wet and get the hell out as quickly as possible. The varsity members had a designated area to sit and change clothes while the scrubs sat where they were told to sit. In the center of the room was a large painted circle. It was off limits to the scrubs and only with permission were they able to enter that circle. Within that circle many times a score would be settled between two scrubs or a veteran and a scrub. Once that altercation was over it was on with the team meeting as the team captain locked the two steel doors. Nobody was permitted to leave until they were told to do so and that never seemed to come soon enough. Free at last is when a scrub was headed for home anxiously hoping to get a much needed hot shower and a hot meal. Of course you never complained to Mom or Dad as you ate dinner, and waited for an opportunity to leave the table to get some much needed rest.

321

One of my cousins (Angelo Aliberti) had to explain to his mother why he had to use the family washing machine every evening; stating that he needed to have clean sweats, socks and the list went on and on for the next days' practice. She could never understand why he had so much excess laundry. Needless to say he was overjoyed when his scrub days were over and he finally made the varsity. He and I had a brotherhood bond that was special, and I was able to console him throughout his days as a scrub. He knew full well how much I wanted to be on the team with him and I constantly listened and supported his determination to persevere. I was quite proud of him when he made the varsity and no longer had to weather the pounding of scrub life. In our spare time we practiced together as if I were a team member learning the plays and helping him as he perfected his timing. This was a way for me to draw closer to the loyalty I had for the team as a bleacher jockey. He did quite well and had a gratifying two years with the Bulldog Varsity as a solid single wing fullback.

After Angelo graduated from Westinghouse, I still had two more years of being a bleacher jockey. I attended every game of the 1952 and 1953 seasons cheering my friends on with every bit of energy and loyalty that I had. I was quite proud of them because I knew what they had gone through to represent the varsity of our Westinghouse Bulldogs. They played there hearts out and I screamed my head off.

There were some individuals who were not anxious to join the ranks of the Room fraternity as they were apprehensive of the mystique that was forthcoming. The desire and determination to play football helped motivate them and adjust to the demands of this close knit fraternity. The initiation began with a military recruit style haircut (shaved head). It was the beginning of what was in store for a determined newcomer to the football program. Whatever took place in **The Room** stayed there and was never discussed with anyone outside. It was likened to a fraternal allegiance that only team members were privy to discuss. The desire to play football for Westinghouse was strongly challenged, as the physical conditioning program was the primary goal.

Back then there was no weightlifting facility for conditioning as there is today. Conditioning was achieved through strenuous workouts consisting of a variety of isometric exercises along with countless pull-ups, pushups, sit-ups, rope climbing, wind sprints and jogging along Washington Boulevard beginning at Silver Lake clear down to the Allegheny River and back. Silver Lake later became an outdoor drive-in theatre and was used during off peak hours for running drills weaving in and out of the speaker posts.

It was a conditioning program that our military forces would appreciate. Many high schools throughout the country exercised similar programs, but the one at Westinghouse was exceptional. Football is a tough sport and getting a team ready physically and mentally for a long season is a challenge.

Extra curricular mind games and discipline were the norm for the scrubs to endure if they wanted to develop the football savvy of a Westinghouse Bulldog. Members of the football team were always well respected as they made their way day in and day out through those hallowed halls of Westinghouse. Wearing that gold and blue uniform for the first time was their reward when they took the field to play their first game as a Bulldog. I know how I felt when I saw any of my family members for

322

the first time taking the field wearing that gold and blue uniform. It was likened to a New York Yankee rookie wearing that pinstripe uniform for the first time.

Usually the scrubs entered the games after a victory was evident for Westinghouse. If the opposition should cross the Bulldog goal line while the scrubs were in the game there would be hell to pay at the following Monday afternoon practice. The varsity would watch and determine who "blew" a defensive assignment. The consequences were not very good. Needless to say a scrub was always under scrutiny on and off the field. He was well aware of the code of conduct and behavioral rules to be observed. Year after year many young men tried and more often than not few survived the rigors of **The Room**.

There were some years when more candidates were willing to put up with the demands and other years when many felt it was not worth the effort. I can recall during the time period leading up to the 1952 and 1953 seasons some sixty or so young men (scrubs) signed up to play football, and Coach Pete Dimperio had to be pleased. I remember seeing that large group of candidates going through the early stages of the conditioning drills in sweats and was impressed with what I saw. There was a lot of talent in that group of hopefuls, but unfortunately it dwindled over a period of time. Only a small number (ten or so) survived the demanding program and made the team. Respect went to the survivors for their courageous effort, and much disappointment to the ones who dropped out as it affected the nucleus of a sizable squad. Many of them were very talented athletes and could have made any other team in the city with a less demanding program. It was a huge loss for our football team as I played on the sandlots with many of them and recognized their talents. They were not willing to put up with or accept the rigorous demands of the program. Sometimes it takes more than talent to achieve a goal, but I might add that the Bulldogs did not win the city title in either one of those two years (1952 Carrick won and 1953 Peabody won).

323

The 1952 and 1953 teams were "Three bricks shy of a load" as they were affected by the loss of some very talented athletes. I really believe the Bulldogs would have excelled even more with some of the talent that left the football program year after year. I remember quite well those two years and realized how foolish certain veterans were in driving away talented athletes with foolish and senseless tactics. I always maintained "Never cast aside what will come back to haunt you later." It cost the Bulldogs a ticket to the city championship in both of those years. They were my peers back then and I shared the disappointments with them. Many years have passed since then, but I for one will always maintain that Westinghouse had the best talent in the city.

There was enough talent walking the halls of Westinghouse to field a sizeable squad every year, but many chose not to accept and challenge the mental and physical demands of the program. Several of my relatives and friends who were members of the football program reflected how the rigors of **The Room** separated the mentally tough from the rest of the hopefuls. When they took to the field they had no fear, were well disciplined and physically and mentally prepared to take on the best. I never saw a Westinghouse team that lacked any of the aforementioned qualities, and I will always be proud of the many that guided the Bulldogs to their winning ways. As the old saying goes – "You can't knock success" – and certainly Westinghouse High School with well over 500 wins and 36 championships (35 City and 1 WPIAL) has gained and earned that respect throughout its storied history. Football is both an aggressive and skillful sport and to be successful at it you must develop the attributes that will produce a winning program. Leaders of **The Room** were expected to control with mature judgement and it took smart levelheaded individuals to be leaders. We must remember that such leadership was to be shouldered by a capable senior every year. Many of those who gave way to the program who were fine athletes in their own right may not agree, but life was never meant to be an easy ride.

Let me share with you a humorous incident that occurred in **The Room** at the time when I was a student there. It so happened one afternoon that two well dressed young men (former students) were looking for one of their friends who was a member of the football team. They decided to enter **The Room** without knocking on the door while a team meeting was taking place. What a foolish move!! Much to their surprise they were greeted by a few of the scrubs and were bodily hustled into the shower room for an unexpected drenching. It happened so quickly, and before they could even think about retaliation they were hustled back outside and were told never to return. You can be sure they never returned, and they will always remember **The Room** at Westinghouse.

At my most recent class reunion we had as our special guest, George Webb, who at the time was head football coach at Westinghouse. He spoke to us with much sincerity and pride of his years as a student athlete at Westinghouse where he played for Coach Pete Dimperio. He revealed a little of his experiences as a player regarding the Room, but not enough to break the code of silence. As he spoke he was kidding me about knowing too much about the Room activities. He indicated that as a coach he would never allow or tolerate such behavior today. That evening Coach Webb and some of my classmates who played football had a great time reminiscing about their experiences. Obviously, the Room of yesterday meant a lot to them and I respect that. As George Webb continued speaking he recalled a former high school teammate coming back to visit him on a game day at Westinghouse. This former player walked into the locker room and stood in the center of that circle and became quite emotional as he took part in a pre-game prayer with Coach Webb and his team. It was apparent that he felt a strong recollection of his own days within that Room. Coach Webb told him that the Room was going to be demolished for major renovation very soon and the former player asked him if he would save a single showerhead for him. Coach Webb saw to it that a showerhead would indeed be given to that proud former Bulldog.

Yes, as Coach Webb alluded, I probably knew too much of what went on in the Room. Even though I may not have been a part of it, many of my closest friends and relatives who played confided in my trust with their experiences. In later years they still often shared with me stories of those experiences, and thus allowing me to fully appreciate what it really meant to each and every one of them. In fact, one of those close friends had expressed to me how he wished I would have been a part of that special camaraderie that I quietly respected. He was right. Even though I was not eligible to play football at Westinghouse I should have volunteered to be a student manager. I regret not having accepted that opportunity. My mindset back then was not what it should have been. I paid the price many times over as I would have enjoyed being with the team. In some small way the 1952 and 1953 seasons would have helped to release some of the bitterness that I had inside of me.

Spiritually, I feel as though I was close at hand because of what I was privy to learn. I may not have agreed with some of the challenges they endured, but I respected their perseverance. As one of my closest friends, Joe Pronio quoted to me, "I was willing to go that extra mile." I knew what he went through as he was one of those who made first team at the young age of fifteen in 1952. When he first entered **the Room** as a scrub he had to deal with the tough varsity members of the 1951 team and they challenged his perseverance. That team consisted of twenty-two seniors and was one of the biggest and most talented teams to come out of Westinghouse. They were rated by the sports writers as one of the top ten high school teams in the past fifty years in Western Pennsylvania. After realizing the challenges my friend Joe went through, it reinforced my decision to include within this chapter a space dedicated to **the Room**.

As I bring this topic to a close I will always remember those few minutes standing at the top of those steps looking in at the **Room** as I spoke with my good friend, "Bronco" Signore. I was privy to sense the mystique of that room that brought these young men who came together as I gazed across the floor with the sunlight penetrating through those tall frosted windows. They shared together the glory and rewards of winning. They needed each other and not one player was big enough to carry the entire team. Coach Pete Dimperio gave them the opportunity to excel on and off the field with his leadership, dedication, wisdom and caring ways.

To this very day I feel as though I always wanted to be a small part of that Westinghouse tradition, and go that extra mile that so many of my friends and relatives traveled. When I see any of them today it seems we never part ways without a story or two about their **Room** and their experience of playing football at Westinghouse. Football at Westinghouse was playing with pain and with pride being the best medicine. What must be realized today is that boys will be boys or men will be men and no matter where they are – high school, college or professional – it is the nature of the beast that exists in the sociology of athletics.

This statement from my good friend Joe Pronio, "Carmen, follow your dream and write about the very sport that you always aspired to play at Westinghouse High School" was so heartfelt and fitting. Recalling these words I was inspired to spend countless hours in putting this book together. Thanks Joe, for your priceless support and encouragement.

## FROM GREENFIELD TO HOMEWOOD

This is a true story of one determined young man who desired to play football for Pete Dimperio and how he went about doing it. It was done in such a way that I would never forget as I was privy to know at that time when it was all unfolding. I met Ray Gorman in the summer of 1952 at the Highland Park Swimming pool. One

325

of our mutual friends Ron "Gus" Spangler (a lifeguard) and I did summer work at the swimming pool. Ray and Gus were teammates at Taylor Allderdice High School and we were talking about the upcoming football season of 1953. Ray had expressed how much he wanted to play for Pete Dimperio and Westinghouse High School. I was quite surprised to hear this as he was already a starting quarterback at Allderdice. Gus, who was the starting fullback, had graduated and would be going on with his life. I remember looking at Ray and seeing the determination in his eyes and knowing that he was dead serious. Of course I thought he was crazy as I knew he would be in for a rude awakening. I knew about "The Room" and what was waiting for him, but I only said, "Ray it will be a lot different than what you experienced at Allderdice." I wished him luck and somehow had a feeling that he was going to face up to all the challenges. Come September of 1953 I began my senior year at Westinghouse and there was Ray Gorman, the kid I met at the Highland Park Pool, sitting in our school cafeteria. I was really happy to see him. This was the beginning of his dream.

The rest of the story was revealed to me some fifty years later. Ray called me at home the early part of 2006 as he had been told that I was writing a book about the history of Westinghouse High School football. We talked for about an hour as he recounted how he was able to accomplish his goal to play football for Pete Dimperio. I was most impressed of the way he sacrificed and planned his objective, and it was done without any special breaks along the way. His father did not agree with his plan, but it did not stop him from pursuing it. He began his journey by dropping out of school for one semester as he moved in with a family member who resided in Homewood. His father was quite upset with him. Ray felt this was the best way for him to make this move without raising any questions by the school board.

Recalling back when I first met Ray with that look of determination it was no surprise that he would end up at Westinghouse. He faced all the challenges of starting over again at a new school. The harassment of being a scrub and putting up with the Room of hard knocks were experiences he would never forget, but he was determined to make the Bulldog varsity and fulfill his dream. This was quite commendable for a young man to possess such a mindset that literally drove him to the top. Pete was proud and very supportive of Ray realizing how determined he was to reach his goal. Ray opened the 1954 season as the starting quarterback for Westinghouse. Ray's father attended every game that season and was quite proud of his son.

The Bulldogs won the Pittsburgh City League Championship that year with a hard fought 7-6 victory over a good Carrick High School team. It was a game that had many of us sitting on the edge of our seats as it was rated as one of the top high school games by Scholastic Sports Magazine. Ray and his teammates really pulled together that night as it was one of the best games that I had seen the Bulldogs play that year. It was a game that could have gone either way and was not over until the final whistle blew.

During my conversation with Ray I could still sense the enthusiasm and satisfaction within his voice as we recounted that experience of fifty years ago. Ray went on to have a fine career in college and later a successful high school football coach. He was the epitome of a determined young man that any coach would love to

326

have leading his football team and you can bet that his coach, Pete Dimperio, was one proud man.

## SILVER LAKE STADIUM – MY FIELD OF DREAMS

I am going back in time, September of the year 1948, my first day as a student at Westinghouse High School. I remember this picturesque setting as I stood atop the grass covered courtyard behind the school overlooking the deep valley below. Within this valley was the football field surrounded on the near side with bleachers, far side and far end was wooded and the open end was bordered by Silver Lake. To access down to this valley below was a long spiral set of cement steps from the courtyard. It was a view that an ambitious photographer would appreciate as the surrounding shadows of nature reflected on the still water of Silver Lake. Many lunch hours were spent atop that courtyard admiring the view below. It was a great place to hang out during our lunch hours watching the fourth period gym classes playing softball or touch football on the field below or the small flocks of wild geese paddling along on the quiet water of Silver Lake.

Our playing field did not have a grass playing surface, but consisted of splotches of tar spread out over a dusty plain of mother earth and gravel. The wooden bleachers were weather-beaten, rotting and splitting at the seams. Stadium lights were non-existent. Many times over I would imagine with wishful thinking how nice it would be if all of the aforementioned items would have been added or upgraded to this valley below. It had all the basic characteristics to be a showcase setting. The mere thought of attending a night football game with those stadium lights reflecting on the still waters of nearby Silver Lake seemed to sanction my imagination.

The lake was a popular community resource long before the new school opened its' doors in 1923. In fact, Silver Lake made news in 1911 with an interesting article depicting its value to the East End community. The following is a brief version of that article that I researched and found in the archives of Carnegie Library Main Branch in Oakland:

327

---

**PITTSBURGH POST**                    **JANUARY 11, 1911**

### Silver Lake and 10 1/2 Acres in 12th Ward
### Proposed Playground Site under Bond Issue

The lake itself has been for years a loved resort of East End youth and the picture taken yesterday (see photo end of chapter 11) shows the frozen surface in use by skaters. By fish planting and the building of bath houses, it would become a mecca for the children of that whole section of the city.

Silver Lake and its beautiful natural surroundings will probably be condemned by the city and used for a playground. The Lincoln Board of Trade has started movement to have the city acquire 12 acres of land including the lake, and has made a report to Mayor Magee and the Pittsburgh Playgrounds Association on the feasibility of the proposition. In the bond issue $800,000 was set aside for acquiring playgrounds sites.

Silver Lake is situated in the heart of the new 12th Ward just below the Brilliant cut-off bridge of the Pennsylvania Railroad. The territory, which the board of trade has in mind, consists principally of a thinly wooded hollow with considerable level ground. Nine and a half acres belong to the Finley estate and three and a half acres belong to the Smith estate.

Rev. C. R. Zahniser, who is Chairman of the Board of Trade Committee which drew up a report on Silver Lake and its' wooded surroundings was an ideal place for a playground. He pointed out that it is within a 15 minute walk for 40,000 people, including 6,000 or 7,000 children. The lake is within a short distance from the Lincoln Avenue, Frankstown Avenue and Hamilton Avenue street car lines and Beechwood Boulevard runs through the proposed site. There is plenty of room for several ball grounds, according to Rev. Zahniser, and one corner of the site is admirably adapted for a nature garden for the children. The slopes of the hollow are wooded, affording a pleasant place for picnics and Silver Lake, covering 2.5 acres, is mostly shallow but of a good quality of water. Residents of the district think if a playground is not made of the hollow it will become a slum district like sections of Junction Hollow and other sections of the city situated near creeks.

The Finley tract is assessed at about $2,000 an acre. The Smith tract includes some land that could be used for building and is a little higher. No attempt has been made to find out what the owners want for the property as it would be taken, if at all, by condemnation proceedings. Councilman Charles Ross, of the twelfth ward, is much interested in the proposition and may later introduce an ordinance to condemn the property if the city administration is agreeable to the idea.

**328**

---

After having read the article above and viewing, several times, one of my favorite movies – "Field of Dreams" - it brought back memories and wishful thinking that I've had for many years. It was a fantasy that I have had for quite some time and would like to share it with you. Many of you who do remember Silver Lake may appreciate what I am about to describe.

But before I begin fantasizing let us go back in time to the year 1949 as it so happened that our City Planning Committee decided to dredge Silver Lake and sell off the property and it's surroundings as it became too much of a problem for them to maintain. It was such a big disappointment for many of us. It was a natural resource fed from a natural underground spring that was part of our school surroundings for many years. In fact our athletic teams were often times referred to as the Silver Lakers. Bordered by Washington Boulevard and tree-lined surroundings it was just as the 1911 article stated - a mecca for many of the young people to enjoy. The city decided not to put the time and money toward maintaining what was once an impressive looking valley. To this very day I can still see a vivid picture of that scene and realize what a loss it was for our community and our school. I would like to share with you a reverie that has been haunting me for many years. Follow along with me on a short journey and realize why it has remained as one of my life's early recollections.

It is a cool Friday night in late September as we begin our fantasy journey from atop the steps of the Lincoln Avenue Bridge. Let's make our way down the long flight of steps leading to the heavily traveled Washington Boulevard. As we reach the bottom of those steps let us pause for a few minutes and take a good look across the boulevard; there facing us is the huge gray stone Brilliant Cut-off Railroad Bridge (a masterful architectural structure) with its huge high arches spanning the quiet water of Silver Lake. As we look through those massive arches out across the lake, there in the background high upon the hill is the back of Westinghouse High School. The gray stone school looms high above a long spiraling set of cement steps leading down to the football field. Back then we affectionately called it the dust bowl (no grass and no lights) where many of our great football teams played. It was our home field, where we enjoyed many thrills and excitement that will always be remembered. We hurry across the boulevard to the other side. We are now heading in the direction of that field to join those enthusiastic and loyal fans of Westinghouse.

With all of this in full view, let us continue walking toward our destination. We make our way over to the worn gravel path (let's call it Silver Lane) along the lake shoreline leading us to this brightly-lit stadium (wishful thinking). With those bright lights reflecting impressively on the calm water of Silver Lake, we can feel the electricity in the brisk night air as we get closer to our destination. From our vantage point we can clearly see and hear the roar of the crowd as our band led by our director Mr. Carl McVicker strikes up a heartwarming rendition of "Westinghouse Forever" at the sight of our football team standing on the school courtyard above awaiting the word to make their way down the long spiraling steps leading to the field below.

The field is a green carpet of Kentucky blue (again wishful thinking) with neatly lined white yard markers. The Bulldogs are fired up as they have reached the bottom of the steps and are making their way onto the field for pre-game warm-up. Our coaches whether it be Pro Burton, Pete Dimperio or George Webb are met by well-wishers as they make their way past the student-body section. The bleachers are full and the crowd is boisterous as they anxiously await the opening kick-off. Many are standing on the surrounding hillsides and behind both end zones. They are here to see one of the finest high school football traditions in America playing under the Friday night lights. Yes, our school was the heart and soul of East Liberty and Homewood. My, it sure feels good to picture this colorful setting before us. Many of the schools across America had what I described above, but we did not. I can attest to that as I visited many during my years of following high school football from coast to coast. We were happy with our antiquated facilities, where we developed great pride, spirit, loyalty and a winning tradition. There were times when we played schools at their home fields with grass and stadium lights and realized what we did not have. The old saying, "you never miss what you don't have" was what we learned to accept.

Just like in the movie – "Build it and They will Come." It was wishful thinking on my part. What a showcase it could have been for Westinghouse High School to go along with its successful football fortunes of the twentieth century. Many of the schools that we competed with outside of the City of Pittsburgh would now visit our home field for a game. The likes of Aliquippa, New Castle, Mt. Lebanon and Altoona

**329**

to name a few would have been great for drawing huge crowds. Parking would not have been a problem as Washington Boulevard and the surrounding areas would have been adequate. A natural bowl-like setting was always there waiting for this panoramic facelift to take place, but it never came. City League football at Silver Lake Stadium – home of the Westinghouse Bulldogs could have been a masterpiece. It was a time when our successful football tradition with well over 500 wins and many championship seasons deserved to be showcased with a beautiful stadium and the adjoining Silver Lake.

This is a panoramic view that I have envisioned many times over. I could see this whole setting reproduced in a water color masterpiece by my friend and fellow alumnus, Mary Lois Verrilla –"The Lady Who Paints Pittsburgh". She would be my choice to paint this scene. Maybe someday she can fit this into her busy schedule and consider doing it.

I will always remember old Silver Lake that was foolishly removed from our community by the City Planning Committee. In its place an outdoor drive-in movie theater was built, and lasted long enough for the novelty to wear off. Today, that area no longer has the drive-in theater as those in the know realized after a while that it was not a feasible location for such a facility. There were more people sitting on the bridge to watch the movies than there were in automobiles.

Today, a car wash establishment and a few small industrial businesses now occupy the land that was once a natural resource. Thanks for the memories of Silver Lake for the many years that it existed, and may our planning committees exercise better judgment when they pursue removing a natural resource in the foreseeable future. This was a treasure that was so much a part of our youthful activities. Every time I drive along this stretch of Washington Boulevard I think of how nice it would be if we could see those huge stone arches reflecting over the quiet water of Silver Lake.

The photos I have saved from years gone by will always be a reminder of that small lake that was enjoyed by so many of us. I realize that time marches on but sometimes tradition is being tarnished along the way. I guess back then it was felt that Silver Lake had lost its luster and was being neglected. Neglect was caused by irresponsible parks and recreation management. The loss of Silver Lake in 1949 was the result of poor planning strategy. The photos I have saved are priceless and the memories will continue to linger each time I drive past that once picturesque scene.

## OUR SONG "WESTINGHOUSE FOREVER"

Some simple definitions of a song could be a melody, a lyric, a strain, a verse, a poem, or a musical expression. The later one defines best, **"Westinghouse Forever"**. The lyrics are very special to all Westinghouse alumni. Every school across America (high school or college) has a song, whether it was a march or an alma mater tribute that is an inspiration to those who still maintain the pride and loyalty of their school days. Many alumni of Westinghouse High School are still quite proud of their song, and that is a known fact. From the time we entered our school until commencement it was an inspiration that was to last forever. Our family get-togethers as I was growing up never ended until we all sang together

330

"**Westinghouse Forever.**" Usually one of the older alumni would raise a glass to toast our alma mater and that would always get the family and friends going as they sang loud and clear the old school song. In fact, many years ago at a family wedding reception, the band leader John Piccolino, a Westinghouse grad, played our song and it brought everyone to their feet with a boisterous round of applause. By the time the song was over a human line had formed and weaved around the reception hall. It was a fun time as family members and friends reflected heartfelt memories of our school days. It was a great wedding reception and a good time was had by all.

Many years after leaving Westinghouse High School, I have heard renditions of this song played out at a football game, at a parade marching down Fifth Avenue in Pittsburgh or at a class reunion, and it still sends chills up and down my spine. I remember several years ago (1955) attending a high school football game in Temple City, California and the home team (Temple City High School) band was on the field and began to play their school song. Much to my surprise it was, you guessed it, the same words as "Westinghouse Forever." It brought me to my feet with chills running down my spine as I sang right along with the local boosters. Here I was 3000 miles away from Pittsburgh singing the words of my alma mater as the tears welled up in my face. How could I ever forget these words? I was in California but my heart was in Pittsburgh.

**Westinghouse forever, loyal and true**
**Nothing can ever change our love for you**
**Rah! Rah! Rah!**
**Westinghouse forever, we're true to you**
**We love our colors of gold and blue**

**331**

Back in Pittsburgh several years later as I was getting ready to leave for work my radio was tuned to station KDKA 1020 and local DJ Jack Bogut – he was spinning a very familiar song. The song happened to be an instrumental version of "Our Director", which was the same exact melody as our school song. When I arrived at my office, I called the KDKA radio station and spoke with the station manager to confirm the song title and arrangement. It was "Our Director," by Henry Mancini, and I thought it would be nice if I could somehow locate a copy of it. I began a search, but without success until one day I mentioned it to a co-worker. Unbeknownst to me this co-worker was a member of a musical group and had a friend that worked for a Musical Record Mart outlet. His friend proceeded to search for a recording of this song for me. Within a few weeks he located a Boston Pop's record album with a selection of "Our Director" – consisting of the same melody that I was searching for. Needless to say, I was quite pleased and purchased the album. Since then I had it put on an audio cassette and a CD. It is one of my musical treasures as I play it from time to time when I need a spiritual lift. Needless to say it is truly a great way to perk up a Westinghouse Class Reunion.

## ANSWERING THE CALL FOR A FRIEND

In the spring of 1980, a call went out to all ex-Bulldogs and alumni to help Pete Dimperio organize a benefit for one of our own. It was for John Cerniglia, a standout from the 1954 Westinghouse High School championship football team who suffered a broken neck from an automobile accident in 1966. It left him a quadriplegic. I got a call to help for this worthy cause from one of my cousins, Bob Merletti, who played on that 1954 team with Cerniglia. I knew John Cerniglia very well as we grew up together in the Larimer section of East Liberty. He had a work ethic that was all systems go and this accident really devastated him and his family. He was a very brave, strong person who showed strength even when the odds were against him.

On the football field he was a tower of strength as he anchored the 1954 Bulldog's line on both offense and defense. He was very instrumental in helping Westinghouse High School win the 1954 city championship, 7-6, over Carrick High School by blocking the crucial extra point attempt.

The word circulated throughout the many ex-Bulldogs and alumni near and far as we assembled for that special evening (May 28, 1980) *"Night with Pete Dimperio"* at the Monroeville Expo-Mart. to help our friend, John Cerniglia. It was great to see all the ex-Bulldogs and alumni pulling together, preparing food and drink for all of John's family, friends and supporters. Pete was as proud as a peacock that night to see many of his former ball players. He always said that he never had a boy who let him down, and that night was certainly an example of how proud he was of all his boys. Many special guests – Steeler's Jack Lambert, former Pirates' Frank Gustine and Dick Groat, Pitt Coach Jackie Sherrill, CMU Coach Chuck Klausing, and Duquesne Coach Dan McCann were in attendance along with Pittsburgh Mayor Richard Caligiuri.

It was a night that I will remember for a long, long time. The strong sense of dedication and togetherness was ever present among the many ex-Bulldogs and alumni. It did not make any difference what years apart they were it was all Westinghouse alumni. Many of us had not seen one another for several years and it brought a bright smile across the face of our friend John Cerniglia – and that was the main purpose for such an occasion. John was a tower of strength before the unfortunate accident and it was very sad for all of us to see him in such a confined position.

God took him from us on July 16, 1982 two years after that memorable evening that we shared with him. John, you will always remain in the hearts of all of us who had the pleasure of knowing you and being your friend. God bless you, until we get together again on the other side to meet our Maker.

## THE UNFORGETTABLE GHOSTS OF WESTINGHOUSE

As I think back to my early years prior to attending Westinghouse High School I heard many stories from family members and neighbors of their fond memories of Westinghouse. It created a sense of curiosity within my young mind as I awaited the

332

time when I would some day be a student there. Would I be as fortunate as they were in experiencing the proud years they seemed to have had as students? The stories and experiences they shared with each other as I listened to them reminisce was fascinating. The names of principals, teachers, coaches, student athletes, musicians, school activities and events were numerous and they really stuck in my mind like a sponge. By the time I arrived there in September, 1948, I was namely familiar with some of those personalities that I had heard so much about. They were there as I could feel their spirits as I walked those halls day in and day out for six enjoyable years. Photos and memorial plaques of many alumni and faculty graced the walls of the main corridor and I could feel the same sense of pride as I walked past them each and every day. They were the ghosts that hung around within those walls at Westinghouse and I would never forget them. To this day I can still sit back and reflect on those memorable years with much gratification. Some alumni may not feel the same as I do, but I sincerely believe that those six years prepared me well for life's journey.

I could walk into our auditorium and remember names of those who preceded me like Erroll Garner, Cornell Cooper, Dakota Staton, Ahmad Jamal, Mary Lou Williams, Billy Strayhorn, Do Do Marmarosa, Joe Ricciardelli, Frank Cunimondo, Adam Wade and many more. They all excelled and went on to stardom as they performed brilliantly in the limelight of the entertainment world. Our music teachers, Mr. Carl McVicker and Miss Hazel Burkholder who spent countless hours in the auditorium teaching and directing some of the finest talent to come out of Pittsburgh are to be commended. They did themselves proud.

333

My friend, Herb Amen, could easily write a best seller about all the talented people who came through the hallowed halls of both Westinghouse and Peabody High Schools. Herb himself is a proud graduate of Westinghouse and is a very talented part-time actor and writer. He was a close friend of one of East Liberty's finest entertainers – the incomparable Billy Eckstein (Peabody High School). I had the pleasure of visiting with Herb Amen at his home a few years ago. He showed me his special room collection of photos and memorabilia of many of the famous and well known entertainers of our time. It was most impressive and priceless and brought back many gratifying memories.

I could walk into our old gymnasium and remember the names of the many that brought the crowd to their feet with their stellar basketball prowess and championship play. There was Charles Cooper, Maurice Stokes, and Ed Fleming (all of them All Americans and NBA stars) whose ghosts will always hang from the rafters of that gymnasium. I can recall when Maurice Stokes was at St. Francis College of Loretto, PA and how he almost single-handedly took them to an NIT Championship in 1955 when he scored 43 points in a semi-final loss to Dayton University in Madison Square Garden. They all left their mark on the floors of many arenas throughout the United States long after their high school playing days. They were a credit to our school and to our community. I was fortunate to see all three of them play at each level of competition (high school, college and pro) and they never forgot where they came from. The old Pitt Pavilion and Fitzgerald Field House were the local arenas where they performed as Pittsburgh City Champions. They brought home the trophies that graced our display cases in our main corridor and made us all proud to be a part of their successful efforts.

Then, of course, I could walk through the short tunnel leading to the football field and passing the laundry room *(Miss Annie's domain)* along the way and still be able to smell the freshness of clean towels going through the spin cycle. As I stand at the top of those steps leading down to the field there are numerous legendary ghosts that come to mind. They made their way down those same steps to mother earth where they learned how to play championship caliber football. Under the leadership of coaches Pro Burton and Pete Dimperio they did themselves proud and gave us the excitement and thrills of a lifetime. The names before, during and after my time are numerous as one would imagine with thirty-five championship years and well over 500 wins.

Before my time there, I remember the old timers repeatedly mentioning by name such stars as *Joe "Showboat" Ware, Bobby Dye and Ken Ormiston*. They were household names in our neighborhood and certainly are three of the most notable football ghosts of Westinghouse high School. There were countless more that followed and unlimited space would be needed to mention them all by name. Every generation had them and they will always be remembered with having that same pride, spirit, loyalty and tradition that existed at Westinghouse. They performed as champions across the gridirons of old Pitt Stadium and Forbes Field and later George Cupples Stadium. Their efforts were acknowledged with numerous awards that decorated our school trophy cases. The past may be long gone, but the stories of the past will be retold with each passing generation. Thanks for those priceless memories.

## WESTINGHOUSE "EAST-WEST GATHERING REUNIONS"

The East-West gathering originated from members of the Westinghouse High School football teams and their beloved coach Pete Dimperio. They came together during the late 1960's at Mr. Steak Restaurant on Rodi Road in Penn Hills. Most of those players were from the late 1940's and early 1950's teams. It was an opportunity for them to remain in touch with each other and their former coach and teacher. It was a loyal camaraderie that is not very common in today's world. When a group of men can continue to remain close from high school days throughout their later years of life is admirable. Coach Dimperio was one who was always ready to help any youth in a time of need and his former players responded with loyal support. This group of men was the heart and sole of Dimperio's domain, as they experienced a special dedication and respect for him.

Later on in time, Joe Pronio and myself, received an invitation to meet with this group for their 50th Reunion at Tivoli's Restaurant in Penn Hills in the fall of 1999, and we were honored. Pete Dimperio, Sr. had passed on but his spirit was strongly felt by so many of us. His son, Pete Jr. was there with us and that was special.

Our most recent gatherings have been held at Café Naples in Verona with good food, laughter and recollections of years gone by. This group of men has a special bond and they continue to carry on the loyalty and respect of a very special era. Westinghouse High School and coach Pete Dimperio is where it all began and many

334

thanks goes to the WHS East-West gathering committee as they will continue to carry on our proud tradition. The committee of Frank Guadagnino, Felix Cutruzulla, Gene Massaro, Joe Nicoletti, Chuck Naser and Len Gallo are the organizers that bring this proud group together. I am looking forward to the next invitation from this fine group of men who epitomize the priceless Westinghouse Bulldog Tradition.

## OPEN ENROLLMENT CHALLENGES NEIGHBORHOOD LOYALTY

Prior to 1970, Westinghouse dominated the City League in football, and during that time period with coaches Pro Burton and Pete Dimperio leading the way, the bulldogs captured twenty-eight city titles. Since the inception of open enrollment, which began in 1979, Westinghouse has no longer dominated. Nevertheless, they have managed to win seven city titles - the same number for both Perry and Brashear with Peabody winning four, Carrick two, and South with one have also claimed city titles during that time span. All things considered, they have managed to do as well as could be expected. Obviously, the open enrollment policy has affected the Bulldogs winning ways of yesteryear and created parity in the City League. Many talented athletes from East Liberty, Homewood and Brushton have not stayed at home to attend Westinghouse, but have decided to go to school elsewhere in the city. Times have changed and so has loyalty.

One morning back around December, 1989, as I was driving my automobile on the way to work, I happened to get behind a PAT bus traveling along Bennett Street in the Homewood/Brushton area. I noticed several young individuals were wearing Perry State Championship jackets waiting to board the bus in front of me. The bus stopped to pick them up. Obviously, they were on their way to Perry High School that is located on the North Side of Pittsburgh. At the time I was surprised to see this since I was passing through the Westinghouse neighborhood. Then I suddenly realized that this was the result of the open enrollment policy. That particular year, 1989 Perry had defeated Westinghouse 7-6 for the City Championship, advanced to the PIAA State Playoffs and beat Berwick 20-8 for the AAA State Title. That was quite a successful year for Perry. Years ago you stayed at home and played for the home school, and that is how loyalty and tradition prevailed at Westinghouse and other schools throughout the city

As time passed I became more aware of how the open enrollment and the so-called magnet programs were affecting many high schools in the city. It became quite obvious that Perry High School (also known as Perry Traditional Academy) seemed to be the one city school that was attracting most of the talented athletes; especially football. I decided it was time to write an article expressing my views to the Pittsburgh Post – Gazette. Below is my article with follow-up rebuttals and comments:

335

## ONE–SIDED CITY LEAGUE

November 2, 2002
**Sports Mailbag, Pittsburgh Post-Gazette**
**34 Boulevard of the Allies**
**Pittsburgh, PA 15222**

Since the inception of open enrollment in the Pittsburgh Public Schools system in 1988, Perry Traditional Academy has harvested the finest athletes from all over the city of Pittsburgh, while the other nine city high schools have paid the price of losing talented athletes.

The 2002 football season has been a real fiasco as Perry has shut out all nine of their opponents by a lopsided average of 53-0. This is a revelation that the best athletes are attending Perry Traditional Academy in hopes of getting a scholarship to play Division I-A College football someday. I do not blame them one bit, but the other nine city schools are losing quality athletes.

Something is wrong with this open enrollment system, as it appears that football has been the main benefactor. In prior years there was no such system and each of the ten city schools were able to compete more effectively and challenge for a city title. Since 1919, the beginning of the Pittsburgh City League and up until 1987, Perry High School had captured only four city titles, but since 1988 (the inception of open enrollment) they have won nine more city titles and one PIAA state title. They have reaped the harvest of the city talent and resemble a city league all-star team playing a schedule of nine undermanned city schools. As far as I am concerned all nine schools could have mailed in the final score of each of their games with Perry. It appears that all nine of Perry's games were nothing more than tune-ups for the upcoming PIAA State Playoffs. Perry will be at the top of the City League year after year and will never be challenged. It does not seem fair to see all the talented athletes heading for Perry Traditional Academy.

It would be interesting to know how many of the boys on the 2002 Perry team actually live in the Perry High School District. I am sure there is a **unique** quota system as to who will attend Perry and that it is well controlled and scrutinized by the powers to be. It would be interesting if the entire WPIAL had open enrollment, allowing a student to attend any high school of choice without having to live in that school district. If it is not permitted in the WPIAL then it should not be permitted in the City League. Time has come for each school district to support and encourage its students to stay at the home school and challenge this unfair open enrollment system. There is no reason for the city school system to be any different than the WPIAL.

No doubt the Perry coaching staff will regard my opinion as sour grapes, but why should they agree with me as they continue to reap the harvest of fine grapes year after year. School loyalty is very important to young students and it is a reflection of community pride. Each school district strives to instill pride and loyalty and that is a reflection of what our country is all about. I am a 1954 graduate of a Pittsburgh city high school (Westinghouse), and I still feel a sense of pride and loyalty for my alma mater.

336

Thank goodness we did not have open enrollment back then as it would have taken away those community values that we cherished so much. City League parity is long gone and will continue that way as Perry fills its horn of plenty.

Carmen Pellegrino
Oakmont

<hr>

## DON'T BLAME PERRY
## REBUTTAL

November 23, 2002

In last week's Sports Mailbag, Carmen Pellegrino stated that "Perry Traditional Academy has harvested the finest athletes from all over the city . . . and that "something is wrong with this open enrollment system."

Does Mr. Pellegrino know that Perry Traditional Academy is a magnet program? Does he know what the requirements are for entering the magnet program? It is not an "open enrollment". There are strict guidelines that are followed.

How then can Perry "harvest the finest" when these guidelines are followed? If there are more applicants than spaces, a computerized lottery is performed. Every student has the choice to make.

Please don't blame Perry or the school system if at this time Perry just happens to have a great team.

Kim Staniszewski
Lawrenceville

<hr>

### Comments from Post-Gazette Sports Writers

**Stan Savran - Column**
November 9, 2002

## TIME FOR PERRY TO JOIN WPIAL

"It's high time for the City League to disband, with those schools being absorbed into the WPIAL. Or at the very least, it's time for Perry Traditional Academy to secede from the City League and pick on somebody its own size."

"Let me make clear that I'm not trying to punish Perry's excellence, but rather to challenge it."

"When the best the competition can do is make an attempt to score, with no chance whatsoever of winning or even being competitive, something is askew. Why, that's downright close to becoming Major League Baseball. As a magnet school, Perry has the advantage of being able to lure players from all parts of the city. Parochial and other private schools compete in the WPIAL, why not them? In addition, the City League has schools that range in classification from Class AA to Class AAAA, so

337

you have the small facing the large. Why not have these schools assimilate into the WPIAL so that they can play teams of like size?"

"And don't think the kids involved wouldn't welcome the challenge. Don't you think the Perry football players would love to compete against the WPIAL Class AAA power of Hopewell, Thomas Jefferson and West Allegheny? Of course they would".

"Some would cite the tradition of the City League."

"As grand as the tradition has been, under the current set up, that tradition isn't being advanced, it's being tarnished. At best, the City Leaguer is ignored. Forbes Field, Pitt Stadium and Duquesne Gardens also had tradition. But time marches on. It's time for Perry and its City League mates, to march into the WPIAL. Who knows? Perry might even give up a point."

**Bob Smizik - Column**
December 4, 2002

"The hullabaloo surrounding the football season of Perry Traditional Academy ignores one key fact: This is basically the City League All-Stars, not your typical neighborhood team, which makes 13 consecutive shutouts remarkable but not historic. Many facts have been unveiled about Perry, but here's the one I most want to know; how many ZIP codes on this far-flung team?"

**338**

**Follow-up Rebuttal**
November 3, 2002
Carmen Pellegrino

"I am not blaming or begrudging **"Perry Traditional Academy"** for their great success as Ms. Kim Staniszewski stated in her response last week to my previous Sports Mailbag article, **"One-sided City League"**. I had stated in my article, that **Open Enrollment** as I perceived it or **Magnet Program** as I stand to be corrected, has contributed greatly to Perry's football success. I have been following high school football for many years, and there are strategic ways of following the proper guidelines for student athletes. The computerized lottery system may justify her opinion, but it does not convince me to change mine. Yes, Perry has a great team this year and I respect that, but the Magnet Program has benefited them greatly. They have had consistent success since the inception of that program – winning eight City League Championships and one PIAA State Championship. Why wouldn't young student athletes want to go with a perennial winner, thereby short changing the other city schools? This creates an extreme one-sided situation

Much credit must go to Perry for a great season as they strongly resemble an all-star team, and I wish them well in the PIAA State playoffs. In closing, I would like to see them step up and join the WPIAL as a City of Pittsburgh representative. They would be a worthy Class AAA member as they reap the harvest of the **Magnet Program**. Then the other nine schools will not have to contend with such overwhelming odds and lopsided scores."

## PROUD AND HUMBLE

This is a story about a man who is ageless and is still getting up every morning to go to work as a security guard at a local hospital here in the Pittsburgh area. I met him several years ago as I drove my wife to and from work every day to her job at that same hospital. One morning after dropping my wife off at the hospital, this security guard waved for me to pull the car over to the side. He extended his hand and introduced himself and with a curious expression asked me what the three letters, WHS on my license plate were meant to be. I told him they stood for Westinghouse High School. Well, he had a smile on his face that was fit for a poster. He proceeded to tell me how he too had attended Westinghouse and played football in the early 40's for coach "Pro" Burton. Well we proceeded in a lengthy conversation as he rattled off many names of guys who he played ball with at Westinghouse. Many of those names I recognized as I had done a lot of research of the early years. He was really excited and proud in telling me of his playing days and how much he enjoyed it. He told me about a particular game he played in where he made several unassisted tackles and was written up in the local newspaper the following day for his efforts. His name is Harry "Boots" Garland and he was quite proud of that newspaper article and well he should be. He expressed to me how much he appreciated coach "Pro" Burton and I was impressed with the way he shared his feelings with me. He said to me, "I really loved old "Pro" because he brought the best out of me and I will never forget him." This really touched me. He was so humble and sincere with his feelings even after all the many years that have passed since his school days.

I still see Harry from time to time at the hospital and he always extends that firm handshake, smiles and waves proudly as I drive by. This is a man who still enjoys talking about Westinghouse and coach Pro Burton. We have had many chats through the years and I look forward to many more. On one of my most recent visits to the hospital I surprised him with a photocopy of his team picture from an old Westinghouse yearbook. He was so happy to receive it as it made his day. Well, Harry, I did not forget – this one is for you. Take care and Go House!

**339**

## SHE WAS INSPIRATION

*By Barbara Cloud*
*The Pittsburgh Press*
*Sunday, August 19, 1990*

"I hadn't been at The Pittsburgh Press too many years when I met Annie McShane."

"Pete Dimperio, the legendary Westinghouse High School football coach, called me one day and suggested I do a story about her."

"I had no idea what an impact she would have on me. With all the hoopla about famous designers and show business personalities I've met, she remains at the top of the list under "memorable."

"Why? Here was a woman, a laundress, who came from Ireland, had a difficult life, held a menial job washing high school football players' uniforms and doing general cleaning at Westinghouse."

"She made it important. And she was loving, generous and trusting when you might have felt she had no right to be."

"The players were her pride and joy until she retired in 1965. Their graduation pictures lined the shelves in the laundry room where she did her work, and later, in her home. And because she felt some of them came to school hungry or with no lunch money, she kept candy bars and loose change in a box open to anyone who needed it".

"I loved her immediately. She gave me a tiny saucer with shamrocks on it which she had brought from Ireland. I just never forgot her, or her brogue, or her goodness."

They called her Miss Annie at school. And as you might have guessed, I am remembering her after all these years because her granddaughter called to tell me she passed away last week at age 92. She had been living with her daughter, Ellen Sheran, in Penn Hills."

"It's one thing to have an opportunity in this job to chat with Bill Blass or Ralph Lauren. I'm far more privileged when I meet the likes of Miss Annie."

---

## MEETING JOE "SHOWBOAT" WARE

**340**

I was probably about nine or ten years of age when I met my father's classmate, Joe Ware. Dad and I were shopping at the time in East Liberty and as we were passing by the Carnegie Library I heard two men call out to each other "Hey Joe, long time, no see". The two shook hands and embraced like all old classmates do. Dad said to me, "Son, this is an old schoolmate of mine, Joe "Showboat" Ware, shake his hand. I looked up at him as I shook his hand and said, "So you are "Showboat Ware". He laughed and said to dad, "Joe what did you tell this young man about me?" They both laughed and began reminiscing about old school days. I sat on the wall in front of the old Carnegie Library located at the corner of Larimer Avenue and Station Street waiting for their long winded conversation to end.

At the time I was too young to appreciate and realize that I had probably met the finest athlete to graduate from Westinghouse High School. Later on, in 1977, the local sports philosophers voted Joe "Showboat" Ware as Westinghouse's greatest athlete of the century.

After much researching on my part I was very impressed with the newspaper articles dating back to 1928, 29, and 30 revealing performances of Joe Ware. I agree with the writers, he was the best of the best to come out of Westinghouse. When I asked my father who is now ninety-three to name the best players he gives me two names: Joe Ware and Bobby Dye. Being from a proud generation, dad still believes they were the best. He smiles broadly at the mere mention of Westinghouse High School and the legends of his time. In fact, he will, upon request, play his harmonica and belt out a nifty version of "Westinghouse Forever" amazing his great grandchildren.

## REMEMBERING A VIETNAM HERO
## CAPTAIN SHERRILL BROWN

As I recall it was around the fall of the year 1950 when a few of us were standing outside in the courtyard during our lunch hour watching as a fourth period gym class was playing a game of touch football on the field in the valley below. We noticed this one little boy was putting on quite a display of speed and agility, and literally impressed the hell out of us. His name was Sherrill Brown and at the time he was no more than thirteen or fourteen years of age – a junior high student at Westinghouse. He was so small and quick and I told my friends, "watch this kid go – he's going to be a star here some day." Sure enough, my words came true. Sherrill Brown became a brilliant little running back for Westinghouse during the 1954 and 1955 seasons making the All–City team in 1955 and excelling on the track team with his God given speed. After high school he went on to Lincoln University and excelled there as well and was a member of the school's ROTC program. After college he served military duty and rose to the rank of Captain. He served his tour of military duty and completed his obligation in 1961. Then two years later he re-enlisted (mid-1963) and was later shipped over to Vietnam. The tour of duty in Vietnam was met with devastating consequences for Sherrill Brown and many of our American soldiers. Unfortunately, on July 10, 1966 he died from shrapnel wounds he suffered when a vehicle he was riding in had passed over a land mine.

When I read about this tragedy in our local newspaper, I was deeply saddened. He was only 27 years old and it was a huge loss for his family. When I knew him from our school days he was quiet and always had such a pleasant demeanor. Coach Pete Dimperio thought the world of him as he was one of his best players at Westinghouse High School.

Around early May of 2000, I had received a phone call from Jonathan Silver, a staff writer for the Pittsburgh Post Gazette. He was preparing to write a special Veteran's Day Memorial about Sherrill Brown. He was told by former Westinghouse football coach George Webb, to give me a call as he thought I would remember Sherrill from my school days. I was so honored to help Mr. Silver as much as I could giving him names of men to call who were teammates of Sherrill at Westinghouse and Don Hudson, a Westinghouse alumni, who coached Sherrill at Lincoln University. Mr. Silver and I spoke at length about my memories of Sherrill Brown. I told him how much I appreciated his efforts to write about one of our own who sacrificed his life for our country. When the article appeared in the Pittsburgh Post Gazette on May 29, 2000 (Memorial Day) I was both proud and sad for the Brown family. Later the following week I phoned Jonathan Silver commending him for such a beautiful article.

The memory of Sherrill Brown will always remain with me, and I will always remember a quote from our former coach Pete Dimperio when he retired in 1967 saying – **"All my athletes to me are Sherrill Brown."**

**341**

## A WESTINGHOUSE CONNECTION

He never played a down of varsity football at Westinghouse High School, but LaVar Arrington did put on a halftime show on the home field of the Bulldogs at a very early age. (See Note below)

It was back in 1984 when LaVar was about six years old. His parents, Carolyn and Michael Arrington, took him to a football game one Friday afternoon at Westinghouse High School field in the Pittsburgh City League. Carolyn and Michael were both graduates of Westinghouse and at halftime they got to talking with some people in the stands. When they looked down for their son, they couldn't find him. Carolyn began to panic and then she heard the crowd cheering. Down on the field there was little LaVar, running every which way with a football tucked under his arm. A delighted Carolyn Arrington said, "This boy's going to do something in sports some day". (See Note below)

It was a sign of things to come for LaVar Arrington as he later excelled at North Hills High School where he performed his football talent at Martorelli Stadium, home of the North Hills Indians.

Martorelli Stadium was named after the former football coach at West View High School before it became North Hills High School and coincidentally, Mario Martorelli before his coaching days, was a star athlete at Westinghouse High School. So there is a trace of Westinghouse in the life of LaVar Arrington. By the time he reached his senior year at North Hills High School, he was a 6'4", 225 pound running back and line backer and one of the most heralded athletes in Western Pennsylvania history. After a fine high school career, he received a scholarship to Penn State where he gained All-American honors as one of the finest linebackers in Penn State's history. After his college career he was drafted in the first round of the NFL draft by the Washington Redskins in 2000 where he is enjoying a fine career as an All-Pro linebacker.

Just as LaVar's mother said several years ago, this young man is going to do something in sports someday. That indeed has happened as today mother's prediction is a reality.

I did get to see LaVar shortly after his playing days at North Hills attending a game at Martorelli Stadium between North Hills and New Castle. He was such a crowd pleaser that night signing autographs for many of the young students attending the game; as he was home on break from Penn State. His presence along the sideline with the North Hills players seemed to spark the Indians as they did upset New Castle that night. The North Hills quarterback in that game happened to be Todd Sczramowski a member of my extended family who played a great game. I was quite proud that night as one of the spectators seated behind me asked if I knew how the stadium got its name "Martorelli Stadium." Of course I was only too happy to reveal my knowledge of the Westinghouse High School connection.

*Note: Taken from "Student Sports" (December 1996/January 1967 issue) feature article "Pittsburgh Power LaVar Arrington" by Mike White who covers prep sports for the Pittsburgh Post-Gazette. He is regarded as one of the best prep writers on the East Coast.*

342

## A ROLE MODEL

I was only twelve years old at the time and a seventh grade student at Westinghouse High School when I first recognized Tommy Costa. He was short like I was and a member of the Westinghouse High School football team. I remember going to all the games and watching him play and I was impressed that someone so small (5'6") and so quick could break away; and take it the distance on any given opportunity. This inspired me into hoping that someday I would be able to follow in his footsteps. Of course later on I found out that it was not so easy to emulate such a talented athlete as Tommy Costa. One could hardly blame me for daydreaming.

In 1948 and 1949 Tommy Costa and Leonard Gallo who was also small and quick were the starting halfbacks for the Bulldogs, and together they gave their opponents fits. Coach Pete Dimperio was quite proud of them and he really loved them a lot better when they could run. When they ran a reverse it was like a guessing game as to who ended up having the ball. I can remember the game against North Braddock Scott – when I was sitting in the stands behind the end zone where Costa and Gallo were awaiting the opening kick-off. They pulled off one of their patented reverses that brought the fans to their feet and before Scott could recover the Bulldogs were on the scoreboard. They were game breakers and gave the Westinghouse faithful many thrills.

As time went on and remembering how I looked up to Tommy Costa as a youngster I was able to meet him and get to know him in later years. At family functions (hosted by one of his sisters) my wife and I had the pleasure of spending some social time with Tommy and his wife. I did get to tell him that when I was a youngster I really looked up to him as a role model. He was very humble to hear that coming from me. It was heart warming for me to be able to talk to Tommy in later years and relate with him about the past and present day happenings. He was a special person to all of us.

Not very long after, on January 18, 1982 Tom passed away of a heart attack and it was a great loss to many of us. He was a man who served his community with the heart of a champion. Unfortunately, his heart was not able to continue supporting the tireless man hours that he had given to so many of the needy and underprivileged. He was an inspector for Penn Hills, honored twice for contributions to Penn Hills, voted "Citizen of the Year" in 1979 and was the subject of a testimonial banquet in 1981. He attended Thiel College and was an officer and director of the Penn Hills Youth Football Association for several years. He was also director of the Shining Arrow Program, where he worked with exceptional children in the Penn Hills area. He was instrumental in raising $25,000 for two injured high school football players, Jeff Boynton of Plum High School and John Cerniglia of Westinghouse High School.

As a member of the city championship teams in 1947, 1948 and 1949, Tom was called "one of the most outstanding players in Westinghouse High School history" by his Coach Pete Dimperio.

As one of his close friends and colleague Clarence Franks said, *"He worked awfully hard with Arrow putting in a lot of man-hours and risked his own*

**343**

*health. He was a rare person, touching so many people. Good friends come along often but great ones like Tom not so often."*

"He was without a doubt a great champion, a fine role model, and I was fortunate to have known him. This book would not be complete without including a special tribute to a genuine human being as my friend Tommy Costa".

## THOSE THREE BRIDGES

Growing up in my old neighborhood of Larimer was an experience that I have valued with much pride. Those early years were ones that have provided me with much to be thankful for. The family upbringing and the community togetherness were worth so much to all of us who grew up during times when most of us appreciated the little things in life. There was a song entitled "Little Things Mean A Lot" recorded by Joni James that was quite popular back then that I always enjoyed listening to on the radio. The title alone was enough to make me appreciate where I came from – **"Larimer, Our Little Italy."** Those little things were numerous values that our parents and grandparents provided for us.

There were three bridges that spanned and bordered our neighborhoods of Lincoln, Larimer and Meadow as we formed many friendships that were priceless. We traveled those bridges many times over as youngsters and probably never really stopped to realize the link each one of them had in the development of our years of growing up in our close-knit Italian village. All three bridges were architectural masterpieces.

Larimer Avenue bridge was built early in 1911 or 12 and was at the time considered second-longest concrete arch in the world with a span of 300 feet. It crossed over a valley below called Washington Boulevard that stretched from the Allegheny River to Fifth Avenue – passing Silver Lake along the way. From the bridge deck it seemed we could see forever looking in all four directions. Looking southwest one could see the Orphan Street mansions with terraced gardens overlooking Washington Boulevard. Looking south we could see the tall bell tower of Larimer Elementary School as it was nestled in the heart of our shopping district. It was a district that was enhanced with all the resources that were needed to feed and clothe our families. It did not stop there as all the amenities to keep a family healthy and sheltered were plentiful. Yes, Larimer was a village that we were quite proud of as our parents and grandparents worked so hard to make a good life for us. The Larimer Bridge stretched north and south between Orphan Street and Deary Street linking us with our Lincoln neighbors.

The Meadow Street Bridge spanned over Chianti Street (later reconstructed and renamed Negley Run Boulevard). Chianti Street was located in a valley below the bridge that always fascinated me. It reminded me of a unique little village of Italian immigrants struggling to someday realize the American dream. They were proud and worked hard to survive during those early years before it was to become Negley Run Boulevard. The bridge was a concrete and masonry structure that overlooked a stretch of small frame houses and cultivated gardens. The east end of the bridge bordered the Larimer community and the west end bordered St. Marie Street which

344

led to Highland Avenue and Peabody High School. Crossing the Meadow Street Bridge on the way to a Westinghouse-Peabody football game was an exciting experience for us. It was a game that both schools looked forward to playing every year.

The Lincoln Avenue Bridge (1906) spanned over Washington Boulevard stretching between Renfrew Street and Atwell Street passing under the Pennsylvania Railroad Viaduct. The Viaduct (1902-03) was a stone masterpiece spanning six arches above the now-vanished Silver Lake. Standing on the bridge deck looking east one can see the back of Westinghouse High School with it's spiraling concrete steps leading to the football field below. Looking west, the Larimer Bridge was in full view. North of the bridge was the Lincoln-Lemington community – the south end was a continuation of Lincoln Avenue winding down to Frankstown Avenue.

The three bridges conveniently funneled into the thriving businesses along Larimer Avenue. They were the heart and soul of life in this little community we called Little Italy. Today each of those bridges have high chain-link fencing secured to the handrails as we are now living in an era when vandalism by unruly behavior takes away the luxury of a more secure way of life. The days of enjoying a leisurely stroll across a bridge are gone along with the memories of yesteryear. Respect for public and private property is lacking today. The weak minded continue to challenge our society and until this changes we will continue to experience their undesirable behavior. Instead of building larger prisons we should be building stronger values for life.

It is very sad to realize that the little things in life that we once appreciated are the same things that many of the youth of today take for granted. They are far more advanced than we were, but sometimes they can't see the trees for the forest. They are missing out on the true meaning of earning, because we give them whatever they want. I blame this on our generation for not doing a good enough job of instilling the respect for life and property that our parents and grandparents impressed upon us.

All I hear today is that we were old-fashioned and square back then. Obviously, there is a wide generation gap. However it is sad to see the youth of today struggling to find a stable comfort zone and the precious values of life. There are so many distractions for them to hurdle. The journeys many of us made across each of those three bridges were priceless and brought many of us together to form friendships that will last forever. We had very little to start with, but we learned from our parents the true values of life. We appreciated all the advancements and enhancements along the way, but we never lost the true value of respect. I will always remember my parent's words "Son, do not ever lose respect for yourself, your family or your neighbors because you will pay dearly." This statement was a constant reminder that I grew up with. Thanks mom and dad for being so firm during my early years. Today I can face up to the challenges of life because I respected both of you for such a beautiful beginning.

## THEY CHALLENGED WESTINGHOUSE

Pete Dimperio once said with a smile on his face, there was no secret to beating Westinghouse. He alluded that a good solid T-quarterback with passing skills always seemed to give Westinghouse problems.

345

Going back to 1946 through 1953 Peabody had a fine quarterback. With the likes of Paul Palumbo, Ross Kemmerer, Pete Neft, and Al Jacks they gave the Bulldogs all they could handle.  The 1946 game ended in a scoreless tie and the following year Westinghouse won a squeaker 14-13 against the Highlanders coached by Dick Meyers.  Kemmerer went on to Pitt after high school and eventually was drafted by the Boston Red Sox as a pitcher.  He had a fine major league career and was a teammate of the late legend, Ted Williams, during his years at Boston.

Then in 1950 both Schenley and Peabody had fine quarterbacks.  Senior, Henry "Model T" Ford was a standout at Schenley as the Spartans defeated Westinghouse that year 12-6.  Schenley won the City Championship that year 6-0 over Carrick as Ford and halfback Joe Moore were the big play guys for Schenley. Ford later was a standout at the University of Pittsburgh. During the same season Peabody junior quarterback, Pete Neft, led the Highlanders in an upset over Westinghouse 7-6 in a rain soaked battle. The Bulldogs struggled that year finishing the season at 4-4-0.

The following year, 1951, Pete Neft was a senior and the Highlanders met Westinghouse at Pitt Stadium.  Both teams were undefeated, but Neft suffered a serious injury early in the game and that really hurt the Highlanders. He was taken out of the game and was replaced by an untested sophomore named Al Jacks. He had to face a strong Westinghouse team that day and was overwhelmed 41-7.  Pete Neft went on to play for Pitt the following year.

Al Jacks did not forget what happened in 1951, and was the returning quarterback for Peabody in 1952. He was now a junior and was developing into a fine leader for the Highlanders.  He had good size and a rifle arm with a fine receiver in Sherman Gardin and a big fullback, Russ Manderville. Peabody defeated Westinghouse that year 7-0 on a touchdown pass from Jacks to Sherman Gardin. Meanwhile Al Jacks still had one more year at Peabody and was the premiere quarterback in the City League who was being sought after by many colleges.

The following year, 1953, he was a senior and led a strong Peabody team to a big win over the Bulldogs 14-6.  He had a strong supporting cast with fullback Chuck Scafuri and halfbacks Jim Thompson and John McNamara and a strong line on both sides of the ball led by Dominic Grande, John Haggerty the Peters brothers (Don and Tom) Dave Rubin and Tom Ewing. The Highlanders went on to capture the City Championship that year over Allegheny 21-0. Al Jacks went on to star at Penn State after graduating from Peabody.  Al Jacks was one of the best quarterbacks to come out of the Pittsburgh City League during that era.

As Coach Dimperio alluded during his coaching career at Westinghouse, a skilled T-quarterback always seemed to be a challenge for the Bulldogs.  Russ Kemmerer, Pete Neft, Al Jacks and Henry Ford were all fine quarterbacks and they surely made a believer out of Coach Dimperio. One thing I remember about Pete Dimperio he always praised the opposition for their talent and efforts. The four quarterbacks he praised were a combined 4-2-1 against his Westinghouse teams. He was known to be helpful and caring for the welfare of all young men regardless of what school or background they came from. He was always willing to help someone in time of need. I for one can personally attest to that.

346

## A SPECIAL RECOLLECTION

This article is from a historical football brochure **(The Old Timers' Golden Jubilee 1900-1956)** that helped me immensely in my research of the early years of Westinghouse High School's football fortunes. I would like to share with you some of the excerpts of the foreword from this brochure written by **C.A. Herman** an accomplished historian/author.

This souvenir brochure was put together for a banquet gathering that was held on November 3, 1956 celebrating fifty years of football in the East End district of Pittsburgh commemorating the names of stellar athletes of yesteryear. It served as an excellent reference source of those very early years.

**The following is one of those excerpts that Mr. Herman so eloquently expressed:**

Fortunately we have a spirited and comprehensive description of football at Westinghouse High School over the early years dating back to 1916 until the present date. Much of the material has been refreshed in our memory of the past from the Year Books obtained from the alumni of Westinghouse High School and the sandlot material is from a reservoir of memories as player, manager, sponsor, and lifelong resident of Homewood-Brushton. On this ground of gratitude with which we look back with pride over the years, we can honestly say, "God has blessed our failures, our opportunities and our calamities."

Memories are so sad, so strange, the days that are no more. The old familiar faces, the rendezvous and places, the joyful days of yesteryear fade in the shadows of time and forms vary in the sunset as the points of vision alter.

Things bygone are the only things that last. Underneath the surface of today lies yesterday; what we call the past are the only things which never can decay.

Oh, there are voices of the past, links of a broken chain – wings that can bear us back to times which cannot come again, yet God forbid that we should lose the echoes that remain. We will pause to pay respect to those who have gone before us. Two empty chairs at the table for our honored guests shall be remembered. Gone but not forgotten we remember **Mr. O.H. Pro Burton ("Builder of Champions" Westinghouse High School 1916-1946) and Ken Ormiston (Westinghouse's All-Scholastic, Pitt's All- American and Homewood's native son).**

We extend greetings to all former athletes and adherents, and to our guests of honor, one of which is **Mr. Peter Dimperio** we pass the title of "Builder of Champions". We live again in retrospect, the joys, the heartaches, the victories, and the defeats. We live in time and the past must always be the most momentous part of it. We have built a bridge and paved the roads to ease the way for youth that is sure to follow us. We have spanned the pitfalls along life's highway, but there are still deep gaps left unguarded where a boy or girl who fails to see is sure to fall in sorrow.

In our time, industry, communities, churches, and civic-minded residents sponsored diversified athletic programs. There were ample vacant lots for children

347

to play. The vacant lots went with the building boom, industry curtailed its financial aid to sports; communities relied on schools and colleges for its athletic leadership. Then came the so-called juvenile delinquency; bigger and larger juvenile courts and so-called houses of correction. Idleness breeds discontent.

Keep a child busy and you keep him out of trouble. An ounce of prevention is worth a pound of cure. Foster and sponsor amateur sports in your community like they did unto you. Give the kids a break, back the American Olympic Fund. A dollar spent in sponsoring amateur sports is a dollar saved. The youth of today are tomorrow's leaders. As we sow so shall we reap at harvest time.

**Yours in sports,**
**C.A.Herman**
**Historian-Editor**

Thanks to Mr. Herman for words so inspirational and appropriate that I am proud to repeat the echoes of their meaningful worth.

## A GIFT FROM WOODY

The following is a copy of a heartwarming letter from a loyal Westinghouse student that appeared in Coach Pete Dimperio's scrapbook. This really epitomizes how much of an impact Dimperio had on so many of us.

Dear Pete,

This is just a little gift to you because I am leaving Westinghouse. The pictures inside were all taken by me last season (1948). I count it an honor at having known you and I hope that someday when you look at this photo book you will remember the red head named Woods who followed your team and you around. Well, Coach, that's a quick look into the past season, but may you have more like them. I got to all but two games and they were pre-season; but to all those games I wore the lucky tee-shirt. I hope the luck it has will stay with you forever and a day.

In closing, I would like to say that there will always be a place in my memory for you and the "48" Squad. And when we go to meet our maker as we all must, when you get to the Valhalla of football I'll be there waiting for you with camera and flashbulbs, and if I am not, just clear a space at the sidelines and get me a field pass and I'll be along shortly.

Goodbye, Good luck and God bless you and the boys.
Charles H. (Woody) Woods
Class of June, 1949

## BRUSHING AWAY THE COBWEBS

As I brushed away the cobwebs and dust from many of the old yearbooks I discovered a plethora of memories of that big house in Homewood. There was one deep seeded value that was always visible within those memories and that was *Pride*. There were so many successful alumni that learned their lessons well and took the pride that they developed at Westinghouse High School right along with them on their journey through life. As our beloved legend *Pete Dimperio* so sincerely expressed at many of our class reunions; *"whatever choice you make in life take pride in what you do and be the best doctor, lawyer or garbage collector that you could be."* Pride was the key element that so many of us seized and maintained throughout our life's journey. It truly has a place in our society and should never waver regardless of what the challenges are that we must endure.

## FROM WESTINGHOUSE TO WESTMINSTER

Walter Sylvester was my friend and my former boss. He was a man who exemplified a strong desire to be successful. While a student at Westinghouse High School, he was determined to be a member of the Bulldogs football team. Unfortunately, Walt was not able to pass the required physical because the doctors said he had a heart murmur. In spite of this he practiced with the team for four years while serving as the team manager. After he graduated from Westinghouse in 1950, Coach Pete Dimperio helped him to get a college scholarship. Walt ended up at Westminster College and was able to pass the physical to play football for the Titans. He played well enough to earn NAIA All-State guard and was inducted into Westminster's Hall of Fame. After his college years Walt found much success in his field of expertise and became owner and CEO of Universal Refractories, Inc. in Wampum, PA. Unfortunately, it was his heart that gave out at a time when it was much too soon. Walt is no longer with us, but the memories we have of him will last forever. Rest in peace my friend we all miss you.

**349**

## PROUD BULLDOG HAS FIVE SUPER BOWL RINGS

Former Pittsburgh Courier Sports Editor Bill Nunn, Sr., and longtime scout with the Pittsburgh Steelers, is one of our own – a graduate of Westinghouse High School. He was born and raised in Homewood and was the son of the first black player known as Hammy Nunn at Westinghouse High School during the "Pro" Burton era. Bill excelled in basketball at both the House and later at West Virginia State. He was a member of the 1942-43 City Champions along with All-American Charlie Cooper of Duquesne University and the Boston Celtics of the NBA. Bill was so well known that he held office with the Negro Leagues and entertained such notable people as Joe Louis, Jesse Owens and many legendary jazz musicians in his Homewood home. His son, actor Bill Nunn of Hollywood fame has starred in 45-plus movies such as "Spiderman," "Regarding Henry" and "Do the Right Thing." He is one proud father, and the owner of five Super Bowl rings having earned them as a longtime member of the Pittsburgh Steelers staff. Today he helps to evaluate college talent.

## PICKING AN ALL-TIME WHS FOOTBALL TEAM MUCH TOO DIFFICULT

Picking an all-time football team from Westinghouse High School is far beyond my reach. I would not even attempt to try as there were too many outstanding players that were deserving of such an acclaim. I will leave this to the many alumni to ponder over when they gather for food and drink. It would be interesting to listen in on some of those choices. But I will mention here that my "FAB 5" WHS basketball team would have to be Chuck Cooper, Maurice Stokes, Edward Fleming, Rickie Richburg and Thomas "Junebug" Howard. I would have enjoyed watching them play together as a team. They all excelled during their years at Westinghouse, and I could not pass up putting this in print. I did manage to follow the glory years of Bulldog basketball as after football season ended the spirit of winning carried over to the hardwood. It was a special time of year.

## WORDS OF WISDOM RECALLING A ONCE PROUD NEIGHBORHOOD

350

Anthony "Herb" Amen and "Cookie" Rizzo have put together editorials that depict so eloquently why I miss my old neighborhood. Before completing this book I would like to share with my readers these words of wisdom that so many of us lived by while growing up in that once proud Italian Community of L.A. My heartfelt thanks goes to both of them for putting together in a special way the words that make me so proud of where I came from.

## BY ANTHONY "HERB" AMEN — 1987

This Editorial is written for the sole purpose of bringing all of our L.A. Families together in friendship as it once was in the past. Our monthly Newsletter is a communication line between the past and the present. All of our memories together make our purpose worthwhile.

Our intentions are not to discriminate against any area, but there is a special feeling inside each one of us when the AVENUE is mentioned.

From the rooftop of Sebastian's Gas Station to the Pinnacle of the no longer existing White Tower Restaurant, once existed a beautiful and close-knit Italian Village. Our kind of town – L.A. was.

LARIMER AVENUE is a feeling of how it used to be. Memories, so many beautiful memories! With generations of children running their hands through the sawdust of Harris-McKeever Meat Market; to the long lines on Friday night to get a fish sandwich at Kreur's Café.

It didn't matter if you lived on Orphan Street or Auburn Street. You could be from St. Marie Street, Collins Avenue or Apple Avenue, you knew in your heart you were in L.A.

Businesses of the past come to mind: Ardolino's, Policastro's, Bloomfield Market and Costa's Grocery. Weekends at the Club Yard—St. Rocco, St. Anthony — on and on went the festivities. The Mayo Clinic couldn't hold a candle to the ills cured at Frank Conte's Drug Store. Our doctors: Dr. Ignelzi, Coscia, Vecchio, Kaiser, Alvin, and Dr. Abbate. Our AVENUE ; what a gem to remember.

Now, they have huge Busy Beaver Building Centers, back then we built and maintained our homes out of Lou's Hardware and Ruffing's Hardware. Our churches – Our Lady Help of Christians, St. Peter and Paul and Rev. DeStazi's Church; Our clubs—I.B.B.A., Sgt. Basilone, Northern Italian Club, and Spigno Club; the wedding receptions at the Alvito Club (St. Mary's) and if you walked in the alley behind the I.B.B.A., you can still see the ridges and gaps in the ground that once was the original Bocci Court of L.A.

Del's Cleaners, Belmont Cleaners, So Chung Laundry — up and down the AVENUE we would stroll. Del Pizzo's Restaurant brought people from all over the city to eat the best homemade Italian food. Moio's Pastries had the greatest Cannoli, Pastaciotti, and Lemon Ice in the world. These places were LARIMER AVENUE.

Listen closely; you can still hear the knocking of Bocci balls behind the high wooden fence at Larimer Avenue and Carver Street. You can even smell the smoke from the DiNobile and Parodi cigars that our grandfathers smoked as they enjoyed their golden years at the Son of Columbus Lodge. My brother knew your brother! My sister knew your sister! Kiss in a greeting. "Hey Compare, Hey Comare, Come Sta?" This was FAMIGLIA! This was LARIMER AVENUE!

351

It is impossible to mention everyone or everything that existed on our AVENUE, but just listing a few brings back so many memories. Marsh's Garage, Allen's 5 & 10, Dutch Sander's Café, Paradise's, Pompa's Market, Labriola's Market, Red Eagle, De Sena's Market, Nick's Market, DeLuca's Market, Sadie Kabosanick's Dry Goods and Arro Furniture. Our home — L.A. was! The Flamingo Skating Rink, The Lexington Skating Rink, The Original Hot Dog Shop, Del Prato's Market, Joe Peep's, Billy and Joe's Dairy, Henry Grasso's Sausage, The Carnegie Library, Sparky's Texaco and everybody's home — The Kingsley House. Our Barbers – Fusco, Cinicola, Mazzotti, Capo, and Tony and Joe Ladico. Our Bakeries – Stagno, Lutz, Rimini, Sabatasso, Pirollo, Gigante, Castellano and Gunzel's.

Easter on L.A. meant Baccala, Smeltz, and Calamarie all lined up in crates of crushed ice along the AVENUE in front of all the market places. Where can you find this in our present lifetime? We, of the L.A.S.C. have preserved all this in our hearts and minds. This is what OUR FAMIGLIA is all about. You know who you are and so until we meet again bring your cherished memories with you.

**Anthony "Herb" Amen**

## "L.A."— BY "COOKIE" RIZZO — 1987

Across the seas in ships they came,
    You know who they are,
    Your name is the same.
To a small Italian Village called "L.A.",
    Far from their Homeland,
    They would venture to stay.
Hard work, dedication with pride, never to make it,
    Without that woman of iron at his side.
    Luxuries were small, families large,
    Children raised on hopes and dreams.
Dinner tables, quite often, filled with only greens.
Social Clubs were formed - St. Mary's of Alvito for the Alvidans,
    Spigno Club the Spignese,
    Northern Italian Club the Pumandese,
    Sargent Basilone, Sons of Columbus, the I.B.B.A.,
    Even the Calabrese would have their day.
But what did it mean?
    A separation of powers?
    No . . . . just fulfilling their dreams.
The day had begun to enjoy a little of life's fun.
    Bocci was their game.
    Mora, Scopa, Padrone e Sotto, Tresette,
    Brought many to fame.
    Laughter was heard from Frankstown to Dean,
    Except in a Mora game when they had to scream.
    Santa Rocco in the streets, in the club yard we'd stay,
    Waiting to hear Nick Isuash and his band . . . . Play.
The Exodus was frightening, a scramble to the Hills,
    Neighbors asking one another, "Will you be leaving . . . .? Still?"
    Decisions made hastily were hard to bear,
    Only much later, did we realize how much we really cared?
L.A., L.A., your heritage runs deep,
    Let us never forget – the memories, and the people that walked our streets.

**Dedicated to the handful of people still living in and around the Larimer Avenue area, and to my father who loved it so.

**"COOKIE" RIZZO**

When Pete speaks, his boys listen. The Westinghouse football coach gives a daily pep talk. After it, the boys hold their own meeting to iron out any difficulties they have as a team or as individuals. They permit no one, not even Pete, to attend.

353

### Pete Dimperio ..... Molder Of Men
By Peter F. Clark, Pittsburgh Press Staff Writer, October 19, 1958

### "THE ROOM"
(Behind closed doors)

354

**A Family Night with Pete Dimperio**

**Benefit for JOHN CERNIGLIA**

Former Westinghouse Star

**WEDNESDAY, MAY 28, 1980 — 7:00 P.M.**

## Program

Welcome

Introduction of M. C.

Toastmaster — PETE DIMPERIO
Former Westinghouse H.S. Coach

Introduction and Remarks by Special Guests:

JACK LAMBERT
and other Steelers

Pirate Parrot

FRANK GUSTINE

DICK GROAT
and other Former Pirates

JACKIE SHERRILL
Head Coach — Pitt Panthers

CHUCK KLAUSING
Head Coach — C. M. U.

DAN McCANN
Head Coach — Duquesne University
and other Celebrites

Former Westinghouse Players

Film Highlights          Dancers — Steel City Angels

Raffles

Refreshments          Music — Renovations

JOHN CERNIGLIA
AND FAMILY

*Special Thanks To:*

FERRY ELECTRIC          COCA COLA
MR. STEAK          DAVE GRIFFIN
IRON CITY          HOWARD KAPLAN

Walter Sylvester a Westinghouse High School graduate went on to Westminster College where he excelled and was named to the 1954 NAIA All-State Team, and the Westminster College Football Hall of Fame.

## PATIENCE IS A VIRTUE

He was determined to play football in high school, but had to forego it due to a medical problem. He practiced and worked out with the team for four years serving as team manager. Walter Sylvester is pictured below (middle row far right in street clothes) with the 1949 Pittsburgh City League Champions Westinghouse High School football team. He was determined to go on to college and fulfill his dream after passing the physical to play football for Westminster College. He excelled in college as an offensive guard and was named to the 1954 NAIA All-State Team and the Westminster College Hall of Fame.

356

1949 Pittsburgh City League Champions

# Three generations of Leonard Gallo

## Westinghouse * Penn Hills * Franklin Regional

### 1948 Westinghouse High School

Sun-Telegraph Photo by Charles E. Brunc

**PILE-UP PLAY . . .** Arms and legs tangle as Carrick High players pile up on Westinghouse High's Left Halfback Leonard Gallo (center) after he skirted right end for an eight-yard gain in championshop game. Westinghouse won, 33-12.

357

Burton • Dimperio • Musilin • Malins • Webb

# Three generations of Leonard Gallo

## Westinghouse * Penn Hills * Franklin Regional

## 1975 Penn Hills High School

D-6     Pittsburgh Press, Sun., Oct. 12, 1975

—Press Photo by Robert J. Pavuchak

*Penn Hills' Len Gallo (7) picks up seven yards against Kiski Area.*

358

## Three generations of Leonard Gallo

### Westinghouse * Penn Hills * Franklin Regional

### 2005 Franklin Regional High School

359

Matt Freed/Post-Gazette photos

Franklin Regional backup quarterback Lenny Gallo breaks free for 23 yards and a touchdown to get the Panthers on the board in their 35-7 win against Selinsgrove at Altoona.

**"WESTINGHOUSE FOREVER"**
(Our Director March, *Bigelow*)
Westinghouse forever, loyal and true,
Nothing can ever change our love for you,
Rah! Rah! Rah!
Westinghouse forever we're true to you,
We love our colors, of Gold and Blue.

360

Carolyn Bright (Behind megaphone D), today she is Carolyn Smith mother of movie actor Will Smith

*Burton • Dimperio • Musilin • Malins • Webb*

## MAJORETTES

### *"High Steppers"*

**Sponsor, Miss Cook**

**1st row**—M. Rhoades, E. Sylvester, M. Angell.

**2nd row**—A. Deluccio, K. McAndrews, M. S. Tigano, G. Dye. L. Graham.

---

*Notre Dame Fight Song*
*Fight, fight, for Westinghouse High*
*Lift high her banner, take up her cry,*
*Lead her on to victory*
*Working together cheerfully,*
*Fight hard, and play the game fair,*
*Shout loud, let cheers rend the air*
*Fight, fight, fight, with might and main,*
*Help Westinghouse win again.*

---

## BAND

### *"Westinghouse Forever"*

**Director, Mr. McVicker**

**1st row**—L. Graham, A. Deluccio, K. McAndrews, M. S. Tigano, M. Rhoads, E. Sylvester, M. Angell, G. Dye.

**2nd row**—W. Smalley, D. Petrucci, M. Richey, D. Himes, A. Grigsby, B. Davis, D. Gardner, W. Booker, G. McCloy, W. Giltrap, B. Tebeau, C. Wright, V. Powers, C. Mack

**3rd row**—R. Santorelli, L. Allen, M. Lee, H. Smith, D. Lee, R. Russell, K. Porter, L. Holt, A. Lake, F. Robinson, J. Scherer, N. Nicholas, P. Moore, W. Hendry, E. Ortiz.

**4th row**—B. Dapper, L. Thomas, B. Davis, W. Jennings, A. Edgar, A. Fentiman, W. Fouch, R. McNulty, F. De-Mark, G. McFalls, R. Cuddy, K. Mack, T. McCray, J. Stewart, W. Davis, M. Johnson, R. Fazio.

**5th row**—D. Simpson, A. Spinola, O. Twist, C. Oden, M. Jackson, B. Taylor, M. Solomon, D. Card, K. Fitts, D. Gardner, A. Hinch, B. Micelli. L. Jackson, C. Jackson, B. Novalis, J. Collis, T. Lehman, J. Burgette, S. Sneed, D. Flemming, R. Holland, M. Yonkers.

*Burton • Dimperio • Musilin • Malins • Webb*

"Hey Bulldog, play
Westinghouse Forever
one more time!"

362

"Ok, here we go one more time!"

Westinghouse forever, loyal and true,
Nothing can ever change our love for you,
Rah! Rah! Rah!
Westinghouse forever, we're true to you,
We love our colors of gold and blue.

Westinghouse Class of 1954
50th Year Reunion

June 19, 2004

363

Burton • Dimperio • Musilin • Malins • Webb

**50th Reunion (10/24/99) Westinghouse High School Football Teams of 1947, 1948, and 1949**

Team members, alumni and guests, front row, left/right, - J. Takacs, A. Cuomo, F. Guadagnino, J. Nicoletti, E. Massaro, R. Gaddie, L. Dell'Aquilla, A. Dent, J. Green, C. Pellegrino. Middle Row, left/right:- M. DeLuca, B. Niccoletti, L. Gallo, E. Twyman, L. Ferragonia, R. Madamma, D. Hudson, B. Antonucci, G. Buccilli, T. Costa, Jr., J. Pronio. Back Row, left/right:- E. Buccilli, S. Migliore, F. Floccari, H. Shellaby, L. Pitacciato, J. Cafino, F. Cutruzulla, C. Naser, J. Alder, P. Dimperio, Jr. Late arrival, G. Moore (not in photo).

We meet twice a year at Café Naples to share fine food and memories of our years at Westinghouse High School and beyond.

**365**

*Burton • Dimperio • Musilin • Malins • Webb*

366

Steve Mellon/Post-Gazette

# Wall of Fame extols Westinghouse High grads

Valeria Williams is the organizer and creator of the Westinghouse High School Wall of Fame, a photographic display of some of the great students and teachers who walked through the school. **See a list of people who have been inducted into the Westinghouse Wall of Fame at post-gazette.com**

# Bill Nunn Sr.

## The Steelers' scout has 5 Super Bowl rings and a well-known actor son

**Bill was born and raised in Homewood, the son of the first black football player at Westinghouse High School. He followed his father to Westinghouse, but the son's sport was basketball. Bill was captain of the 1943 Westinghouse team that won the Pittsburgh City League Championship.**

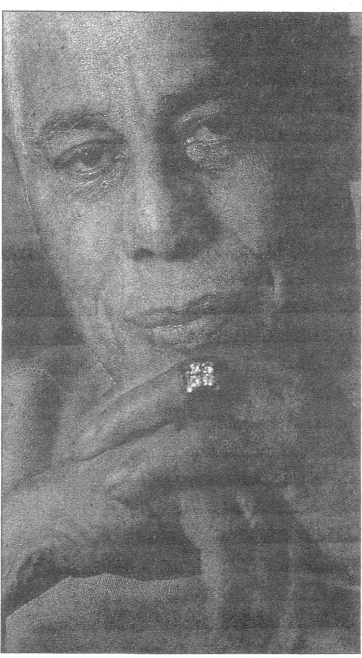

Peter Diana/Post-Gazette

Former Pittsburgh Courier sports editor Bill Nunn, 81, was a longtime scout with the Steelers and now helps evaluate college talent.

367

*Burton • Dimperio • Musilin • Malins • Webb*

*"Across the seas in ships they came, to settle in the village below"*

368

*"Crossing the Larimer Avenue Bridge to their new Italian community"*   John Kane, 1932

Burton • Dimperio • Musilin • Malins • Webb

### "The bridge that I crossed over many times walking between my home in Little Italy to Westinghouse High School"

Larimer Avenue Bridge, largest Concrete Span in the World, Pittsburgh, Pa.

369

LARIMER AVENUE

Pittsburgh's Little Italy

*Burton • Dimperio • Musilin • Malins • Webb*

370

The house where my family lived up until I was 6 years of age.

SCHREIBER TRUCKING CO.

ORPHAN STREET "SKYLINE" - A STUNNING VIEW OF L.A. MANSIONS

LARIMER SCHOOL
Corner of Winslow St. & Larimer Ave.
East Liberty

371

# PETE DIMPERIO
## 1987 HALL OF FAME INDUCTEE

372

The successful career of Pete was predicted in the year book of his graduating class at Fifth Avenue High School where Pete was a star in football. The class prophet saw him as a second Knute Rockne. Certainly this has been fulfilled to the fullest extent.

After a year of prep at California Normal where he starred on the greatest of California's football teams, he matriculated at Thiel College. At this school Pete was an outstanding lineman. He was captain of the team and was selected as an All-American on the small colleges All-Star Team. His graduate work was done at Springfield College where he received his Masters Degree. Further graduate work was done in administration at Pitt.

The scene of his boyhood was the beginning of his long and successful coaching career. Pete managed and coached independent teams in Hazelwood. During the summer vacations, he conducted very interesting programs on the playgrounds of that district. It was during these sessions that he observed the potential of many local boys that he sent

on to college and higher education. Pete's first school assignment was as physical education teacher and basketball coach. His success in the roundball sport was phenomenal. At Herron Hill he won 117 games and lost 8. When a football coach was needed at Westinghouse, Pete was the first choice. His career at Westinghouse High School has surpassed all expectations and he leaves behind a career that will go down in scholastic annals as unequaled for all time. He has won 187 league games and lost 5. he has won 17 city championships in 21 years.

From such fantastic physical achievements it was evident that they would be reflected in the personal lives of the players and their coach. Hundreds of his players were given college scholarships. Today, we find many of his boys successful men in the professional and business world. They took advantage of the opportunities given to them by their coach. Pete gained fame and renown from his success, and it opened up a new field to him; namely, as an after-dinner speaker. He as appeared at Michigan State, Philadelphia Sportswriters Banquet, Atlantic City National clinic, University of Pittsburgh, and many others. Pete was clinic manager for fourteen years of the Coach of the Year Clinic. This clinic enjoys the largest attendance of all the clinics. In addition, we might list such honors as Junior Chamber of Commerce "Man of the Year" in Sports, Dapper Dan Award, National Prep Magazine Coach of the Year in 1954, Bnai Brith Service Award, and induction into Pennsylvania Sports Hall of Fame in 1964.

The legend of Pete Dimperio will live long in the hearts of his players and friends.

# JOSEPH B. NATOLI
### 1987 HALL OF FAME INDUCTEE

In Joe Natoli's life-long career in organizing athletics for young people, a career that runs the gamut from basketball to baseball to football, there is one achievement which is his piece de resistance, his magnum opus, his labor of love. This is his Morningside Bulldogs Football Club.

Here is an organization which started as a neighborhood team playing against other neighborhoods and became an instant winner. A team that grew to become Pittsburgh's Morningside Bulldogs, Incorporated, preparing hundreds of young men for high school and college football.

And here is an organization which played 298 games, having lost but 19 times over a 30-year span. When you have written that last sentence you have stated something so incredible that it almost defies belief. It is a record that may well surpass that of anyone else who ever coached the game.

In sporting circles in a hundred cities and towns in the eastern United States and Canada, the Bulldogs were known as the ultimate football team in their class. It was not uncommon for Joe's Bulldogs to arrive in a city in one of the 13 states in which they played, be given the key to the city by the mayor, read in the newspaper that "The winningest team in the world is coming to town," run a 40-0 score on a team the locals thought was a great one, and leave town the next day with the local people nearly awe-struck by the display of precision and power they had witnessed. Such was the unbelievable success of Joe's Bulldogs.

And he did it all without any of the helmet slapping and abusive techniques employed by lesser men. There was always a camaraderie, an esprit de corps, a closeness, that made the Bulldogs something special.

Pittsburgh's Morningside Bulldogs Football Club is now a fraternal organization made up of the 879 people who played for or were associated with the team. Joe Natoli built his house so well that it will stand for many years. It is a football legend, a legend of excellence.

Some unbelievable Morningside Bulldog statistics are:
Once went 12 seasons with only 3 losses.

For each touchdown the opponents scored, the Bulldogs scored 9 points.

The Bulldogs averaged over 30 points per game for their entire 30 years.

The Bulldogs came within one play of being ungained-upon rushing one year.

The Bulldogs recorded 184 shutouts.

In 1961, the Bulldogs were unscored upon.

Joe Natoli and his wife, Helen, have two sons, Tommy and Joey.

373

*Looking back in time:*

*I cannot forget how close I came to playing for Coach Joe Natoli and the Morningside Bulldogs. I missed the age cut-off date by two months.... just another disappointment during my life's journey.*

# Bo Silvio

## Frank A. Santamaria Lifetime Achievement Award

374

Albert "Bo" Silvio was born on March 3, 1934 at home in the Larimer section of East Liberty. Born at home, Albert was the ninth child of ten children born to Thomas and Louise Silvio. Albert's family included three sisters and six brothers. He went to Larimer Grade School before going onto Westinghouse High School, where he played football for three years under the late Pete Dimperio. He was on the 1951 undefeated City League Championship team. His last year of high school, he began working evenings at Ward Baking Company due to family hardship. He never got to realize his dream of going onto college and becoming a high school coach. He continued to help his family financially, and soon met his beautiful wife, the former Catherine "Kay" Shullo, shortly after. They were married on February 12, 1955 and then quickly started their family by having two daughters, Anna Louise and Marie, along with son, Angelo. He accepted a job with Equitable Gas where he worked for 32 years, 28 of which he was a foreman with the company.

He joined the Order of Italian Sons and Daughters of America in 1972 and has been a faithful member ever since. He has been President of the Frank DiLeo Lodge #219 for the past 18 years. He is currently the Vice President of Western Pennsylvania, a position which he has held for the past 6 years. He has also held previous positions, such as National Representative and National Councillor. For the past 5 years, he has been the chairperson of Italian Day at Kennywood Park, located in West Mifflin, PA where the Order of Italian Sons and Daughters of America host over 900 special needs children and their supervisors to a day of fun, food, and rides at the park. This involves obtaining contributions, organizing the

volunteers, and overseeing one of the biggest days at Kennywood Park. It is so wonderful to see these children have a day where they can forget their problems and have fun.

Bo is a member of the Umberto DiNardo Council #116 Sons of Columbus and has been involved with Columbus Day Parade and participated since its inception. He helps with and serves as Christopher Columbus on his float, the Santa Maria. He is a member of and represents the Order of Italian Sons and Daughters of America at the Coalition of Italian American Organizations (CI AO).

At Christmas time, Bo chairs the Operation Shoebox charity where members of the Order of Italian Sons and Daughters of America donate their time, money, and gifts to the less fortunate and also visit them and provide entertainment. His lodge also supports a Christmas visit with the special children at Camp Shining Arrow, where they bring a cake and money for the camp. Bo is also a member of the Sheriff's Reserve of Allegheny County.

With all this on his plate, he is still a devoted and loving husband, father, pappy and greatgrandpa to his family, who are very fortunate to have him in their lives. He and his wife, Kay, just celebrated their 50th Wedding Anniversary, which is one of his proudest accomplishments. Along with their three children, they also have eight grandchildren, Daniel Silvio, Matthew Sagi, Brittany Silvio, Karmen Silvio, Angelo Silvio, Alyssa Orr, Cody Orr, and Brandy Orr, and one greatgrandchild, Christopher Ball. He also has a great circle of friends and fellow lodge members and considers himself to be one lucky man.

*My Friend and WHS Classmate*

## WHS ALUMNUS TONY "HERB" AMEN
## AN EXTRA IN NUMEROUS MOVIE FILMS

My friend, Tony, has enjoyed a priceless journey meeting and sharing stage time with so many famous movie stars and musical legends.

We grew up in the same neighborhood with hopes and aspirations of some day fulfilling them. Tony loved the arts and I loved football, and we both possessed a passion to someday find our nitch.

Tony has indeed found his nitch meeting so many entertainers and movie stars too many to mention by name. After several visits with Tony and his wife Dianne I left their home with such a nostalgic reward. His room of wall mounted photos of so many celebrities is the most impressive collection that I have ever seen. It is more than just a room full of photos there is a personal experience that Tony expresses with each well-known star. It is literally a priceless plethora of fascinating experiences that would make for a coffee table gem of a book. Hopefully, some day he will put it all in that unwritten book.

A sincere thank you, Tony, for your interest and support of my book, "Memories of a Foregone Era". It was a huge boost to hear you say, "Carmen you should be proud of your endeavor."

375

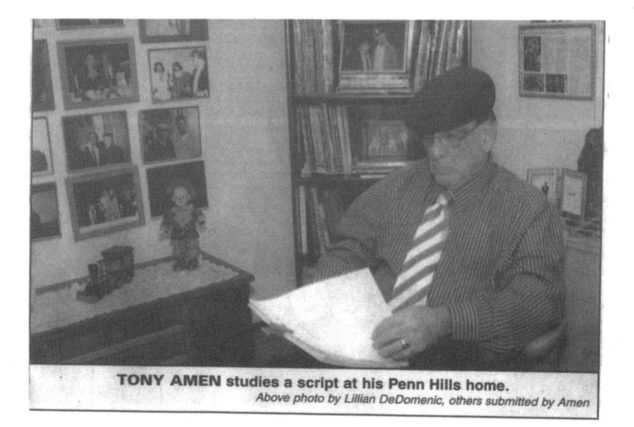

**TONY AMEN studies a script at his Penn Hills home.**
*Above photo by Lillian DeDomenic, others submitted by Amen*

**Pittsburgh Post-Gazette**

### AS YEARS GO BY CLASS REUNIONS ARE FILLED WITH BITTERSWEET EMOTIONS

Tuesday, June 17, 1997

## Westinghouse High, Class of '37, stages bittersweet reunion every year

By Gretchen McKay

It's funny how a few years can cast a shadow of doubt over even the fondest of teen-age memories.

Though Linda (Valentine) Keefe and Rose Marie (Accetta) Wells both attended their senior prom at George Westinghouse High School, neither could agree on where, exactly, the dance was held.

Wells swore it was in the crepe paper-decorated school cafeteria while Keefe, the senior class secretary, was just as adamant she and her classmates danced the night away in a smoky Downtown club.

"Don't you remember?" Keefe demanded, as a smile broke over her face. "Our chaperones were stoned out of their minds!"

John Heller/Post-Gazette

Anthony Corrado, 78, of Oakland greets classmates at the Westinghouse High School Class of '37 reunion at the Churchill Valley Country Club last Saturday.

Location aside, they both concurred that the dance — like their entire senior year more than a half-century ago — was wonderful, perhaps even magical.

"This class was always such a close

group," said Keefe, recalling that night so long ago in 1937. "And our reunions have always been very happy occasions."

And so last Saturday, close to three dozen of the January 1937 graduating class of Westinghouse High and their guests lingered over drinks and dinner at the Churchill Valley Country Club, creating yet one more happy memory: that of their 60th class reunion.

"It's more important now to get together because we're getting older," explained Charles Castleforte of Swisshelm Park, 77, one of the event's organizers. And though most of the class doesn't see each other on a daily basis, "they are all still good friends."

Like many reunions, the gathering

SEE **REUNION**, PAGE F-5

**REUNION** FROM PAGE F-1

allowed the old classmates to catch up on such life events as grandchildren, vacations and retirements, as well as trade information with one another on other alums who couldn't make the trip.

But mostly, it was about reminiscing about the good old days.

"What I remember most is the way the teachers treated us," said Ralph Eberle, 79, of Leechburg, Pa. "They were always so concerned. If you didn't understand something, they kept you after school until you got it."

"In those days, there were no school buses," noted Danny Nardozzi, a life-long Pittsburgher who worked for the Pittsburgh Sun-Telegraph and Pittsburgh Post-Gazette before retiring in 1982. "We had to walk, rain or shine, with street cars passing us by."

For many, with a war looming overseas and the country in the midst of a financial crisis, there were no thoughts of college.

"We went to school during the Great Depression, so money was

always tight," recalls Raymond Pritchett, 78, of Chippewa, Pa, who, like many of his schoolmates, served in the military during World War II. To help support his family, in fact, Pritchett could only go to school a half a day during the last two years so he could work in the afternoons putting up siding and brick.

After so many years, old friends weren't always immediately recognizable — more than one grad had to peer at the name tag stuck on a former classmate's chest before making a connection. But however delayed, the response was always one of sheer delight.

"My kids thought I was crazy, going so far away," admitted Marie (Pragliola) Beltz, who drove the four hours from a retirement home in Quincy, Pa., to attend. "But just seeing your old friends — it feels so good!"

The class first got together in 1957, after 20 years on their own; at their 55th reunion, due to everyone's advancing ages, someone suggested they make the affair a yearly event, as opposed to once every five years.

A few reunions ago, there was

live music or DJs and jitterbugging until the wee hours of the night. But nature has taken its course over the decades, and this year, most partygoers' joints were a little too stiff for dancing, their eyesight a bit foggier, their hearing not quite as sharp.

"I'll see for you if you walk for me," quipped class president and former football star Guy Guadagnino, walking with the help of a cane, to a classmate recovering from cataract surgery.

The numbers, too, have dwindled, to where just 20 graduates made it out of a class of a graduating class of 158.

"In the early years, there was always a tremendous response," says Velma Martiner, who mailed out more than 60 invitations. "But things do change as you get older."

Some of the letters, she said, come back from alums who are either homebound or can't drive at night; others tell about health problems, such as cancer, or the death of spouses.

Still other invitations go unanswered, leaving the surviving graduates to wonder if yet another classmate has left their ranks

PITTSBURGH POST-GAZETTE ■ TUESDAY, JUNE 17, 1997

### AS YEARS GO BY CLASS REUNIONS ARE FILLED WITH BITTERSWEET EMOTIONS

# Westinghouse Class of '37 stages emotional reunion

forever.

But for those who remain, the enthusiasm — and camaraderie — has never been stronger. And most of the alums gathered are as active as someone 10 years younger.

Martiner, a self-described "career gal" who never married, still works 40 hours a week as a paralegal for a Downtown law firm; Ray Pritchett finds it difficult to stay away from the insurance and investment business he's run for more than 50 years; Linda Keefe, who has retired twice, continues to log time part-time as a secretary.

Even Anthony Corrado, who is hooked to nasal oxygen and missed the last three reunions due to illness, still makes it to the office once a week to do the accounting.

"There aren't too many couch potatoes here," observed Corrado's nephew John.

Ten years ago, the class held their 50th reunion jointly with the class that graduated in June 1937. Though it was a nice affair, "they just took over so completely," recalled Martiner. "It just wasn't as enchanting and engaging as having it on our own."

The 1935 city championship baseball team, pictured in the Westinghouse High School Class of '37 yearbook. Gus Guadagnino is middle row, second from right.

As a result, they never joined forces again.

Yet as hard as Martiner admits it is to get the old gang together every year, she is looking forward already to next year's event.

---

*Have you celebrated a joyous event in an unusual way? Gotten engaged while climbing Everest or married canoeing down the Ohio, for example? If so, drop us a line (or drop the dime on a friend) and we'll consider featuring your story in this space above our Celebrations package each Tuesday. Send your stories to: Mark Murphy, Features Dept., Pittsburgh Post-Gazette, 34 Blvd. of the Allies, Pittsburgh, Pa. 15222. These stories do not replace the classified announcements in Celebrations, so for information about how to use that space, call 263-1236.*

377

*Looking back in time:*
*Guy Guadagnino, a member of this WHS Class of 1937 later went on to teach and coach baseball for many years at West View High School (later renamed North Hills High School.) North Hills honored him by naming its baseball diamond Guadagnino Field. Another Westinghouse alumnus that excelled and made us all proud.*

## Under the Lights at Martorelli Stadium
## 1999

Todd Szramowski played football for North Hills High School much to the delight of so many of us. He made us proud when he was chosen at the end of the season as a member of the Post-Gazette 1999 High School Football Fabulous "22" Team. I followed Todd's football career from the midgets to high school as he is a member of my extended family. I could not be more proud of this young man for what he has accomplished in his life since high school – earning a college degree and working in the field of his choice. He is one of my many memories of a foregone era.

**Todd Szramowski**
**North Hills**
**Senior QB**
**6-0, 185**
One of WPIAL's biggest surprises. Did not play QB as a junior. This year, had more than 2,000 yards offense for 9-1 team. Completed 103-189 for 1,663 yards, 14 TDs. Team's leading rusher with 532 yards on 146 carries.

**Top player**

North Hills quarterback Todd Szramowski has been named the North Hills News Record Offensive Player of the Year. "He always seemed to make something positive" happen, said his coach, Jack McCurry. "He had the ability to improvise and make something happen." For more on Szramowski, as well as who was named Defensive Player of the Year and Coach of the Year, **see** pages 9-10.

File photo

---

*Burton • Dimperio • Musilin • Malins • Webb*

379

**Coach George Webb, Carmen Pellegrino and Joe Pronio**

**\*An Accolade from a Classmate\***
As he scans over pictures of Westinghouse High
He smiles and he breathes a happy sigh
As he revels in memories of days gone by
A truer "Bulldog" may never be known.
His spirit and heart he has always shown
And so I would like to say in a sincere Bulldog way
Carmen Pellegrino we applaud you today
May God bless you always along life's way
Your Friend,
Joe Pronio

380

*June 17, 2000*
As the cake says GO! Westinghouse Reunion Committee!
Our Class of 1954 celebrated the New Millennium in grand style.
*Churchill Valley Country Club*

My wife Pat and former Westinghouse coach George Webb collectively surprised me with this jacket on my 65th birthday.

HOW PROUD WE WERE

382

TO WEAR THIS LETTER

# PART 4

# RECORDS AND SUMMARIES

*Throughout the better part of the twentieth century Westinghouse High School managed to uphold a special winning tradition. The storied history of all the winning seasons epitomizes a special loyalty that existed in a school district that lasted until the Pittsburgh Public School System deemed it necessary to make changes. Those changes through open enrollment enabled students to choose where they desired to pursue their high school careers. The following summary reflects a remarkable football record that will always hold a special place in the hearts of the many proud alumni that were a part of that special winning tradition. There was something special about attending the high school where you lived. It brought a unique bond to the communities of Homewood, Brushton, Lincoln and Larimer and it all came together at Westinghouse High School.*

## RECORDS AND SUMMARIES
## WESTINGHOUSE HIGH SCHOOL
### PITTSBURGH, PA
## FOOTBALL RECORD

**1913 (2-3-1)**

| WHS | 6  | FIFTH AVE | 12 |
|-----|----|-----------|----|
| WHS | 12 | EDGEWOOD  | 13 |
| WHS | 6  | MUNHALL   | 6  |
| WHS | 27 | RIVERSIDE | 0  |
| WHS | 0  | TARENTUM  | 38 |
| WHS | 77 | WOOSLAIR  | 0  |

**Note:** No City Champion crowned until 1919 season

**1915 (4-1-3)**

| WHS | 6  | ALLEGHENY    | 0  |
|-----|----|--------------|----|
| WHS | 0  | PGH CENTRAL  | 12 |
| WHS | 8  | PEABODY      | 6  |
| WHS | 6  | ASPINWALL    | 0  |
| WHS | 7  | BEAVER FALLS | 7  |
| WHS | 6  | CRAFTON      | 6  |
| WHS | 18 | PARNASSUS    | 0  |
| WHS | 0  | WILKINSBURG  | 0  |

**1917 (2-5-1)**

| WHS | 0 | ALLEGHENY   | 12 |
|-----|---|-------------|----|
| WHS | 6 | FIFTH AVE   | 0  |
| WHS | 0 | PEABODY     | 6  |
| WHS | 7 | SCHENLEY    | 7  |
| WHS | 6 | SOUTH       | 0  |
| WHS | 0 | PARNASSUS   | 7  |
| WHS | 0 | WEST NEWTON | 39 |
| WHS | 0 | WILKINSBURG | 33 |

**1919 (5-1-1)**

| WHS | 0  | ALLEGHENY    | 33 |
|-----|----|--------------|----|
| WHS | 0  | FIFTH AVE    | 0  |
| WHS | 6  | PEABODY      | 0  |
| WHS | 6  | SCHENLEY     | 0  |
| WHS | 25 | SOUTH        | 0  |
| WHS | 34 | SOUTH HILLS  | 0  |
| WHS | 30 | TURTLE CREEK | 0  |

**ALLEGHENY CITY CHAMPION (NO PLAYOFF)**

**Note:** This was the first year a City Champion was crowned

**1914 (2-6-0)**

| WHS | 0  | PGH CENTRAL | 20 |
|-----|----|-------------|----|
| WHS | 0  | FIFTH AVE   | 13 |
| WHS | 0  | PEABODY     | 6  |
| WHS | 0  | ASPINWALL   | 21 |
| WHS | 9  | CRAFTON     | 6  |
| WHS | 15 | PARNASSUS   | 12 |
| WHS | 0  | TARENTUM    | 21 |
| WHS | 7  | WILKINSBURG | 35 |

**1916 (1-4-1)**

| WHS | 6  | ALLEGHENY      | 9  |
|-----|----|----------------|----|
| WHS | 0  | PEABODY        | 9  |
| WHS | 38 | CARNEGIE       | 0  |
| WHS | 0  | CONNELLSVILLE  | 46 |
| WHS | 7  | PARNASSUS      | 7  |
| WHS | 0  | WILKINSBURG    | 33 |

**1918 (0-1-0)**

| WHS | 0 | JOHNSTOWN | 23 |
|-----|---|-----------|----|

Note: Short Season World War I

385

**1920 (5-3-0)**

| WHS | 6  | ALLEGHENY   | 0  |
|-----|----|-------------|----|
| WHS | 0  | FIFTH AVE   | 21 |
| WHS | 0  | PEABODY     | 2  |
| WHS | 6  | SCHENLEY    | 7  |
| WHS | 10 | SOUTH       | 0  |
| WHS | 6  | SOUTH HILLS | 0  |
| WHS | 21 | McDONALD    | 0  |
| WHS | 13 | SWISSVALE   | 0  |

**FIFTH AVE CITY CHAMPION (NO PLAYOFF)**

**1921 (7-0-1)**

| WHS | 6 | ALLEGHENY | 0 |
|---|---|---|---|
| WHS | 51 | FIFTH AVE | 0 |
| WHS | 13 | PEABODY | 7 |
| WHS | 20 | SCHENLEY | 0 |
| WHS | 7 | SOUTH | 0 |
| WHS | 20 | SOUTH HILLS | 7 |
| WHS | 35 | SWISSVALE | 0 |

WESTINGHOUSE CITY CHAMPION
(NO PLAYOFF)
WPIAL AA PLAYOFF
WHS  0    ROCHESTER 0
(CO-CHAMPIONS)

**1922 (5-2-1)**

| WHS | 13 | ALLEGHENY | 17 |
|---|---|---|---|
| WHS | 40 | FIFTH AVE | 7 |
| WHS | 26 | PEABODY | 0 |
| WHS | 0 | SCHENLEY | 6 |
| WHS | 34 | SOUTH | 6 |
| WHS | 14 | SOUTH HILLS | 0 |
| WHS | 0 | MONACA | 0 |
| WHS | 27 | SWISSVALE | 0 |

ALLEGHENY CITY CHAMPION
(NO PLAYOFF)

**1923 (3-4-1)**

| WHS | 6 | CARNEGIE | 6 |
|---|---|---|---|
| WHS | 0 | ALLEGHENY | 32 |
| WHS | 0 | FIFTH AVE | 6 |
| WHS | 19 | LANGLEY | 6 |
| WHS | 0 | PEABODY | 6 |
| WHS | 6 | SCHENLEY | 12 |
| WHS | 45 | SOUTH | 0 |
| WHS | 7 | SOUTH HILLS | 6 |

ALLEGHENY CITY CHAMPION
(NO PLAYOFF)

**1924 (5-3-0)**

| WHS | 7 | SWISSVALE | 15 |
|---|---|---|---|
| WHS | 20 | ALLEGHENY | 9 |
| WHS | 6 | FIFTH AVE | 12 |
| WHS | 0 | LANGLEY | 27 FW/WHS |
| WHS | 3 | PEABODY | 0 |
| WHS | 0 | SCHENLEY | 28 |
| WHS | 21 | SOUTH | 7 |
| WHS | 13 | SOUTH HILLS | 0 |

SCHENLEY CITY CHAMPION
(NO PLAYOFF)

386

**1925 (5-2-1)**

| WHS | 53 | ALLEGHENY | 0 |
|---|---|---|---|
| WHS | 27 | FIFTH AVE | 0 |
| WHS | 6 | LANGLEY | 0 |
| WHS | 0 | PEABODY | 0 |
| WHS | 0 | SCHENLEY | 6 |
| WHS | 33 | SOUTH | 0 |
| WHS | 0 | SOUTH HILLS | 7 |
| WHS | 2 | OLIVER | 0 FW/WHS |

CITY CHAMPIONSHIP PLAYOFF
SCHENLEY 35   SOUTH HILLS 0

**1926 (4-3-1)**

| WHS | 0 | YOUNGSTOWN RAYEN, OHIO | 19 |
|---|---|---|---|
| WHS | 14 | CORAOPOLIS | 0 |
| WHS | 6 | SWISSVALE | 7 |
| WHS | 40 | FIFTH AVE | 0 |
| WHS | 12 | LANGLEY | 0 |
| WHS | 26 | PEABODY | 0 |
| WHS | 0 | SCHENLEY | 13 |
| WHS | 0 | SOUTH HILLS | 0 |

SCHENLEY CITY CHAMPION
(NO PLAYOFF)

**1927 (7-0-1)**

| | | | |
|---|---|---|---|
| WHS | 67 | S. BROWNSVILLE | 6 |
| WHS | 42 | SWISSVALE | 0 |
| WHS | 0 | WILKINSBURG | 0 |
| WHS | 61 | FIFTH AVE | 6 |
| WHS | 23 | PEABODY | 6 |
| WHS | 6 | SCHENLEY | 0 |
| WHS | 20 | SOUTH | 0 |

**CITY CHAMPIONSHIP PLAYOFF**

| | | | |
|---|---|---|---|
| WHS | 13 | OLIVER | 6 |

**1928 (7-1-1)**

| | | | |
|---|---|---|---|
| WHS | 12 | INDIANA | 0 |
| WHS | 7 | NEW CASTLE | 25 |
| WHS | 19 | WAYNESBURG | 0 |
| WHS | 0 | ALLEGHENY | 0 |
| WHS | 27 | FIFTH AVE | 6 |
| WHS | 31 | PEABODY | 0 |
| WHS | 6 | SCHENLEY | 0 |
| WHS | 46 | SOUTH | 6 |

**CITY CHAMPIONSHIP PLAYOFF**

| | | | |
|---|---|---|---|
| WHS | 19 | SOUTH HILLS | 0 |

**1929 (5-3-0)**

| | | | |
|---|---|---|---|
| WHS | 20 | NEW CASTLE | 13 |
| WHS | 0 | ROCHESTER | 6 |
| WHS | 0 | JEANNETTE | 6 |
| WHS | 30 | ALLEGHENY | 0 |
| WHS | 40 | FIFTH AVE | 0 |
| WHS | 12 | PEABODY | 7 |
| WHS | 0 | SCHENLEY | 12 |
| WHS | 40 | SOUTH | 7 |

**CITY CHAMPIONSHIP PLAYOFF**

| | | | |
|---|---|---|---|
| SCHENLEY | 15 | SOUTH HILLS | 0 |

**1930 (7-2-0)**

| | | | |
|---|---|---|---|
| WHS | 0 | ALTOONA | 19 |
| WHS | 13 | GREENSBURG | 20 |
| WHS | 52 | ALLDERDICE | 7 |
| WHS | 25 | CARRICK | 0 |
| WHS | 66 | FIFTH AVE | 0 |
| WHS | 19 | PEABODY | 7 |
| WHS | 6 | SCHENLEY | 0 |
| WHS | 20 | SOUTH | 6 |

**CITY CHAMPIONSHIP PLAYOFF**

| | | | |
|---|---|---|---|
| WHS | 12 | SOUTH HILLS | 6 |

**1931 (2-5-1)**

| | | | |
|---|---|---|---|
| WHS | 0 | WILKINSBURG | 35 |
| WHS | 0 | GREENSBURG | 39 |
| WHS | 13 | ALLDERDICE | 12 |
| WHS | 31 | FIFTH AVE | 0 |
| WHS | 0 | LANGLEY | 0 |
| WHS | 0 | PEABODY | 13 |
| WHS | 0 | SCHENLEY | 14 |
| WHS | 6 | SOUTH | 7 |

**CITY CHAMPIONSHIP PLAYOFF**

| | | | |
|---|---|---|---|
| SOUTH HILLS | 7 | SCHENLEY | 0 |

**1932 (4-4-1)**

| | | | |
|---|---|---|---|
| WHS | 0 | WILKINSBURG | 7 |
| WHS | 0 | MT. LEBANON | 7 |
| WHS | 13 | ALLDERDICE | 0 |
| WHS | 0 | ALLEGHENY | 6 |
| WHS | 41 | FIFTH AVE | 0 |
| WHS | 12 | PEABODY | 6 |
| WHS | 14 | SCHENLEY | 0 |
| WHS | 7 | SOUTH | 7 |

**CITY CHAMPIONSHIP PLAYOFF**

| | | | |
|---|---|---|---|
| PERRY | 13 | WESTINGHOUSE | 6 |

387

**1933 (4-2-2)**

| | | | |
|---|---|---|---|
| WHS | 14 | RANKIN | 7 |
| WHS | 12 | BRADDOCK | 0 |
| WHS | 0 | ALLDERDICE | 0 |
| WHS | 13 | FIFTH AVE | 0 |
| WHS | 7 | PEABODY | 13 |
| WHS | 0 | SCHENLEY | 0 |
| WHS | 0 | SOUTH | 12 |
| WHS | 21 | SOUTH HILLS | 6 |

**CITY CHAMPIONSHIP PLAYOFF**
**PEABODY 13 SOUTH HILLS 0**

**1934 (6-0-3)**

| | | | |
|---|---|---|---|
| WHS | 0 | JEANNETTE | 0 |
| WHS | 0 | BRADDOCK | 0 |
| WHS | 6 | BUTLER | 0 |
| WHS | 13 | ALLDERDICE | 0 |
| WHS | 6 | FIFTH AVE | 0 |
| WHS | 13 | PEABODY | 7 |
| WHS | 13 | SCHENLEY | 0 |
| WHS | 19 | SOUTH | 0 |

**CITY CHAMPIONSHIP PLAYOFF**
**WHS 6 CARRICK 6**
**(CO-CHAMPIONS)**

**1935 (4-3-2)**

| | | | |
|---|---|---|---|
| WHS | 20 | DERRY TWP. | 12 |
| WHS | 0 | FORD CITY | 0 |
| WHS | 0 | JEANNETTE | 20 |
| WHS | 19 | ALLDERDICE | 0 |
| WHS | 6 | FIFTH AVE | 0 |
| WHS | 0 | PEABODY | 3 |
| WHS | 0 | SCHENLEY | 0 |
| WHS | 13 | SOUTH | 0 |

**CITY CHAMPIONSHIP PLAYOFF**
**SOUTH HILLS 6 WESTINGHOUSE 0**

**1936 (6-3-0)**

| | | | |
|---|---|---|---|
| WHS | 20 | WELLSVILLE, OH. | 18 |
| WHS | 0 | JEANNETTE | 6 |
| WHS | 12 | McKEESPORT | 18 |
| WHS | 13 | ALLDERDICE | 7 |
| WHS | 12 | FIFTH AVE | 9 |
| WHS | 13 | PEABODY | 7 |
| WHS | 20 | SCHENLEY | 0 |
| WHS | 25 | SOUTH | 6 |

**CITY CHAMPIONSHIP PLAYOFF**
**SOUTH HILLS 12 WESTINGHOUSE 0**

388

**1937 (4-3-1)**

| | | | |
|---|---|---|---|
| WHS | 0 | NEW KENSINGTON | 0 |
| WHS | 7 | MT. LEBANON | 25 |
| WHS | 13 | ALTOONA | 25 |
| WHS | 12 | ALLDERDICE | 7 |
| WHS | 13 | FIFTH AVE | 0 |
| WHS | 13 | PEABODY | 15 |
| WHS | 20 | SCHENLEY | 6 |
| WHS | 14 | SOUTH | 0 |

**CITY CHAMPIONSHIP PLAYOFF**
**SOUTH HILLS 8 PEABODY 0**

**1938 (7-1-0)**

| | | | |
|---|---|---|---|
| WHS | 0 | ALTOONA | 14 |
| WHS | 14 | ALLEGHENY | 7 |
| WHS | 12 | FIFTH AVE | 6 |
| WHS | 25 | OLIVER | 0 |
| WHS | 7 | PEABODY | 0 |
| WHS | 20 | PERRY | 0 |
| WHS | 4 | SOUTH | 0 |
| WHS | 13 | SOUTH HILLS | 0 |

**WESTINGHOUSE CITY CHAMPION**
**(NO PLAYOFF)**

**1939 (8-0-0)**

| WHS | 12 | ALTOONA | 7 |
|---|---|---|---|
| WHS | 20 | ALLDERDICE | 6 |
| WHS | 13 | CARRICK | 0 |
| WHS | 31 | LANGLEY | 0 |
| WHS | 12 | PEABODY | 6 |
| WHS | 21 | SCHENLEY | 0 |
| WHS | 25 | SOUTH | 0 |
| WHS | 14 | SOUTH HILLS | 0 |

**WESTINGHOUSE CITY CHAMPION (NO PLAYOFF)**

**1940 (4-3-0)**

| WHS | 0 | ALTOONA | 20 |
|---|---|---|---|
| WHS | 12 | KISKI SCHOOL | 0 |
| WHS | 20 | ALLDERDICE | 6 |
| WHS | 6 | PEABODY | 18 |
| WHS | 12 | SCHENLEY | 0 |
| WHS | 6 | SOUTH | 12 |
| WHS | 26 | SOUTH HILLS | 0 |

**SOUTH HILLS-OLIVER CO-CHAMPIONS (NO PLAYOFF)**

**1941 (5-1-1)**

| WHS | 12 | PENN HILLS | 0 |
|---|---|---|---|
| WHS | 7 | ALTOONA | 20 |
| WHS | 7 | ALLDERDICE | 0 |
| WHS | 19 | PEABODY | 0 |
| WHS | 6 | SCHENLEY | 6 |
| WHS | 32 | SOUTH | 0 |
| WHS | 19 | SOUTH HILLS | 12 |

**WHS-OLIVER CO-CHAMPIONS (NO PLAYOFF)**

**1942 (6-2-1)**

| WHS | 8 | PENN HILLS | 0 |
|---|---|---|---|
| WHS | 0 | ALTOONA | 27 |
| WHS | 0 | MT. LEBANON | 14 |
| WHS | 19 | ALLDERDICE | 0 |
| WHS | 26 | PEABODY | 0 |
| WHS | 18 | SCHENLEY | 0 |
| WHS | 32 | SOUTH | 0 |
| WHS | 25 | SOUTH HILLS | 0 |

**CITY CHAMPIONSHIP PLAYOFF**

| WHS | 6 | OLIVER | 6 |
|---|---|---|---|

**(CO-CHAMPIONS)**

389

**1943 (6-1-1)**

| WHS | 6 | PENN HILLS | 0 |
|---|---|---|---|
| WHS | 0 | ALTOONA | 0 |
| WHS | 13 | MT. LEBANON | 0 |
| WHS | 19 | ALLDERDICE | 13 |
| WHS | 19 | PEABODY | 6 |
| WHS | 0 | SCHENLEY | 23 |
| WHS | 33 | SOUTH | 6 |
| WHS | 13 | SOUTH HILLS | 0 |

**CITY CHAMPIONSHIP PLAYOFF**

SCHENLEY 21    ALLEGHENY 7

**1944 (7-2-0)**

| WHS | 6 | N.B. SCOTT | 7 |
|---|---|---|---|
| WHS | 0 | ALTOONA | 7 |
| WHS | 13 | MT. LEBANON | 0 |
| WHS | 31 | ALLDERDICE | 0 |
| WHS | 14 | PEABODY | 0 |
| WHS | 35 | SCHENLEY | 0 |
| WHS | 20 | SOUTH | 6 |
| WHS | 40 | SOUTH HILLS | 7 |

**CITY CHAMPIONSHIP PLAYOFF**

| WHS | 18 | PERRY | 13 |
|---|---|---|---|

**1945 (8-1-0)**

| WHS | 27 | N.B. SCOTT | 26 |
|---|---|---|---|
| WHS | 0 | DONORA | 27 |
| WHS | 12 | ALTOONA | 0 |
| WHS | 14 | ALLDERDICE | 7 |
| WHS | 14 | PEABODY | 0 |
| WHS | 20 | SCHENLEY | 0 |
| WHS | 34 | SOUTH | 12 |
| WHS | 13 | SOUTH HILLS | 0 |

**CITY CHAMPIONSHIP PLAYOFF**

| WHS | 13 | ALLEGHENY | 0 |
|---|---|---|---|

**1946 (7-1-1)**

| WHS | 7 | N.B. SCOTT | 0 |
|---|---|---|---|
| WHS | 12 | CONNELLSVILLE | 6 |
| WHS | 6 | ALTOONA | 20 |
| WHS | 27 | ALLDERDICE | 0 |
| WHS | 0 | PEABODY | 0 |
| WHS | 19 | SCHENLEY | 6 |
| WHS | 25 | SOUTH | 7 |
| WHS | 15 | SOUTH HILLS | 13 |

**CITY CHAMPIONSHIP PLAYOFF**

| WHS | 27 | ALLEGHENY | 7 |
|---|---|---|---|

**1947 (8-0-1)**

| | | | |
|---|---|---|---|
| WHS | 14 | N.B. SCOTT | 7 |
| WHS | 12 | CONNELLSVILLE | 6 |
| WHS | 0 | ALTOONA | 0 |
| WHS | 40 | ALLDERDICE | 0 |
| WHS | 14 | PEABODY | 13 |
| WHS | 20 | SCHENLEY | 0 |
| WHS | 19 | SOUTH | 0 |
| WHS | 13 | SOUTH HILLS | 12 |

**CITY CHAMPIONSHIP PLAYOFF**

| | | | |
|---|---|---|---|
| WHS | 19 | CARRICK | 0 |

**1948 (8-1-0)**

| | | | |
|---|---|---|---|
| WHS | 26 | N.B. SCOTT | 7 |
| WHS | 12 | ELLWOOD CITY | 9 |
| WHS | 13 | ALTOONA | 14 |
| WHS | 46 | ALLDERDICE | 0 |
| WHS | 33 | PEABODY | 14 |
| WHS | 33 | SCHENLEY | 0 |
| WHS | 33 | SOUTH | 6 |
| WHS | 41 | SOUTH HILLS | 6 |

**CITY CHAMPIONSHIP PLAYOFF**

| | | | |
|---|---|---|---|
| WHS | 33 | CARRICK | 12 |

**1949 (8-1-0)**

| | | | |
|---|---|---|---|
| WHS | 28 | N.B. SCOTT | 7 |
| WHS | 31 | ALTOONA | 14 |
| WHS | 0 | DUQUESNE | 13 |
| WHS | 56 | ALLDERDICE | 0 |
| WHS | 47 | PEABODY | 0 |
| WHS | 27 | SCHENLEY | 7 |
| WHS | 40 | SOUTH | 0 |
| WHS | 28 | SOUTH HILLS | 0 |

**CITY CHAMPIONSHIP PLAYOFF**

| | | | |
|---|---|---|---|
| WHS | 13 | ALLEGHENY | 0 |

**1950 (4-4-0)**

| | | | |
|---|---|---|---|
| WHS | 0 | JOHNSTOWN | 21 |
| WHS | 13 | ALTOONA | 20 |
| WHS | 20 | DUQUESNE | 13 |
| WHS | 38 | SOUTH | 0 |
| WHS | 19 | SOUTH HILLS | 0 |
| WHS | 70 | ALLDERDICE | 0 |
| WHS | 6 | SCHENLEY | 12 |
| WHS | 6 | PEABODY | 7 |

**CITY CHAMPIONSHIP PLAYOFF**

| | | | |
|---|---|---|---|
| SCHENLEY | 6 | CARRICK | 0 |

**1951 (9-0-0)**

| | | | |
|---|---|---|---|
| WHS | 48 | ALLEGHENY | 19 |
| WHS | 34 | ALTOONA | 0 |
| WHS | 18 | DUQUESNE | 7 |
| WHS | 40 | SOUTH HILLS | 7 |
| WHS | 53 | ALLDERDICE | 12 |
| WHS | 64 | SOUTH | 8 |
| WHS | 41 | PEABODY | 7 |
| WHS | 41 | SCHENLEY | 7 |

**CITY CHAMPIONSHIP PLAYOFF**

| | | | |
|---|---|---|---|
| WHS | 20 | CARRICK | 7 |

**1952 (5-3-0)**

| | | | |
|---|---|---|---|
| WHS | 6 | DONORA | 13 |
| WHS | 27 | ALTOONA | 0 |
| WHS | 0 | DUQUESNE | 14 |
| WHS | 21 | ALLDERDICE | 6 |
| WHS | 13 | SCHENLEY | 0 |
| WHS | 0 | PEABODY | 7 |
| WHS | 33 | SOUTH | 0 |
| WHS | 19 | SOUTH HILLS | 13 |

**CITY CHAMPIONSHIP PLAYOFF**

| | | | |
|---|---|---|---|
| CARRICK | 27 | PEABODY | 6 |

**1953 (6-2-0)**

| WHS | 6 | DONORA | 12 |
|-----|-----|--------|-----|
| WHS | 13 | ALLIQUIPPA | 6 |
| WHS | 20 | ALTOONA | 6 |
| WHS | 6 | PEABODY | 14 |
| WHS | 61 | SCHENLEY | 6 |
| WHS | 33 | SOUTH | 12 |
| WHS | 27 | SOUTH HILLS | 12 |
| WHS | 33 | ALLDERDICE | 7 |

**CITY CHAMPIONSHIP PLAYOFF**
**PEABODY 21 ALLEGHENY 0**

**1954 (8-1-0)**

| WHS | 28 | DONORA | 0 |
|-----|-----|--------|-----|
| WHS | 7 | ALLIQUIPPA | 0 |
| WHS | 7 | ALTOONA | 19 |
| WHS | 39 | ALLDERDICE | 0 |
| WHS | 25 | PEABODY | 0 |
| WHS | 33 | SOUTH HILLS | 13 |
| WHS | 46 | SOUTH | 0 |
| WHS | 27 | SCHENLEY | 12 |

**CITY CHAMPIONSHIP PLAYOFF**
**WHS 7 CARRICK 6**

**1955 (8-1-0)**

| WHS | 12 | DONORA | 0 |
|-----|-----|--------|-----|
| WHS | 0 | ALLIQUIPPA | 35 |
| WHS | 14 | ALTOONA | 13 |
| WHS | 25 | PEABODY | 0 |
| WHS | 20 | SOUTH HILLS | 7 |
| WHS | 38 | SOUTH | 0 |
| WHS | 28 | ALLDERDICE | 0 |
| WHS | 34 | SCHENLEY | 6 |

**CITY CHAMPIONSHIP PLAYOFF**
**WHS 37 CARRICK 6**

**1956 (7-2-0)**

| WHS | 6 | DONORA | 0 |
|-----|-----|--------|-----|
| WHS | 0 | ALLIQUIPPA | 13 |
| WHS | 0 | ALTOONA | 33 |
| WHS | 19 | SOUTH HILLS | 14 |
| WHS | 28 | ALLDERDICE | 14 |
| WHS | 12 | SCHENLEY | 6 |
| WHS | 6 | PEABODY | 0 |
| WHS | 39 | SOUTH | 19 |

**CITY CHAMPIONSHIP PLAYOFF**
**WHS 20 CARRICK 6**

391

**1957 (8-1-0)**

| WHS | 28 | ALLIQUIPPA | 12 |
|-----|-----|--------|-----|
| WHS | 34 | McKEESPORT | 13 |
| WHS | 13 | ALTOONA | 34 |
| WHS | 40 | SOUTH HILLS | 0 |
| WHS | 33 | SCHENLEY | 7 |
| WHS | 31 | PEABODY | 0 |
| WHS | 27 | ALLDERDICE | 6 |
| WHS | 38 | SOUTH | 6 |

**CITY CHAMPIONSHIP PLAYOFF**
**WHS 39 FIFTH AVE 13**

**1958 (7-2-0)**

| WHS | 19 | ALLIQUIPPA | 7 |
|-----|-----|--------|-----|
| WHS | 19 | MT. LEBANON | 40 |
| WHS | 6 | ALTOONA | 8 |
| WHS | 31 | SCHENLEY | 6 |
| WHS | 46 | SOUTH | 19 |
| WHS | 48 | SOUTH HILLS | 12 |
| WHS | 39 | PEABODY | 6 |
| WHS | 33 | ALLDERDICE | 7 |

**CITY CHAMPIONSHIP PLAYOFF**
**WHS 38 ALLEGHENY 0**

**1959 (5-3-1)**

| WHS | 0 | ALLIQUIPPA | 13 |
|-----|-----|--------|-----|
| WHS | 6 | WINDBER | 31 |
| WHS | 40 | HAR-BRACK | 43 |
| WHS | 0 | PEABODY | 0 |
| WHS | 34 | SOUTH | 6 |
| WHS | 31 | SOUTH HILLS | 0 |
| WHS | 33 | ALLDERDICE | 13 |
| WHS | 35 | SCHENLEY | 0 |

**CITY CHAMPIONSHIP PLAYOFF**
**WHS 35 CARRICK 12**

**1960 (7-1-1)**

| WHS | 14 | ALLIQUIPPA | 14 |
|-----|-----|--------|-----|
| WHS | 13 | HAR-BRACK | 7 |
| WHS | 0 | MT. LEBANON | 28 |
| WHS | 44 | SOUTH | 13 |
| WHS | 41 | SOUTH HILLS | 13 |
| WHS | 33 | ALLDERDICE | 0 |
| WHS | 39 | SCHENLEY | 26 |
| WHS | 25 | PEABODY | 7 |

**CITY CHAMPIONSHIP PLAYOFF**
**WHS 39 ALLEGHENY 7**

**1961 (8-1-0)**

| | | | |
|---|---|---|---|
| WHS | 0 | ALLIQUIPPA | 6 |
| WHS | 12 | MT. LEBANON | 6 |
| WHS | 26 | N. CATHOLIC | 0 |
| WHS | 42 | ALLDERDICE | 7 |
| WHS | 14 | SCHENLEY | 6 |
| WHS | 20 | SOUTH HILLS | 19 |
| WHS | 55 | SOUTH | 0 |
| WHS | 19 | PEABODY | 0 |

**CITY CHAMPIONSHIP PLAYOFF**

| | | | |
|---|---|---|---|
| WHS | 27 | LANGLEY | 7 |

**1962 (6-2-1)**

| | | | |
|---|---|---|---|
| WHS | 21 | ALLIQUIPPA | 6 |
| WHS | 14 | MT. LEBANON | 21 |
| WHS | 20 | HAR-BRACK | 6 |
| WHS | 20 | SOUTH HILLS | 0 |
| WHS | 20 | SCHENLEY | 0 |
| WHS | 12 | PEABODY | 13 |
| WHS | 48 | SOUTH | 12 |
| WHS | 46 | ALLDERDICE | 6 |
| WHS | 7 | PEABODY | 7 |

(PLAYOFF)*

*Note:Peabody declared winner on first downs 8-7

**CITY CHAMPIONSHIP PLAYOFF**

**PEABODY 9  LANGLEY       0**

**1963 (8-1-0)**

| | | | |
|---|---|---|---|
| WHS | 25 | NEW CASTLE | 0 |
| WHS | 13 | MT. LEBANON | 0 |
| WHS | 7 | BISHOP McCORT | 9 |
| WHS | 39 | SCHENLEY | 6 |
| WHS | 33 | PEABODY | 0 |
| WHS | 48 | SOUTH | 6 |
| WHS | 41 | ALLDERDICE | 0 |
| WHS | 34 | SOUTH HILLS | 6 |

**CITY CHAMPIONSHIP PLAYOFF**

| | | | |
|---|---|---|---|
| WHS | 46 | ALLEGHENY | 6 |

**1964 (9-0-0)**

| | | | |
|---|---|---|---|
| WHS | 20 | NEW CASTLE | 6 |
| WHS | 13 | BISHOP McCORT | 12 |
| WHS | 35 | NORTH CATHOLIC | 12 |
| WHS | 27 | PEABODY | 6 |
| WHS | 27 | ALLDERDICE | 0 |
| WHS | 43 | SOUTH | 6 |
| WHS | 41 | SOUTH HILLS | 6 |
| WHS | 46 | SCHENLEY | 6 |

**CITY CHAMPIONSHIP PLAYOFF**

| | | | |
|---|---|---|---|
| WHS | 45 | LANGLEY | 6 |

**392**

**1965 (9-0-0)**

| | | | |
|---|---|---|---|
| WHS | 6 | NEW CASTLE | 0 |
| WHS | 19 | CHARLEROI | 7 |
| WHS | 34 | STEUBENVILLE CATH. | 6 |
| WHS | 40 | SOUTH | 0 |
| WHS | 47 | ALLDERDICE | 7 |
| WHS | 27 | SOUTH HILLS | 0 |
| WHS | 46 | SCHENLEY | 7 |
| WHS | 42 | PEABODY | 12 |

**CITY CHAMPIONSHIP PLAYOFF**

| | | | |
|---|---|---|---|
| WHS | 41 | GLADSTONE | 7 |

**1966 (6-2-0)**

| | | | |
|---|---|---|---|
| WHS | 25 | NEW CASTLE | 27 |
| WHS | 0 | WARREN HARDING, OHIO | 12 |
| WHS | 33 | ALLDERDICE | 12 |
| WHS | 47 | SOUTH HILLS | 7 |
| WHS | 40 | SCHENLEY | 0 |
| WHS | 40 | PEABODY | 14 |
| WHS | 32 | SOUTH | 0 |

**CITY CHAMPIONSHIP PLAYOFF**

| | | | |
|---|---|---|---|
| WHS | 27 | GLADSTONE | 0 |

**1967 (8-1-0)**

| WHS | 26 | CARRICK | 19 |
|-----|----|---------|----|
| WHS | 35 | FIFTH AVE | 19 |
| WHS | 33 | GLADSTONE | 6 |
| WHS | 41 | LANGLEY | 0 |
| WHS | 67 | OLIVER | 0 |
| WHS | 40 | PEABODY | 27 |
| WHS | 25 | SCHENLEY | 0 |
| WHS | 13 | SOUTH HILLS | 12 |

**CITY CHAMPIONSHIP PLAYOFF**
**ALLDERDICE 20    WESTINGHOUSE 13**

**1968 (5-3-0)**

| WHS | 34 | ALLDERDICE | 13 |
|-----|----|------------|----|
| WHS | 40 | ALLEGHENY | 0 |
| WHS | 18 | FIFTH AVE | 0 |
| WHS | 12 | LANGLEY | 7 |
| WHS | 0 | PEABODY | 13 |
| WHS | 7 | PERRY | 33 |
| WHS | 0 | SCHENLEY | 12 |
| WHS | 46 | SOUTH | 6 |

**CITY CHAMPIOSHIP PLAYOFF**
**SOUTH HILLS 14 CARRICK 6**

**1969 (6-3-0)**

| WHS | 24 | ALLDERDICE | 0 |
|-----|----|------------|----|
| WHS | 48 | ALLEGHENY | 12 |
| WHS | 6 | CARRICK | 44 |
| WHS | 36 | GLADSTONE | 0 |
| WHS | 28 | OLIVER | 18 |
| WHS | 22 | PERRY | 14 |
| WHS | 0 | SOUTH | 14 |
| WHS | 18 | SOUTH HILLS | 12 |
| WHS | 12 | SOUTH | 14 (Playoff) |

**CITY CHAMPIONSHIP PLAYOFF**
**CARRICK 30 PEABODY    6**

**1970 (9-0-0)**

| WHS | 26 | ALLDERDICE | 6 |
|-----|----|------------|----|
| WHS | 44 | ALLEGHENY | 6 |
| WHS | 26 | CARRICK | 6 |
| WHS | 40 | GLADSTONE | 0 |
| WHS | 26 | LANGLEY | 0 |
| WHS | 44 | PEABODY | 20 |
| WHS | 22 | PERRY | 0 |
| WHS | 28 | SOUTH HILLS | 6 |

**CITY CHAMPIONSHIP PLAYOFF**
**WHS   26    CARRICK    6**

393

**1971 (7-1-0)**

| WHS | 52 | FIFTH AVE | 0 |
|-----|----|-----------|----|
| WHS | 20 | GLADSTONE | 10 |
| WHS | 14 | LANGLEY | 2 |
| WHS | 28 | PEABODY | 32 |
| WHS | 32 | PERRY | 8 |
| WHS | 18 | SCHENLEY | 0 |
| WHS | 50 | SOUTH | 6 |
| WHS | 48 | SOUTH HILLS | 12 |

**CITY CHAMPIONSHIP PLAYOFF**
**PEABODY 44 ALLDERDICE        12**

**1972 (5-2-1)**

| WHS | 0 | ALLDERDICE | 6 |
|-----|----|------------|----|
| WHS | 33 | FIFTH AVE | 0 |
| WHS | 8 | LANGLEY | 12 |
| WHS | 26 | OLIVER | 0 |
| WHS | 34 | PEABODY | 0 |
| WHS | 8 | PERRY | 8 |
| WHS | 16 | SCHENLEY | 6 |
| WHS | 36 | SOUTH HILLS | 0 |

**CITY CHAMPIONSHIP PLAYOFF**
**CARRICK  28 ALLDERDICE        20**

**1973 (4-4-0)**

| WHS | 30 | ALLEGHENY | 0 |
|-----|----|-----------|----|
| WHS | 10 | CARRICK | 6 |
| WHS | 6 | LANGLEY | 8 |
| WHS | 0 | PEABODY | 16 |
| WHS | 0 | PERRY | 6 |
| WHS | 25 | SCHENLEY | 6 |
| WHS | 6 | SOUTH | 24 |
| WHS | 20 | SOUTH HILLS | 12 |

**CITY CHAMPIONSHIP PLAYOFF**
**PERRY 38    SOUTH        6**

**1974 (4-4-0)*        *(7-1-0)**

| WHS | 6 | GLADSTONE | 0 *(FL) |
|-----|----|-----------|----|
| WHS | 22 | OLIVER | 8 *(FL) |
| WHS | 32 | PEABODY | 6 *(FL) |
| WHS | 14 | ALLEGHENY | 18 |
| WHS | 22 | CARRICK | 6 |
| WHS | 50 | LANGLEY | 0 |
| WHS | 8 | PERRY | 6 |
| WHS | 46 | SOUTH HILLS | 0 |

**CITY CHAMPIONSHIP PLAYOFF**
**PEABODY 20 PERRY        0**
*(FL) Forfeit 3 games for ineligible player.

**1975 (7-2-0)**

| | | | |
|---|---|---|---|
| WHS | 32 | ALLDERDICE | 0 |
| WHS | 8 | FIFTH AVE | 0 |
| WHS | 16 | GLADSTONE | 0 |
| WHS | 20 | LANGLEY | 6 |
| WHS | 30 | OLIVER | 0 |
| WHS | 14 | PEABODY | 0 |
| WHS | 0 | PERRY | 14 |
| WHS | 12 | SOUTH HILLS | 8 |
| WHS | 12 | CARRICK | 20 (PLAYOFF) |

**CITY CHAMPIONSHIP PLAYOFF**
**PERRY 14    CARRICK    0**

**1976 (7-0-2)**

| | | | |
|---|---|---|---|
| WHS | 45 | ALLDERDICE | 0 |
| WHS | 33 | ALLEGHENY | 0 |
| WHS | 27 | BRASHEAR | 0 |
| WHS | 26 | CARRICK | 14 |
| WHS | 50 | OLIVER | 0 |
| WHS | 14 | PERRY | 0 |
| WHS | 30 | SOUTH | 6 |
| WHS | 12 | SOUTH HILLS | 12 |

**CITY CHAMPIONSHIP PLAYOFF**
**WHS    20    PEABODY    20**
**(CO-CHAMPIONS)**

**1977 (7-2-0)**

| | | | |
|---|---|---|---|
| WHS | 18 | ALLDERDICE | 6 |
| WHS | 18 | BRASHEAR | 0 |
| WHS | 14 | LANGLEY | 9 |
| WHS | 20 | PEABODY | 18 |
| WHS | 20 | PERRY | 0 |
| WHS | 20 | SCHENLEY | 6 |
| WHS | 10 | SOUTH | 14 |
| WHS | 18 | SOUTH HILLS | 0 |

**CITY CHAMPIONSHIP PLAYOFF**
**SOUTH 22    WESTINGHOUSE 0**

**1978 (3-5-0)**

| | | | |
|---|---|---|---|
| WHS | 16 | ALLDERDICE | 0 |
| WHS | 14 | ALLEGHENY | 8 |
| WHS | 14 | BRASHEAR | 26 |
| WHS | 12 | CARRICK | 8 |
| WHS | 6 | OLIVER | 18 |
| WHS | 0 | PERRY | 8 |
| WHS | 16 | SCHENLEY | 18 |
| WHS | 20 | SOUTH | 42 |

**CITY CHAMPIONSHIP PLAYOFF**
**PEABODY 13 PERRY    8**

**1979 (4-3-1)**

| | | | |
|---|---|---|---|
| WHS | 14 | ALLEGHENY | 14 |
| WHS | 6 | LANGLEY | 0 |
| WHS | 6 | OLIVER | 0 |
| WHS | 16 | PEABODY | 18 |
| WHS | 8 | PERRY | 0 |
| WHS | 6 | SCHENLEY | 12 |
| WHS | 52 | SOUTH | 0 |
| WHS | 0 | SOUTH HILLS | 13 |

**CITY CHAMPIONSHIP PLAYOFF**
**BRASHEAR 8    PEABODY 7**

**1980 (5-3-1)**

| | | | |
|---|---|---|---|
| WHS | 14 | PUNXSUTAWNEY | 22 |
| WHS | 20 | ALLDERDICE | 6 |
| WHS | 12 | ALLEGHENY | 6 |
| WHS | 8 | BRASHEAR | 24 |
| WHS | 8 | CARRICK | 12 |
| WHS | 20 | OLIVER | 0 |
| WHS | 18 | PERRY | 6 |
| WHS | 21 | SCHENLEY | 21 |
| WHS | 42 | SOUTH | 20 |

**CITY CHAMPIONSHIP PLAYOFF**
**BRASHEAR 8 PEABODY    0**

394

**1981 (10-1-0)**

| WHS | 13 | PUNXSUTAWNEY | 0 |
|---|---|---|---|
| WHS | 58 | ALLEGHENY | 7 |
| WHS | 18 | LANGLEY | 14 |
| WHS | 26 | OLIVER | 0 |
| WHS | 6 | PEABODY | 7 |
| WHS | 17 | PERRY | 13 |
| WHS | 7 | SCHENLEY | 0 |
| WHS | 37 | SOUTH | 6 |
| WHS | 24 | SOUTH HILLS | 0 |
| WHS | 19 | CARRICK | 12 (PLAYOFF) |

**CITY CHAMPIONSHIP PLAYOFF**
**WHS  12    PEABODY    7**

**1982 (8-2-0)**

| WHS | 19 | INDIANA | 27 |
|---|---|---|---|
| WHS | 20 | CLAIRTON | 19 |
| WHS | 34 | ALLDERDICE | 6 |
| WHS | 21 | BRASHEAR | 8 |
| WHS | 21 | CARRICK | 13 |
| WHS | 14 | OLIVER | 6 |
| WHS | 22 | PERRY | 0 |
| WHS | 22 | SCHENLEY | 12 |
| WHS | 50 | SOUTH | 6 |

**CITY CHAMPIONSHIP PLAYOFF**
**BRASHEAR 13  WESTINGHOUSE 6**

**1983 (6-4-0)**

| WHS | 6 | CLAIRTON | 14 |
|---|---|---|---|
| WHS | 14 | ERIE CATH. PREP | 34 |
| WHS | 0 | LANGLEY | 28 |
| WHS | 28 | OLIVER | 6 |
| WHS | 42 | PEABODY | 6 |
| WHS | 16 | PERRY | 8 |
| WHS | 20 | SCHENLEY | 0 |
| WHS | 28 | SOUTH | 0 |
| WHS | 20 | SOUTH HILLS | 8 |
| WHS | 0 | CARRICK | 23 (PLAYOFF) |

**CITY CHAMPIONSHIP PLAYOFF**
**CARRICK 13 LANGLEY    6**

**1984 (6-3-0)**

| WHS | 12 | KNOCH | 40 |
|---|---|---|---|
| WHS | 0 | ALLDERDICE | 7 |
| WHS | 7 | BRASHEAR | 8 |
| WHS | 40 | CARRICK | 0 |
| WHS | 34 | OLIVER | 6 |
| WHS | 7 | PERRY | 0 |
| WHS | 52 | SCHENLEY | 0 |
| WHS | 22 | SOUTH | 6 |
| WHS | 25 | SOUTH HILLS | 0 |

**CITY CHAMPIONSHIP PLAYOFF**
**BRASHEAR 7  LANGLEY  6**

395

**1985 (4-4-0)**

| WHS | 6 | GERMAN TWP. | 19 |
|---|---|---|---|
| WHS | 21 | LANGLEY | 14 |
| WHS | 24 | SCHENLEY | 12 |
| WHS | 13 | OLIVER | 6 |
| WHS | 0 | RIVERVIEW | 20 |
| WHS | 29 | SOUTH | 20 |
| WHS | 6 | PERRY | 15 |
| WHS | 13 | PEABODY | 18 |

**CITY CHAMPIONSHIP PLAYOFF**
**BRASHEAR 31 PERRY        0**

**1986 (5-6-0)**

| WHS | 0 | ELLWOOD CITY | 19 |
|---|---|---|---|
| WHS | 34 | CARRICK | 6 |
| WHS | 8 | LANGLEY | 6 |
| WHS | 26 | OLIVER | 7 |
| WHS | 12 | PEABODY | 7 |
| WHS | 14 | PERRY | 48 |
| WHS | 8 | SCHENLEY | 6 |
| WHS | 0 | SOUTH | 14 |
| WHS | 0 | ALLDERDICE | 6 |
| WHS | 6 | BRASHEAR | 61 |

**PLAYOFFS**
**CITY LEAGUE SEMI-FINALS**
PERRY 35     WESTINGHOUSE 6
BRASHEAR 21          SOUTH     0
**CITY LEAGUE FINAL**
PERRY 26     BRASHEAR          0

## 1987 (5-4-0)

| | | | |
|---|---|---|---|
| WHS | 7 | CARRICK | 26 |
| WHS | 10 | LANGLEY | 12 |
| WHS | 7 | OLIVER | 0 |
| WHS | 54 | PEABODY | 0 |
| WHS | 7 | PERRY | 12 |
| WHS | 23 | SCHENLEY | 0 |
| WHS | 16 | SOUTH | 8 |
| WHS | 27 | ALLDERDICE | 14 |
| WHS | 7 | BRASHEAR | 18 |

**PLAYOFFS**
**CITY LEAGUE SEMI-FINALS**

| | | | |
|---|---|---|---|
| BRASHEAR | 19 | CARRICK | 0 |
| PERRY | 14 | LANGLEY | 9 |

**CITY LEAGUE FINAL**

| | | | |
|---|---|---|---|
| BRASHEAR | 22 | PERRY | 0 |

## 1988 (5-3-2)

| | | | |
|---|---|---|---|
| WHS | 7 | BRASHEAR | 34 |
| WHS | 20 | CARRICK | 0 |
| WHS | 19 | LANGLEY | 19 |
| WHS | 7 | OLIVER | 0 |
| WHS | 14 | PEABODY | 6 |
| WHS | 12 | PERRY | 15 |
| WHS | 0 | SCHENLEY | 0 |
| WHS | 26 | SOUTH | 0 |
| WHS | 7 | ALLDERDICE | 0 |

**PLAYOFFS**
**CITY LEAGUE SEMI-FINALS**

| | | | |
|---|---|---|---|
| BRASHEAR | 36 | WESTINGHOUSE | 0 |
| PERRY | 15 | LANGLEY | 0 |

**CITY LEAGUE FINAL**

| | | | |
|---|---|---|---|
| BRASHEAR | 28 | PERRY | 12 |

**PIAA STATE AAAA SEMI-FINAL**

| | | | |
|---|---|---|---|
| CENTRAL CATH. | 19 | BRASHEAR | 14 |

**PIAA STATE AAAA FINAL**

| | | | |
|---|---|---|---|
| CENTRAL CATH. | 14 | CEDAR CLIFF | 7 |

**Note:** First year for City League in PIAA Playoffs

## 1989 (9-3-0)

| | | | |
|---|---|---|---|
| WHS | 56 | QUIGLEY | 0 |
| WHS | 34 | ALLDERDICE | 8 |
| WHS | 14 | BRASHEAR | 0 |
| WHS | 24 | CARRICK | 6 |
| WHS | 21 | LANGLEY | 0 |
| WHS | 20 | OLIVER | 8 |
| WHS | 7 | PEABODY | 22 |
| WHS | 0 | PERRY | 8 |
| WHS | 20 | SCHENLEY | 8 |
| WHS | 25 | SOUTH | 0 |

**PLAYOFFS**
**CITY LEAGUE SEMI-FINALS**

| | | | |
|---|---|---|---|
| WHS | 27 | PEABODY | 21 |
| PERRY | 22 | BRASHEAR | 0 |

**CITY LEAGUE FINAL**

| | | | |
|---|---|---|---|
| PERRY | 7 | WESTINGHOUSE | 6 |

**PIAA STATE AAA SEMI-FINAL**

| | | | |
|---|---|---|---|
| PERRY | 20 | GREENSBURG SALEM | 0 |

**PIAA STATE AAA FINAL**

| | | | |
|---|---|---|---|
| PERRY | 20 | BERWICK | 8 |

NOTE: PERRY WON BOTH CITY LEAGUE AND STATE AAA TITLES

## 1990 (6-5-0)

| | | | |
|---|---|---|---|
| WHS | 6 | BUTLER | 37 |
| WHS | 46 | SOUTH | 0 |
| WHS | 0 | ALLDERDICE | 13 |
| WHS | 19 | BRASHEAR | 6 |
| WHS | 40 | CARRICK | 0 |
| WHS | 45 | LANGLEY | 6 |
| WHS | 13 | OLIVER | 14 |
| WHS | 21 | PEABODY | 6 |
| WHS | 0 | PERRY | 43 |
| WHS | 32 | SCHENLEY | 14 |

**PLAYOFFS**
**CITY LEAGUE SEMI-FINALS**

| | | | |
|---|---|---|---|
| PERRY | 13 | WESTINGHOUSE | 6 |
| OLIVER | 40 | ALLDERDICE | 0 |

**CITY LEAGUE FINAL**

| | | | |
|---|---|---|---|
| PERRY | 6 | OLIVER | 0 |

**PIAA STATE AAA SEMI-FINAL**

| | | | |
|---|---|---|---|
| SETON LA SALLE | 10 | PERRY | 6 |

**396**

## 1991 (8-4-0)

| | | | |
|---|---|---|---|
| WHS | 0 | BUTLER | 35 |
| WHS | 41 | SCHENLEY | 20 |
| WHS | 26 | SOUTH | 0 |
| WHS | 8 | ALLDERDICE | 14 |
| WHS | 12 | BRASHEAR | 14 |
| WHS | 13 | CARRICK | 12 |
| WHS | 37 | LANGLEY | 0 |
| WHS | 14 | OLIVER | 6 |
| WHS | 27 | PEABODY | 0 |
| WHS | 16 | PERRY | 8 |

**PLAYOFFS**
**CITY LEAGUE SEMI-FINALS**

| | | | |
|---|---|---|---|
| WHS | 13 | SCHENLEY | 0 |
| PERRY | 39 | BRASHEAR | 0 |

**CITY LEAGUE FINAL**
PERRY 14 WESTINGHOUSE 11
**PIAA STATE AAA QTR. FINAL**
LOCK HAVEN 14 PERRY 6
**PIAA STATE AAAA QTR. FINAL**
STATE COLLEGE 9 BRASHEAR 6

## 1992 (11-1-0)

| | | | |
|---|---|---|---|
| WHS | 17 | PERRY | 3 |
| WHS | 52 | SCHENLEY | 0 |
| WHS | 32 | SOUTH | 6 |
| WHS | 45 | ALLDERDICE | 0 |
| WHS | 44 | BRASHEAR | 0 |
| WHS | 49 | CARRICK | 7 |
| WHS | 47 | LANGLEY | 0 |
| WHS | 54 | OLIVER | 0 |
| WHS | 54 | PEABODY | 0 |

**PLAYOFFS**
**CITY LEAGUE SEMI-FINALS**

| | | | |
|---|---|---|---|
| WHS | 56 | SCHENLEY | 0 |
| PERRY | 14 | ALLDERDICE | 0 |

**CITY LEAGUE FINAL**
WHS 15 PERRY 6
**PIAA STATE AAA QTR. FINAL**
LOCK HAVEN 20 WESTINGHOUSE 19
**PIAA STATE AAAA QTR. FINAL**
STATE COLLEGE 38 ALLDERDICE 0

397

## 1993 (10-2-0)

| | | | |
|---|---|---|---|
| WHS | 20 | PEABODY | 0 |
| WHS | 35 | PERRY | 13 |
| WHS | 20 | SCHENLEY | 28 |
| WHS | 53 | SOUTH | 0 |
| WHS | 36 | ALLDERDICE | 0 |
| WHS | 14 | BRASHEAR | 12 |
| WHS | 34 | CARRICK | 0 |
| WHS | 44 | LANGLEY | 0 |
| WHS | 36 | OLIVER | 8 |

**PLAYOFFS**
**CITY LEAGUE SEMI-FINALS**

| | | | |
|---|---|---|---|
| WHS | 22 | PEABODY | 13 |
| PERRY | 20 | SCHENLEY | 14 |

**CITY LEAGUE FINAL**
WHS 40 PERRY 0
**PIAA STATE AAA QTR. FINAL**
LOCK HAVEN 13 WESTINGHOUSE 8

## 1994 (4-4-1)

| | | | |
|---|---|---|---|
| WHS | 22 | OLIVER | 22 |
| WHS | 12 | PEABODY | 26 |
| WHS | 20 | PERRY | 14 |
| WHS | 14 | SCHENLEY | 19 |
| WHS | 64 | SOUTH | 0 |
| WHS | 26 | ALLDERDICE | 0 |
| WHS | 40 | BRASHEAR | 41 |
| WHS | 16 | CARRICK | 0 |
| WHS | 14 | LANGLEY | 19 |

**PLAYOFFS**
**CITY LEAGUE SEMI-FINALS**

| | | | |
|---|---|---|---|
| PEABODY | 40 | ALLDERDICE | 8 |
| SCHENLEY | 21 | PERRY | 14 |

**CITY LEAGUE FINAL**
PEABODY 8 SCHENLEY 7
**PIAA STATE AAA QTR. FINAL**
SHARON 29 PEABODY 7
**PIAA STATE AAAA QTR. FINAL**
ERIE CENTRAL 24 SCHENLEY 0

**1995 (9-3-0)**

| WHS | 22 | LANGLEY | 16 |
|---|---|---|---|
| WHS | 16 | OLIVER | 21 |
| WHS | 6 | PEABODY | 2 |
| WHS | 6 | PERRY | 7 |
| WHS | 35 | SCHENLEY | 0 |
| WHS | 41 | SOUTH | 6 |
| WHS | 14 | ALLDERDICE | 0 |
| WHS | 49 | BRASHEAR | 6 |
| WHS | 20 | CARRICK | 0 |

**PLAYOFFS**
**CITY LEAGUE SEMI-FINALS**

| WHS | 14 | SCHENLEY | 0 |
|---|---|---|---|
| PEABODY | 20 | PERRY | 12 |

**CITY LEAGUE FINAL**

| WHS | 24 | PEABODY | 12 |
|---|---|---|---|

**PIAA STATE AAA QTR. FINAL**

| SHARON | 34 | WESTINGHOUSE | 0 |
|---|---|---|---|

**PIAA STATE AAAA QTR. FINAL**

| ERIE McDOWELL | 42 | SCHENLEY | 6 |
|---|---|---|---|

**1996 (10-2-0)**

| WHS | 30 | CARRICK | 6 |
|---|---|---|---|
| WHS | 54 | LANGLEY | 6 |
| WHS | 24 | OLIVER | 13 |
| WHS | 18 | PEABODY | 27 |
| WHS | 22 | PERRY | 12 |
| WHS | 17 | SCHENLEY | 13 |
| **WHS** | **21** | **SOUTH** | **0 (500th win)** |
| WHS | 33 | ALLDERDICE | 6 |
| WHS | 48 | BRASHEAR | 0 |

**PLAYOFFS**
**CITY LEAGUE SEMI-FINALS**

| WHS | 19 | PERRY | 3 |
|---|---|---|---|
| PEABODY | 14 | SCHENLEY | 12 |

**CITY LEAGUE FINAL**

| WHS | 40 | PEABODY | 12 |
|---|---|---|---|

**PIAA STATE AAA QTR. FINAL**

| GREENVILLE | 29 | WESTINGHOUSE | 6 |
|---|---|---|---|

**PIAA STATE AAAA QTR. FINAL**

| ERIE McDOWELL | 25 | SCHENLEY | 6 |
|---|---|---|---|

398

**1997 (7-3-0)**

| WHS | 21 | BRASHEAR | 20 |
|---|---|---|---|
| WHS | 56 | CARRICK | 0 |
| WHS | 44 | LANGLEY | 0 |
| WHS | 6 | OLIVER | 0 |
| WHS | 45 | PEABODY | 0 |
| WHS | 0 | PERRY | 39 |
| WHS | 0 | SCHENLEY | 27 |
| WHS | 40 | SOUTH | 6 |
| WHS | 14 | ALLDERDICE | 12 |

**PLAYOFFS**
**CITY LEAGUE SEMI-FINALS**

| SCHENLEY | 33 | WESTINGHOUSE | 28 |
|---|---|---|---|
| PERRY | 59 | BRASHEAR | 0 |

**CITY LEAGUE FINAL**

| PERRY | 34 | SCHENLEY | 6 |
|---|---|---|---|

**PIAA STATE AAAA 1ST ROUND**

| ERIE McDOWELL | 45 | SCHENLEY | 12 |
|---|---|---|---|

**PIAA STATE AAA 1ST ROUND**

| PERRY | 41 | GREENVILLE | 0 |
|---|---|---|---|

**PIAA STATE AAA 2ND ROUND**

| PERRY | 27 | HUNTINGDON | 19 |
|---|---|---|---|

**PIAA STATE AAA SEMI-FINAL**

| PERRY | 29 | W. ALLEGHENY | 17 |
|---|---|---|---|

**PIAA STATE AAA FINAL**

| BERWICK | 17 | PERRY | 14 |
|---|---|---|---|

**1998 (5-4-0)**

| WHS | 24 | ALLDERDICE | 6 |
|---|---|---|---|
| WHS | 20 | BRASHEAR | 40 |
| WHS | 44 | CARRICK | 6 |
| WHS | 56 | LANGLEY | 6 |
| WHS | 6 | OLIVER | 7 |
| WHS | 32 | PEABODY | 24 |
| WHS | 0 | PERRY | 47 |
| WHS | 6 | SCHENLEY | 46 |
| WHS | 20 | SOUTH | 17 |

**PLAYOFFS**
**CITY LEAGUE SEMI-FINALS**

| PERRY | 28 | OLIVER | 14 |
|---|---|---|---|
| SCHENLEY | 34 | BRASHEAR | 14 |

**CITY LEAGUE FINAL**

| PERRY | 26 | SCHENLEY | 6 |
|---|---|---|---|

**PIAA STATE AAAA 1st ROUND**

| ERIE CATH PREP | 36 | SCHENLEY | 0 |
|---|---|---|---|

**PIAA STATE AAA 1st ROUND**

| PERRY | 54 | OIL CITY | 6 |
|---|---|---|---|

**PIAA STATE AAA 2ND ROUND**

| HUNTINGDON | 44 | PERRY | 18 |
|---|---|---|---|

**1999 (2-7-0)**

| WHS | 19 | SOUTH | 36 |
|---|---|---|---|
| WHS | 0 | ALLDERDICE | 20 |
| WHS | 8 | BRASHEAR | 29 |
| WHS | 24 | CARRICK | 14 |
| WHS | 54 | LANGLEY | 6 |
| WHS | 12 | OLIVER | 21 |
| WHS | 19 | PEABODY | 22 |
| WHS | 14 | PERRY | 30 |
| WHS | 7 | SCHENLEY | 35 |

**PLAYOFFS**
**CITY LEAGUE SEMI-FINALS**

| OLIVER 20 | PERRY | 14 |
|---|---|---|
| SCHENLEY 24 | BRASHEAR | 21 |

**CITY LEAGUE FINAL**

| SCHENLEY 41 | OLIVER | 27 |
|---|---|---|

**2000 (5-4-0)**

| WHS | 11 | SCHENLEY | 21 |
|---|---|---|---|
| WHS | 26 | SOUTH | 8 |
| WHS | 18 | ALLDERDICE | 20 |
| WHS | 21 | BRASHEAR | 14 |
| WHS | 20 | CARRICK | 6 |
| WHS | 34 | LANGLEY | 0 |
| WHS | 12 | OLIVER | 22 |
| WHS | 23 | PEABODY | 8 |
| WHS | 9 | PERRY | 34 |

**PLAYOFFS**
**CITY LEAGUE SEMI-FINALS**

| ALLDERDICE 39 | BRASHEAR | 7 |
|---|---|---|
| PERRY 35 | OLIVER | 0 |

**CITY LEAGUE FINAL**

| PERRY 6 | ALLDERDICE | 0 |
|---|---|---|

**2001 (9-2-0)**

| WHS | 0 | PERRY | 46 |
|---|---|---|---|
| WHS | 27 | SCHENLEY | 22 |
| WHS | 27 | SOUTH | 0 |
| WHS | 33 | ALLDERDICE | 13 |
| WHS | 21 | BRASHEAR | 17 |
| WHS | 44 | CARRICK | 0 |
| WHS | 38 | LANGLEY | 6 |
| WHS | 16 | OLIVER | 0 |
| WHS | 21 | PEABODY | 15 |

**PLAYOFFS**
**CITY LEAGUE SEMI-FINALS**

| WHS 22 | PEABODY | 0 |
|---|---|---|
| PERRY 46 | BRASHEAR | 0 |

**CITY LEAGUE FINAL**
**PERRY 14 WESTINGHOUSE 6**

**PIAA STATE AAAA 1ST ROUND**
**ERIE CATH. PREP 41 BRASHEAR 9**

**PIAA STATE AAA 1ST ROUND**
**PERRY 35 WILMINGTON 7**

**PIAA STATE AAA 2ND ROUND**
**PERRY 41 BRADFORD 7**

**PIAA STATE AAA SEMI FINAL**
**WEST ALLEGHENY 28 PERRY 14**

**PIAA STATE AAA FINAL**
**W. ALLEGHENY 28**
**STRATH HAVEN 13**

399

# No. 1: Donora in '45

Donora High's 1945 Dragons, from left: linemen Bill Samer, Ed Duda, Rudy Andabaker, Ernest "Pappy" Ross, Tom Buchak, Karl Pell, Andy Lelik, and backs Lou Cecconi, Roscoe Ross, Dan Towler, Francis DeFelicis.

400

## The readers' top 20

| School | Year | Votes |
|---|---|---|
| 1. Donora | 1945 | 20 |
| 2. Monessen | 1961 | 17 |
| 3. Donora | 1944 | 15 |
| 4. New Castle | 1970 | 14 |
| 5. Mt. Lebanon | 1981 | 11 |
| 6. Central Catholic | 1951 | 10 |
| 7. Beaver Falls | 1960 | 8 |
| Central Catholic | 1964 | 8 |
| 9. Westinghouse | 1951 | 7 |
| 10. North Braddock Scott | 1934 | 6 |
| North Allegheny | 1982 | 6 |
| 11. Brownsville | 1940 | 5 |
| Penn Hills | 1979 | 5 |
| 12. Latrobe | 1968 | 4 |
| North Catholic | 1970 | 4 |
| 13. Clairton | 1954 | 3 |
| Connellsville | 1941 | 3 |
| New Kensington | 1947 | 3 |
| Thomas Jefferson | 1980 | 3 |
| Westinghouse | 1948 | 3 |

## The experts' top 10

| School | Year | Pts. |
|---|---|---|
| 1. Donora | 1945 | 14 |
| 2. Monessen | 1961 | 8 |
| 3. New Castle | 1970 | 5 |
| 4. Beaver Falls | 1960 | 4 |
| 5. Butler | 1964 | 3 |
| Wilkinsburg | 1957 | 3 |
| North Catholic | 1970 | 3 |
| Braddock | 1958 | 3 |
| Westinghouse | 1951 | 3 |
| Mt. Lebanon | 1981 | 3 |

# THE WESTINGHOUSE BULLDOG'S
# VAUNTED SINGLE WING OFFENSE

When Pete Dimperio arrived at Westinghouse in 1946 he inherited a single-wing offense that had existed at Westinghouse since 1916. He fine tuned it with his own strategic variations that required precision timing, speed and deception in an effort to confuse the defense. In practice he believed in running the same play over and over until he was satisfied that it was perfectly executed. This was his way of making sure everyone was on the same page. Many marveled at the way the Bulldog offense performed the single wing offense as it was likened to watching a clinic. The following plays reflect this explosive offense that Coach Pete Dimperio generated so effectively for twenty-one years (1946-1966) at Westinghouse High School.

## LEGEND:

[X] Offensive center
O   Offensive player
•   Intended ball carrier
◑   Optional ball carrier
X   Defensive player

**401**

O O O[X] O O O   Balanced line

O O [X] O O O O   Unbalanced line right

O O O O [X] O O   Unbalanced line left

**NOTES:** In this offense the following is essential:

1. Speed, deception and timely execution of blocks.
2. Quarterback is a versatile back in this offense.
3. Pulling linemen are keys to effective lead blocking.
4. Overall team speed, execution and timing are a must.
5. Center position is the take charge leader.
6. Fullback has the ability to spin smoothly and handle the ball with precision timing.
7. Knowing what every position player is required to do on each play.

### 1.  Left Halfback Off-tackle

*On this play the left halfback takes center snap and follows his convoy of blockers around the right side.*

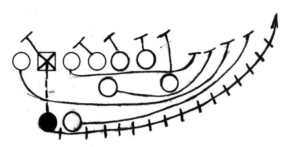

### 2.  Fullback Inside Tackle(inside power play)

*On this play the fullback takes center snap and follows the blocking of his quarterback and right halfback going inside right tackle.*

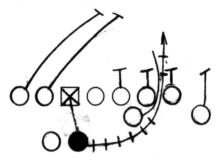

402

### 3.  Right Halfback Reverse with Option to Pass (a misdirection play)

*On this play the fullback takes center snap and runs right. The left halfback also runs right.  However on a slick maneuver the right halfback takes a hand off from the fullback and runs around left side following the blocking of his quarterback and tackle.*

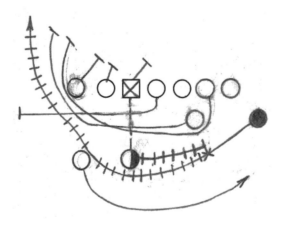

**4. Fullback Inside Trap Option Pass (a misdirection play)**

*Both left halfback and right halfback run left as the fullback takes the center snap and fakes a hand-off to the quarterback (who also runs left), the fullback then runs up the middle behind the trap block by the right tackle.*

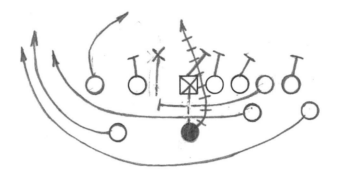

**5. Right Halfback (in motion) Sweep**

*On this play the fullback takes snap from center and hands off to the right halfback (who is in motion to the left). The right halfback takes the ball and follows his blocking around the left side.*

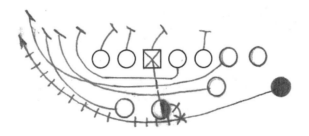

**403**

## FULLBACK SPINNER SERIES

**NOTE: In this series of plays the fullback executes a 360 degree spin after receiving the snap from center as he hands off or keeps the ball. Overall execution of movement, faking and timing by the all the backs is the key to confusing the defense.**

**6. Fullback Keeper With Right Halfback in Motion**

*On this play the fullback will spin and fake to both halfbacks and will keep the ball and take it up the middle behind the left pulling guard.*

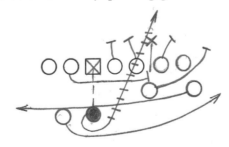

### 7. Right Halfback (in motion) Reverse

*On this play the left halfback takes a handoff from a spinning fullback then in a split second the left halfback hands off to the right halfback who is in motion left. Two linemen have pulled to the left to block along with the quarterback who is also blocking for the ball carrier (left halfback).*

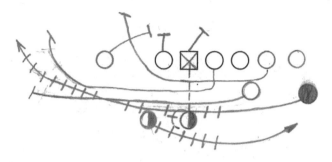

### 8. Left Halfback Run or Pass

*On this play the left halfback takes a handoff from the spinning fullback and has the option of either running right or passing down field.*

**404**

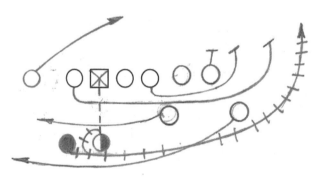

### 9. Right Halfback Inside Reverse

*On this play the spinning fullback takes center snap, fakes to both the left halfback and quarterback but hands off to the right halfback who follows the left tackles trap block up the middle.*

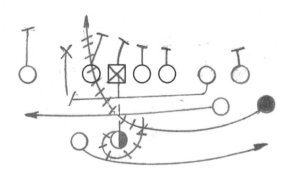

## BUCK LATERAL SERIES

**NOTE:** The buck lateral series has two important variations that enable the quarterback to be positioned so he can receive handoffs and/or handle the ball for pitchouts.

### 10.  Quarterback Pitchout to Left Halfback Sweep
*On this play the quarterback takes handoff from the spinning fullback, runs to the right and pitches to the trailing left halfback who also sweeps wide to the right.*

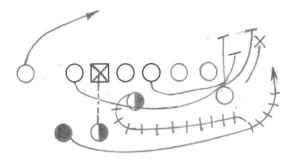

### 11.  Right Halfback Inside Reverse
*On this play fullback takes center snap starts toward the offensive line and hands off to the quarterback who then hands off to the right halfback who runs behind a trap block by the right tackle.*

**405**

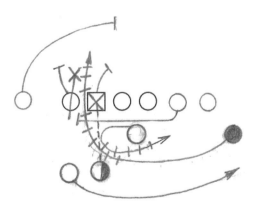

## 12. Fullback Keeper

*On this play the fullback takes center snap and takes off through the right tackle hole. The fake executed by the quarterback that is intended to fool the defensive player while the two halfbacks are also moving left and right respectively. This is a power run up the middle with the quarterback and both halfbacks executing fakes to fool the defense.*

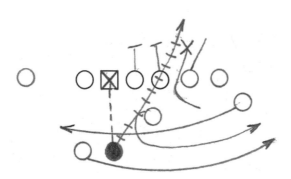

**NOTE: In this offense any one of the backs or receivers could be called upon to pass the ball.**

## 13. Quarterback Pass

*On this play fullback takes center snap and hands off to the quarterback to pass down field. The two halfbacks and the two ends break out to run pass patterns - flat, over the middle, side line and deep.*

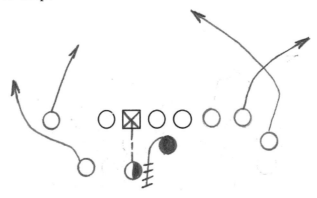

## 14. Short Punt With Option to Pass

*On this play quarterback takes center snap, motions to punt, but instead resets to pass long or short screen pass to back in the left flat.*

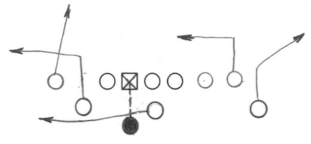

### 15. Fullback Pass Play

*On this play fullback takes center snap, spins and flips a short pass to the right halfback who follows a trap blocking right tackle up the middle.*

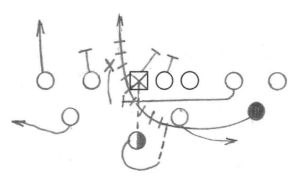

407

# PITTSBURGH CITY LEAGUE FOOTBALL CHAMPIONS

| | | | | |
|---|---|---|---|---|
| 1919 | Allegheny | | 1973 | Perry |
| 1920 | Fifth Avenue | | 1974 | Peabody |
| 1921 | Westinghouse | | 1975 | Perry |
| 1922 | Allegheny | | 1976 | Westinghouse, Peabody *(20-20 Tie)* |
| 1923 | Allegheny | | 1977 | South |
| 1924 | Schenley | | 1978 | Peabody |
| 1925 | Schenley | | 1979 | Brashear |
| 1926 | Schenley | | 1980 | Brashear |
| 1927 | Westinghouse | | 1981 | Westinghouse |
| 1928 | Westinghouse | | 1982 | Brashear |
| 1929 | Schenley | | 1983 | Carrick |
| 1930 | Westinghouse | | 1984 | Brashear |
| 1931 | South Hills | | 1985 | Brashear |
| 1932 | Perry | | 1986 | Perry |
| 1933 | Peabody | | 1987 | Brashear |
| 1934 | Westinghouse, Carrick *(6-6 Tie)* | | 1988 | Brashear |
| 1935 | South Hills | | 1989 | Perry |
| 1936 | South Hills | | 1990 | Perry |
| 1937 | South Hills | | 1991 | Perry |
| 1938 | Westinghouse | | 1992 | Westinghouse |
| 1939 | Westinghouse | | 1993 | Westinghouse |
| 1940 | Oliver, South Hills *(Co-champs)* | | 1994 | Peabody |
| 1941 | Westinghouse, Oliver *(Co-champs)* | | 1995 | Westinghouse |
| 1942 | Westinghouse, Oliver *(6-6 Tie)* | | 1996 | Westinghouse |
| 1943 | Schenley | | 1997 | Perry |
| 1944 | Westinghouse | | 1998 | Perry |
| 1945 | Westinghouse | | 1999 | Schenley |
| 1946 | Westinghouse | | 2000 | Perry |
| 1947 | Westinghouse | | 2001 | Perry |
| 1948 | Westinghouse | | 2002 | Perry |
| 1949 | Westinghouse | | 2003 | Perry |
| 1950 | Schenley | | 2004 | Perry |
| 1951 | Westinghouse | | 2005 | Perry |
| 1952 | Carrick | | 2006 | Oliver |
| 1953 | Peabody | | | |
| 1954 | Westinghouse | | | |
| 1955 | Westinghouse | | | |
| 1956 | Westinghouse | | | |
| 1957 | Westinghouse | | | |
| 1958 | Westinghouse | | | |
| 1959 | Westinghouse | | | |
| 1960 | Westinghouse | | | |
| 1961 | Westinghouse | | | |
| 1962 | Peabody | | | |
| 1963 | Westinghouse | | | |
| 1964 | Westinghouse | | | |
| 1965 | Westinghouse | | | |
| 1966 | Westinghouse | | | |
| 1967 | Allderdice | | | |
| 1968 | South Hills | | | |
| 1969 | Carrick | | | |
| 1970 | Westinghouse | | | |
| 1971 | Peabody | | | |
| 1972 | Carrick | | | |

**408**

# PITTSBURGH CITY LEAGUE FOOTBALL CHAMPIONS

| SCHOOL | NO. OF TITLES (YEARS) |
|---|---|
| ALLDERDICE | 1 (1967) |
| ALLEGHENY | 3 (1919,1922,1923) |
| BRASHEAR | 7 (1979,1980,1982,1984,1985,1987,1988) |
| CARRICK | 5 ( *1934,1952,1969,1972,1983) |
| FIFTH AVENUE | 1 (1920) |
| GLADSTONE | 0 ( Title games appeared in-1965,1966) |
| LANGLEY | 0 ( Title games appeared in-1961,1962,1964,1983,1984) |
| OLIVER | 4 ( *1940, *1941, *1942, 2006) |
| PEABODY | 8 (1933,1953,1962,1971,1974, *1976,1978,1994) |
| PERRY | 15 (1932,1973,1975,1986,1989,1990,1991, 1997,1998,2000, 2001,2002,2003,2004,2005) |
| SCHENLEY | 7 (1924,1925,1926,1929,1943,1950, 1999) |
| SOUTH | 1 (1977) |
| SOUTH HILLS | 6 (1931,1935,1936,1937,*1940,1968) |
| **WESTINGHOUSE** | **35** **(1921,1927,1928,1930,*1934,1938,1939,*1941,*1942, 1944,1945,1946,1947,1948,1949,1951,1954,1955, 1956,1957,1958,1959,1960,1961,1963,1964,1965, 1966,1970,*1976,1981,1992,1993,1995,1996)** |

**409**

*Indicates shared title (co-champion)

**NOTES:**

1) Westinghouse has qualified for playoff contention in 49 different years since 1919 (the first year Pittsburgh began crowning a City League Champion).
2) Westinghouse has qualified to play for the city title 44 times – winning 31

outright, sharing 4 as co-champions for a total of 35 while losing 9 title games and being runner-up (see 3 below).

3) Westinghouse finished the following 9 years as runner-up for the city title: 1932, 1935, 1936, 1967, 1977, 1982, 1989, 1991and 2001.

4) Westinghouse appeared as a play-off contender but were eliminated in the following 5 years: 1962, 1986, 1988, 1990, and 1997.

5) Westinghouse had to forfeit 3 games in 1974 due to an ineligible player, thus eliminating them from title contention.

**410**

## WESTINGHOUSE HIGH SCHOOL FOOTBALL RECORD

| YEARS | COACH | WHS vs City League | | | | WHS vs WPIAL/PIAA | | | | OVERALL | | | |
|---|---|---|---|---|---|---|---|---|---|---|---|---|---|
| | | W | L | T | Pct. | W | L | T | Pct. | W | L | T | Pct. |
| 1913 - 1915 | Hugh Robinson | 2 | 3 | 0 | 0.400 | 6 | 7 | 4 | 0.462 | 8 | 10 | 4 | 0.444 |
| 1916 - 1945 | O.H.'Pro' Burton | 123 | 34 | 13 | 0.783 | 26 | 31 | 10 | 0.456 | 149 | 65 | 23 | 0.696 |
| 1946 - 1966 | Peter P. Dimperio | 116 | 5 | 3 | 0.959 | 35 | 24 | 2 | 0.593 | 151 | 29 | 5 | 0.839 |
| 1967 - 1970 | Rudy Musilin | 28 | 7 | 0 | 0.800 | DNP | DNP | | | 28 | 7 | 0 | 0.800 |
| 1971 - 1977 | Fred Malins | 41 | 15 | 3 | 0.732 | DNP | DNP | | | 41 | 15 | 3 | 0.732 |
| 1978 - 2001 | George Webb | 153 | 68 | 5 | 0.692 | 3 | 14 | 0 | 0.176 | 156 | 82 | 5 | 0.655 |
| 1913 - 2001 | Overall | 463 | 132 | 24 | 0.778 | 70 | 76 | 16 | 0.479 | 533 | 208 | 40 | 0.719 |
| PLAYOFFS | | 39 | 14 | 5 | 0.736 | 0 | 4 | 1 | 0.000 | 39 | 18 | 6 | 0.684 |

411

Burton • Dimperio • Musilin • Malins • Webb

| WESTINGHOUSE HIGH SCHOOL FOOTBALL RECORD BY DECADES | | | | | | |
|---|---|---|---|---|---|---|
| YEARS | RECORD | PCT. | TITLES | | | COACHES |
| DECADES | W-L-T | | CITY | WPIAL | PIAA | |
| 1913-1919 | 16-21-7 | 0.432 | 0 | 0 | 0 | Robinson / Burton |
| 1920-1929 | 53-21-7 | 0.716 | 3 | 1 | 0 | Burton |
| 1930-1939 | 52-23-10 | 0.693 | 4 | 0 | 0 | Burton |
| 1940-1949 | 67-13-5 | 0.837 | 8 | 0 | 0 | Burton / Dimperio |
| 1950-1959 | 67-19-1 | 0.779 | 7 | 0 | 0 | Dimperio |
| 1960-1969 | 72-14-2 | 0.837 | 6 | 0 | 0 | Dimperio / Musilin |
| 1970-1979 | 57-23-4 | 0.712 | 2 | 0 | 0 | Musilin / Malins / Webb |
| 1980-1989 | 63-33-3 | 0.656 | 1 | 0 | 0 | Webb |
| 1990-1999 | 72-35-1 | 0.672 | 4 | 0 | 0 | Webb |
| 2000-2001 | 14-6-0 | 0.7 | 0 | 0 | 0 | Webb |
| 1913-2001 | 533-208-40 | 0.72 | 35 | 1 | 0 | Robinson/Burton/Dimperio/Musilin/Malins/Webb |

**NOTE: 1913 was first official season for Westinghouse**

412

# WESTINGHOUSE HIGH SCHOOL FOOTBALL SINCE 1913
## ROAD TO 500 WINS

| *YEAR | WON | LOST | TIED | PCT. |
|-------|-----|------|------|------|
| 1926 | 50 | 38 | 12 | 0.568 |
| 1936 | 102 | 61 | 23 | 0.625 |
| 1945 | 157 | 75 | 27 | 0.676 |
| 1951 | 201 | 82 | 29 | 0.71 |
| 1959 | 255 | 97 | 30 | 0.724 |
| 1965 | 302 | 102 | 32 | 0.748 |
| 1973 | 352 | 118 | 33 | 0.749 |
| 1982 | 407 | 140 | 37 | 0.744 |
| 1990 | 453 | 172 | 39 | 0.725 |
| 1996 | 504 | 189 | 40 | 0.727 |
| 2001 | 533 | 208 | 40 | 0.72 |

413

**\*Note:Years indicated are season ending.**

# From Westinghouse to the National Football League

Tony Liscio – Westinghouse High School Class of 1959
Dallas Cowboys – 1963 - 1971
*Source: NFL Encyclopedia*

Jon Henderson – Westinghouse High School Class of 1963
Pittsburgh Steelers – 1968 - 1969
Washington Redskins – 1970
*Source: NFL Encyclopedia*

Mark Ellison – Westinghouse High School Class of 1967
New York Giants – 1972 - 1973
*Source: NFL Encyclopedia*

David Kalina – Westinghouse High School Class of 1966
Pittsburgh Steelers 1970
*Source: NFL Encyclopedia*

Wesley Garnett – Westinghouse High School Class of 1966
San Diego Chargers
*Source: WHS Hall of Fame*

Eugene Harrison – Westinghouse High School Class of 1966
Pittsburgh Steelers
*Source: WHS Hall of Fame*

Melvin Myricks – Westinghouse High School Class of 1962
Kansas City Chiefs
*Source: WHS Hall of Fame*

**414**

# *A SPECIAL TRIBUTE*

415

**Maurice Stokes**

**Charles Cooper**

**Edward Fleming**

*Burton • Dimperio • Musilin • Malins • Webb*

## THE PRIDE FLOWED FROM SEASON TO SEASON

The key element of **Pride** at Westinghouse was a year round attribute ....
Regardless what the activity was the student body thrived on achievement .... When
a student or any of our teams or groups excelled we paid tribute to them in our
auditorium. Whether it was athletics, music or any other qualifying feat it was
honored at center stage. Our football team and its' winning ways was a prime
motivational feeder to the rest of the student body. Regardless of what was at stake
or on the line the pride factor was the mindset of every student. There were so many
individuals that excelled in so many endeavors that another book would have to be
written. I can recall one of my classmates, Tony Treser, a good all around student
athlete who excelled in swimming and won top honors in both City and State and was
awarded a full scholarship to the University of Pittsburgh. He was a fine example
who strived to be the best. Through hard work and perseverance Tony Treser
achieved his goal. I might add he carried that work ethic long after high school,
succeeding as a successful business entrepreneur. This is what Westinghouse High
School was all about.

Reflecting on how our winning ways continued from the football field to the
basketball arenas was priceless. Beginning way back in 1919 when the so called
"marvel team" took top honors in the City the Bulldogs contended and excelled on the
hardwood, but it wasn't until 1943 when Westinghouse finally took the city title
again. This was a time period when the winning ways of football carried over to the
winning ways of basketball, and became an obsession to be the best in the city in both
sports. The winning ways continued throughout the next three decades.

## FROM WESTINGHOUSE TO THE NBA

Although this book covers primarily my recollections and fond memories of
Westinghouse football, I cannot forget the glory years that our basketball program
had endured.  The first city championship of Pittsburgh in basketball was the 1919
Westinghouse Bulldogs.  They were called at that time the "Marvel Team".  It was the
first major sport championship that the Bulldogs had won.  Back then, it was huge
since it was the first year that the City of Pittsburgh crowned a high school city
champion in basketball.

It was many years later that Westinghouse basketball reached that championship
level again.  Football seemed to be the major interest of the young men who donned
the gold and blue of the Bulldogs during the early years.  Then by the early 1940's a
young man by the name of Charles Cooper emerged and made his presence known as
he guided the Westinghouse basketball program back to a championship playoff
contender.

The Bulldogs won back-to-back city titles in 1943 and 1944 as All-City and All-
State center Charles Cooper led the way. He was later to star at Duquesne University
where he had made All-American. I remember him quite well as he was a neighbor
who lived only a block away from our family.  We looked up to him with respect and

admiration. He was a credit to Westinghouse High School, Duquesne University and our City of Pittsburgh. He later broke the color barrier in the NBA as the Boston Celtics drafted him number one. We were quite proud of Cooper and since he was from my old neighborhood that made him very special to us young guys. He was the first to make it to the NBA from Westinghouse High School and that was quite an accomplishment. But there were two more to follow in his footsteps as the Homewood school produced basketball greats Maurice Stokes and Edward Fleming. They were both at Westinghouse when I was a student there. They gave us championship performances that many of us will long remember – especially the memorable playoffs in both the City League and PIAA States. The Bulldogs were basketball City Champions in 1948, 1950, 1951, 1952, 1953 and 1954. All of these teams were a credit to Westinghouse and the basketball program. Certainly our alumni were quite proud and inspired by the stellar performances of Cooper, Stokes and Fleming. During those championship years the Bulldogs had several good players who later went on to college and did quite well. But it was Cooper, Stokes and Fleming that gave Westinghouse High School that prestigious link to the NBA.

**Charles Cooper** – Westinghouse High School Class of 1944
    Duquesne University All-American
    Boston Celtics (NBA First round pick)
    Head of Parks and Recreation in Pittsburgh, PA
**Maurice Stokes** – Westinghouse High School Class of 1951
    St. Francis of Loretto, PA All-American
    Rochester Royals (NBA Rookie of the Year 1955-56)
    NAIA Basketball Hall of Fame
    Naismith Memorial Basketball Hall of Fame Class of 2004
**Edward Fleming** – Westinghouse High School Class of 1951
    Niagara University All-American
    Minneapolis Lakers (NBA)
    High School Basketball Coach (Westinghouse & Wilkinsburg)

**417**

The next time Westinghouse won a City Title in basketball was in 1972 led by Reggie Cox and Gary Stevens. That gave the Bulldogs their tenth City Title. So even though Westinghouse did not have the same consistency of success in basketball as they had in football they still produced many fine performers. They were playoff contenders year after year since that first title in 1919. Sometimes it is not always how many titles you win, but how well you performed to make people remember where you came from. The 1950s reflected an era of basketball at Westinghouse that produced some of the finest talent to come out of the Pittsburgh City League. Cooper, Stokes and Fleming set the stage for so many talented players in and around the Pittsburgh area. It became a hot bed for high school basketball throughout the following years. So many talented teams... Fifth Avenue, Schenley, Perry and Peabody were showing up year after year competing for State honors. There were so many talented players too many to mention by name who made it to the next level.

To this day the Pittsburgh City League can play with the best of the best. Looking back in history the following schools won PIAA State Titles: South High School in 1934 and 1937; Schenley High School in 1966, 1971, 1975, 1978 and 2007; Fifth Avenue High School in 1976. They were all great high school teams from the Pittsburgh area. The last time Westinghouse won a city title in basketball was 1998. The Bulldogs were led by Ricky Richburg that year as they captured the eleventh City Title in school history. Richburg later went on to star at Robert Morris University.

In recent years the open enrollment policy or magnet programs have affected Westinghouse in all athletics and basketball is certainly one program that has really felt the wrath of this proposition. I sincerely feel this enrollment re-alignment has created more negatives than positives for all of the city schools in Pittsburgh. In fact I would gladly sit down to discuss and/or defend my heartfelt feelings with any school administrator regarding this present day system. In one strong statement and I quote: "Why try to fix something that does not need to be fixed." It literally took away the values of school and community pride. How sad to see such a wholesome value disappearing from our Pittsburgh communities.

## THEY PERSEVERED WITH A SQUAD OF SEVEN

**418**

The 1999/2000 basketball season at Westinghouse began with thirteen pretty good ball players, but coach Nate Lofton ended up with only seven on the squad. In spite of this unfortunate development, they still managed to make it to the final four in the City League Playoffs before losing a heart breaker 38-37 to Peabody in the semi-finals. The seven young men who stayed with Coach Lofton are to be commended as they represented a loyal and spirited Westinghouse team. Its young people like those seven who will realize that the loyalty they gave to Westinghouse will always be a valuable asset to their future. They never quit and that is a true Westinghouse characteristic that so many of their predecessors possessed. Cooper, Stokes and Fleming possessed that burning desire to be the best and they made Westinghouse High School quite proud of their accomplishments.

## "JUNEBUG" WOWED THEM AT THE ROUNDBALL CLASSIC

The Dapper Dan Roundball Classic was the game if you were a high school basketball player in Western Pennsylvania. It was an opportunity to show off your basketball skills in front of a packed house of curiosity seekers. In 1981 when Thomas "Junebug" Howard arrived for his tryout at the Mellon Arena, he was a 5-foot-10-guard who had played on mediocre basketball teams at Westinghouse High School. He was at best a long shot to make the Pennsylvania All-Star Team, but all he wanted was a chance to show what he could do. Sonny Vaccaro the Roundball talent coordinator was so impressed with the performance of Junebug during the tryouts. "He was so quick, blowing by every other player on the court," remembered Vaccaro. There was little doubt in Vaccaro's mind that Howard belonged on the Pennsylvania team stating - "He had one of the most memorable practice sessions. I had never even heard of him going into the practice, but as the day wore on everyone was talking about him. He was also one of the nicest and most appreciative kids we've ever had."

Junebug played in the big game against the United States All Stars who had Patrick Ewing on their team. This did not faze him one bit as he excited the Civic Arena crowd with his lightning – quick penetrating moves. He deftly dribbled the ball through his legs and behind his back and moved with ease past the much more publicized United States players. The crowd reacted with his every move as he pleased them with his stellar play. Joe Butler of the Metro Index College Scouting Service alluded at the time that Howard had the best quickness of the 15,000 kids he had seen play during his seven years of running a scouting service.

Unfortunately two years later (August 1981) Howard was killed in an automobile accident on the Ohio Turnpike. He was to be a sophomore at Alderson-Broaddus College in Philippi, W.Va., where he was a member of the basketball team. The Roundball Classic was undoubtedly one of the biggest highlights of his basketball career. The Homewood-Brushton YMCA dedicated its outside basketball court to the former Westinghouse star by renaming it "The Thomas Junebug Howard Basketball Court." Also his uniform and number were retired at Westinghouse.

## PICKING AN ALL-TIME WHS QUINTET

As I expressed in an earlier Chapter I would never attempt to pick my All-Time WHS football team, but for basketball I will oblige. I will make mention here that my favorite Bulldog basketball team would have to be Chuck Cooper, Maurice Stokes, Edward Fleming, Rickie Richburg and Thomas "Junebug" Howard. They all excelled during their years at Westinghouse, and it would have been a real treat to see them play together as a team. The mere thought of watching "Junebug" and Richburg bringing the ball up the floor to complete an offensive play with Cooper in the post flanked by Stokes and Fleming in the corners would have been worth the price of admission to see this taking place. Yes basketball at Westinghouse High School during those glory years was very much in the limelight... As the many playoff games at the old Pitt Pavilion and the Fitzgerald Field House were priceless memories that I will always cherish. The classic contests with Farrell High School and its legendary coach Ed McCluskey were real thrillers to the final horn. How can I not include my memories of basketball at Westinghouse?

## LADY BULLDOGS TAKE CENTER STAGE

I could not complete this book without paying a special tribute to the successful girl's basketball program at Westinghouse led by Coach Phyllis Jones. She has done a paramount job of guiding the Lady Bulldogs to thirteen consecutive city title appearances since 1995. That is an incredible accomplishment at any level of competition and they deserve a place in this book. To the best of my recollection this has never been accomplished by any high school basketball program (boys or girls) in the City League of Pittsburgh or the WPIAL. If so, I would stand to be corrected.

419

While the boy's athletics have declined in recent years, the girls have really stepped up and carried on the winning tradition that always flowed through those portals on Murtland Avenue. I might add that the girls at Westinghouse have also excelled in track and much to my surprise supported the struggling boy's football program. Congratulations to Phyllis Jones and the Lady Bulldogs for a job well done.

420

# A SPECIAL TRIBUTE

## TO THE GLORY YEARS OF BOYS BASKETBALL AT WESTINGHOUSE HIGH SCHOOL

### PITTSBURGH CITY LEAGUE CHAMPIONS
### 1919 • 1943 • 1944 • 1948 • 1950
### 1951 • 1952 • 1953 • 1954 • 1972 • 1998

421

------

## TO THE GLORY YEARS OF GIRLS BASKETBALL AT WESTINGHOUSE HIGH SCHOOL

### PITTSBURGH CITY LEAGUE CHAMPIONS
### 1983 • 1984 • 1995 • 1997
### 2001 • 2003 • 2007

*Burton • Dimperio • Musilin • Malins • Webb*

**Maurice Stokes**

## The Scoreboard

4-18-70

# Maurice A Model

### By Pat Livingston

They'll lay Maurice Stokes to his eternal rest tomorrow, a well-deserved rest, under a blanket of pine needles in the simple priests' cemetery at St. Francis College.

And the remains of this anguished athlete will sanctify the ground he lies in.

Death mercifully came for Maurice Stokes in a Cincinnati hospital on Tuesday. Tomorrow, his body will be flown, in a private plane donated for the occasion by Purdue University, to the Loretto campus where he achieved the first measure of fame he was to enjoy in his brief, forsaken life.

It's not a normal procedure, interring the remains of a layman in Franciscan Cemetery, the unpretentious resting place of the college's departed clerics. The gravesite lies just below Doyle Hall, the tiny gym where Stokes played basketball while he was a student at the school.

In a dying wish, Maurice asked to be buried there, and such is the regard of the priests at this school for their happy carefree, brown-skinned brother that they leaped at a chance to grant it. Maurice Stokes will be remembered as a black man, but his great heart and his immortal soul were the color of love.

## St. Francis Remembers

St. Francis never lost its infatuation for the big, powerful athlete who led its basketball teams into the big time. Starting at the moment of Stokes' death, the Rev. Vincent Negherbon, the president of the college, ordered the flag flown at half-staff, and tomorrow, while Stokes' body lies in state in the school's Immaculate Conception Chapel, classes will be suspended.

The college has never forgotten Stokes' final triumph there, the 1955 season when he almost led the Frankies to the National Invitation Tournament championship. The 6-5, 235-pound giant won the Most Valuable Player Award that year with a display of individual brilliance that is still a conversation piece when basketball fans gather in New York for the NIT.

Maurice Stokes was always a prolific scorer, one of the leaders in the professional National Basketball Association, and he was, in his heyday with the Cincinnati Royals, as fine a rebounder as there was in the league—a brilliant combination of talents.

Yet there was no personal hunger in Stokes' approach to basketball. In a game where one's ability to score is of paramount importance, he was constantly one of the league leaders in assists. His own scoring suffered because of his unselfish zeal to get the ball to an open man with a better shot.

## DEAD AT 36

# Stokes Loses Long Battle

Pittsburgh's Maurice Stokes, author of one of the most heroic chapters in the history of American athletics, died yesterday in Cincinnati. He was 36 years old.

He suffered a heart attack March 30 in Good Samaritan Hospital, Cincinnati, where for the last 12 years he struggled back from near death after sustaining severe brain damage.

Stokes was stricken with post-traumatic encephalopathy on March 15, 1958. The attack was believed to have been the result of a blow on the head during a National Basketball Association game. He was in his third season as a star with the Cincinnati Royals at the time.

Stokes' body will be on view from 6 to 9 p.m. tomorrow at Good Samaritan Hospital, then will be flown to Loretto, Pa., for burial at St. Francis College, his alma mater, on Thursday.

Stokes, a 6-7 basketball star at Pittsburgh Westinghouse High School, went on to lift St. Francis to national prominence. He set 11 of the school's 13 basketball records from 1951 through 1955, and in that final season led the Frankies to fourth place in the National Invitational Tournament. He was named the Most Valuable Player in that tournament.

Stokes is survived by his parents, Mr. and Mrs. Tero

**MAURICE STOKES**

Stokes, a sister, Mrs. Clarice Washington, all of Pittsburgh, and a brother, Tero Jr., of Denver, Colo.

Jack Twyman, his former Cincinnati teammate and his legal guardian during his 12-year struggle against paralysis, was directing funeral arrangements.

423

## A Message Here

But Stokes' real triumphs came, not within the boundary lines of the basketball court, but in the dignity with which he handled his own adversity. After he was stricken by encephalitis, a puzzling disease which left him immobile and helpless for the last third of his life, his cheerful acceptance of his fate and his painstaking struggle for survival became an object lesson for those of us who panic at irrelevant problems.

In a way, I suppose, one might find a degree of symbolism in Stokes' burial in the pine-scented hills of white exurbia. It might symbolize, perhaps, a black man's escape from the ghetto, but Maurice Stokes, by the force of his own personality and his concern for his fellow man, made that escape a long time ago.

Stokes' death did end, though, his brotherly relationship with Jack Twyman, his white guardian, and there was a valid symbolism in that bond between black man and white.

"If Mo's illness and Jack's devotion show somebody that races can co-exist," said a mutual friend of each at a testimonial to Maurice last year, "this is not in vain."

# At long last, Stokes in Hall of Fame

By Chuck Finder
Pittsburgh Post-Gazette

After decades of raising donations, after a generation of writing letters, after naming a booster club and building a gymnasium and exhausting every plausible other manner of commemorating the name of Maurice Stokes in perpetuity, St. Francis University of Loretto and Jack Twyman last night were able to celebrate perhaps the highest homage yet.

They personally inducted the late Stokes into the Naismith Memorial Basketball Hall of Fame.

"It's kind of a bittersweet moment," said Twyman, Stokes' Pittsburgh playground companion, his pro basketball brethren, his legal guardian and his guardian angel.

"I'm excited for Maurice," Twyman said yesterday by phone from Springfield, Mass. "But I regret he's not here to experience it himself."

Stokes' story has become something of a legend and was a made-for-TV movie. The former Westinghouse High School standout — who scrapped with Central Catholic's Twyman and Westinghouse's Ed Fleming and Pottstown's Dick Ricketts on the Mellon Park courts — and St. Francis star wound up reunited with his buddy on the Rochester NBA team that moved after their rookie season to Cincinnati. In their third season together, with the powerful forward already a three-time All-Star on his way to all-time greatness, Stokes got entangled with a Minneapolis Lakers rebounder and fell with a thud, landing on his head.

Three days later, after a 12-point, 15-rebound playoff game March 15, 1958, Stokes collapsed in Twyman's arms on a team plane. He was diagnosed with post-traumatic encephalopathy. He remained unconscious for months and paralyzed the remainder of his life.

On April 6, 1970, Stokes died of a heart attack at age 36.

On April 5, 2004, the veterans committee announced he was its choice for the Class of 2004 for the basketball Hall of Fame. He joins Clyde Drexler, Lynette Woodard, coach Bill Sharman, executive Jerry Colangelo and foreign standout Drazen Dalipagic.

Last night, in a ceremony televised by ESPN Classic, the six were inducted into the hall.

About five dozen St. Francis fans, alumni and faculty, including president the Rev.

SEE **STOKES**, PAGE B-11

---

**STOKES,** FROM PAGE B-1

Gabriel Zeis, gathered in the Springfield Marriott to celebrate and watch the telecast of the festivities that, down the street and inside the hall, cost a pricey $350 per person.

Twyman represented them. First, Hall of Famers Oscar Robertson — a Cincinnati college and pro player who often visited a hospitalized Stokes — and Bob Pettit introduced Stokes, at Twyman's request. Then up to accept the enshrinement came Twyman, who oversaw his friend's care and the letter-writing campaign for the Hall of Fame and the fund-raising that started out as a way to pay the hospital bills but then transformed into an NBA-wide alumni effort.

In an emotional acceptance, his voice cracking at times, Twyman last night spoke of "Maurice the man," how for 12 years as a paraplegic Stokes inspired so many others. "Whatever I've done for Maurice, I've gained tenfold. Let me just say, congratulations big fella, you made it."

Before the ceremony, Twyman offered: "It took a little work, but it was inevitable. Earl Lloyd said at the luncheon [yesterday], if Maurice had not played a minute of pro ball, he would have been more than qualified to be in the Hall of Fame because of his collegiate career.

"There's no question that it needs to happen and would have happened. I'm really very pleased for Maurice. And I'm grateful that I'm still around to see it happen."

Twyman, inducted in 1982, plans to give Stokes' posthumously-awarded hall blazer, ring and trophy to St. Francis officials this morning at a university breakfast reception.

"I think this will be great for St. Francis," Twyman said. "There aren't many guys who have a fieldhouse named after him. And they're planning a big, new display case in the lobby for these three items. I think it's appropriate."

Coincidentally, the Hall gave its John Bunn Lifetime Achievement Award Thursday to longtime NBA commissioner's office representative Zelda Spoelta, who worked with the Maurice Stokes Foundation and NBA Legends in her role with league alumni and their families. She told reporters in Springfield, "The fact that the Hall of Fame is also recognizing Maurice Stokes makes this an even sweeter occasion for myself and all the people who've helped keep the foundation going."

Tomorrow, at the Indiana Country Club, the 23rd annual Maurice Stokes Golf Outing will take place.

Meanwhile, in Springfield, the living hall inductees will be in a parade and available at an autograph party.

"You know, we have a lot of fond memories," said Twyman, who gathered his children and grandchildren in Springfield for the hall ceremonies. "They grew up with Maurice. He was part of our family.

"I guess this puts a little closure on Maurice as an athlete. You'll never put full closure on the experience we had when he was sick. We miss him. But he deserves to be recognized by his peers."

*Chuck Finder can be reached at cfinder@post-gazette.com or 412-263-1724.*

---

*Burton • Dimperio • Musilin • Malins • Webb*

Sun-Telegraph Photo by Paul Hunter

**CITY CHAMPIONS** . . . Westinghouse High School basketball team which will represent District VIII (the City League) in the PIAA Class A basketball tournament opening this week. W. Peatross, E. Phelps, J. Nunlist, M. Stokes, E. Fleming and D. Savio, left to right, are the first six on Coach Willard Fisher's squad. Bulldogs play Bradford High School of District IX at DuBois on Wednesday night. They have lost only once

*City Basketball Champions --- 1950-1951*

l. to r.:—BACK ROW, Coles (Manager), MacNamara, Miller, Hefflin, Nixon, Robinson, Anthony, Vita, Federeci (Manager). FRONT ROW, Coach Fisher, Prunty, Peatross, Fleming, Stokes, DeStefano, McMasters, Predmore (Manager).

426

Edward Fleming

Charles Cooper

J. Bisceglia, W. Nunn, C. Cooper, P. DeVaughn, A. Bonomo, Coach R. Zahniser
**1943 Pittsburgh City League Champions**

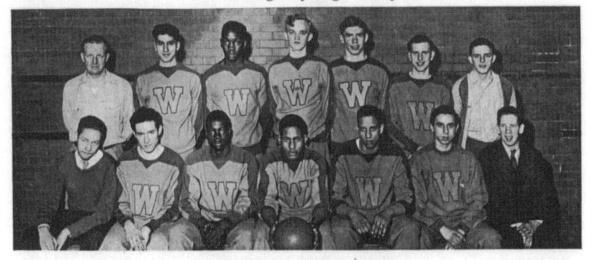

BASKETBALL TEAM—1942-43

PLAYERS: *First Team*, Paul De Vaughn, William Nunn, Charles Cooper, Jorden Bisceglia, Albert Bonomo. *Substitutes*: William Lo Presti, Robert Coles, Nelson Beam, Ralph Burkhouse, William De Wall, Robert Craven. *Managers*: William Johnson, William Connolley, Anthony Garland.

**26**—POST-GAZETTE: Thurs., Feb. 24, 1983

# Roundball was special for Junebug Howard

**By Steve Hecht**
Post-Gazette Sports Writer

The Dapper Dan Roundball Classic. It is *the* game if you're a high school basketball player in Western Pennsylvania.

When the Roundball Classic holds its annual tryouts this Sunday afternoon, from 12:30 to 6 at Allegheny Community College, 80 players will be there trying to latch on to a dream.

They will be there trying to make the 11-player Pennsylvania All-Star team (or the City-Catholic or West Penn team) and get the chance to play in front of 15,000 fans at the Civic Arena ... to have the spotlight trail them as they are introduced to the crowd ... and to get the chance to play against the best high school basketball players from around the United States.

These were dreams not unlike Thomas "Junebug" Howard's when he arrived for his tryout two years ago.

He was a 5-foot-10 guard who had played on mediocre basketball teams at Westinghouse High School. He was, at best, a longshot to make the Pennsylvania All-Stars.

But when that tryout session of 1981 had ended, there was little doubt in Roundball talent coordinator Sonny Vaccaro's mind that "The Junebug" belonged on the Pennsylvania team.

"He was so quick, he just blew by every other player on the court that day," remembers Vaccaro. "He was one of the quickest players, if not the quickest, to ever play for Pennsylvania.

"He had one of the most memorable practice sessions. I never had even heard of him going into the practice, but as the day wore on everyone was talking about him. He was also one of the nicest and most appreciative kids we've ever had."

Last August, Howard, 19, was killed in an automobile accident on the Ohio Turnpike. He was to be a sophomore at Alderson-Broaddus College in Philippi, W.Va., where he was a member of the basketball team.

This season, in tribute to Howard, members of the Westinghouse basketball team wore black arm bands. In Westinghouse's final regular-season game against Schenley, his number was retired and a plaque was presented to his mother.

The Homewood-Brushton YMCA has dedicated its outside basketball court to the former Westinghouse star by renaming it "The Thomas Junebug Howard Basketball Court."

It was a fitting move.

"My son would spend sometimes four and five hours down there practicing," remembers Ruthie Howard, Junebug's mother. "If he could find one player to practice with, he'd stay down there all night.

## Roundball tryouts

Tryouts for the 19th annual Dapper Dan Roundball Classic will take place this Sunday from 12:30 to 6 p.m. at Allegheny Community College on the Northside. There will be three different tryout sessions. Players will be trying out for the Pennsylvania, City-Catholic and West Penn All-Star teams.

This year's Roundball is slated for Sunday afternoon, April 17, at the Civic Arena. Tickets to the Roundball costing $8.25, $6.25 and $4.25 can be obtained by writing to: Dapper Dan Club, P.O. Box 957, Pittsburgh, Pa. 15230. Checks should be made payable to the Dapper Dan Club. A self-addressed stamped envelope should be included with each order.

The list of players eligible to try out:

**WPIAL Class AAA** — Marion Ferguson, Center; Brian Brezicki, Greensburg, C.C.; Bob Bauer, Central Catholic; Rick Bell and Ron Rink, Bethel Park; Ron Reynolds, Swissvale; Paul Grubb, Greensburg Salem; Jim Majetic, Ambridge; Jim Kollar, Derry; Brian Neil, Belle Vernon; Matt Knizner, Greg Farrell and Mike Shincovich, Hempfield; Mike Gadsby, Burrell; Bill Leonard and Todd Preston, McKeesport; Jim Robick, Shaler; Chris Frizzell, Uniontown; Mike Ryan and Steve Vandiver, Wilkinsburg; Don Henderson and Darrin Modrak, Norwin; Duane Johnson, Canon-McMillan; Darol Lee, Beaver Falls; Brian Condron, Plum; Wendell Rogers and Dave Gestrich, Penn-Trafford; James Barton, Aliquippa; Paul Thomas and Bill Graham, North Hills; Bruce Beichner, Butler; Mike Runski, Valley; Chris Seneca, Todd Lee and Sean Hall, Penn Hills; Fred Reynolds, Connellsville; Roland Shannonhouse, Farrell; Tom Boney, Latrobe; Dwayne Todd, Steel Valley; Rich Dickinson and Darryl Gatlin, Blackhawk; Bill Urso, Fox Chapel; Gary Parker, West Mifflin North.

**WPIAL Class AA** — Rich Kunselman, Laurel; Dale Hawkins, Duquesne; Mike Kurka, South Allegheny; Eric Campagna, Brentwood; John Watt, Turtle Creek; Jim Stepoli and Craig Nard, Monessen; Mark Beavers, Sto-Rox; Les Ward, Hampton; Mike Hensel, Mars; Mike Kolessar, Apollo-Ridge.

**WPIAL Class A** — Andre Carey, St. Thomas; Dave Timko, Father Geibel; Brian Stewart, Midland; Dave Santucci, Cornell; Jeff Trebac, Riverview; Tony Conn, Bentworth; Carl Mickens, Fairchance-Georges; Kris Gomory, Rochester.

**City League** — Eric Pinno, Allderdice; Chris Wilson and Brian Minniefield, South; Norris Thompson, Schenley; Harold Hamlin and Gerald Lovelace, Peabody; Jerome Henderson and Bill Gist, Oliver; Ron Stevenson, Ken Snyder and Maurice Vason, Langley; Carl Wilson, Perry.

**Others** — Jamie Schaaf, Erie Prep; Dean Kartsonas, Shady Side Academy; Bob Iuotzzino, Bishop Guilfoyle; Dave Aiken, Ligonier Valley; Mike Burtness, Indiana; John Bowen, Warren; Brad Heckert, Chief Logan.

'Mamma, there's two other kids down there with him and he's still hooping.' "

Mrs. Howard says the Roundball Classic was undoubtedly one of the biggest highlights of Junebug's basketball career.

"He said when he came home after the Roundball that he'd long remember this night," she says. "He was very proud to be able to participate in that game and get the chance to play against the United States and especially Patrick Ewing."

The United States, led by Ewing's 12 points, 12 rebounds and six blocked shots, gave Pennsylvania its worst beating ever that night, 108-73.

Junebug's lightning-quick penetrating moves were one of the few things Pennsylvania fans had to cheer about. Howard would deftly dribble the ball through his legs and behind his back and move with ease past the

**Thomas "Junebug" Howard**

and pepped things up," says Joe Butler of the Metro Index College Scouting Service. "He was entertaining as a player and he was just perfect for the Roundball.

"In my seven years of running a scouting service and watching players from around the country, Junebug had the best quickness. I've seen about 15,000 kids play, too.

"If it's possible, he might have been too quick. Kids had trouble handling his ability. He'd throw a pass and it would be right there, but they couldn't adjust to his ability."

Westinghouse Coach John Sparvero admits that sometimes Junebug would play a little out of control and that he'd have to remind him to settle down.

"But at the Roundball tryouts, I went up to him and said, 'Bug, put on a show. All the things I told you not to do during the season, go out and do them,'" remembers Sparvero.

"I'd most likely say the Roundball Classic was the highlight of his life. Myself, and the

429

430

12-11-1997                                    Joyce Mendelsohn/Post-Gazette
Ricky Richburg: Averages 28 points a game for Westinghouse.

*1951-1952*

**IN TITLE GAME . . .** Westinghouse High School team which will oppose Carrick for the City League basketball championship at the Pitt Field House tomorrow night. Left to right: Back row—Rippy Nixon, Charles Robinson, and Jim Vita. Front row—Pat Wade, Charley Hefflin, John Miller, coach Willard Fisher and Bill Peatross. The Bulldogs won the Section I title and Carrick Raiders the Section II crown.

Sun-Telegraph Photo.

431

432

**1952**

*City Champions*

**1st row**—D. Carl, Manager; C. Heflin, L. Nixon, C. Robinson, W. Peatross, J. Miller, W. Wilkerson, R. Beasley, J. Vita.

**Standing**—L. Prunty, Manager; N. Jamison, Manager; R. McNamara, L. Saunders, F. Griham, P. Wade, J. Dorsey, F. Federici, D. Nunlist; J. Schram, Manager; M. Fisher, Coach.

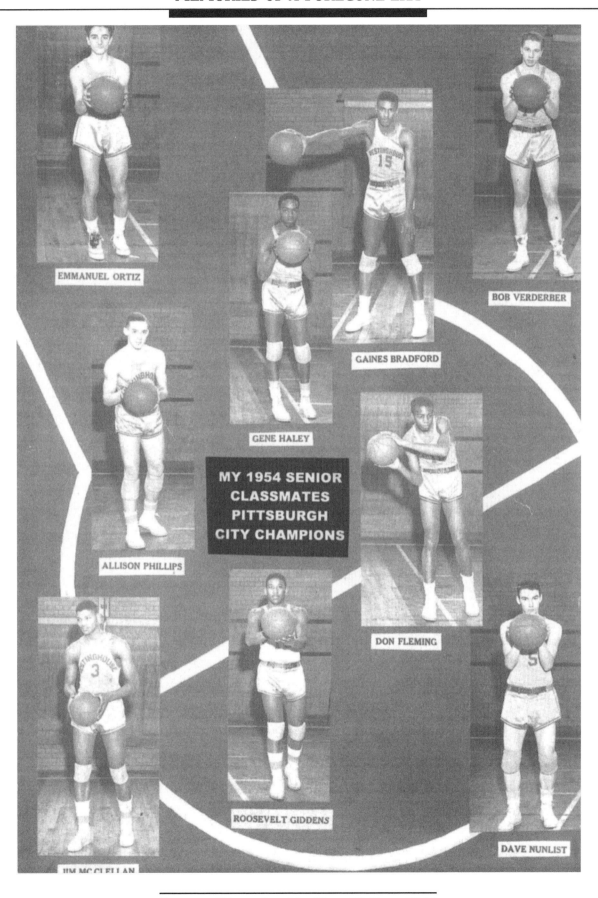

EMMANUEL ORTIZ

GAINES BRADFORD

BOB VERDERBER

GENE HALEY

MY 1954 SENIOR
CLASSMATES
PITTSBURGH
CITY CHAMPIONS

ALLISON PHILLIPS

DON FLEMING

JIM McCLELLAN

ROOSEVELT GIDDENS

DAVE NUNLIST

THURSDAY, MARCH 1, 2001    **HIGH SCHOOLS**

Christopher Horner/Tribune-Review

Westinghouse junior Sidney Thomas drives to the basket around Schenley's Kim Jackson (35) and O'naje Thompson in the City League championship on Wednesday.

| Westinghouse | 56 |
| Schenley | 48 |

# At last

## Westinghouse ends Schenley's run of City titles

434

16—POST-GAZETTE: Fri., Feb. 25, 1983

**High**

## Athlete of the week

Darrell Sapp/Post-Gazette

**Westinghouse junior Stacey Williams is the City League's latest standout.**

### By Steve Hecht
Post-Gazette Sports Writer

At Allderdice, there was Parade All-America guard Mary Myers. Carrick produced Pitt's outstanding Jennifer Bruce, a Big East All-Star. This past season, Brashear had an outstanding player in Penn State-bound Lisa Faloon.

But the way Westinghouse Coach Frank Barnes figures it, his 5-foot-11, 160-pound junior, Stacey Williams, has a shot at becoming the best girls basketball player ever to come out of the City League.

"Stacey has everything it takes," says Barnes. "She has all the instincts. Her stats show what a complete, all-around ballplayer she is: She already has 1,198 career points. This season she is averaging 23 points, 12 assists and 10 rebounds a game.

"I don't think in high school Jennifer Bruce was the ballhandler that Stacey is. Mary Myers was an assist person. She controlled the ball. She was a great team leader. She had charisma. But she can't rebound with Stacey.

"Stacey is the total basketball player. She can dribble, she can shoot, she's an assist person and she can rebound."

At Tuesday's girls city championship, Williams wowed the crowd by dribbling behind her back and through her legs and throwing several no-look passes. The Post-Gazette Athlete of the Week also managed a game-high 21 points and 14 rebounds to help Westinghouse (22-3) past Oliver, 53-48.

Williams' flashy, playground-style play is exciting to watch. It comes from years of practice. "This girl plays basketball year-round. She's been doing it since she was six years old," says Barnes.

Rita Williams, Stacey's mother, confirms that her daughter has been shooting baskets at the local city playgrounds for quite a while.

"She's the baby of the family (the youngest of seven children), and by being the baby, she always got a lot of attention," says the elder Williams. "She'd always follow her older brothers to the playground, and they'd shoot with her."

Now she may be a better player than some of those older brothers.

"I play basketball with the guys a lot," says Williams. "Sometimes the older guys won't let me in their games. I'll just walk away. If they let me in, though, I try to show them I can play. The next time, they usually let me in without asking."

While Williams has some outstanding attributes, there are some facets of her game she must work on during her senior year.

"She's becoming more and more competitive," says Barnes. "But she needs to gain that fiery competitiveness. I think it will come. Stacey's still only 16 years old."

On the basketball court, it's a very sweet 16.

435

Mark Murphy/Post-Gazette

**Westinghouse's Stacey Williams (55) and Dionne Morris share a high five after the Bulldogs crushed Oliver, 71-36**

436

# Morris, Williams lift 'House to title

By Mike White

Westinghouse's Dionne Morris and Stacey Williams are a pretty potent one-two punch. Just ask the Oliver Bears.

Morris and Williams did just about anything they wanted to Oliver yesterday in leading Westinghouse to a 71-56 win in the girls' City League basketball championship at Brashear.

On bombs from the outside, on drives to the hoop and on nifty passes, Morris and Williams ate Oliver (12-7) alive, allowing the Bulldogs (19-5) to capture their second straight City League championship.

Morris, a 5-foot-6 junior guard, scored 27 points, grabbed nine rebounds and made six steals. Williams, a 5-11 senior guard-forward, had 17 points, six rebounds, three steals and seven assists.

"They're outstanding. They play so well together," Westinghouse Coach George Webb said of his co-captains. "The thing about them is that they always know where the other is. They blend together just like one."

Last year, Westinghouse played Oliver in the title game, and the Bulldogs squeaked out a 53-48 victory. Thanks to Morris and Williams, this game was much easier.

"People talk about Seton-LaSalle and Suzie McConnell, but when you think of Dionne and Stacey, you think of two good players," said Webb. "I think Dionne is one of the best guards in Pennsylvania."

Oliver barely had its warmups off before Morris and Williams broke into their act. Williams fed Morris with a behind-the-back pass for the first hoop of the game, then made another pretty pass

to Morris on a fast break for the second hoop. Morris then hit an outside shot, and Williams followed with six straight points to give the Bulldogs a 12-0 lead.

Westinghouse increased its margin to 32-11 at halftime. Morris and Williams had 26 of the 32 points.

"They had a lot of nice outside shots," said Oliver Coach Pat Sharkey. "Our team was cold and off, though."

Westinghouse enjoyed a hefty lead throughout the second half, the biggest being 37 points at 69-32. Near the end, Williams had the Westinghouse crowd rocking as she put on a dribbling and passing show that would've made Magic Johnson proud.

"I like to impress the fans a lot," said Williams.

She and Morris did a pretty good job of that.

## "Thanks to the Girls at Westinghouse For upholding our Proud Tradition"

*Burton • Dimperio • Musilin • Malins • Webb*

# EPILOGUE

## "THANKS FOR THE MEMORIES"
By Carmen Pellegrino

"This essay of my sentiments was expressed to my classmates at our 50th Class Reunion on June 19, 2004 and I would like to share it with my readers. It is my way of bringing this book to a closure by giving thanks for the many proud years and memories I enjoyed at Westinghouse High School."

For many of us our roots originated in the proud communities of Homewood, Brushton, Lincoln and Larimer where we enjoyed our early years of elementary learning. We heard so much from our older siblings about this great high school that we could not wait to see for ourselves. Then came September of 1948 and it was time to make that long awaited journey. We came together from our neighboring elementary schools to the big house in Homewood to form the future class of 1954 at Westinghouse High School. There was much apprehension as we were facing a major adjustment in our young lives. The anticipation of arriving at our new school that had such a proud tradition was somewhat overwhelming for many of us. The seniors were there waiting to greet us with much patience and understanding. They showed us what pride and tradition were all about. We could feel those attributes as we made our way through those hallowed halls. It was like a mystique that we were finally privy to realize.

Our first week there we were treated to our first pep rally in the school auditorium to initiate the start of the 1948 football season. It really lifted our spirits as we sat there and read the words of our school motto inscribed very clearly above the stage **"HERE YOUTH AND OPPORTUNITY MEET."** It was a statement that was so meaningful. We were greeted by Mr. Harsky leading the cheerleaders and our marching band with Mr. McVicker at the helm leading us with a heartwarming rendition of, **"Westinghouse Forever."** To us seventh graders it was awesome as the spirit of Westinghouse High School was unfolding on that stage right before our very eyes. The1948 football team was introduced and the entire student body responded with such enthusiasm that we had never seen before. The Bulldogs were in high gear and we were impressed by this overwhelming display of school spirit. It was a spirit that was there for us to seize, and we soon realized how special it was.

During that first year our football and basketball teams were crowned, City Champions of Pittsburgh. What a way to start our first year at the "Big House" in Homewood. Some two years later we met the rest of our classmates as they came in from Baxter Junior High, Lemington, Our

437

*Burton • Dimperio • Musilin • Malins • Webb*

Lady Help of Christians and Corpus Christi, and thus the balance of the class of 1954 was formed. Now we were all together and it was all systems go. Our winning ways continued as we were the "City Champions" again in football in 1949 and 1951, and in basketball from 1950 through 1954. Much gratitude went to our coaches, Pete Dimperio, Willard Fisher, Austin Grupe and Joseph Harsky for a job well done. They prepared and motivated us well as we enjoyed our winning ways.

Yes, the late forties and early fifties were for us unforgettable and memorable years at our big house in Homewood. It was a time in our lives that shall never be forgotten. We had three fine principals during those six years – Mr. Kistler, Mr. Dean and Dr. Felton. They, along with a fine faculty staff of 75 members, too many to mention by name, collectively prepared us for life's journey. A fine job they did. We were a spirited class under the same roof and blended together very well. Many friendships were formed and to this day camaraderie still exists between many of us. Tonight some of us will be seeing each other for the first time since our two commencements – January 29th and June 18th, 1954. Back then we had two senior classes, but tonight we are together as one class. Some fifty years ago we were teens and today many of us are grandparents and great-grandparents. It is hard to believe as I stand here looking out at all those familiar faces that it is the year of 2004. This is truly a great reunion, filled with so much to be thankful for. Let us celebrate with a toast that we will come together again in five more years.

438

Tonight let us look back, reminisce and call to mind some of the happenings that we experienced during that memorable year: Remember when . . . Our first day as seniors and how important we thought we were . . . Picture taking day for the Sketchbook and how sharp we wanted to look . . . Our class rings arrived and it was the first piece of jewelry for many of us . . . The pep rallies that fired us up especially the ones before the Peabody game . . . Our bus and trolley rides to and from the football and basketball games and God Bless the poor drivers . . . Our Homeroom Christmas parties and how we stuffed ourselves . . . Report card day and not too many of us were smiling . . . Our parents paid our teachers a visit and found out just how smart we really were . . . Senior Day and we were proud Bulldogs . . . Ribbon Day Dance and the girls had to show many of us guys the latest ballroom techniques . . . The Spring Concert and our music department excelled . . . Our Variety Show and oh what talent many of us had as we took center stage . . . Then finally, our last day of school and many of us had mixed emotions . . . We said good-bye to all the underclassmen and members of our faculty . . . Commencement night and how proud our parents were as we marched to the sounds of "Pomp and Circumstance" to receive our diplomas . . . We gave our grand old alma mater our last look as we left the auditorium . . . Good-bye Westinghouse; we shall never forget you . . . There was no turning back as it was time for us to face the outside world . . . We took with us the learning skills and tools that our faculty so effectively placed within our young minds and in our hands . . . Now it was up to us to put them to good use…We went our separate ways to pursue our endeavors and ambitions.

Tonight, some 50 years later, we come together to celebrate this milestone occasion with much to be thankful for. We fondly remember those who are not with us . . . those who are separated by distance, by illness, and those who have departed this life. Together let us rejoice and pay homage to our grand old alma mater and proudly say, "Thanks for the memories, the education, the spirit and the proud tradition that you bestowed upon us. There were friendships that were short-lived and there were friendships that were long-lasting, but all in all they were special. Coming together for this reunion rekindles what makes life so precious. In closing let us sing "Westinghouse Forever" one more time. Thank you and God Bless.

**"WESTINGHOUSE FOREVER"**
(Our Director March, Bigelow)
**Westinghouse forever, loyal and true,**
**Nothing can ever change our love for you,**
**Rah! Rah! Rah!**
**Westinghouse forever we're true to you,**
**We love our colors, of Gold and Blue.**

*"I have learned after many years to find peace of mind somewhere between my ambitions and my limitations. God has helped me to realize that he will always be there when it is time to rise above all of life's challenges as he has blessed me in so many ways. Much of my happiness has come in later years and it was well worth the wait...and Thanks be to God."*

*Carmen Pellegrino*

**439**

**CLASS OF 1954**
**50 YEAR REUNION**
JUNE 19, 2004
CHURCHILL VALLEY COUNTRY CLUB

440

*Sketchbook*

**WESTINGHOUSE HIGH SCHOOL**
**PITTSBURGH, PA**

441

"Sharing memories of a foregone era with my classmates"

*Burton • Dimperio • Musilin • Malins • Webb*

442

Carmen Pellegrino      Larry Modena      Dominic Ruffa

We were classmates for 12 years.....beginning at Larimer Elementary in 1942 and ending at Westinghouse High School in 1954

Back together again for our 50th Class Reunion ...... Weekend of June 18, 2004

# In Memoriam

My Friend Joe:

Every once in a while someone touches our lives and leaves a lasting impressing. This was my friend Joe Pronio. God took you with Him before this book made it to press, but you knew what it reflected from cover to cover. May god Bless You for being what you meant to so many of us. Until we meet again on the other side in the Valhalla of Football, save me a place next to you on the 50 yard line.

Your Friend,
Carmen

*Joe Pronio passed away on August 9, 2007.*

# ABOUT THE AUTHOR

*"My journey ended with a surprise induction into the Westinghouse High School Commission of Recognition (WHSCR) Hall of Fame."*

Pittsburgh native, Carmen Pellegrino sacrificed his eligibility to play varsity sports in order to graduate from Westinghouse High School. His family had moved away from Homewood in 1952 but Carmen opted to remain with his class and graduate from his beloved Westinghouse High in 1954.

As a student at Westinghouse, he received the American Legion School Award for Scholastic Achievement, was a member of the Yearbook Staff, played intramural sports and earned a scholarship offer to the Art Institute of Pittsburgh.

After having served six years with the U.S. Army National Guard, he pursued his desire for engineering earning degrees in both Electrical and Mechanical Engineering Technology from Point Park University.

His love for the game of football and his high school inspired him to track the storied history of football at his alma mater. After retiring in 2001 as an Interiors Engineer and Technical Documentation Specialist for US Airways, Carmen began to research and write his long-awaited documentary.

Carmen and his wife, Pat, make their home in Oakmont, PA.